Berlin is the historic symbol of Germany, but it is the most un-German of cities; it is the heart of Prussia, but the most un-Prussian of cities; it was the capital of Imperial and Nazi Germany, but it was never trusted by its rulers.

Today it is a sundered city: one half the capital of East Germany, the other half an island of democracy one hundred miles behind the iron curtain. The division is marked by the infamous Berlin Wall and miles of impassable barbed wire between the Western Sector and the Eastern.

Berliners defy easy labeling. They are tough, sentimental, sardonic, and so brash they make other Germans wince. And beneath a staid façade, there has always been a licentious side to the city that has made it the most uniquely uninhibited city in Europe.

Walter Henry Nelson examines the city and its people today, and enough of its history as well to explain how it acquired its personality. In this book he has brought alive the city's essential beat and its enduring mystique.

(continued on back flap)

THE BERLINERS

Their Saga and Their City

by

Walter Henry Nelson

DAVID McKAY COMPANY, INC.

New York

THE BERLINERS: THEIR SAGA AND THEIR CITY

FOR MY MOTHER
who introduced me to Berlin

acknowledgments

I interviewed more than 1,000 persons while living in Berlin to write this book; I cannot list them all, though I am indebted to each of them. Many of those mentioned have had to be given pseudonyms to protect them or their relatives from harassment by the East Berlin authorities; I am grateful to all who spoke openly with me, often at considerable risk to themselves. My notes and reference materials weighed half a ton when I left Berlin; I cannot list all my sources here either, for reasons of space. The Berlin newspapers, their editors and their files, were invaluable to me; so was *Der Spiegel,* West Germany's liberal, thorough news magazine. The Berlin Information Center and its staff were a great help, as was the Landesarchiv Berlin and the Information Officers of the U.S. Mission, the U.S. Command, and the U.S. Air Force at Tempelhof. Rolf and Karin Leinweber, Albert and Edith Noack, Bill and Vinnie Fish, Hermann Thibaut and others whom I interviewed came to be helpful friends who were generous with advice and suggestions. Waltraut Rodewald and Cornelia Jacobsen assisted in researching, as did the late Audrey Rosenthal; I am indebted to them for their help, as I am to Katya Sheppard for her valuable editorial advice and to Nicole Shulthes and Ann Woodley for their work on the manuscript. My mother, who lived in Berlin for nearly 30 years, 17 of them as an officer of the U.S. Mission after the war, reviewed the manuscript and offered helpful suggestions. Of course none of those mentioned here are responsible for my own interpretation of events, nor for any of the book's shortcomings.

The text mentions several works from which I have quoted; those not specifically mentioned are acknowledged below.

I am grateful to Deutsche Verlags-Anstalt, Stuttgart, for permission to quote from Arnold Brecht's *Aus nächster Nähe* and to Verlag Ullstein GmbH for permission to quote from Wolfgang Leonhardt's *Die Revolution entlässt ihre Kinder.* The diary entries of Ursula von Kardoff are here reprinted from her *Diary of a Nightmare,* copyright © 1962 by Biederstein Verlag München; english translation © 1965 by Rupert Hart-Davis Ltd., by permission of the John Day Company, Inc., publisher. The diary entries of William L. Shirer are quoted from his *Berlin Diary,* by kind permission of Alfred A. Knopf, Inc., New York. Anecdotes concerning Arno Scholz derive partly from interviews and partly from his *Nullvier,* here quoted by kind permission of the author. Rudi Thurow's experiences were first documented in *Kontrollpunkt Kohlhasenbrück,* edited by Rainer Hildebrandt, and quoted from by kind permission of Hohwacht Verlag, Bad Godesberg. Quotations of Arthur M. Schlesinger, Jr., are taken from *A Thousand Days: John F. Kennedy in the White House,* and cited here by kind permission of Houghton Mifflin Co., Boston. Quotations of Walter Kiaulehn have been taken from his *Berlin,* by kind permission of Biederstein Verlag, Munich. The quotation of Michael Ratcliffe appeared in the January 2, 1966 edition of *The Sunday Times,* London, and is here reprinted by permission of that newspaper. The letter of Gottfried Benn first appeared in Wolfgang Paul's *Kampf um Berlin* and is here reprinted by kind permission of Albert Langen Georg Müller Verlag, Munich. The quotation of A.J.P. Taylor is taken from his *The Course of German History* and is here reprinted by kind permission of Hamish Hamilton Ltd., London. "The Solution," the poem attributed to Bert Brecht, first appeared in "Aus Bertolt Brechts späten Jahren" by W. Paul, *Neue Deutsche Hefte,* Guetersloh, November 1958.

THE BERLINERS

chapter one

IN BERLIN'S WOODED GRUNEWALD, ONE CAN CLIMB TO THE TOP
of the Trümmerberg, a hill made of air-raid debris, where so much
rubble is piled up that it is even higher than the Müggelberg, the
highest natural point in Berlin. The Trümmerberg, about 390
feet high, is the biggest of three such artificial mounds in the city;
the Insulaner in District Schöneberg, also in West Berlin, and the
Bunkerberg in East Berlin's District Friedrichshain are somewhat
smaller. A third or more of what used to be Berlin lies buried
under them.

The Grunewald, in which the Trümmerberg (literally "Rubble
Mountain") stands, is in itself a relic of the old Berlin, and along
with it, suffered grievous damage. It was for two centuries a pine
forest, fifteen and one half square miles in size, or about half as big
as Manhattan Island; it lost forty-four percent of its trees during
and immediately after World War II, but most of these have been
replaced, just as most of Berlin's Western sectors have been rebuilt. It took two thousand workmen two full years to fill in all the
bomb craters and trenches in this forested park preserve; ultimately, it was replenished with more than 24 million new trees.
Not all of these were pines, however: The Grunewald has changed,
just like Berlin.

Young boys were picking about the Trümmerberg the day I
visited it; they were in search of buried treasure, but found only
junk and mortar. Beneath us lay 18 million cubic meters of ruins
—bricks, stones, cornices, archways, window frames, bathtubs,
and marble fragments—most of it now covered with grass and the
poplars, maples, alders, and robinias planted there in later years.
In winter, a ski-and-toboggan run, as well as two ski jumps, allow

1

the young Berliners of today to soar above their past, as though they were overcoming the remnants of their heritage and leaving behind the accumulated trash of their parents' Nazi years. I had the thought that some excited archaeologist, perhaps a thousand years hence, may excavate this hill. Indeed, if such a man digs here, he will find part of my own past as well, for I spent many years of my youth in the Berlin that lies buried beneath the Trümmerberg.

The last time I saw that old Berlin still standing was nine months after the start of World War II; there was a feverish bustle about the city, for it was from Berlin that the marching orders were being issued. I was a boy then, and in May, 1940, at Tempelhof Airport, my mother and I boarded a darkened Lufthansa Heinkel passenger plane bound for Venice. It would be eight years before I would see Berlin again.

My father was in the Foreign Service, attached to the American Consulate General in Berlin, where he remained after we had left the city. After Pearl Harbor, he was interned and exchanged for German diplomats in the United States. And so Berlin, while being the city of my childhood, does not altogether claim me; although the Berliners are the people I remember from my early youth, I was not one of them, but an American living among them. Later, as an adult, I returned to visit and to live there for awhile, most recently to research this book, but I am still not one of them. My view of the Berliners is necessarily trans-Atlantic, and my feelings about them, ambivalent.

The first time I saw postwar Berlin was during the Blockade of 1948-49. I had arrived at Tempelhof during the airlift, in uniform, as a member of the United States Army Military Intelligence. The Cold War was on and the city hungered and shivered, yet I felt strangely at home as I drove through its dark streets that cold and rainy winter evening in 1948, trying to find my old neighborhood. Few people were about and those I saw seemed lost in this sea of damp stone ruins. Perhaps they were not sure as yet of their identity—were they still regarded as despised remnants of Hitlerism, or had they already been reassessed as Cold War heroes, fighting for freedom a hundred miles behind the Iron Curtain?

I approached the street in which I had lived as a boy, off the

2

Hundekehlestrasse, near the Roseneck. The cinema in which I remembered seeing Erich Kästner's *Emil und die Detektive* was now gone, bombed out, as was the garage that had serviced our family's envied Buick throughout the 1930's and most of the little stores in which we had shopped. The shells of burned-out houses stood everywhere, much as they must have looked the day after the raids that had ruined them. These were interspersed with leveled, stone-strewn places where walls had been knocked flat to keep them from collapsing on their own. Most of the trees in the neighborhood seemed to be missing also, or to be shorn of their branches; the desperate postwar need for firewood in the city had stripped Berlin of its great pride, its greenery. My old neighborhood looked eerie, as though it were welcoming me home with a ghastly grin, made gap-toothed by the missing buildings.

Then I came upon Sulzaerstrasse, the street in which we had lived. It looked completely out of place: It had not changed a bit. None of the apartment houses on either side of it had been hit by bombs; the only sign of war it showed were small holes in the concrete frontages of the buildings, the result of small-arms fire during the Soviet conquest of the city.

I walked down the street toward the end house on the west side. There, I pressed the bell to the basement flat to see if Otto Ahrensdorf, the janitor, was still about; he was the only one in the street I would remember. The only others we had known well on Sulzaerstrasse had been two Jewish families. They had managed to emigrate in 1938, one settling down in Long Island, the other near London.

"*Tja*, we survived, *junger Herr*," Ahrensdorf said a little later in his flat, smiling with delight over the coffee and cigarettes I had brought along in the hope there might be a reunion. He looked thinner, but otherwise just as I remembered him—a face like cracked leather, hands like grimy steel. He had greeted me at the door still wearing the blue visored workingman's cap I recalled from my youth. I noted that, unlike some other Germans, he had kept the small Hitlerian moustache he had always worn; he had, after all, grown it long before Hitler came to power. "It's almost indecent, our surviving," he said smilingly, "considering how many bombs you dropped to kill us."

Frau Ahrensdorf showed me a photograph of their daughter,

who had been about eighteen when I had left the city. She had become a handsome woman, and beside her in the picture, stood a man in uniform.

"Yes, she's engaged now," Ahrensdorf said with pride, "and to an English officer!"

"She's done well for herself," I commented. "I hope everything will turn out well for you two, also."

"Fantastic, how times have changed!" Ahrensdorf replied. "In the old days, she might have become a sergeant's wife, me being only a janitor, but now she's about to marry a major! His family even owns a business of their own."

"As soon as this blockade is over and we can get permission," Frau Ahrensdorf added, "we're to travel to England for the wedding."

I asked her if she were worried about the Russians.

"*Lieber Pomm als 'Frau, komm!,'* is what we say in Berlin," she replied, referring to the *Pomm* that stood for the airlift's dehydrated potatoes; she'd rather have those, she meant, than Soviet rule, for "Woman, come!" had been the mating call of Red Army rapists in the city after its surrender.

After an hour, I left, wishing them luck. By the time I returned to Berlin, in the 1960's, they had moved away from Sulzaerstrasse. No one knew where, for Ahrensdorf had retired. This was recently, on the first of several visits to research this book.

Once again, I arrived at Tempelhof to see that everything had changed. What had been ruined had become modern—glass office-buildings, new apartment houses, and wide boulevards crowded with cars had replaced much of the rubble. I walked down the Kurfürstendamm, then went through Checkpoint Charlie into East Berlin, where I ate goulash at the Hotel Sofia. The Berlin Wall, which had developed into a prime tourist attraction of the city, had already been up for several years. Again, in both West and East Berlin, I was overcome with a sense of eerieness, but this time it was due not to bomb craters and burnt-out houses being everywhere, but rather to the division of the city. One felt that there was an unreal air about the city and that the Berliners themselves perhaps contributed to it.

For awhile, trying to analyze the atmosphere, I found only new questions. At that time, I spent nearly a year there, living among

4

the Berliners, for it seemed to me I needed to understand, at least a little, the entire life of this city. It became clear that its riddle might lie buried in a series of small events scattered throughout its years, scarring all of them to form a pattern. Furthermore, the city of Berlin seemed human in another way: Like a man, it also has its contradictions. Berliners, as a matter of fact, seem to be full of them.

A pattern—albeit a superficial one—did emerge almost immediately, and fascinated me. For one thing, in some ways the city has ended up today almost as it began hundreds of years ago. It was then a frontier bastion, remote from the main commerce of Western life, and that's just what many think it is right now. For another, early Berlin was backward compared with other German cities, both economically and culturally; I met many Germans (Berliners included) who thought it was becoming that way again today. Even the division of the city into east and west ironically reflects its state at birth for then, as now, it was divided into two separate municipalities. In those early years, just as today, a harsh despotism kept it from uniting, and as has been the case in recent years, Berliners who revolted against tyranny were killed in the city's streets, or fled Berlin. Furthermore, this is not the first time Western powers have occupied Berlin, nor are the Red Army soldiers now ringing the city the first Russians quartered there.

All sorts of parallels—and contradictions—emerged, all bringing new questions in their wake. More and more, the city struck me as a living being that had endured a great deal. Was it dying of old age? And what of the Berliner himself? Would he survive? Or would he change? For he was, and still is, a different sort of German, one worth recording.

And where does hope lie for this city and its people? If Germany is ever reunited, it will again be governed from Berlin. Once more, Berliners will help shape our destiny, wherever we live. Even today, they can determine our future, for what goes on inside Berlin could start a nuclear war.

I therefore chose to examine Berlin minutely, as a diagnostician, fearing cancer, might. If I have also examined it subjectively, I did so like a lover, trying to understand the Berliners and what types they are. Throughout a year of mingling with the city's crowds, a host of impressions came to me; many turned my feel-

5

ings bitter-sweet. Often I began to feel that special melancholia which is so much a Berlinese emotion; soon I had to leave the city to sort out my thoughts more clearly. Today, living away from it, I occasionally feel homesick for Berlin. My friends there warned me that I would. They said they had no doubt they'd see me back there again, once more on the Kurfürstendamm. They're probably right.

One of the most popular songs in Berlin is called "I've Still Got a Suitcase in Berlin" (*"Ich hab' noch einen Koffer in Berlin"*). The words mean something special to Berliners and to all those who've lived in Berlin for any length of time. Most of them, myself included, still do keep a suitcase in Berlin. It amounts to emotional baggage.

Berlin has lived through the kind of history that produces a lot of legends—and inevitably, a lot of dreary clichés. West Berlin, for example, can be identified in any number of ways—"bastion of democracy," "beleaguered city," "citadel of freedom"—even by those who cannot locate it accurately on a map. The real Berliner ends up suffocated in a smog of meaningless, if well-meaning, platitudes. One wonders how many know the significant geographical fact that West Berlin is actually situated 110 miles behind the Western frontiers of East Germany and closer to Communist Poland than to the West. A former *New York Times* reporter asserts that few New Yorkers are believed to know it. When he wrote for the "Week in Review" section of the Sunday *New York Times,* standard editorial procedure, he says, was to identify the city's exact location in the lead of any story about it. ("West Berlin, a Western enclave located 100 miles behind the Iron Curtain . . ." was more or less the accepted introductory form.) There is even a story current in Berlin press circles which tells of a United States Senator who did not realize where he was. Asked in a Berlin press conference what he felt like standing 100 miles inside the Communist world, he reportedly sputtered, "Does the Amurrican people know of this?"

The isolation of the city from the Western world, as well as its unnatural and dangerous division, is the special agony of Berlin today. It's a commonplace to say this was caused by Soviet villainy and/or American naïveté, but it makes for a simple morality-play reading of history. Americans who accept the explanation believe it dramatically reveals Soviet perfidy; they do not mind admitting American policy might have been naïve in those far, distant days. Some of our wartime allies like it because it makes Americans seem ingenuous adolescents. And there are Germans who prefer this reading of history, for it suggests they had no alternative but to play the role of victim. Others, however, believe that the "Wall of Shame" (*Schandmauer*), as Berliners call the Berlin Wall, may be part of the Germans' penance for their national disgrace. A West Berlin city official suggested as much during a luncheon talk he gave to a delegation of West German diplomat trainees visiting the city when he said that the "invisible writing above the Berlin Wall," consisted of the words that used to appear on Nazi construction projects. "Also for this can we thank our Führer!"

This wall, of course, defines the division of the city and runs in a zigzag line from north to south, along Berlin's district boundaries. Looking at a map of Berlin, one has the impression that the wall tears, rather than cuts, the city in half. Such a map strongly resembles a spider's web. The inner hub from which the city's concentric circles spin is District Mitte (appropriately meaning "Berlin-Center"), which was Berlin's banking, insurance, governmental, and cultural center before the war. Today, as the heart of East Berlin, it stretches from the Brandenburg Gate through Unter den Linden and the Marx-Engels Square, out to the Alexanderplatz and the Karl-Marx-Allee, and is now being developed into the tourist, entertainment, and governmental showcase of East Germany.

In the concentric circles which lie beyond, there used to be traditional city gates (of which only the Brandenburg Gate remains standing), the position of all of which can still be located by reference to streets and squares that bear their names if not their portals. The "ring" formed by these city gates enclosed the oldest Berlin districts, actually suburban when first settled, but very built up and central today. The next concentric circle is formed by a circular railway, the Ringbahn, which encloses six Berlin districts, some of them in East and others in West Berlin.

The radii of the web are the city's roads and railways, both the underground system of the U-Bahn and the surface and elevated lines of the S-Bahn. They run out to the city limits, the last of the concentric circles. Here farmland can still be encountered, even

7

today, with the result that some of these Berlin sections retain a peaceful, bucolic air. The farther out from the center one gets, the quieter and more elegant West Berlin's districts become. These sections are known as *Villenviertel,* or villa-quarters, and some of the mansions are very handsome indeed, even though most of them are now subdivided into small apartments, and in many cases, furnished rooms. East Berlin's aspect, once one gets away from its central hub, is far less elegant. Travelers into East Berlin should not assign all the blame for this to Communism, for the Soviet sector of the city was never Berlin's prettiest. Its one truly handsome section, Berlin-Mitte, lay devastated by the time the war ended, and the workers' tenements that survived the war have not survived the ravages of time as well. There are a good many workers' sections in West Berlin, too, of course, and it is in such proletarian neighborhoods that one sniffs real Berlinese air, that *Berliner Luft* of which the Berliners are so proud.

East Berlin's city limits imperceptibly merge with the East German countryside, but West Berlin's are more precisely defined, for the three Western sectors are completely surrounded by an impassable fortified frontier.* Toward East Berlin, this takes the form of the Berlin Wall, but the frontier facing the countryside north, west, and south is just as formidable. While researching this book, we lived in West Berlin's Marienfelde section, in the south of the city. The frontier was just a half-mile from our house, and consisted of barbed-wire entanglements, a plowed "death strip," mine fields, and guard towers. Take a wrong turn in West Berlin and you are likely to run either into the wall or this fortified border, just as we did on several occasions. The experience is valuable: It helps one to realize how much the West Berliners are imprisoned.

Their way out lies through East Germany or over it by air. The road, rail, and air "access routes" are all strictly defined, and their continued availability to the West Berliners has required the presence of British, French, and American troops in the city.

* Actually neither frontier nor boundary, but a *demarcation line.* This latter term being too cumbersome, I have adopted one or another of the first-named; both are commonly used in the Western press. In West Germany and West Berlin, however, the press avoids using them, for fear of implying that the "German Democratic Republic" (East Germany) is a sovereign state with national frontiers.

8

Nowhere else in the world do these armies confront Soviet Russian troops as immediately as in Berlin. The city, even today, remains a shrine to the Cold War, and one has the sense that here it has always been maintained, even if it may have thawed elsewhere from time to time. Although the wall and its effects on the Berliners will be discussed in later chapters, a glance at some early events may help put the present in perspective.

Berlin's postwar situation was actually determined in part during the two days which preceded the surrender of the city on the morning of May 2, 1945. Two men who now play prominent roles in Germany were participants; two others, who formed the past, were leaving this city's always dramatic stage. Forty-eight hours before Hitler's forces surrendered in Berlin, a party of German civilians boarded a Douglas aircraft in Moscow and left for Germany; it was early in the morning of April 30, and just a few hours after Adolf Hitler had received a last report telling him Berlin could not, after all, be relieved. At Frankfurt on the Oder, where the plane from Moscow landed, the Germans climbed aboard a truck, and eventually, were driven in Russian and American limousines to Bruchmühle, a village eighteen miles east of Berlin.

In the capital, meanwhile, the top floors of the Reich Chancellery on the Wilhelmstrasse had been destroyed; Soviet artillery had been trained on it since the early hours of the day. A few hours before the Germans from Moscow reached Bruchmühle, Adolf Hitler committed suicide in his *Führerbunker* underneath the Chancellery. The "Brown" dictatorship he personified was ending; the "Red" dictatorship the Germans from Moscow were importing was just about to begin.

Walter Ulbricht, the man leading the Germans from Moscow, lunched with political officers of Marshal Zhukov's staff and passed the night. While he and his nine companions rested, the battle for Berlin continued to rage. Six days earlier, the *Völkischer Beobachter* carried a proclamation by Hitler ordering that anyone hampering the defense of the city by deeds or defeatist talk, as well as anyone countenancing this, be hanged or shot on the spot. This set the tone: The Berliners were to do the rest—which meant the dying. Uniformed hangmen roamed the streets, festooning lamp posts with "traitors." A ragtag army of old men and young boys, often ridiculously armed, were pressed into defending the capital with the few troops left; those who failed to report received no food. While Ulbricht slept and German generals anguished over the morality of surrender, Berliners died on every corner. Berlin Gauleiter Joseph Goebbels' assurances that Germany would somehow still win were met with sneers. "Sure we believe in final German victory," the Berliners would say, "especially now that we can travel from the Western to the Eastern front on the subway!" Yet, perversely, they had a sneaking admiration for the clubfooted propaganda minister whom they had derided as "Gimpy" or "the Gimp" (*"Hinkebein"* or *"Hinkefuss"*); they knew he'd been lying to them for years, but they admired the sheer, outrageous nerve of his brash lies. *"Det iss jekonnt!"* they'd say in their Berlinese dialect, meaning "You've got to hand it to him. That's masterly!"

Some Berliners who knew Goebbels suspect he was less a fanatic Nazi than an opportunist gambler, who'd put his cards on Nazism to build a career under Hitler. Accurate or not, it was clear by the morning of May 1, as Ulbricht entered Berlin for the first time, that Goebbels was played out. He'd lost, and knowing it, had himself and his family killed off rather than face bankruptcy. With the Nazi Gauleiter removed, Ulbricht had a clear field (although it was a field of rubble) in which to operate. The few Nazis still alive had either fled the city with forged papers, were burning or burying their uniforms, or fighting to the death.

That same evening, a thousand miles away in Stockholm, Sweden, a young Socialist strode up to the platform of a mass meeting called by the International Workers' Council to make a few remarks. He was Herbert Ernst Karl Frahm, thirty-one years old, a relative unknown, and overshadowed at this meeting by the two main speakers, authors Gunnar Myrdal and Sigurd Hoel. As he reached the microphone, he was handed a note saying Hitler had committed suicide the previous day. He read the news to the assembled anti-Nazis. A stunned silence followed the announcement. The night of the truncheons was over. Frahm, who was known only by the code name that he had assumed when he started to fight the Nazis, thirteen years earlier, stepped down. In his future role in Germany, he continued to use his adopted name, Willy Brandt.

The night was indeed over, but the dawn of May 2 did not mark a new day, for the battle for Berlin continued to rage. Today, Soviet divisions ring the city, while a much smaller force of British, French, and American troops maneuvers in the Grunewald. The struggle for this city has already exhausted many, the greatest among them Ernst Reuter, from 1948 to the time of his death in 1953 West Berlin's mayor and the live symbol of defiance during the Blockade. From 1957 to 1966, Willy Brandt had that post and today Klaus Schütz is the mayor. Yet, in a certain sense, the Berliners in this confrontation between East and West have very little to say. Ulbricht comes from Saxony and obeys orders that come from Moscow while Foreign Minister Brandt, the son of a poor salesgirl from Lübeck, North Germany, and Chancellor Kiesinger determine policies from Bonn. None of these men, nor the soldiers who back them up, are Berliners. Berliners always seem to be caught in the middle. They are expected to do little more than endure, struggle, and sometimes die; they are also expected to do all this heroically.

Germans who have lived in Berlin for any length of time tend to become Berliners, no matter where they hail from originally, for Berlin claims loyalties fast. The *Tagesspiegel,* West Berlin's most highly reputed newspaper, says, "One moves into the city, lives here a couple of years, and one day, when asked where one comes from, one answers, 'From Berlin—that is, actually I was born elsewhere . . .'" No West Berliner, therefore, ever questioned the authenticity of Brandt's Berlin credentials, though Walter Ulbricht, who is contemptuously referred to as "the Saxon" even by East Berliners, could never say, "I am a Berliner," as John F. Kennedy did. To become a Berliner means to become a partisan of the city and of its people. Ulbricht may enjoy letting himself be photographed receiving flowers from little uniformed girls, just as Hitler used to do, but it has not helped his image; the youngsters may be Berliners, but the man with them is not, even though he's been around for a long time.

The region from which Ulbricht comes is the birthplace of many Berliners, however. Most of those Berliners who weren't born in the city come from Saxony, Silesia, North Germany (specifically the Mark Brandenburg surrounding Berlin), East Prussia, or Pom-

11

erania. Sixty years ago, just about sixty percent of all Berliners had been born elsewhere, which shows how fast the city was then growing and attracting new people; today, about fifty percent of the city's population are immigrants, but few of them are fresh from other regions, for the city is no longer growing. Still, one out of every two Berliners at one point or another had to learn how to be a Berliner. It is amazing how fast many of them learned.

I certainly did not always find it easy to understand the Berliners, but consoled myself with the thought that I did not have to start by trying to understand the Germans, whom no one, including Tacitus, seems ever to have been able to figure out. For to call the Berliners "Germans" is like calling the Parisians "Frenchmen"; this takes you only part of the way—and often in the wrong direction.

Most people who've met Berliners are fascinated by them, and most visitors to the city for even a few days find the Berliner likable—as well as puzzling. "He's just different," said an American businessman in the Berlin Hilton's cocktail lounge, "and easier to like than most Germans." A Londoner said Berliners have "a Cockney air about them," and a Jewish attorney in West Berlin told me that this is the only city in Germany to which a Jew can return without misgivings (though Hamburg, it might be noted, today has a Jewish Lord Mayor). I heard the same in East Berlin, where a Jewish cabarettist from Vienna said the Viennese were too anti-Semitic for him; being a Communist, he came to East Berlin, rather than to the Western sectors, but in any case he felt comfortable among Berliners. Indeed, so unusual is this city that John F. Kennedy could make his famous "I am a Berliner" statement without outraging even anti-Germans. One cannot even conceive of his saying, perhaps in Munich, "I am a German!"

What makes the Berliner so different? Perhaps the *Steppke,* the typical Berlin street urchin, is illustrative, for he seems unlike other German children, a fact that goes far toward explaining why he ends up being unlike other German adults.

He is not necessarily charming. Indeed, little German children from the provinces may well win your heart more readily. This Berlin gamin may be spitting or urinating in the streets, but nevertheless one cannot deny that there is something fetching about the *Steppke.* His Berlin brashness is rooted in unconcern and lack of

12

affectation; rough as he is, he betrays a certain innocence. There is a story about him which, while apocryphal, goes a long way toward explaining both "the Berlin type" and the special Berlinese humor. It is about Emil, a Berlin boy evacuated in 1943 to escape the heavy air raids that began in March of that year and whose fate was to land in a Rhineland village convent school.

The atmosphere here was foreign. The local children seemed simple, sweet—and also, duller than those back home. Their mothers were pious and straight-laced; Emil was accustomed to the open-hearted, rough, and often loud-mouthed workers' wives of Berlin. The village men were given to ponderous meditations and mysterious silences; Emil longed for the Berliners' coarse and rapid repartee. He was out of his element and felt lost.

The nuns regarded him as underprivileged and were, perhaps, over-solicitous. In any case, they were so sweet to Emil that it made him feel sick. *"Iss ja zum kotzen!"* one can hear him say in his Berlinese slang—"It's enough to make you puke!"

But he tried hard to please, for Berliners are by and large open-hearted, if at first reserved. They boast that they can get on anywhere, even if they are a bit provincial in their pride of being from Berlin. And so, Emil fell to and worked hard to fit in.

One day, during a class on nature-lore, his convent teacher turned to Emil with the question, "What is it that is tiny, has bright eyes, a bushy tail, likes to chew nuts, and hops from branch to branch?"

Emil, to whom nature was as much of a mystery as was the Catholic religious instruction given by the nuns, mulled the question over for awhile.

"Well, it naturally figures to be a squirrel," he said brightly. "But on the other hand, after six weeks of seeing how this joint here operates, it just might be our sweet little infant Jesus."

It is now more than twenty-five years later; Emil is an adult, back where he belongs, on the banks of the River Spree, in Berlin. It does not matter whether he lives in Prenzlauer Berg in East Berlin or in the West's Neukölln or Wedding; he is a Berliner and considers himself a special type. Like all Berliners, he is a big-city character: tough, cynical, and a little coarse. These attributes have not always made him a popular figure, for many of his fellow countrymen find his ways unfamiliar and even somewhat "un-

German." They may be amused by the Berliner, titillated even, but usually are also a little shocked, embarrassed, and outraged by his "vulgarity." Most of all, they resent the fact that the Berliner, no matter what his social station may be, never allows people to look down on him, dismissing all other Germans as coming from "the provinces." This rankles today more than in the past, for many of the citizens of West German cities such as Düsseldorf, Hamburg, and Munich are now more prosperous than Berliners and consider themselves more urbane than ever. The Berliner, by and large, concedes their prosperity, but still tends to dismiss them as *kleinbürgerlich,* as having the ways of narrow-minded petits bourgeois. As for the government at Bonn, Berliners, of course, feel far superior to that, as well. As one young Berlin actor said, sipping a Manhattan in the chic Volle Pulle bar on the Steinplatz, "Bonn may be old and quaint, but as a capital of Germany, it is ridiculous!" The only thing Bonn has in common with a capital, he added, is the capital letter "B" it shares with Berlin.

It does not take long in Berlin to learn that the Berliners regard their city as the center of Germany even though they are painfully aware of its isolated position. They remain convinced it is the nation's rightful hub and that hope for Germany exists only once the city has resumed its historical place.

In West Berlin's unofficial tourist center, the Breitscheidtplatz, where the elegant Kurfürstendamm begins at the Kaiser Wilhelm Memorial Church and the Europa Center, a huge sign looms above the crowds. It reads *"Berlin bleibt doch Berlin."* The city's unofficial slogan, it means, more or less, "Berlin remains Berlin, *no matter what!"*

Berliners have had to reconcile themselves to a good deal, having gone through much more than most of us, but they have a strong knack for survival, as we shall see. A Berlinese expression says that "it's all right to be stupid, as long as you at least know how to take care of yourself." Getting along under adverse conditions, even collaborating (the art of *Mitmachen*) to save your skin, is a Berlinese talent that it is likely to save them in the future just as it has in the past. Berliners are supposed to be especially courageous, this being their Cold War stance, but it seems questionable whether they are so in actual fact. A Berlin psychiatrist told me he doubts they are "tougher" than other people, no matter what the Berlin legend says. "The difficulties the Berliners endured, the tests of strength they met," he says, "simply made them tough. Similar difficulties and tests might have made any other Germans just as tough."

He believes non-Germans would probably have proved even better suited to such tests of resolution. "Americans," he says, "have a frontier tradition of helping the community to survive. The British have an equally well-developed community loyalty. Neighborly help is largely foreign to Germans. If the British or the Americans had been threatened as the Berliners have been, I think they might have met the danger more resolutely."

Be that as it may, the Berliner has shown a good deal of courage and resolution already. If it was exciting to live through the past thirty years in Berlin, then most Berliners would probably agree that they've had more than their fair share of thrills and would just as soon have a little peace and quiet.

Yet the Berliner remains proud of his city, of its sufferings, of what it has had to endure, and proud also of the way the Berliners responded. His civic pride appears to be stronger than his national patriotism. You won't often hear Berliners declare nationalistically that they are Germans; they will identify themselves as Berliners always, just as many New Yorkers and Romans will evoke the name of their city first before they call themselves Americans or Italians.

It is one of the paradoxes of this city that this capital of illiberal Prussia should seem to regard itself today as Germany's liberal conscience. This former stamping ground of Germany's officer caste, this home of German militarism and hatchery of German wars, sees itself as the hope of German democracy, and although the headquarters of the Nazi dictatorship, considers itself a defense against German Right-Wing extremism. Some Berliners, as a matter of fact, even seem to regard a Germany whose leadership does not come from Berlin as potentially dangerous.

Yet there is not mere boastfulness here, for it is tempered also by other typically Berlinese traits: detachment and cynicism. Professor Hans-Joachim Lieber, scholar and former *Rektor* (president) of West Berlin's Free University, makes the point that this detachment existed even when Berlin was the capital of the Kaiser's empire.

15

"Of course, the Berliner was impressed by the pomp around him when Berlin was the center of the German *Kaiserreich*," Lieber says, "but even then there would come a time when he'd back off in cynical detachment. Watching all the *Glanz und Gloria,* the glitter and glory, he'd say, 'Now, hold it a minute, let's not overdo it!' "

Detachment has helped make the Berliner famous for his impudence and his contempt for authority. Countless Berlinese stories, more legends than jokes, chronicle his cheek and gall. One is about Friedrich von Wrangel, the Berlin military governor whose troops subdued the Berliners after their 1848 revolution. Strolling down Unter den Linden one day late in his life, Field Marshal Wrangel noticed that a young urchin on the sidewalk stopped whistling when he saw him. Flattered by what he assumed to be a show of respect, Wrangel called the boy over.

"You there!" he said. "Why have you stopped whistling? Is it because of my uniform?"

The *Steppke* backed off a safe distance and shouted back, "It's because when I see you I want to laugh, and when I laugh, I can't whistle!"

Fifty-six years after Wrangel's death, when President Paul von Hindenburg affixed his signature to the document that named Adolf Hitler chancellor, this side of the Berliner remained the same.

"Now they'll have to sweep the Wilhelmstrasse at least twice a day," Berliners said. "Hindenburg is likely to sign any scrap of paper lying around the street."

Political satirist Rolf Ulrich claims that such wisecracks demonstrate the Berliner's "sure ability to spot what is phoney, pretentious, hollow or ridiculous." His troupe of cabaret artists, who called themselves the *Stachelschweine,* or Porcupines, serve up a caustic bill of fare and deliver, in rapid-fire Berlinese, one debunking and irreverent crack after another.

Berlin, says Ulrich, is "the dream city for a political satirist, for the Berliners' comprehension of politics is instinctive." On tour "out in the provinces," on the other hand, Ulrich's actors have to slow down their delivery by fifty percent; non-Berlin audiences, he says, don't catch on as fast.

16

A good deal of the Berliner's humor has consisted of laughing at adversity. It is gallows humor stemming from a capacity for joking about the rope around his neck. Berliners undergoing wartime air raids took mocking leave of each other with, "Stay healthy, survive—and make sure to tend my grave!" or else they wisecracked, "If you're still alive, it can only be your own damn fault; they certainly dropped enough bombs!"

When wit fails them, Berliners often make do with sheer brash. Even this amuses them, and as with the reaction of some of them to Goebbels, they can admire a man's big-mouth bravura even if they both dislike him personally and what he says. It is technique which many a Berliner admires even more than substance. This has led many of them to the sidelines, content to watch other actors in their city and to criticize their performances. It has also led them into difficulties, for many of them tended to forget the drama was real and played for keeps.

It is an astounding fact that when the Berliners celebrated the seven hundredth anniversary of their city in 1937, they could look back on only fifteen years of genuine democratic self-government in the preceding five centuries. Why this was so will be explored later, but part of the answer was given by author Emil Ludwig. Writing of those who acclaimed Kaiser Wilhelm I on Unter den Linden after his 1871 victory over France, Ludwig called them "courageous, strong, and devoted" but also "inherently less liberty-loving than submissive." It was one of the contradictions of the Berliners that the Hohenzollern monarchs (and Hitler) never trusted them, but that in fact they had little to worry about most of the time.

To say that is not to denigrate those Berliners who have many times fought and died for their ideals of liberty, notably during the uprisings of 1848 and 1918, as well as in East Berlin in 1953. Others in Berlin fought Hitler on his homeground. Yet, by and large, these seem exceptions. Berlin has always been an occupied city and Berliners in the past have for the most part grudgingly done the bidding of their masters, choosing to perform acts of resistance or sheer humanity individually. As we shall see, there were many such acts; put together, they make for a history of inner disengagement, but not of popular resistance. It took the Cold War to enlist the masses, yet the Berliner derides the heroic Wagnerian mantle hung about him by the world press. He knows he is a pragmatist who likes to survive. If that makes him less "heroic," at least it shows him as utterly human.

chapter two

ANY WAY YOU SLICE IT—AND IT HAS BEEN SLICED IN HALF—
Berlin is a big city. Its 341 square miles could easily encompass the
three major West German cities of Frankfurt, Stuttgart, and
Munich; either portion of it is bigger than any of these three. Berlin
is bigger than all of Chicago, five times as big as the District of
Columbia, fifteen times the size of Bermuda, and just about as
large as all five boroughs of New York City put together. It is three
miles wider than New York is at its widest point, stretching twenty-
eight miles west to east, and covers twenty-eight and one-half
miles north to south, or thirteen and four tenths miles longer than
the length of Manhattan Island. Even if you split Berlin as Ulbricht
did, it remains big: West Berlin, with fifty-four percent of the
city's territory, covers as much as 185 square miles.

Like London, Berlin grew out from a nucleus at a river's edge.
Its Thames is the River Spree but, unlike London, Berlin is criss-
crossed by canals, lakes, and smaller rivers. The Spree itself flows
from the Müggelsee in the east right through the city's center,
skirting Tiergarten Park, until it empties into the Havel River opposite West Berlin's District Spandau. Sometimes the erratic course
of the frontier between East and West Berlin runs along the river's
edge. Looking at this peaceful river, patrolled by gunboats, one
is struck not so much by the wall's much discussed inhumanity as
by its sheer insanity.

That all this has more than an ideological effect can be seen
particularly when one looks at West Berlin's population, the structure of which can be construed as a sign that the city is dying.

For the pessimists, the case is easy to summarize. The city, they
point out, is today dying of old age. More than twenty percent of

19

the Berliners, East and West, are over sixty-five years of age; further, Berlin is, specifically, a city of old ladies, for women far outnumber men in both East and West Berlin. Every second West Berliner is over forty years of age and may be regarded as queuing up behind the thirty-nine thousand Berliners who die each year, about thirteen thousand more dying than are born. West Berlin has more than seven hundred cemeteries, as crowded as its buses, because the large, spacious forest cemeteries that used to serve the city are inaccessible today to even the dead of West Berlin, for they lie in East Germany, on the city's outskirts. If there were no influx of West German workers into West Berlin, sheer biology would turn this part of the city into another Fort Lauderdale or similar urban graveyard by 1975, and every fourth West Berliner will then be over sixty-five years of age. Already, West Berlin's two hundred and six old-age homes are so crowded that large numbers of volunteer workers are needed to help staff them; many more homes are needed if all those requiring such institutionalization are to be helped. The total number of people over sixty-five years of age in all of Berlin comes to roughly six hundred thousand, about the same number as live in Pittsburgh, Pennsylvania, or in the states of Hawaii, New Hampshire, or North Dakota. Two-thirds of the city's aged live in the Western sectors; these oldsters are equal in number to all the Germans living in Boston, Chicago, Cleveland, Detroit, Los Angeles, New York, Philadelphia, San Francisco, and Oakland, *combined*. As for East Berlin, the entire populations of either Jacksonville or of St. Petersburg, Florida, could almost be replaced by its one hundred and eighty thousand old people.

Whether it is due to climate, heredity, or way of life, Berliners seem to live a long time, which, of course, only aggravates the problem. West Berlin, for example, currently has more than two hundred and seventy-five thousand persons over seventy years of age and almost four thousand over ninety. A lot are widows and widowers, of course, but the latter figure even includes ten bachelors, who are presumably being pursued by the 181 spinsters who are over ninety years of age. Although it might appear that Berliners go on living forever (eighteen are more than one hundred years old), they do eventually prove themselves mortal and after death, almost half their number are cremated. This is a space-saving technique that has always been more in vogue in Berlin than elsewhere, but today it is a necessity due to the scarcity of graves. Smoke may be seen curling out of the Wilmersdorf crematorium in West Berlin almost any time one passes it. The building has a dome which resembles that on the Capitol in Washington, D.C., and the smoke rising from a chimney recessed in this dome tends to make the building somewhat eerie. The dead are dressed in their best clothes before being consigned to the flames; I mention this because there was a scandal some years back which sheds light on the conditions Berliners have had to endure. Shortly after the war, when everything was hard to come by, it was discovered that certain crematorium employees were not only reselling old wreaths, but were actually stripping the corpses before burning them—a fact reported by a horrified relative who insisted on having one last look at his deceased, only to find the corpse stark naked inside its box.

Apparently Cold War tensions do not cause despair of any great intensity, for those in the city who have accelerated the death rate by committing suicide did so, apparently, for other reasons. Berlin has always had an incredibly high suicide rate. About nine hundred West Berliners succeed in such attempts each year and about two thousand more fail. It appears that most of them are in despair over incurable disease or family strife, or clearly emotionally unbalanced. In Berlin, most male suicides hang themselves, while women turn to gas. The failures predictably try poison, since it is easier to swallow a non-lethal dose and have the police flying squad, or *Überfallkommando,* pump it out than it is to regulate ropes or gas fumes. Further, unlike in many other countries, survivors have nothing to fear in Berlin. Although the police there, as elsewhere in Germany, seem to have a regulation to cover any act at all, suicide attempts are not verboten in Berlin.

The marital strife and family difficulties promoting such despair have receded somewhat lately, a little more in West Berlin than in the East. Presently, only one out of every five West Berlin marriages break up, versus a staggering one out of every two in 1950. That year there seemed little reason to bother trying. The crippling blockade of the city had ended in May, 1949, but it had drained West Berlin of its energies. In 1950 the unemployed, who today do not even exist statistically in West Berlin, totalled more than three hundred thousand. West Berlin started late and has not yet caught up with West Germany's economic recovery; the early hard times reflected themselves, as they always seem to do—in divorce. Even now, the greater difficulties that East Berliners face may be seen in East Berlin's higher divorce rate. Three out of every ten "socialist marriages" wind up on the rocks.

Five years after the end of the war, Berlin was a city of unemployed workers, unhappy families, and old people. The excess of women, coupled with the shaky family life, created its own special problems. One elderly couple who lived through those years supply an illustration by no means untypical. Born Berliners, Gerda and August (as I shall call them) were then in their late fifties; they had been married since 1919, when August was mustered out of an Imperial Hussars regiment. In 1950 they were trying to start their prewar automobile business again. They needed financial advice and found it in a forty-five-year-old woman, a tax consultant, who soon became a friend of the family and began to come over for dinner several times a week. Meals were valuable then and being served at table two or three times a week by Frau Gerda was a form of extra payment. August drove the tax consultant home in the late evenings, and after awhile, began to spend more and more time with her. They became lovers; the mid and late fifties are regarded by many Germans as a man's "best years." Gerda, aware of the relationship, found serving her husband's mistress meals every second day increasingly annoying. Late one night, when August was absent from home, Gerda strolled over to the tax consultant's apartment house. There, in front of the building, Gerda encountered the woman with August in tow. She had decided to have a showdown with the consultant and told her that she had some nerve letting Gerda serve her dinner and then helping herself to "dessert," as it were, later the same night. The consultant's eyes went wide with anger and disbelief.

"You listen here!" she shouted back at Gerda. "It's *you* who has the nerve! What your husband does is his own business, and as far as I am concerned, you know very well how few men are left around here. You'd better realize they've got to be shared!"

A lot of sharing went on in those days. Not only was every second marriage breaking up, but the birth rate was catastrophically low. The population of both West and East Berlin was sinking. Many of the young had by now deserted the city, most of them for far healthier West Germany. The postwar exodus seemed like a deathblow. It is, after all, the beat of young hearts, the vigor in young hands, and the enthusiasm of youth's spirit that make a city come alive. Berlin, like Matthew Arnold's Oxford, seemed to be the "home of lost causes, and forsaken beliefs, and unpopular names, and impossible loyalties."

The war had done its part in reducing the number of Berliners. When Hitler started World War II, the city's population was 4,200,000, and by the time he had committed suicide not quite six years later, it had been cut almost in half. By no means had all of these people been killed—some had been relocated along with portions of Berlin's industry, most of it important to the war effort; others had left for shelter in the countryside. In the summer of 1943, when the heavy raids began and war work had raised the population to almost 4.5 million, the Nazis appealed to all women not engaged in vital industry, and particularly to those with small children, to let themselves be evacuated or to go to relatives living outside Berlin. (Many of these Berliners later bypassed the city when they fled west to escape the Russians.) Even today, a million ex-Berliners continue to live in West Germany, swallowing their traditional prejudices against "provinces."

After the restrictions on moving into Berlin were lifted, the city's population began to pick up again, though not energetically. About half a million drifted back between 1945 and 1951, two-thirds of them moving into the three Western sectors of the city. Today, about 3.3 million live in East and West Berlin combined, making Berlin a fraction smaller than Chicago in population, but still more populous than Paris. Of course, this is a comedown for a capital that had once ranked just behind New York, Tokyo, and Greater London. West Berlin alone now ranks just behind Mukden, China, but ahead of Rome, in terms of population, while East Berlin is somewhat smaller than Detroit.

Berlin has always reacted rather speedily to its changing political atmosphere. Whenever the Russians turn on the screws, the population tends to drop a little (and real estate values to plummet). Then when the Western allies respond with resolution, both stabilize themselves again. This is not to imply that there are Berliners who move in and out of the city in accordance with the amount of heat put on it by the Soviets, for those who move out usually do not return. As one Berliner said to me, "Those we can do without!" The newcomers who replace the irresolute are often of sturdy stuff. Five percent of the three million Germans who have left East Germany since the end of World War II (a fifth of the entire East German population) chose to remain in West Berlin. Many of them are young and not easily cowed. Much has been done to influence young West Germans to work and live in West Berlin. A massive recruitment drive was begun after the erection of Ulbricht's wall in 1961 cut off new blood from the East. These efforts have slowed the decline of West Berlin's population, but by no means ever made it into the "boom town" that journalists have sometimes called it.

Young West Germans have been brought into West Berlin by means of advertising ballyhoo, financial grants, and other inducements. In East Berlin, the problem of a declining population was not solved until August 13, 1961, when Ulbricht—apparently not able to rely on persuasive advertising techniques—dealt with the matter by means of brick, cement, barbed wire, and submachine guns.

West Berlin has managed to attract several thousand new Berliners a year since 1961, slightly more than the number who leave. Whenever the monthly average begins to dip a fraction, the West Berlin Senat, which administers the city by leave of the three Western military commandants, tends to boost its advertising budget and intensify its efforts. It even got those imported workers already employed in Berlin to write their friends back home, saying in effect, "Come on in, the water's fine!" Despite this, there remain Cassandras who predict a thirteen-percent population decline by the 1970s.

One of the reasons for this becomes apparent during a walk in Berlin's streets. One wonders whether some strange Germanic prudery or ill-placed modesty keeps pregnant women indoors after the fourth month, for one hardly ever sees any. Of course, there aren't many for few babies are born in Berlin. While the United States was worried when its birth rate dropped to about eighteen live births per one thousand inhabitants, such a rate would delight West Berlin, which currently has twelve per thousand, and might even please East Berlin, with only seventeen.

24

The low birth rate explains the need for importing West German workers, for municipal aid to young couples getting married, and for the financial help given to young parents. Today's Berliners like a good wedding almost as much as they like a birth. One sportive Berlin woman did her bit for the city by having an illegitimate child at age forty-six. Eleven percent of all new West Berliners (and slightly more in East Berlin) are born on the wrong side of the bed. It is interesting to note that half the gallants involved in West Berlin had pangs of conscience afterward, for that many legitimize their offspring before they are three years old. They do this by admitting paternity and by providing the children with their surnames, though only five of the fourteen hundred who did so were willing to marry the mothers.

In addition to new births and newly imported workers, West Berlin also gains new citizens from other countries. Almost twenty thousand foreigners have liked the city so much in the years since the war that they have applied for and received German citizenship. The largest single contingent, somewhat surprisingly, are the Israelis. About forty thousand foreigners live in West Berlin, three thousand of them from the U.S.A. These figures do not include Allied soldiers or civilian officials. Another eleven thousand come each year to stay for awhile, about three thousand more than those who leave. Visitors to West Berlin annually include one hundred sixty thousand foreigners and four hundred thousand West Germans. On any one day in West Berlin, at least every fifth person one sees on the streets is sure to be a visitor.

The erection of the wall in 1961 has, of course, eliminated large-scale emigration from East to West Berlin, yet almost four thousand do make the move each year. Almost all of them are women over sixty-five years of age, Ulbricht being happy to add to West Berlin's welfare budget while reducing his own. Naturally, they aggravate the old-age problem in the Western sectors. The traffic here is not entirely one-sided: About 150 women and 130 men knock on the wall and move from West to East Berlin each year. A few of these are young men who escaped to the West and later, unable to endure the "utter chaos" of a free society, felt compelled to take their chances on returning East again. One escapee called them "Mama's boys," products of Mother Russia's smothering educational embrace.

What they return to has at least one distinction that West Berlin, for all its prosperity, has not been able to get: East Berlin is the official capital of East Germany, the *Haupstadt* of the "German Democratic Republic." As such, it acts as a magnet for that nation's youth and is more of a center for them than an outpost. Despite its leaden air, it has a youthful atmosphere; one seems to see more young people about its streets than in the Western sectors.

Still, East Berlin has changed and much of it is no longer "Berlinese" in character. It has been overshadowed by the doctrinaire regime and the humorless man who runs it. Those who know Ulbricht claim they have never seen him genuinely laugh. He has made his regime into a government of petits bourgeois and has provincialized his capital with Saxons.

Not only is Ulbricht himself from Saxony, but so are most of his functionaries and troops in Berlin. If they are not Saxons, they come from other distant areas, for Ulbricht found out that the Berliners in his army could not be trusted to shoot other Berliners. "Today we have fewer real Berliners in East Berlin than West Berlin has," one East German official admitted to me. "Our city and its government has become Saxon, right to the very top." To say this is not to denigrate Saxony, which has its attractions; it is merely to note that the milieu in East Berlin has changed. Along with its freedoms, it has lost its sophistication.

Because Berlin is an industrial city, it is safe to portray today's typical Berliner as a factory or construction worker. In the west he is likely to live in a district like Neukölln, which—with 275,000 people jammed into 120,000 apartments—is the most populous area in West Berlin. Like Wedding and Kreuzberg, it is one of the best-known workers' sections and perhaps among the most interesting. Other West Berlin districts are Tiergarten, Charlottenburg, Spandau, Wilmersdorf, Zehlendorf, Schöneberg, Steglitz, Tempelhof, and Reinickendorf—each a city in itself, with upward of 100,000 inhabitants.

In East Berlin, Prenzlauer Berg is the most crowded district, perhaps because it suffered comparatively little from wartime bombings. The workers there are used to enduring Russians: In 1813, Russian soldiers bombarded Berlin from Bötzowberg, the site of an old brewery. The city was then occupied by the French. Like many neighborhoods inhabited by Berlin workers,

Prenzlauer Berg has a revolutionary tradition, one that is glorified by the East Berlin press but carefully watched by its People's Police. It was in Prenzlauer Berg that a famous gathering of revolutionary workers took place in 1848 and there also that Karl Liebknecht, the early German Communist leader, directed revolutionary soldiers and workers in January, 1919. The ferment that was so commonplace in the streets of districts like this gave the Reich capital the name of "Red Berlin" in earlier years.

These districts are still extremely crowded. Prenzlauer Berg has almost nineteen thousand inhabitants per square kilometer; West Berlin's Kreuzberg, with more than eighteen thousand, is not far behind. West Berlin's workers' districts are thinning out a little, however, partly because of the new housing being put up elsewhere in the city and partly because greater prosperity has allowed the worker to seek a bit more comfort. Many Berliners are dissatisfied with the living conditions they endured for decades, ever since the *Gründerjahre* following the founding of the German Reich in 1871. This event launched an unprecedented boom for those nine hundred thousand Berliners who suddenly found themselves citizens of the Imperial Capital. In the forty years that followed, the city grew—exploded, really—to a population of almost four million. Peasants who owned Berlin acreage during those years were transformed almost overnight into *Millionenbauer;* they lived the "tony" life in huge villas in District Schöneberg and died like Pharaohs beneath splendid mausolea near the Hauptstrasse.

Tenements shot out of the sandy Berlin soil in those years on every street and corner, like fungi. These districts may look picturesque to those who do not live in them, but it seems clear that the builders who put them up ruthlessly tried at the time to pack the maximum proletariat into the minimum space with the least possible investment. Several generations of occupancy have not improved these tenements, and some Berliners say that, if they had their way, they would not even want to be *photographed* in Neukölln.

"The British and the Americans," one Berlin housing official once said to me ironically, "bombed out the wrong sections of the city." He was referring to the fact that many of Berlin's handsomest villa sections were leveled, along with the town's center, but

27

that many of the workers' slums were not hit too severely. This, of course, is not quite true, for many districts jammed with workers and their families were bombed and burned to the ground. Kreuzberg, for instance, was a sea of flames during the worst raid of the war on February 3, 1945. Wave after wave of bombers roared over Berlin, laying what the Berliners call "carpets of bombs," and entire districts disappeared. In the process, the bombs cleared away a lot of the old slums. These houses have in a large measure been replaced; a quarter of a million new apartments have been built in West Berlin alone since the end of the war. Some, like those built in the Hansa section as part of a 1957 city-boosting international architectural competition, are handsome and equipped with the most modern comforts. Others, which seem modern on the outside, lack such facilities as central heating and centrally supplied hot water, not to speak of elevators. Even in such "model" housing developments as Gropiusstadt, partly designed by Walter Gropius, a former Berliner now of the United States, many residents who rely on tiled coal stoves for their heat lug pails of briquets up the stairs each day from storage places in the cellars. Hot water is provided by small-capacity, gas-heated tanks above each sink. This rather primitive arrangement is not mentioned on official tours of the apartment site; one learns of it only after coming to know some tenants personally. The city officials understandably prefer to concentrate on Berlin as Beulah Land. They like to cite the fact that the number of apartments built in West Berlin in thirteen years equals the total of all new flats put up during that period in Austria, Belgium, Hungary, Norway, and Yugoslavia. The tiled stoves, or *Kachelöfen,* it is pointed out, keep the rents low.

This is not to suggest in the least that the new developments are undesirable. All have their own flush toilets, and to have that is to have a good deal. For many Berliners who grew up in the old workers' slums, a bathroom with a flush toilet is a white-tile El Dorado. The old housing, in which three out of four Berliners continue to live, often have toilets half a flight down the stairs or even in outhouses in rear courtyards. The tenants have keys to the stalls, in which they sit and freeze in the winter. Wedding and Neukölln have the most old apartment houses in West Berlin—

seventeen thousand in all, mostly four to six stories high, with a total of two hundred thousand flats.

Certainly the new housing is a step up the ladder, though a mixed blessing. Life in them may be clean and airy, but for many it is often also excruciatingly dull. Berliners are extremely social creatures. One lady who moved to a new apartment is so depressed that she is trying to move out, even though she may have to use an outhouse. She is lonely in the new development, she says, because whenever she looks out the window, she sees only a patch of grass and another apartment house. In Neukölln, she leaned out of her window to watch the life of the taverns, shops, restaurants; she enjoyed the sounds of cars, trolleys, buses, vans, and trucks, the smells and noises of people and animals everywhere. There she knew everyone, while in Gropiusstadt she feels alone—"like in a prison." The novelty of having a flush toilet is not much comfort, she adds, for "how much time can one spend there?"

The circumstance of loneliness as an acute problem in Berlin is one which seems difficult to believe, considering the density of its population and the natural gregariousness of the Berliner. Yet it affects large numbers, particularly women. In Neukölln alone, there are as many widows and divorced women as there are people of all kinds in Danville, Illinois, or Montclair, New Jersey. This is not a local district problem. As many widows and divorced women live in West Berlin as there are men, women, and children populating Venice, Italy, or Fort Worth, Texas. One sees these women everywhere in Berlin; three-hundred fifty-thousand-strong, they walk alone, like stragglers in an army of the solitary, wearing those ugly German women's hats that author Hans Habe aptly described as "felt helmets" and toting enormous leatherette shopping bags to market, sitting somewhat defiantly in Kurfürstendamm cafés if they have the money, or, if they have not, resting with arms folded aggressively over their large bosoms on park benches. They vastly outnumber the widowers and divorced men. In Neukölln specifically, the proportion of widows to widowers is seven to one.

The reason for this is not just that in Berlin, as on Madison Avenue, men fail to survive the weaker sex. Many of these widows lost their husbands during World War II. As for the larger number of divorced women than men, this is due to the relative ease with which those men who wish to can get back on the rolls of the married. West Berlin alone has three hundred thousand more women than men. Not all of these ladies are elderly, either, and even if one excludes the merrier widows and divorcees of marriageable age, there still remain one hundred thousand West Berlin women between eighteen and forty who are on the hunt for their first husbands. Thus divorced men are frequently and, I suspect, rather triumphantly, trotted off to the *Standesamt* for a new license, while their ex-wives can only console themselves with a sense of moral outrage.

The elderly of West Berlin who receive small pensions don't have much surplus money left for entertainment. The same holds true for a lot of workers; they live comfortably, but modestly. The average weekly wage in West Berlin is 148.14 marks ($37), and even those workers who earn more rarely top 200 marks ($50) a week. While rents are low, food prices are high, even by United States standards. Such items as coffee are virtual luxuries, a pound costing 8 marks ($2) in West Berlin and 30 marks ($7.50) in the East. This represents a big chunk out of the household budget; it hurts even more than it would hurt an American worker who has to pay this in dollars. A pound of meat alone costs the Berlin worker more than an hour's earnings, while in the U.S.A. he might earn the price of a pound of hamburger in fifteen minutes.

Everything, of course, is relative and it would be wrong to paint a picture of the West Berlin worker as poorly housed, poorly fed, and generally underprivileged. Factory and office canteens provide cheap noon meals; evening meals in Germany traditionally consist of cold cuts, which are inexpensive. Many of the requirements Americans make of life are simply not made by the 1,500,000 working men and women of Berlin, such as the "need" for central heating or a centrally supplied source of constant hot water. A young Berlin woman I know recently spent about six months in New York City and energetically toured its streets, the slums included. When she returned to her round of nursing duties in Neukölln, she was asked about what she had seen. "It isn't like in the movies, eh?" the Neuköllners said to her. "Tell us, did you see the slums?"

"Well, I can tell you one thing," she answered back rather

sharply. "What they call slums there a lot of us might call luxury housing! Even some of those slums have central heating, central hot water, and even elevators!" She still doubts whether she was believed. Such extras are elements of the soft way of life and the Berliner has been raised to be more rugged. Albert Noack, an eighty-six-year-old Berliner whom I came to know quite well, takes a cold shower every morning, never heats his apartment unless he has guests, and bicycles every day. People like that don't mind hiking up four flights of stairs, a bucket of briquets in hand.

No matter where they live in the city, or on which side of the wall, most Berliners—at least the older ones—still think of their city as a whole, rather than as two separate entities. As for the youngsters, one teacher told me, "We start them off with nonpolitical, topographical maps, the kind that show Berlin without its sectors."

This may work; Berliners think it important that it should. However, the editor-in-chief of a Berlin newspaper told me, "My son hasn't got the vaguest idea what East Berlin looks like. Furthermore, he doesn't care, when you come right down to it. To him, Berlin is just West Berlin and what's across the wall is simply *drüben* [that over there]."

Still, as the young man may find out some day, the people being walled in are not too different from those being walled out. While the West Berliner despises the Ulbricht regime, he is nevertheless happy to arrogate to himself those few of its accomplishments of which he approves. The fact that East Berlin's architectural style has been modernized and brought into conformity with that of West Berlin pleases Western city planners, all of whom are busy devising visionary, courageous, if sometimes Utopian, plans for the politically free, de-walled and united city hoped for in five, ten, twenty, 100 years, no one dares speculate when.

When that comes, West Berliners will want to stream across the Spree River to head to such green oases as the three-hundred-acre *Tierpark* or zoo in Friedrichsfelde. It was built by the East German Government in 1955, and is one of the few monuments to the S.E.D. regime that is likely to remain popular. This is because West Berliners are in one respect worse off than their walled-in brothers to the east, for the latter can spend weekends and holidays in the countryside surrounding the city, while the West Berliner cannot. For West Berliners a holiday in the country means a trip to West Germany or beyond, and not all of them can afford the cost of such vacations, particularly now that the East Germans demand they buy transit visas. Fortunately for them, West Berlin is lavishly supplied with parks and lakes or, as one city official said to me, "the people would really have cracked up long ago." French author-diplomat Jean Giraudoux, who saw Berlin before the war, said, "Berlin is no city of gardens—it is a garden in itself!" And it is true that more than twenty percent of Berlin's acreage consists of almost two hundred lakes, canals, rivers, and streams, as well as thousands of acres of parkland and woods. About twenty-five thousand acres are in West Berlin alone.

The greenery is enough to turn any New Yorker green with envy. Berlin reportedly has more trees than any capital on earth, a fact that points up the quality of its dry, stimulating, and clean air and that explains the pleasing aspect of its boulevards. The lengths to which Berliners will go to preserve trees is amazing to an American accustomed to seeing them bulldozed to clear a construction site or to watching parkland chopped up to make room for highways. When Berlin widens or extends its already wide avenues, it adds more trees, many of which, because of the unpolluted air, grow to majestic size.

It has a temperate climate, though it lies farther north than Newfoundland or Winnipeg, Canada, level with the southern tip of Kamchatka, Siberia, and with London. A line drawn 1,541 miles from the Kremlin to Paris runs right through Berlin, and helps explain its historic interest in East-West commerce and contacts. (A line drawn through the city in the other direction would, first of all, pretty well define the Berlin Wall, then head north to just east of Copenhagen and south to Naples.)

Berlin today lies farther east than ever before, the Poles having "moved west" since World War II. This eastward orientation is welcomed in East Berlin, of course, but the West Berliners continue to underscore their ties to the West, ignoring the fact that the city has always been situated in a somewhat remote and eastern part of Central Europe. This has had its effect on the Berliners of past centuries, as we shall see, and it is fortunate for the city that it has always been able to attract such foreigners as the Slavs, Austrians, and French.

This helps explain why the Berliner is romantic and sentimental, especially regarding his city. One can hardly think of any other city that has as many songs written about it, Paris excepted. And Berlin's songs even have a distinctly Parisian tone at times, being melancholy when they are not rousing and defiant, or simply boisterous, German-style. Though most of them were composed a long time ago, they remain popular even today. The unofficial city motto, *Berlin bleibt doch Berlin,* stems from one of its most popular songs, written by Walter Kollo for the revue *Drunter und Drüber.* Called "So lang noch Unter'n Linden," it was written around the turn of the century, when Berlin boomed; it is inexplicably defiant —as though Berlin, even then, was being undermined by rascals.

"So lang noch 'Unter'n Linden'
Die alten Bäume blühn,
Kann nichts uns überwinden,
Berlin bleibt doch Berlin—

"Wenn keiner treu Dir bleibe
Ich bleib Dir ewig grün,
Du meine alte Liebe,
Berlin bleibt doch Berlin!"

"So long as the old trees still bloom on Unter den Linden, Berlin remains Berlin and nothing can vanquish us," the lyrics proclaim. "Should no one else prove faithful, I'll always remain true to you, my old love—Berlin is *still* Berlin!"

There is another song inextricably associated with Berlin. Written by a contemporary of Kollo, it has become just as popular among Berliners, and even far more so among foreigners visiting the city for awhile. Entitled "Berliner Luft" it hails the Berlin "air," or atmosphere. I heard it almost every day in the small office across from the Europa Center that I used while researching this book. It drifted up from a *Leierkasten,* the hurdy-gurdy, or barrel organ that is the most typically Berlinese of all instruments. It is a simple, if throbbing, march that lacks even the subtleties Sousa offers, and that goes on forever repeating its theme hypnotically. Yet, one's step quickens to it involuntarily, one's stride becomes bouncier, and one feels that perhaps one could, after all, take on the world. One feels, in short, like a Berliner.

The travel posters and the motion pictures portray a different Berliner from the one encountered in reality. This Berliner, on the placards in the West, seems either to be on the way to the Opera, or ready to demonstrate his solidarity with the Western allies on the square in front of the Rathaus Schöneberg. His counterpart in the East is presented as either marching off to conquer new production norms, to protest United States bestiality in Viet Nam or Mississippi, or to applaud a Bulgarian folk-dance troupe at some S.E.D. cultural hall.

It is true that *some* Berliners do all these things. The portrait presented, however, is incomplete; it is a caricature created by those who want either to drum up the tourist trade or drum home the Cold War. Such propagandists, whether they are from Berlin or Washington, do not necessarily serve the best interests of the Berliners, no matter how well-meaning they consider themselves to be.

The city and its people cannot be truthfully portrayed by means of the usual collage: a photograph of Peter Fechter, the most famous victim of the wall, pasted alongside some tickets for last year's Festival Weeks. Berlin, perhaps more than other cities, is an interlacery whose hundreds of elements are related to, but not identical with each other.

The city in all its variety has been a rack and a cross for its people for nearly seven hundred years, as well as their joy and glory. In the process, it has captured the imagination of mankind, as well as consistently engaged its attention and energies. How all this happened is the story of the making of Berlin, as well as of its destruction and rebirth.

34

chapter three

BERLIN MAY BE ISOLATED FROM THE WESTERN WORLD TODAY, approachable only by means of access routes kept open by threat of Western arms, but it was even more remote in its beginnings. This city did not spring initially from out of the Western world, but from a border region guarding the west from Eastern incursions, the frontier, or "Mark" Brandenburg. The place within this Mark through which the River Spree flowed was a marshy region filled with swamps, forests, and roving robber barons. Where the Spree branches to embrace an island, a number of fishermen settled, calling the place Cölln. They built some huts, grouped about a square like Conestoga wagons drawn up for protection around a fire in the frontier. Soon others came and settled on one of the river banks, forming a new community. A mill dam, the Mühlendamm, connected them; this was to become a river crossing of importance. The new community across the Mühlendamm from Cölln called itself Berlin. No one knows the origins of either name for certain: Cölln may have derived from *colonia,* Latin for "colony," but it is just as likely that it stems from *Kollen,* German for a swelling or a hill rising from the water. Berlin probably derived its name from any one of several Slavic words for swamp, puddle, marsh, wallow, or creek—which pretty well describes what it must have looked like at the start.

It soon began to look a little better, for merchants crossing the Mühlendamm for trade with the East eventually brought a measure of prosperity to the two towns; Berlin and Cölln grew to be rivals, bickering with and maintaining their independence from each other, though they did unify some administrative functions. A joint city hall stood symbolically in the middle of a long bridge connecting the two towns. Like today's nineteenth-century Rathaus in East Berlin, this original building had a reddish tint; it was intricately carved, topped with pretty wooden towers bearing the twin cities' two flags, and was certainly the most handsome structure there. Clay, mud, and occasionally, wooden shacks made up the rest, separated by tiny alleys and unpaved roads which stank of garbage and ordure. Everywhere dungheaps steamed and barefoot boys prodded cows through the slime. Pigs and occasional wild boars snorted about, rummaging for slops. At a time when German cities to the south and west were large, prosperous, and handsome, Berlin-Cölln was a medieval farm settlement. The twin cities were even smaller than nearby Brandenburg, and hundreds of years behind such cities as Nuremberg, Cologne, Augsburg, Munich, and Hamburg. The citizens knew it and worked hard to catch up.

Gradually their prosperity increased and in 1391 they became completely self-governing communities, left at peace by their rulers, the margraves of Brandenburg. They were even important enough to be allowed to join the Hanseatic League, which was not only a benefit to trade, but a great honor and privilege. Membership in this association of commercial towns only went to cities that were free and independent. The people of Berlin-Cölln were proud to be just that. Left to themselves, they might have followed the path of other cities and states, developing a politically powerful middle class and a resulting tradition of self-government. Instead, a different fate was to befall them.

Friedrich Hohenzollern, burgrave of Nuremberg and a member of a then undistinguished line of South German nobility, had bought the Mark Brandenburg at the start of the 15th century. It then consisted of not more than ten thousand square miles of lands still terrorized by robber barons and rebellious knights; the new margrave, who had also bought himself the title of elector of Brandenburg, entered with a strong force. The townspeople were grateful to see him subdue the rebellious nobles but when his son, Johann the Alchemist, moved to subdue Berlin and Cölln, they united to oppose the threat to their independence. Faced with this, Johann withdrew to Spandau until he was replaced by his brother, Friedrich II, called *Eisenzahn,* or "Iron-Tooth," who repudiated this weak stand. In 1442, disunity within Berlin and Cölln gave Iron-

Tooth the chance to act. Certain guilds and citizens had offered him the keys to the cities if he would defend their interests against the joint Berlin-Cölln magistrates; Iron-Tooth moved in, settled the dispute, and stayed. He forbade all union between the towns, compelled Cölln to cede him a portion of land, and began to build a palace, soon called the *Zwingburg,* meaning a fort built to coerce. The local citizens were outraged by the brutality and harshness of his rules, and in 1448, they revolted. Apparently the leaders were Berliners, for the rebellion went down in the Hohenzollern annals as a first example of *Berliner Unwille,* German for the Berliners' refractoriness, their indisposition to obey. The citizens seized and imprisoned the margrave's local judge, chased his officials out of town, stormed his chancellery, burnt books, letters, and decrees, and reestablished their cities' joint administration in the Rathaus on the Lange Brücke. Opening their dam, they flooded part of the land on which Iron-Tooth was building his *Zwingburg,* and put up a fence to replace the Cölln city walls which the margrave had destroyed.

Six hundred armored knights charged in and bloodily suppressed the rebellion. Its leaders, including the Mayor of Berlin, were banned from the Mark Brandenburg. All moves to unite Berlin and Cölln were forbidden. Henceforth the Hohenzollerns spoke only of their two residences, Berlin and Cölln, issuing all decrees from Cölln. For the next five hundred years Berliners would be subject to Hohenzollern rule.

To symbolize his position, Iron-Tooth gave Berlin a new coat of arms. The "Berlin bear," standing upright, had first appeared toward the end of the 13th century; at that time, the Brandenburg eagle played a secondary role on the shield. Iron-Tooth put the bear in chains and placed him on all fours. He even went so far as to perch his eagle on the bear's back. It took hundreds of years for the Hohenzollern rulers to allow that Berlin bear to stand upright again, and they kept a slave collar about its neck until 1875.

Shortly after Iron-Tooth's victory, the Hohenzollerns moved their court to the *Zwingburg,* on the site where Ulbricht today parades his troops, the Marx-Engels Platz. These rulers were harsh, fierce, and forbidding; they made no attempt to welcome the Renaissance sweeping the rest of Europe. The spirit of independence that marked the earliest stage in Berlin's history was over. The Hohenzollern era taught the Berliners order and obedience.

Brewers, potters, and printers pursued their trades in Berlin and Cölln, merchants and traders prospered, and lively leather, textile, and paper industries were established. Then came the Thirty Years' War. While the electorate of Brandenburg managed to remain neutral for a while, it was ultimately engulfed. In 1631 the Swedes swarmed over the region and captured the Spandau fortress outside Berlin-Cölln. By the end of the war the population of the twin cities had been cut in half, to six thousand.

Elsewhere in Germany, cities suffered even more. Magdeburg, just eighty-eight miles away from Berlin, was sacked by the Swedes and almost all its forty thousand citizens were massacred. Wolfenbüttel lost seven out of every eight inhabitants. Altogether the death toll reached eight million.

Elector Georg Wilhelm fled to Königsberg in East Prussia during the war, sending his son to Holland. The Berlin-Cölln councillors petitioned his help, reporting that "pestilence, arson, robbery, and extortion" were leading citizens "to slash, drown, or hang themselves to end their lives." There was nothing Georg Wilhelm could do except pass away, leaving matters to his son, in 1640.

The task facing the new elector, Friedrich Wilhelm, barely out of his teens, was formidable. The twin cities had been reduced to cinders, and their people to destitution. Half of all the houses were burned to the ground and a third were untenable. Furthermore, outside the towns almost nothing had survived. Friedrich Wilhelm's annual income was less than an eighth of his father's, all his best estates were mortgaged to the hilt or sold, his undisciplined troops sustained themselves by robbing, and he himself couldn't even enter his palace because the roof was about to collapse. What he inherited was described by one of his advisors in these terms: "Pomerania is lost, Jülich is lost, we hold Prussia like an eel by the tail, and have no choice but to mortgage the Mark Brandenburg."

The young elector was optimistic and energetic. He hoped to pattern his *Residenzstadt* after the prosperous cities he'd seen in Holland during four years as a university student in Leiden. The spotless Dutch streets and busy Dutch commerce had impressed him, and with more faith than either wherewithal or reason for hope, he began to build Berlin-Cölln in that image. Wood was handed out free of charge to all those willing to rebuild their homes;

he even cleared the area in front of his palace of trees for this purpose.

To fortify the city along Dutch lines, he later started a construction program which lasted a quarter of a century. As there weren't enough Berliners to do the job, troops brought in to help were quartered among the citizens, in five hundred homes. Every able-bodied citizen was compelled to work. A wall more than thirty feet high in some places began to rise; twenty feet thick, it jutted into thirteen bastions, and was surrounded by a moat one hundred and sixty feet wide in places. Berliners were skeptical, noting the structure was literally built on sand and that the walls merely defined a target for enemy cannoneers. Furthermore, the troops quartered among them were rough, often thieving, types and the fortifications rendered even more perilous the situation of those citizens living outside the walls in suburban districts like Dorotheenstadt.

This community was the brainchild of the elector's second wife, who in 1670 had received as a gift from her husband a parcel of land outside the gates. She had it subdivided into plots offered for sale as a *Quartier des Nobles*. To make it more attractive, she had one thousand linden (or lime) trees planted four abreast, about 325 feet down the road to Spandau, thus defining what was to become Berlin's most historic avenue. The plots sold briskly and Dorothea made a nice profit.

The elector, who yearned to build a great society in Berlin, was, in fact, beginning to produce results. He had defeated the Swedes and chased them out of all his lands. He had rebuilt much of the city and had cleaned up the rest. (Typical was an order issued in 1660: "Pigsties, stables, and all other like places offering a similar stink are to be removed from public streets!") He was complex: tough and unscrupulous, yet devout and idealistic. He asserted his right over East Prussia by cynically tearing up a treaty with the Poles and he relentlessly pressed his fight against aristocrats who resisted his moves to centralize Brandenburg by cutting their power. He also saw that armies consisting of a rabble recruited by press gangs were outmoded and that a permanent, well-trained, and highly disciplined force was needed.

The Junkers grumbled, but tax funds were finally coming into Berlin from their estates. A standing army was formed, first from among Swedish deserters; an officer corps was built out of aristocrats impoverished by the war.

More important to the Berliners, he fostered trade and commerce and set an example of religious tolerance. Believing a mixed population better for tax purposes than a handful of "pure" beggars, he invited both Jews and Catholics into his lands, though he himself was a conscientious Protestant. In short, he chose a melting pot instead of an empty one.

Again in 1685, when France sent thousands of Protestant Huguenots searching for new homes outside that country, he immediately issued an edict opening Berlin-Cölln to these *refugiés*. It was a move dictated by his strong Protestant conscience, but it was also a shrewd act. Until then Berliners had been a mixture of various German and some Slavic strains. Now, with a stroke of the pen, Friedrich Wilhelm brought in an enormously industrious and intelligent group of Frenchmen. Overnight it seemed, the city that boasted twenty thousand inhabitants had gained another five thousand. Every fifth Berliner was a Frenchman.

"Today everything has to be French!" a Berlin author wrote four years after the Huguenots settled in Berlin. "You can't even hope to be received at court any more if you don't speak French! Children four or five years old, even those just barely able to crawl, are being introduced to French gallantries, their parents busy finding them French language and dancing masters. Let a young man hope to succeed with a girl, then he must show up wearing French hats, vests, and silk stockings. No one cares if he has a hunchback, crooked legs, calf's eyes, a buzzard's beak, buck teeth—no matter, so long as he behaves French. The German language is dying out and another has insinuated itself. Anyone who doesn't speak French today reveals himself as stupid!"

These were boom times: the sort to which Berliners respond best. Trade increased six hundred percent within a few decades. The city was developing an important manufacturing industry and countless crafts; trade and commerce flourished, thanks in part to the new Friedrich Wilhelm Canal built in 1668. This first Berlin canal connected the Oder and Spree rivers through intervening waterways, linking cities as far-flung as Breslau in the east and Hamburg on the North Sea, and making Berlin-Cölln into a major distribution center for East-West traffic. Ultimately, Fried-

40

rich Wilhelm's canal sparked others, followed later by roads and railways, all of which further developed the city into a transportation hub.

Dutch artists, architects, and craftsmen made their way to the twin cities, attracted by their burgeoning prosperity and the electoral welcome. Friedrich Wilhelm, already called "the Great Elector," was a Germanic "Sun King," the model of the benevolent autocrat. He even looked the part: majestic, portly, with an imperious glance and prominent Roman nose. The only thing he saw that saddened him was his third son, the misshapen successor to his throne, who had outlived two older brothers.

The new elector, Friedrich III, determined to make up for the bitter years of his childhood. As he was unable to look as regal as his father, he planned to become regal in fact—to become king, not just remain margrave and elector. Yet only Leopold I, the "Holy Roman Emperor of the German Nation," could permit this promotion, and since only the Hapsburg Emperor held a royal title within the German Empire, Friedrich would have to be king outside this territory, not in the Mark Brandenburg, but in far-off Prussia, of which Friedrich was hereditary duke. To become king served no particular purpose of statecraft at the time, though it proved important enough for the future; Friedrich was simply interested in reigning gloriously—far more than in ruling well. He proceeded to win Imperial consent by providing Brandenburg troops for the emperor's wars. Meanwhile, he and his brilliant and beautiful wife, Sophia Charlotte, turned to the task of making their city look regal, cost what it might.

West of Friedrichswerder, a portion of the city developed by his father, and south of Dorotheenstadt, he built his own suburb. On the left side of Unter den Linden, as seen from the palace, it is now the center of East Berlin. (Bahnhof Friedrichstadt is located there.) In Friedrich's day, this suburb proved popular for two reasons: It lay outside the city, and also brought its residents special privileges. These included freedom from compulsory labor, levies, tribute, and quartering of troops, all by-products of electoral rule endured by the rest of the citizens. An excise tax, originally begun by his father, was kept on the books, and oddly, the poor rather liked it, for they thought it meant that those who could afford the biggest meals would pay the highest taxes, since the tax was passed on to the consumers by millers and butchers in the city. This tax helped feed Friedrich's lavish court.

Sophia Charlotte had attracted large numbers of artists, philosophers, and architects to Berlin, men like Andreas Schlüter of Hamburg, the great baroque sculptor. He created an equestrian statue of the Great Elector that is his masterpiece. A year later, he built a palace for Sophia Charlotte that became her principal salon until she died in 1705. Around this developed a small community of houses, a hundred in all; the pioneers here were settling the wilderness, for Charlottenburg lay on the road to Spandau and both the king and queen had to ride through the woods to it with an armed escort. Here, Sophia Charlotte surrounded herself with all that was exquisite and luxurious. One of the few who remained unimpressed by the court was the heir to the throne, Friedrich Wilhelm. He had small liking for perfumes, pleasure palaces, and pretension. He plotted to clean house.

No sooner had the queen's palace been finished than Friedrich III ordered an arsenal built for himself. The Zeughaus, 295 feet long and built in a hollow square, still stands on Unter den Linden today, just off the Marx-Engels Platz, site of the old palace. In that location, it nicely centered the city and the state on a munitions shed (later an armaments museum) presaging the militarism yet to come. Outside, it is decorated with fine antique helmets and trophies, but sculptor Andreas Schlüter chose a different decorative element for the interior court. Here he carved twenty-two heads of dying warriors, portraits in agony, their mouths torn open in suffering grimaces, a mute tribute to war's reality.

Across the west arm of the Spree—on the site of Friedrich Eisenzahn's original *Zwingburg*—lay the palace; Schlüter took this hodgepodge of buildings and awkward wings in hand, turning them into a structure with form and unity, if not beauty. His one mistake was that he forgot that he was building the palace on sand and marsh; overestimating his foundation, he almost brought about the collapse of the dome. A commission that included a rival Swedish architect found him guilty of error, and the rival, Eosander von Göthe, finished the job after Schlüter resigned. Schlüter remained a favorite of the king, and continued working in Berlin until he was finally chased out of town, along with all the other architects and artists, by Friedrich's son when he succeeded to the throne. He fled to St. Petersburg, where he died a year later. All his major work, however, was done in Berlin and the city remained his monument at least until World War II, when much that he had built was destroyed.

The city was emerging rather regally. In addition to Schlüter's palace and Zeughaus, there were Göthe's spun-sugar pleasure palace, Schloss Montbijou, and Schlüter's post-office building. An Academy of Art was formed in 1696 by Schlüter and a Dutch painter, Augustin Terwesten, and in 1700, an Academy of Science was organized under the philosopher Leibnitz, its first president.

All this activity on so many fronts cost a great deal of money, but for sheer lavish expenditure, it is hard to beat the events surrounding Friedrich's coronation. This took place in East Prussia, and in December of 1700, the court began its journey to Königsberg, using more horses (thirty thousand) for this trip than Berlin had inhabitants. These vast expenses were being incurred just a few years after the Great Elector had exhausted the cities' finances by his twenty-five year program of building a wall around the towns, and just fifty years after the Thirty Years' War. Difficult or not, the necessary horses were assembled in relays, the court moved ponderously eastward, and on January 18, 1701, Elector Friedrich III crowned himself Friedrich I, King "in" Prussia, placing the crown on his head with his own hands.*

On May 6, he returned to Berlin-Cölln, where the citizens prepared a major welcome. Six huge, decorative gates of honor had been placed where the Alexanderplatz lies today. Thousands of Berliners cheered, the bells of all churches rang simultaneously, and two hundred cannons boomed from ships in the Spree, from the city walls, and even from the roof of the Marienkirche. Afterward, as many places and objects as possible were renamed in the new king's honor. The Georgenstrasse was renamed Königsstrasse; the Georgentor, or gate, became the Königstor; and the Festungsgraben, or fortress-moat, became the Königsgraben. With this, the Berliners began their noxious tradition of changing the names on streets and squares almost with each major change in their political fortunes.

The festivities, the king's building programs, and the lavish

* King *in,* not *of,* Prussia as half of Prussia was still Polish.

43

court life plunged the city so much into debt that the king periodically hoped alchemists might bail him out. When such schemes failed, he put the Mark Brandenburg further into debt, not to speak of the Berliners, already groaning under taxes. The citizens came to resent their new king, for their municipal magnificence was not matched by general prosperity. Indeed, it had been achieved by bleeding them dry. Yet Friedrich's buildings and the infusion of art and culture he gave Berlin proved to be of enduring value. And it was he who, in 1709, finally united Berlin, Cölln, and their suburbs into one capital city, Berlin.

chapter four

GLITTER AND GLORY HAD BEEN ACHIEVED BY MORTGAGING BRAN-
denburg to the hilt. Even those who had enjoyed the reign of King
Friedrich I were confronted with the sobering dawn. The heir to
the throne, Friedrich Wilhelm I, or "Fatty," as he was called, was
their hangover.

He, more than any other, fathered "Prussianism" and brought
about the birth of the modern Prussian state. His scrupulous personal attention to duty rescued his people from the financial ruin
his father had bequeathed them, but his brutish temperament
helped even more to shape their destiny. The army was his abiding
love and his closest companion was Prince Leopold von Anhalt-
Dessau, who built it up during this reign. Yet Anhalt-Dessau and
Friedrich Wilhelm I had more in common than a love of soldier-
ing; their view of life and its obligations ran parallel. Both were
devout Lutherans, with a passion for frugality. Both were pious
and brutal. Both believed that a good shepherd canes lost sheep
and beats piety into the prodigal. Together, they turned Berlin
and all of Brandenburg-Prussia into a reform school.

Once in power, they built a perfectly drilled Prussian Army,
using the Roman legionnaires' cadenced march tempo, which
had somehow been forgotten for centuries. Cadence allowed units
to be wheeled about like machines, and to fire volleys. The method
had first been tried out on the Potsdam "Giants' Guard," which
Friedrich Wilhelm had organized while still crown prince; once
he became king, it was perfected in the army as a whole. Anhalt-
Dessau didn't bother with niceties; he used the lash and hangings
to produce terrified automatons upon the drill fields.

Before he could build an army, however, the new king needed

45

funds. Unlike his father, he did not plunge the state further into debt to get them, but tried instead to cut expenditures and improve the economy of the land. He was generous enough to give his father a fancy funeral, but scorned the expense of a coronation for himself. No sooner was Friedrich I laid to rest than the new king returned to his palace and stripped off the hated peruke and fancy coat he had always been compelled to wear. In shirt-sleeves, he helped servants tear down the palace wall hangings; he banned carpets and upholstered chairs; he sold his father's wines and diamonds; and he turned the palace itself into an office building, selecting a five-room suite for himself and his family. Desks, files, and bureaucrats were moved into the remaining space. Palace personnel was cut from 141 to a round dozen; an army of courtiers, artists, architects, musicians, and learned men were fired.

In many ways it was a Herculean task to clean out Berlin's perfumed palaces and to turn them, in effect, into stables, but the twenty-five-year-old king was equal to it. Cultural life completely ended throughout his reign. Even the theater was banned. Friedrich Wilhelm not only thought amusements sinful, but worse yet, a waste of time. Thinkers seduced men into questioning Constituted Authority, which Luther had proclaimed as being divinely ordained. Under Friedrich Wilhelm, the Berliners were taught that obedience was the highest virtue.

What life for the Berliners was like at that time may be gauged from some of the royal decrees. Everything had to produce "a plus," that is, every activity, public or private, had to produce *ein Plus,* "something extra." He ordered Berlin's market women no longer to sit idly about waiting for customers, gossiping among themselves; they were to keep their fingers busy knitting socks. Pastors were told exactly how long their sermons were to be, so as not to keep anyone from other tasks. His son, Crown Prince Friedrich, was told precisely what he was to do every moment of every day. Friedrich Wilhelm considered the idle ungodly, and if others neglected to administer the rod to them, he caned them himself. He used to do this during the brisk walk he took daily when, if he saw any Berliners lazing about, he'd grab them by the coat and thrash them thoroughly with his stick.

It was not long before he had personally terrorized most of the Berliners, as well as the countryfolk. Berlin wasn't big at the time and a morning's constitutional might take the king most anywhere; people fled at his approach, or having received advance warning, stayed home. Yet he did all this, it would seem, without conscious malice. He simply regarded himself as father to his people and therefore thrashed them paternally if they displeased him. He never believed for a moment that the Berliners feared and hated him. On one occasion, he seized hold of a young man in the street who had tried to run away when he saw the king coming.

"Why are you running away?" Friedrich Wilhelm demanded, raising his rattan cane above the young man's head.

"I was afraid, Your Majesty!" stammered the trembling wretch.

"Afraid? Afraid?" the king shouted, livid with rage and beating the young man with his stick. "You are supposed to love me! Love me, scum!"

Of course, he was more than eccentric. The Berliners suspected he was a bit mad. He was a short, red-faced, fat man who never wore anything but army uniform: the "Soldier King," as he liked to call himself; "the drill sergeant," as his Berliners called him.

Gradually, his reign shaped society anew. He took charge of everything. If he had the instincts of a barroom bouncer, he had a great deal of shrewdness and intelligence as well. He made his ministers mere errand boys, built a huge bureaucratic machine to collect taxes, and laid the foundations for the "incorruptible" Prussian civil service and the "impartial" Prussian system of justice, both of which in fact often proved less than the stated ideal.

Most fatefully, however, he neutralized all opposition. Under him, the members of Berlin's middle class could not become political opponents because they either served in the bureaucracy, which made them dependent on the king's purse, or because they profited from the king's build-up of the army. As for the aristocracy, Friedrich Wilhelm took care never to give them positions of influence in his administration, particularly on their own lands, for local loyalties might make them local foci of power. Instead, he gave them positions in his army, which made them powerless. As these Junkers cared little for their own freedoms, they cared nothing for those of others.

In time, Friedrich Wilhelm's harsh policies paid off and the Berliners began to prosper. The king redeemed the lands his father had pawned and that had further been decimated by a plague in 1709. Thousands of Protestant immigrants from West Germany and from Salzburg emigrated to Prussia, upon offer of homesteads and fruitful work; they repopulated and revitalized agriculture, which soon accounted for half the state's income.

What bloomed most luxuriantly, however, was the Prussian Army, which he developed into a force of eighty thousand men, each man conscripted for a term of twenty years. This gave Friedrich Wilhelm the fourth largest army in Europe, though Prussia ranked only thirteenth in size in terms of population. Service was so harsh that, when conscription began in Berlin, most of the city's young skilled workers and apprentices fled; the king had to exempt Berlin from conscription in order to keep its industry going and bring the young men back. To make up for the loss, Prussian recruiting agents roamed not only through the king's territories, but throughout all Europe, even into England. Those whom they could not persuade to join, they drugged or knocked senseless and kidnapped. No traveler was safe in Prussia during Friedrich Wilhelm's reign; if one attempted to flee the army into which he had been dragooned, he was treated as a deserter. Despite the threat of death, desertions were so high that the rate made the Prussian Army a standing joke in Europe at that time. Many who failed to escape killed themselves, and the suicide rate in the Berlin garrison alone averaged two a week.

One victim of the king's brutality who won the greatest sympathy among the Berliners was his handsome, cultured crown prince, Friedrich, who later became Frederick the Great. For a time, when he was very young, the king doted on him. The moment, however, that the boy was old enough to have a mind of his own, he began to dislike him. Humiliations soon followed, especially as Friedrich Wilhelm now suspected that the prince and his mother were pro-British. In full view of the court, the king would force the young Friedrich to kiss his boots. Finally, the prince attempted escape with the help of a friend, an officer in the Berlin guards garrison. Betrayed, he was seized, caned bloodily by his father, and thrown into Küstrin fortress. There he was forced to watch his friend, Lieutenant von Katte, being beheaded. The only thing that saved him from a similar fate was enormous pressure from European courts, finally from even the emperor himself.

Ultimately, the "convicted deserter" was allowed to resume his military rank. He had earlier hated uniforms, but was now grateful to put one on again. Uniforms meant a great deal in Berlin in those years: Any man wanting any claim to society (which then meant court society) had to be a military officer. In fact, any officer, no matter how lowly, outranked any civilian, no matter how venerable. During the succeeding reign, which merely consolidated this social structure, Cabinet Councillor Count Schwerin was outraged one day when a young officer-cadet, a *Fähnrich,* usurped his place at an official dinner in Berlin. The dignitary complained to the king who told him there should never have been any dispute at all, since it was well-known that in Prussia any cadet outranked any cabinet councillor (whereupon Schwerin resigned his office and joined the army as a *Fähnrich*).

If an officer-cadet ranked so high, the gulf separating a captain of horse from a Berlin merchant can be imagined. Indeed, civilians counted for nothing, and as commissions went only to aristocrats, all was "scum" beneath the aristocratic military junta ruling Berlin. The city was turning into a garrison town that bristled with uniforms, with parades and military reviews as its main entertainments. The state was becoming a military dictatorship with a table of organization instead of a social structure. Industry was growing, but the main business in town was to supply the army. The bourgeoisie either worked toward this end, or administered the regime to the satisfaction of the generals. Inevitably, a society organized on this basis develops a militaristic ethos. The relationship between those in authority and the people was simply that of the drill sergeant and the recruit.

Berlin intellectuals believe its vestiges still linger on. Even in Berlin, where the citizens have a built-in tendency toward refractoriness, one can note the truth of Nietzsche's statement: "The eleventh commandment in Germany is: One must always take that view of a matter which the Good Lord commands!" The "Good Lord" was all too often a military despot.

It came to be a standing joke in Berlin that one could out-bully any official by out-shouting him. The flabbergasted bureaucrat naturally assumed that anyone barking at him must be obeyed, for no one but a superior would dream of acting that way. It worked, and was more sad than funny, underlining the fact that all too many

Germans have the reactions and responses of people who have been whipped too long. What made the Berliner more disrespectful of authority was the sophisticated and cosmopolitan nature of his city. He was a Berliner first, a Prussian second; "Prussia" meant Potsdam and the countryside to him. He loved the importance and "glory" Prussia achieved, but he loved even more the urbane character of Berlin.

Universal education was introduced in Prussia under Friedrich Wilhelm ahead of most other countries in Europe. He also tore down his grandfather's famous fortifications and replaced them with a customs barrier and fourteen gates. These, finally, enclosed the suburbs and left room for some civic expansion. The king's commercial and agricultural policies were equally enlightened, but his methods often prevented his subjects from appreciating them. Everything he touched had a military harshness. All the streets he planned led to parade grounds, all the houses he built were meant to quarter troops, and all the squares he planted accommodated military reviews. The beautiful "Lustgarten" that his father had terraced and decorated with exotic plants and fountains was turned into a parade ground.

Pariser Platz, at the end of Unter den Linden, was now taking shape, as were Leipziger Platz, Wilhelmplatz, and Dönhoffer Platz. The Friedrichstrasse, which intersects Unter den Linden and on which "Checkpoint Charlie" today affords non-Germans entry into East Berlin, had been built only because the king wanted a direct route to Tempelhof, a large field that he turned into the principal drill and parade ground for Berlin's guard regiments.

He devised a unique way to "sell" new plots in Friedrichstadt, that settlement of one thousand homes his father had established and that Friedrich Wilhelm had extended by another fourteen hundred. No effort was made to persuade potential customers, and the fact that many of the parcels of "land" sold were actually swamp didn't interest him. A colonel, "Obrist" von Derschau, was relieved of military duties and put in charge, along with a civic official, Mayor Koch. The colonel listed prospective members of the aristocracy, the mayor prospects among the burghers. Those selected were then informed that they need only pay ninety percent of the building costs, as the king had graciously made them a gift of the land and ten percent of the expenses. No arguments were tolerated; only immediate flight from Berlin saved anyone who did not want to build. As for those who capitulated and put up homes, they found that the king insisted that all new houses in Berlin were to have attic rooms in which he could quarter troops.

One handsome building that stemmed from his reign is the Kammergericht, the Prussian "Supreme Court." Designed by Philipp Gerlach and erected on the Lindenstrasse, it's more noteworthy today than it was in Friedrich Wilhelm's time, for it's now the only example of Berlin baroque remaining in the city's Western sectors. Appropriately enough, the damaged building, restored in recent years, now houses West Berlin's "Berlin Museum" and is a temple of nostalgia.

More and more, the king suffered from gout, and it was felt, was dying. Dropsy swelled his already enormous body with fluids; his organs—lungs, kidneys, heart, as well as his arteries—were diseased and gave him no rest. Yet he took a tour of East Prussian farm provinces, spurning all comforts, racing across wretched roads, hardly resting at any one stop. When the journey was finished, so was he.

Returning to Berlin, the king prepared for death with all the matter-of-factness with which he had always run the state. He had reconciled himself with his son during his last journey; now he was prepared to reconcile himself with God. The court preacher, Roloff, insisted he must forgive his enemies, but that was too much to ask and he sent the cleric packing. Finally, he checked out the size of his coffin and had it placed next to his bed. Then he insisted on watching a dress rehearsal of his funeral procession from a window. During this, he saw a groom make a mistake and immediately ordered a general attending him to go down and thrash the fellow personally, after which he lay back to linger on for a few days. When he finally expired, the Berliners celebrated, for the hour of liberation had arrived—or so they thought.

chapter five

AT FIRST, FRIEDRICH II SEEMED TO LIVE UP TO THE BERLINERS' expectations. He liberalized laws, abolished torture, and even asked the advice of Berlin's merchants on matters concerning industry and commerce. Unfortunately, many of his promises soon vanished in the smoke of battle. He attacked and conquered Silesia and then, shortly afterward, had to fight a "Second Silesian War" to retain the territory. Taxes rose sky-high and conscription mounted.

Furthermore, war was changing the idealistic king more each year until there was little but cynicism left. His friend, the architect Knobelsdorff, was among the first to note the change. Years earlier, he and Friedrich had planned the dramatic architecture that the prince intended to give Berlin: It was to be a plunge into a "Prussian style" inspired by the classical lines of Greece and Rome. A *Forum Fridericianum* was to be built by Knobelsdorff, the Opera its first building, but no sooner was this completed than Knobelsdorff found out Friedrich no longer shared his vision. The forum was started, but arbitrarily altered by the king. Friedrich grew misanthropic and withdrew to his new palace, Sans Souci, in Potsdam for it pleased him while Berlin did not. In 1735, Knobelsdorff died, broken-hearted, but he had left his stamp on Berlin. Aside from the Opera, his most popular work was the transformation of the Tiergarten into a beautiful public park.

Friedrich, writing countless poems and histories in Potsdam, had little direct effect on the cultural life of Berlin, but the mere existence of this "philosopher king" did encourage the growth of literary life. Among those who fostered it most was a nineteen-year-old fugitive who arrived in Berlin in 1748, in full flight from his creditors. He was Gotthold Ephraim Lessing.

The customs guards had their misgivings about letting him pass through Brandenburg Gate (then only a small wooden structure hardly higher than a man), for Berlin was attracting its fair share of rogues now that its population was approaching one hundred thousand. It was growing fast under Friedrich II and would reach one hundred fifty thousand by the time he died. Lessing got through despite his wretched appearance (he arrived with little more than the clothes on his back), but only after he agreed to present himself each Friday at the gate, as though on parole, even though he could give the name of a respectable local citizen as sponsor.

This was his cousin, Christoph Mylius, editor of one of Berlin's two newspapers, whose publisher, Johann Rüdiger, hired Lessing to catalog his library and help out on the paper as well. Berlin's intellectual life then centered around the famous philosopher, Moses Mendelssohn, and the city's three book publishers, two of whom also produced the newspapers. Newspaper life was lively, for the Berliners' newspaper habit—really an addiction, even today—began early. Berlin had its first paper in 1617, five years before London, though London was then fifty times as big as Berlin. The city has always been a *Zeitungsstadt,* a city of newspapers— indeed, a sea of them; by 1928 the Berliners would be able to choose from among 147 daily and weekly newspapers published in the city. Two of the oldest and most famous were the Voss and Spener papers, nicknamed "Auntie Voss" and "Uncle Spener."

Mendelssohn, the publishers, and Lessing were not, however, the most famous literary figures in Berlin at the time. Its most exalted litterateur was the king himself, but as he wrote in French and despised German, his influence was remote. So Francophile was the Berlin court that when Voltaire visited Friedrich he wrote a friend, "I am in France here. French is the only language; German is used only with soldiers and horses . . ."

Lessing, however, used German—to polemicize against the Francophile atmosphere, to urge a popular cultural awakening, and to write about art, literature, philosophy, and God in fresh, daring, liberal ways.

When Voltaire was invited to remain in Potsdam for a long stay,

Lessing acted as his secretary and interpreter. The two men were impressed with each other, for Lessing had already made a name for himself with three plays, one of which (*Die Juden,* or *The Jews*) was a scathing attack on anti-Semitism. Mylius, Rüdiger, and Nicolai had taught Lessing journalism, but Voltaire broadened his outlook and engaged his spirit. The Frenchman was intellectually incorruptible and utterly independent. Lessing saw in him the ideal after which he himself would strive.

The relationship between Friedrich and Voltaire eventually soured. Voltaire left Berlin, and Lessing returned to journalism and to the theater. In one year, 1755, he produced *Miss Sara Sampson,* regarded as the first German tragedy of everyday life, co-authored with Mendelssohn a treatise on poetry, and published (at age twenty-six!) a six-volume set of his own collected works. Somehow he also managed to be everywhere and to meet everyone in Berlin, to dance, to fence, to be seen in all salons and coffeehouses, and to attend every public event. But, at the end of that year, Lessing already had enough of the city, for its atmosphere was becoming more autocratic than ever and Lessing's literary circle found the growing royal and military despotism burdensome. As Lessing wrote Nicolai after leaving Berlin, freedom of expression under the atheistic Friedrich II consisted of freedom to attack religion, but not royal absolutism.

Autocracy, in fact, was growing; fateful changes were being made in Berlin society. Unlike his father, who had excluded Junker aristocrats from top government posts, Friedrich welcomed the nobles. He mistrusted the middle classes, whom his father had employed as civil servants. He chose instead to fill all the lower ranks of the bureaucracy with former non-commissioned officers or with privates disabled in service. Thus he set a policy of relying on military men and aristocrats. Inevitably, that *Kadavergehorsam,* or "cadaver-like obedience" of the barracks square came to infest the administration. Still, good must coexist alongside evil and there was, of course, another side to this coin: Officials who dared not disobey or question also never dared to steal. The administration came to be as incorruptible as it was inflexible, as unstinting in its zeal to serve the state as it was to resist all change within that state. This incorruptibility also extended to the courts, whose reform under Friedrich II was both badly needed and much welcomed. His deep personal sense of justice (which never left him, however autocratic he became) made him yearn for a *Rechtstaat*, a rule of law to which even he himself might be subject. In practice, he often violated the concept, but by and large his dream was fulfilled. In future years, Berlin's judges proved remarkably incorruptible; what came to be corrupted were the laws themselves.

After ten years of peace, the Berliners found themselves once more plunged into a war, this time against Austria, France, Russia, and Saxony, an overwhelming coalition meant to destroy Prussia forever. Soon, they found themselves occupied by Russian and Austrian soldiers, who marched into Berlin in late 1760, even as thousands of Berliners fled their homes. When City President Kircheisen heard the conquerors demanding four million talers in tribute, he fainted.

They might as well have asked a hundred times that sum; there just wasn't that much money left in Berlin. These facts were presented to the Russians not by Berlin's commander, General von Rochow, nor by City President Kircheisen, both of whom the news had paralyzed, but by a merchant named Gotzkowsky who carried out all negotiations during the occupation of Berlin, and who has become a legendary figure as the city's "merchant patriot." He succeeded in getting the levy reduced to 1.5 million talers and in many other ways alleviated the suffering of the citizens.

Shortly afterward news that Friedrich II was approaching with a relief army caused the conquerors to retreat. After four years of war, his reputation in the field had grown so much that the very mention of his name sent a chill of fear through his enemies.

The occupation of Berlin in 1760 (and a brief raid on the city three years earlier) were the only occasions the Berliners experienced the Seven Years War at first hand. Finally, when the Prussians exhausted their enemies, a peace was signed, terms being *status quo ante bellum*. One thing, however, was very different: Ever after, Berlin was taken seriously in the capitals of Europe, for if a European coalition the size of the one just disbanded could not destroy Prussia, no individual state would even try.

Friedrich returned to Berlin, determined to restore the state's economy and to rebuild his decimated army, for it alone seemed

55

to guarantee Prussia's existence. Later, Mirabeau was to comment, "War is the national industry of Prussia." Certainly it engaged the energies of the entire state, and even now all hopes that the general welfare might benefit from a reduction of the army to pre-war levels were dashed. Friedrich ordered the army maintained at a permanent wartime footing of one hundred fifty thousand, cost what it might. Disbanding some of the "free battalions" he had formed alongside regular units, he also weeded out all members of the middle classes from the officer corps.

A vast reconstruction program was begun. Colonists were encouraged to immigrate, lands were rehabilitated, and industry was fostered. A new Prussian state bank opened in Berlin with the king's money, and a new porcelain factory was established on Leipziger Strasse. (To help it, Friedrich forbade not only the import of Saxony's Meissen china, but even its transit through his lands en route elsewhere.) The printing and cloth-manufacturing industries were encouraged and silks, woolens, linens, satins, and cottons soon came to be the state's largest export items. A Silesian mining department began coal mining, ironworking, lead mining, and smelting.

Tobacco, coffee, and salt monopolies were established by the state, their prices set sky-high so as to provide large profits. Nor could anyone evade them; citizens were simply ordered to buy. They brought the state large revenues. As it turned out, they also brought the Berliners some of their traditional culinary delights.

Sacks of salt stood in all homes, for Friedrich II didn't care what the Berlin housewives did with it, so long as they could show by means of their "salt books" that they had bought the required quantities. As a result, the resourceful Berliners hit upon the idea of using salt to pickle the small cucumbers which could be obtained inexpensively near the Spree forest. The sour pickle that resulted has been a gustatory delight Berliners continue to crave today. Sauerkraut also came into its glory in Berlin as a result of Friedrich's salt monopoly, but perhaps the tastiest result came when a Berlin master butcher named Kassler offered for sale specially smoked pork chops which had been placed in a salt solution. Kassler's pork ribs, or *Kassler Rippchen,* as these were ever after called, still appear along with sauerkraut and the Berliners' beloved puréed yellow peas on days of celebration.

The Frederician era made popular one additional food the Berliners had not earlier known—the potato. The vegetable had been brought to Europe from South America in the late 16th century, but was not known in Berlin until the mid-18th. When they were first promoted as fit for consumption, the Berliners reacted with extreme skepticism. City officials summoned citizens to the marketplace to display the strange tubers, and in good Prussian fashion, an elaborate instruction was read aloud. The citizens tasted them and threw them down to the dogs. When it was noted that the dogs refused to eat them, the Berliners walked away.

The bad harvests and near-famine that followed the Seven Years' War finally forced the Berliners to eat what the dogs had rejected. Berlin newspapers now hailed the potato as a substitute for bread, meat, cheese, and butter, as "suitable in every dish," and "Auntie Voss" even provided a recipe for making a coffee substitute from potatoes, which it claimed looked and tasted exactly like the real thing. In time the Berliners became not only accustomed, but addicted to these roots, and together with other Germans, made them central to their cuisine by working them into a bewildering array of dishes unknown to man outside their territories.

The near-famine made reconstruction difficult and huge subsidies needed to be financed with sky-high taxes. Resentment grew and Friedrich II decided to establish Prussia's first secret state police, modeled on the existing French organization. A Berlin official was sent to Paris to study French methods; he returned, recommending infiltration of the underworld. The king approved. After a notorious murder, the chief of the new secret police told the king that this crime showed that it was not enough to place police spies in apprentices' quarters and similar breeding places of crime, but that agents (*geheime Vertrauensleute*) ought to be infiltrated into each and every level of Berlin society. This Friedrich refused to do, but similar proposals in later reigns received more sympathetic royal hearing. Thus began a horror that, in one form or another, never again left Berlin.

The police also kept a sharp eye on the press. "Hard" news and even reporters were virtually unknown; despite its struggles, the press in Berlin could not free itself from the shackles imposed by the very man who in his youth had condemned press censorship.

Rousseau noted that Friedrich's policies deliberately denied the middle and lower classes any chance at political education; indeed, his aristocratic-military autocracy cast an icy chill over all thought in the capital.

Unter den Linden in these years began to reflect Berlin's new position as capital of a major European power, even if much of the rest of the city remained poor and shabby. Forty-eight old houses built on the avenue during Friedrich Wilhelm I's reign were torn down and replaced at state expense by thirty-three larger ones; these soon housed government offices and gave the avenue a distinctly new and official character.

The Forum Fridericianum received its final touches. A few blocks south of it, Carl von Gontard completed the French Cathedral, decorated with sculptures by Berlin's Daniel Chodowiecki, and located on what was then famous as the Gendarmenmarkt, Friedrichstadt's chief marketplace. It was named after the *Gens d'armes* regiment of cuirassiers, which had its stables and guardhouse there from 1736 to 1782. Today the church is ruined, and the square is renamed Platz der Akademie.

The *Alte Bibliothek,* that library which the Berliners nicknamed "the book-cabinet," was completed and equipped with eighty thousand books. A librarian and two "servants" were hired. ("They must not just be lackeys," read the original instruction, "but ought to know enough to find the books requested and to put them away again afterwards.") Friedrich II himself thought up the motto below the building's cornice, *nutrimentum spiritus* ("food for the spirit"), which the Berliners dismissed as pompous, saying it really meant, "Spirits also are nutritious."

In 1785, Prince Ferdinand opened Schloss Bellevue in the Tiergarten, on a plot where the architect Knobelsdorff had built himself a dairy farm, which became a love nest for him and his mistress. Bellevue Palace, from which most Hohenzollern state processions down Unter den Linden began, served the Nazis as a guesthouse for people like Molotov. Then called the *Gästehaus des Reiches,* the palace is today the official residence of the West German president. Knobelsdorff's Meierie came to be the prestigious home of some of Berlin's famed theatrical figures—Max Reinhardt, and later, Gustav Gründgens.

The new palace prompted wealthy Berliners to build their own villas at the edge of the Tiergarten, thus defining what came to be Tiergarten Strasse, soon one of the most imposing in the city. Prosperity gradually was returning, at least to the aristocracy. The Berliners in general were still suffering from the effects of the war. An old engraving shows the *Weihnachtsmarkt* (the Christmas Market) jammed with almost as many beggar boys as officers. The existence of the beggars was a problem, especially when times were bad, and the newspapers and police regularly warned against them.

Robberies and assaults took place throughout the city, for street lighting was inadequate where it existed at all. So dark were some of the streets that one Berlin merchant who tried to cross the palace bridge leading to Unter den Linden fell into the Spree and drowned, there being no railings at water's edge. "Our streets are so poorly paved," wrote a Berliner, "that every stranger to the city seems to complain that the soles of his feet ache. There are hills and valleys in each sidewalk and at night one is in constant danger of falling and breaking one's bones."

Houses didn't have street numbers then; these were first introduced at the end of the 18th century. The city was still small enough so that a Berliner would describe his home by its distance from the corners or by its decorative elements. He lived in the third house on Breite Strasse, or the house bearing two lions, or the one with six sculptured maidens over its door. Everyone knew where most everyone lived.

Goethe's *Goetz von Berlichingen* was produced by Berlin's Koch theatrical company in 1774, the year Goethe became world famous at twenty-five years of age because of his novel, *Werther*. The company apologized for the play's "Shakespearean" character, but the *Vossische Zeitung* gave it a favorable review, noting that it familiarized the Berliners with their own history, about which they were not taught "a particle" at school. This was a subtle criticism of the king's contempt for things German.

"In order to convince oneself of the lack of taste prevalent in Germany in our times, one need only frequent the public theatres," the king wrote (in French, of course). "There one may see those wretched Shakespearean plays translated into our language and note how the entire audience goes wild with joy at watching ridiculous buffooneries, which are suitable for wild men in Canada. Laborers and gravediggers appear in them and make speeches worthy of their lot; then princes and kings appear. How can one be touched or pleased by such a bizarre mixture of the lowly and the mighty, of buffoonery and tragedy? One might forgive Shakespeare his peculiar aberrations, for a period in which the arts are born is not the time of their maturity. But now there appears on stage a *Goetz von Berlichingen,* a nauseating imitation of these bad English plays, and the public applauds and demands that such tasteless platitudes be repeated."

Four years later, at twenty-nine, Goethe visited Berlin (without visiting the king); his diary shows he watched the cavalry being drilled at Potsdam, toured the Berlin porcelain factory, spent an evening in the Tiergarten, walked through the exhibits in the arsenal, went out as far into the Berlin suburbs as Tegel and Zehlendorf, and spent whatever free time he had left meeting and conversing with Anton Braff, Daniel Chodowiecki, Anna Louise Karsch, and others of the city's small artistic community. He also visited Moses Mendelssohn, who at that time was Berlin's leading thinker and who had translated the Pentateuch into German. Mendelssohn was the only Jew in the city who had free access to the king.

The king, as he grew older, slipped into legend even before his death. Devastatingly witty, as malicious as he could be charming, he affected an elaborate shabbiness, hobbling about in stained and even patched clothing. He personally ran everything: not a postal clerk could be appointed without his consent. He was feared and loved as "old Fritz" (*der alte Fritz*); those veterans who had survived his wars worshiped him and called him "Father." On visits to Berlin, some people even rushed to kiss his garments, even lick his boots. Others held back. Intellectuals like Nicolai had doubts, for they saw the autocrat as well as the legendary figure.

Foreign observers alone spoke their minds. Mirabeau even ventured to ask Friedrich personally why "the German Caesar was not also their Augustus," to which Friedrich replied that the arts flourish best when left alone. Far more daring was a British diplomat who told the king he'd rather be a monkey in Borneo than a subject of the Prussian Crown, which understandably threw Friedrich into a rage.

When Friedrich died at age seventy-four, he had ruled for forty-six years. Against his wishes, he was buried beside his father in Potsdam's Garrison Church. His niece, Princess Luise, says everyone "dissolved in tears" and that "all his faults disappeared," everyone thinking "only of his wonderful qualities." Mirabeau, who was in Berlin at the time, was more interested in the reactions of average Berliners. He says they were happy to see Friedrich II go and claims there was rejoicing in the streets, even as there had been when his father had died.

chapter six

JOURNALIST FRIEDRICH NICOLAI DESCRIBED THE CITY AFTER THE death of Frederick the Great as having 110,000 inhabitants, a garrison of 30,000 soldiers, 5,000 *refugiés,* and 3,372 Jews. He placed himself, along with all other Berlin burghers, at the bottom of Berlin's three-layer society, noting that above was the aristocratic officer class and the officials serving them. Yet there was a fourth class as well who had neither citizenship nor any rights, only privileges, and these were the Jews. As outsiders, they were at least in one sense freer than Berlin's burghers, for they could govern themselves through their elders. They were, therefore, free of the stratified social system, as a poor man is free of any worries about the stock market.

Of course, they were burdened with restrictions. They couldn't trade in wool, leather, fur, tobacco, wine, wood, and many other commodities. Still, life had improved for them under the old king. They didn't live in ghettos, and they were allowed to lend money at interest, which, despite the special taxes imposed on them, had helped to establish banking fortunes. Their situation was much the way novelist Gustav Freytag described it in 1859. Germany's Jews, he says, were "indispensable, yet deeply hated; necessary, yet cursed; in daily danger of fire, robbery, and murder, yet the quiet masters of the property and welfare of hundreds; in an unnaturally precarious position, yet always steadily occupied; living amidst the densest mass of Christians, yet separated from them by iron barriers . . ."

One thing that set them apart in Berlin was the extent of their education and culture. Jewish Berliners of that day taught their children art, science, literature, and philosophy long before non-

Jewish Berliners did, for they had traditions of scholarship which were then foreign to Christian Berlin. They were also far more cosmopolitan, for their extensive contacts with other Jewish communities throughout Europe opened their eyes to the outside world whereas their non-Jewish contemporaries were distinctly provincial. Most Christian Berliners had never been outside Prussia, much less German-speaking lands, while these Jewish Berliners corresponded with and traveled to all Europe. No wonder many Christian Berliners found them fascinating. Among the most famous were two unusual women, Henriette Herz and Rahel Levin. Each founded a salon encouraging cultural growth and mixing groups in society that had little chance of meeting elsewhere. In fact, Rahel Levin, whose father died destitute, later entertained Prince Louis Ferdinand, who became her close friend.

What was most exciting to the Berliners, however, was the fact that this new intellectual life was of their own making, not imposed on them by their rulers. It was thanks to Henriette Herz and Rahel Levin that Berlin seemed more than a garrison town, and the Berliners themselves suddenly more than provincials.

The visits Prince Louis Ferdinand paid to the home of Rahel Levin show what an unusual Hohenzollern this young man was. His sister, Princess Radziwill, was equally cultured. Both were prominent in Berlin society, yet recognized that the dissolute court was letting Prussia slide to rack and ruin. Frederick the Great had been childless and was succeeded by a drunken, depraved nephew who spent his time and money on mistresses, setting a tone which the Prussian aristocracy was only too happy to follow after years of asceticism under Frederick the Great. Ironically, Prussia vastly increased her territories under Friedrich Wilhelm II; this tended to make Berlin society think there was nothing wrong when in fact the army, the foundation of Prussia, was deteriorating more each day. This became very apparent to Louis Ferdinand and everyone else, at Valmy, when a revolutionary French "rabble" defeated the Prussian military machine and destroyed the image of Prussian invincibility.

Prussia's army had lacked spirit, its generals boldness, and its tactics were fifty years behind the times. Depressed and confused, Louis Ferdinand sought answers and found them during a dinner party at which he met Baron vom Stein, a Prussian civil servant. Stein recognized that Prussia desperately needed to find new sources of inner strength among the people. "Despotic governments," he later told the prince, "destroy the peoples' character by denying them participation in public affairs and by entrusting such affairs entirely to an army of professional, intriguing bureaucrats." It was a perfect description of the situation in Berlin. The situation did not improve when Friedrich Wilhelm II died. The new king, Friedrich Wilhelm III, faced Napoleon Bonaparte, not a rabble; he sought neutrality by trying to appease the French, but in fact only isolated himself and left his country almost defenseless. Eleven years elapsed between the time Prussia made peace with revolutionary France and the time Napoleon entered Berlin: They were little more than a decade of illusion. Nothing—not even Napoleon's occupation of nearby Hanover—could move the court to decisive action. Baron vom Stein, who was called to Berlin as minister for trade a year before Napoleon's conquest, discovered that he was powerless to reform the frozen, rigid, immovable state.

Berlin itself was filled with contradictory rumors. Some Berliners were terrified; others urged immediate action and were ready to fight. Many continued business as usual, while still others prepared to save themselves while it was still possible. Extravagance, licentiousness, and luxury continued. The court set an example of foolish bravado, continuing its festivities, balls, and ceremonies until August, 1806, mere weeks before Napoleon destroyed Prussia. Even as their soldiers marched west towards the Napoleonic front throughout all August and September, the Berliners were led to believe these were routine exercises; they even cheered them on. Louis Ferdinand, who understood that it was all deadly serious, groaned. "We live day by day in a kind of paralysis," he said. "Unbelievable, when one considers the importance of every moment!" Then he also rode off to war and to his death in the battle of Saalfeld.

The mood among the Berliners soon changed radically. The immediacy of the danger finally dawned on them, not because they were notified by the court but because on September 19 they saw Queen Louise, dressed in the uniform of her own cuirassier regiment, riding at its head down Unter den Linden, as far as Brandenburg Gate. Late next day, a long train of carriages and wagons rumbled unannounced down Unter den Linden, accompanied by hussars bearing torches. All the carriages were closed, affording no view of who might be inside. When the news got out that the cargo actually was the king and queen and the immediate court circle, dismay and horror spread throughout the city.

Count von der Schulenburg, the Military Governor in Berlin, had been left behind. For nearly a month, he kept the Berliners completely in the dark, feeding them rumors of non-existent victories. Then, on October 17, Schulenburg received news that the Prussian Army had suffered a calamitous defeat at Jena and Auerstädt. He prepared to flee Berlin, but continued to keep the news from the Berliners. The notices he published that day merely stated: "The king has lost a battle. Now the first duty of all burghers is to maintain order!" *Jetzt ist Ruhe die erste Bürgerpflicht* (his actual words) mean more than that: Their first duty was not only order or calmness, but silence as well.

When his carriage and the wagons carrying his possessions appeared on Unter den Linden, the Berliners realized the truth about their situation. An enraged mob attacked the wagons and succeeded in halting Count von der Schulenburg in front of the Brandenburg Gate.

"Traitor!" they shouted at him.

"What do you want?" Schulenburg yelled. "After all, I'm leaving my children behind!"

His coachmen lashed at the horses. They reared, bolted, and charged through the crowd, through the gate, and out of Berlin.

Now other citizens tried to flee. The wealthy rushed their treasures to Stettin, Küstrin, or Silesia, where some of the most militant of the city's journalists—those who'd urged a strong stand against Bonaparte—fled as well. At the same time, farmers from the surrounding countryside rushed in with their possessions, for their farms were in immediate danger of being overrun. They, and all those Berliners who didn't have the wherewithal to flee, were left behind.

The first French soldiers to arrive marched through Brandenburg Gate five days after Schulenburg had escaped. No more than a small advance guard, they were led by the adjutant to General Hulin. The Frenchmen, having exchanged polite greetings with the Civil Governor at the Rathaus, took possession of all palaces and important civic buildings, and prepared to bivouac. Later that same day, the first elements of Marshal Davout's armies entered the city. They were shocked when the vanquished Berliners cheered them enthusiastically.

Bonaparte himself lingered in Potsdam to see the grave of Friedrich II in the Garrison Church; when he left, he issued orders to leave the church unmolested. Three days later, on October 27, he entered Berlin.

French elite regiments, forming a guard of honor, had lined Unter den Linden ever since early morning. Scores of thousands of Berliners and Prussians from the nearby countryside packed the avenue behind them. The rest of Berlin was deserted, its streets empty and silent. At four in the afternoon, the military display began. As the emperor himself reached within a hundred paces of the gate, the bands struck up the "Marseillaise." A roar of *"Vive l'Empereur!"* greeted Napoleon. The cheering continued as he rode down Unter den Linden toward the palace. He himself remained dour, silent, unsmiling as he watched the cheering, conquered multitudes. Those who were there—and among them were Rahel Levin and Alexander von Humboldt—say he looked at the Berliners with cold contempt.

He did not understand them. He believed he was their conqueror. They thought he was their liberation.

chapter seven

ALTHOUGH THE FRENCHMEN IN BERLIN BROUGHT A REFRESHING
note to social occasions, as well as much elegance and culture,
it was clear to the Berliners that they had merely exchanged one
military dictatorship for another. Their own love affair with their
French conquerors soon ended.

Not that the French were worried. When the philosopher,
Fichte, delivered his rousing "Speeches to the German Nation" in
Berlin, it was noted that much of the applause came from French
officers in the audience; they enjoyed the rhetoric and regarded
it as little more than that. They missed a subtle, yet important,
note: the idea that the Berliners owed their allegiance less to
Prussia than to the concept of a unified "Germany." It was a spark
which would rekindle passions Napoleon had quenched.

Reform was in the air. In Königsberg, Friedrich Wilhelm III had
invested Baron vom Stein with wide powers. Within five days, Stein
abolished serfdom, canceled all distinctions between land held by
peasants and aristocrats, and did away with those distinctions of
class with respect to employment, trades, and commerce. He further
strengthened Cabinet reforms initiated by Karl von Hardenberg,
and a year later, granted self-government along modern lines to
every Prussian city and town. The reforms had been easy to under-
take; they had needed only non-interference from the king. The
spirit of change infested the Prussian generals, too, who planned
the modernization of the army.

But Napoleon became wary of Stein and the baron had to flee
for his life, finding refuge first in Prague and then among the
Russians. Not only was reform now in the air in Berlin, but revolt as well. When an officer named Major von Schill tried to lead

his Hussar regiment against Napoleon, it cost him his head, which was severed in the Berlin Rathaus and sent to Napoleon's brother Jérome in an alcohol-filled bottle. King Friedrich Wilhelm III, depressed and indecisive, tried only to pacify the French, even after Napoleon's defeat in 1812 and the mounting patriotic fever in Berlin. Finally, General Hans Yorck von Wartenburg acted on his own. He was no Major Schill, matters had changed, the wind was different, and in this turbulent time, the king did the best he could have done: nothing at all. The French armies had staggered out of Russia, and in December, 1812, Wartenburg opened all Prussia to the czar's armies, now a liberating force. In their front ranks was Baron vom Stein as the czar's administrator for West and East Prussia. Stein immediately convened the first Prussian parliament, and it promptly established a national militia and reserve. With Stein prodding from the east and Hardenberg tugging in Berlin, the king reluctantly called his people to arms. In the "Battle of Nations," as Napoleon's defeat at Leipzig came to be called, the Prussian force included its first volunteers— ten thousand patriots, most of them Berliners.

The aftermath was exhilarating. Everywhere restless, freedom-seeking students left classrooms, paraded, demonstrated, shouted slogans, formed patriotic fraternities. The wind of change was in the air and swept the king along. In May, 1815, he promised his people a constitution; hopes were high. Soon, however, the reactionary coalition forged by Metternich at the Congress of Vienna rallied; the king never kept his word. The promise of a real constitution was betrayed, no assembly was called, and agricultural reforms ended. After having risen in the war of liberation, the Berliners found themselves less liberated than ever. One of the few benefits their sufferings brought them was the return of Schadow's "Quadriga," that Berlin goddess riding a chariot atop Brandenburg Gate that Napoleon had taken to Paris eight years earlier. When the Congress of Vienna divested Prussia of its Polish territories and its aristocracy of three million serfs, by way of recompense, Friedrich Wilhelm was given land far-off along the Rhine. This, however, was filled with three million freemen whom the Junkers feared were poisoned with French liberalism and Roman Catholicism. The Junkers didn't realize they'd won the Ruhr

Basin, that enormous depository of iron and coal. It was this reservoir—more than even Prussian "glory"—that was to transform Berlin into a major metropolis.

The "wars of liberation" had produced a lot of cripples. One of these, Fritz Werkmann, became legendary in Berlin as "an authentic Berlin type." He was also one of the first recorded street musicians to play the hurdy-gurdy or barrel-organ in the city. Werkmann, who had lost both legs at Leipzig and had to balance precariously on two wooden stumps, had been rewarded by the king with an Iron Cross and a permit to perform in the capital. The tiny cripple became a familiar sight in fashionable quarters where people with money congregated. Stumps banging on sidewalks, Werkmann lurched about unsteadily, pushing his *Leierkasten* and cranking out popular airs. A favorite was "I am a Prussian: Do you recognize my colors?" Coming from so mutilated a veteran, with an Iron Cross joggling grotesquely on his chest, this evoked special sympathy—but also the anger of officers, who regarded the song as a reproach.

Worse yet were verses of Werkmann's own composition, which he sang to attract new audiences. Freely translated from the Berlinese idiom, these tell his story:

> When my legs were shaved off me
> In the war that has just passed
> Then my king, as though for payment,
> Slapped a medal on my breast.
>
> And he uttered, "Dearest Fritze,
> So that you may live in ease,
> We now further here reward you:
> Let you crank songs in the streets."
>
> Thus it is through royal mercy
> A small pittance comes to hand:
> Ah, it proves too short for living,
> And for dying, it's too grand.
>
> Still, despite it, this old warrior
> Can, among the living, sing—

Standing stiff and at attention—
"Let us hail our glorious king!" *

It was an odd mix of patriotic slogans and bitter words, the type
which today would be called Brechtian. Over the years, the young
army officers in Berlin found these songs ever more vexing, just
as they found the sight of a decorated cripple hobbling to military
music distasteful. They finally decided to do something about it:
They drove Werkmann to despair, and ultimately, to attempt
suicide.

The atmosphere in Berlin encouraged such meanness of spirit.
A ruthless suppression of all liberal thought, writings, and associations had begun; what followed were called "the quiet years" in
Berlin. Baron vom Stein retired from public life in anger. Having
failed to establish a representative society, he concentrated on
establishing at least a society for historical research. Such a retreat
into scholarship was always to provide a refuge to Berlin states-
men made impotent by their despotic regimes. Karl von Hardenberg, for his part, became increasingly conservative. Even the Prussian Army, although based on a national call-up, remained much
the same as before. Now that the Government had again swung
over to complete reaction, its army had once more become its instrument for oppression.

As repression mounted, even some of Fichte's speeches were
banned from circulation in printed form, and the police watched
for subversive content in the sermons of Friedrich Schleier-
macher, professor at the university in Berlin and one of the leading
Protestant theologians of the 19th century. Even generals like Hermann von Boyen were dismissed because they had been on the
army reform commission. Wilhelm von Humboldt—philologist,
writer, diplomat, privy councillor—had, like Stein, retired in protest against the Government's betrayal.

* Als ma wurden in dem Krieje
   beede Beene abrasiert,
   hat mein König als Belohnung
   ma de Heldenbrust jarniert.
   Un' jesajt: "Mein lieba Fritze,
   det et dir mög wohlajehn,
   derfste ferna als Belohnung
   eenen Leiakasten drehn!"

So vadien durch Königs Jnade
ick mir eenen Pappenstiel,
ach—für't Leben is't ze wenig,
und zum Sterben is't ze viel.
Dennoch olla Freiheitskrieja
lebste heute immer noch,
stehste stramm und rufst bejeistat!
"Unsa König lebe hoch!"

70

It was during these years that Fritz Werkmann's enemies tried to prevail. His permit to perform was rescinded, and rather than starve to death, he tried suicide. He failed in the attempt, but became a *cause celèbre* instead. Outraged Berliners protested the persecution of the veteran; thousands collected funds for him. Eventually, they set Werkmann up in business as a publican, in a *Kellerkneipe* (cellar tavern) on the Artillerie Strasse, allowing him to live out his years in dignity in a trade much respected in Berlin.

Unable to participate in public life, the Berliners sought relief in private amusements. Heinrich Heine, who then came to the city at the age of twenty-two, exclaimed on seeing it, "Isn't the present splendid!" He had been attracted to Berlin by the presence there of classical scholar Friedrich Wolf, as well as the philosopher Hegel, who had replaced the dead Fichte at the new Friedrich Wilhelm University, established in 1810 in a former palace on Unter den Linden. Here among his new Berlin friends, Heine's restless, democratic spirit first found direction and form. Here, in the capital of Prussia, he learned to loathe Prussia's militarism and absolutism, yet here he also learned to love the Berliners themselves.

He furnished articles to a South German newspaper and tried to temper his enthusiasm. "As soon as I begin to praise my good Berliners," he wrote, "I know my reputation among them is finished. They shrug their shoulders and whisper, 'That fellow's become insipid; now he's even praising us!'" Still he could not help being enthralled by the city's elegance, for Berlin was now truly big and fashionable. He wrote of its Hôtels de Rome and de Petersbourg, of the fine cuisine for which the Café de Commerce was famed, of the bonbons that brought renown to the Café Royal, and of the street scene.

"Now it's noon, the time the world of elegance comes out to stroll," Heine observed in one dispatch. "What a polished crowd surges up and down these 'Linden'! See that dandy with his many gaily colored vests? Hear him whispering earnest words to his lady? He ogles her through his lorgnette, smiles, fusses his hair. What beautiful women one sees and what a lot of men glittering with medals! Those countless decorations everywhere! Have a coat fitted here, and your tailor asks immediately, 'With or without a notch for the ribbons?' "

It was a sight which also enchanted a young actress named Karoline Bauer, who came to Berlin a couple of years after Heine.

"It had only two hundred thousand inhabitants then," she wrote, "no gas, no railroad, no running water, only three theatres, two newspapers, no stock-market fever. Its cry was, 'Long live bagatelles; long live trifles!' "

Not all was rosy, however. The first Berlin tenements— those *Mietskasernen,* or "rental-barracks,"—were already springing up near the Hamburg and Oranienburg Gates, sure portents of industrial prosperity and misery. (Later, an inflation struck, sending large numbers of the fainthearted from the city.) The first gaslights arrived in Berlin two years after Karoline Bauer entered it; then came the machine factories, railways, arterial roads, steamers along the Spree River. One Berlin institution then established was the Café Kranzler, on the corner of Friedrichstrasse and Unter den Linden; it exists today, amost 150 years later, on the Kurfürstendamm in West Berlin.

These were solid, respectable, Victorian "Biedermeier" years, the quiet years that stretched from the Congress of Vienna to 1848. It was a time when several archetypal Berlinese characters became famous. Madame du Titre was one of them, noted for her *Schlagfertigkeit,* her ability to deliver a withering verbal riposte in Berlinese. Another was Dr. Ernst Ludwig Heim, who had fourteen hundred patients, each month paid for as many as 975 prescriptions for the poor out of his own pocket, and never paused for a moment. He even saw patients while he shaved at five in the morning. He embodied that Berlin *Tempo* then emerging and of which the Berliners are so proud, apparently thriving on it, for when he died at 87, he was still working. Johann Gottfried Schadow, the sculptor, was another. A tailor's son, he had risen to court sculptor, or *Hofbildhauer,* and to membership in the Academy of Arts two years after Frederick the Great's death. A year before Napoleon conquered the city, he had been made rector of the academy, and in 1816, its director. He dominated the city's artistic life until his death in 1850, as much through his personality as his artistic ability. Karl Friedrich Zelter was another outstanding Berliner. Although a master bricklayer by trade, he came to be one of the city's most influential musicians. He founded a choral group, which soon came to be known in Berlin as the *"Singakademie,"* and eventually, he was made a professor and its academic head. Like Schadow, Zelter also was famed for his gruff Berlin manner and his mastery of the city's dialect.

"At first meeting," Goethe said about him, "he seems harsh, perhaps even coarse, but this is merely superficial. I know almost no one who is at the same time so *gentle* as Zelter. And don't forget he's lived for more than half a century in Berlin. I see in everything that this is a city filled with such an impertinent species of mankind that one doesn't get far using delicacy with them; to keep above water in Berlin, one has to be somewhat coarse oneself . . ."

Zelter, who rediscovered the music of Bach for the Berliners and who established its Institute for Church Music, died in 1832, his death-bed remarks adding to the many stories told about him. "Don't just smear that off as though it's nothing, doctor," he murmured to the physician who mopped his brow. "That's something the likes of you won't see every day—honest bricklayer's sweat." With that, he died.

In Weimar, Goethe was dead; in Berlin, Zelter, old Dr. Heim, Rahel Levin, and many others of the old days were dead as well. A new salon, founded by Bettina von Arnim, had attracted Berlin's intellectuals. The times had changed: Bettina, with her aristocratic name and radical social conscience foreshadowed the future. So did a young law student at Berlin's university, who arrived in 1837 and stayed four years—Karl Marx.

Bettina von Arnim wrote two books that caused sensations in Berlin. The first was a three-volume masterpiece, purporting to be and known as *Goethe's Exchange of Letters with a Child*. When it was later revealed that Bettina herself had written all of Goethe's letters in this book, she became famous for having fooled the experts. The second book appeared later, after Friedrich Wilhelm III died and Friedrich Wilhelm IV became king. Bettina was so shocked by the hopeless misery of Berlin's poor that she described the wretched social conditions of the city in a book she entitled, *This Book Belongs to the King* (*Dieses Buch gehört dem König*), hoping to arouse his conscience. It failed to do so.

In Paris in February, 1848, Karl Marx published *The Communist Manifesto*. While it inflamed many, it merely reflected a revolutionary atmosphere already in the air throughout Europe. In Berlin the year before, the king had even agreed to convoke the members of Prussia's provincial diets, or parliaments, calling them to a United Diet in the capital. The delegates weren't satisfied, however. They wished to meet regularly and to be given a share in government. To this Friedrich Wilhelm IV could not agree. His romantic nature was attracted by the "mystical" bond between absolute monarch and people. When the March, 1848 revolution broke in Berlin, it caught him completely by surprise and left him horrified.

It had been ignited in February, when the news of the French upheaval reached Berlin. King Louis Philippe had been deposed and France again became a republic. Once more the spirit of revolution spread from Paris. Berlin was ready for it. Murmurs of rebellion had continued ever since the United Diet broke up in June.

Finally, on March 18th, masses of citizens gathered outside the palace to present their demands. In dispersing them, soldiers accidentally fired the two shots that transformed the demonstration into an uprising. Within hours, more than one thousand barricades had been thrown up in the streets of Berlin. More than two thousand troops, firing cannons as well as rifles, battled for fourteen hours with tens of thousands of Berliners.

"The barricades," wrote an eyewitness, "began to form as though by magic. Old and young, rich and poor, joined together on every street corner to build these barriers. Booths, wagons, busses, carriages, huge freight, postal or farmers' carts, construction lumber—everything—were torn up, overturned, and brought together. Women and children worked alongside the rest. Everyone was equal. One saw, for example, two men carrying a beam, one of them in rags, the other in fine clothes. The basic materials used were torn-up paving stones, large boulders, beams, boards; to these were added beds hauled out of houses, along with sacks and other furniture. Everyone willingly contributed whatever he could. Women brought coffee, slices of bread, and handed food to the workers and fighters in the streets. Men everywhere formed bullets and hammered themselves lances . . ."

74

Yet the king still took no action. Torn with fears and inner contradictions, he remained immobile and weeping inside the palace.

The street fighting cost the lives of eighteen soldiers and 183 Berliners, and by the time the day ended, it certainly seemed as though the army were in firm control. Yet the king's generals had not reckoned with their eccentric king, who was unwilling to subjugate his city and unhappy that his somewhat romantic notions of a United Diet should have been met with further demands. Finally, he collapsed. First he said he would withdraw the troops if the Berliners would remove their barricades; then he agreed to remove them from the city even if the Berliners did not do their part. By March 21, Berlin was in the hands of the revolutionaries.

An eyewitness account reports that the citizens mocked and jeered the soldiers as they withdrew through Brandenburg Gate. The last units to leave, members of Guards regiments, even arrived in Spandau without their weapons and in complete disorder, spat upon and splattered with mud.

The Berliners' rage had also turned on the fifty-one-year-old Prince of Prussia, Wilhelm, brother of and successor to the childless king, who had helped lead the troops against barricades. They called him the "Cartridge-Prince" (*Patronenprinz*) and demanded he be delivered up to them. Unwilling to comply, yet also unwilling to shelter Wilhelm, the king had him transported clandestinely to Spandau, and after he was discovered there, to the Peacock Island in the Havel. Later he was secretly moved to London. Then the king waited to see what would happen.

The tragedy is that nothing much did occur, despite the fact that the Berliners were now in complete control of the city for the first time since Friedrich Eisenzahn had moved into Berlin. They had even established a citizen militia to replace the army, but instead of arresting the king, it mounted guard in front of the palace to protect him. It would have been possible to seize all public buildings and declare a republic or a popular democracy; instead, measures were taken to prevent just that. When some revolutionaries threatened such moves, they were prevented from seizing the palace of Prince Wilhelm by a handful of Berlin's university students—not by force, but by the sign that the students had posted in front of the palace reading, *Nationaleigentum,* or "National Property."

Three centuries of Hohenzollern rule had their effect. While other countries arrested their kings, the Berliners assembled in front of the palace to hear what the voice of Constituted Authority had to say.

On March 21 Friedrich Wilhelm IV stepped out on his balcony and told the citizens he would appear on horseback in the palace square. He asked them to hand him one of their revolutionary banners, the black-red-gold *Reichsbanner* which became the flag of Weimar and is today the flag of both Germanies.

At 11 A.M., the king rode out in uniform, followed by his ministers and princes; every one of them wore tri-color ribbons about their sleeves, including the king. Perhaps they thought he had capitulated; in fact, having failed to quell the revolution, he was proceeding to join it.

A guard of burghers bearing tri-colored flags flanked him as he rode along Unter den Linden. Cheers accompanied him down the avenue, as tens of thousands lined the street waving. Tri-colored flags and brightly colored cloths—anything that could flutter—hung from all the windows.

An honor guard of three students met him at the university, where the entire student body and all the professors had excitedly assembled. They may have hated Prince Wilhelm and the military, but this was different: This was their king, order incarnate, *die Obrigkeit*—"Authority" itself. They seemed to have forgotten that all effective power was in their hands. They did not insist that he accede to their demands. They simply assembled in orderly rows and waited for him to speak.

He gave a virtuoso performance. He promised nothing, but inspired them all, gave not an inch yet seemed almost democratic. "I wish only Germany's freedom, Germany's unity, and order!" he shouted.

Raising his hand heavenward in the kind of gesture which appealed to him and his people, he announced he was placing himself at their head and that henceforth, "Prussia is merged into Germany!"

It seemed a promise of German unification, which all liberals wanted; in return, the Berliners were prepared to accept Order.

In October, Wrangel led thousands of Prussian soldiers back into the city and overthrew the liberal parliament, reestablishing autocracy. Bowing to overwhelming military force, the Berliners settled again for an easeful search after prosperity. Those among them who had most yearned for freedom abandoned their city in sadness and disgust.

A tidal wave of Germans swept across the Atlantic after 1848—more than a quarter of a million of them came to America *each year* during the 1850's, seeking to find what they had not been able to establish at home. Those liberals who chose to remain in Berlin were rendered totally ineffective or became "practical" moderates; an example is David Hansemann, Prussian minister in 1848, and the most liberal of them. He had tried to create democratic institutions, but later founded a bank instead.

Briefly, the revolt brought the Berliners freedom of the press (an illustrated weekly named *Kladderadatsch* was founded, offering the satire Berliners love so well), a Parliament had been formed and Berliners had even won the right to smoke in the streets, but the course toward renewed autocracy was in fact irreversible.

chapter eight

REVOLUTIONS HAVE ALWAYS BEEN MORE EFFICIENTLY SUP-
pressed than mounted in Berlin and most Berliners, as it has been
said, have learned to accommodate themselves to autocrats, rather
than rise up against them. The reasons for this can be dated back,
to a large extent, to their experience in 1848. They had won freedom on the barricades and earned it with their blood, but it
had lasted only from March until October. Wrangel, the city's new
military governor, had again placed the Berliners under military
occupation. All the guns were in the hands of the ruling junta; the
soldiers who wielded them were ruthlessly divorced from any
sympathetic connection with the people. Civilians in Berlin
were, of course, necessary to the economic life of this garrison
city, but were more tolerated than welcomed, and allowed to remain only if they obeyed the military rule.

Soon the king divested himself of the tri-color he had affected
to win the loyalty of the Berliners and swung completely about to
reaction. Berlin liberals were furiously persecuted for years. When
the king suffered a stroke that left him insane, Cartridge-Prince
Wilhelm replaced him as regent, and after his brother's death, succeeded him as king. Unification would finally be achieved under
Wilhelm, thanks to his chancellor, Otto von Bismarck. When
King Wilhelm I first offered him the reins of government in 1862,
he asked if Bismarck were ready to serve "even against the majority" in the new but powerless Parliament. Bismarck assured him
he was. He had few illusions about the citizens around him, for
he rightly saw the Berliners as being at the very root of liberal
discontent. He neither liked nor trusted them, nor ever entertained the idea that they liked him.

"They hate and slander me because I am a Junker and not a professor," Bismarck told Dr. Moritz Busch, a sycophantic journalist who was his sometime Boswell.

He was referring to the delegates in Parliament. The ones he most disliked were the members from Berlin. He said Berliners "must always be in opposition and have their own ideas," but admitted they had "their virtues—many and estimable ones—they fight well, but would not consider themselves to be as clever as they ought to be unless they knew everything better than the Government."

His dislike of them grew over the years; he never even got to like their city. In later life, he told some Berlin students, "Berlin has grown too big for me industrially and politically." In fact, it had by then grown too proletarian and socialistic. It had become an anomaly in Germany, "the absolute antithesis of everything that provincial Germans regarded as Germanic," *Der Spiegel* wrote in a cover article about Berlin. The city in Bismarck's day, it said, seemed "booming, noisy, tolerant, a melting-pot . . . cold, soulless, 'degenerate,' 'Jewish,' a cosmopolitan conglomerate drawn along the lines of Paris and New York." Indeed, much of the description was true, which helps explain why foreigners found it attractive.

Bismarck, however, even considered the possibility of moving the Reichstag out of Berlin altogether, perhaps to Potsdam. A French journalist quoted him as saying he'd much rather have picked a city older than Berlin as the capital of his united Germany. One special reason for moving Parliament, he told Busch, was the Berlin delegation in that body. Not only were there too many Berliners in the Reichstag, but they always seemed to attend each session. He checked the *Parliamentary Guide* on this occasion and read off the names of Berliners to Busch; there were forty-six among the delegates. Not more than two hundred Reichstag members regularly attended sessions, he stated, "and of these the Berliners are probably always present." This was, in his view, "a monstrous condition of affairs," giving the Berliners nearly a fourth of the "effective representation of Germany," and worse yet, leading to the possibility of liberal majorities.

"They are always in their places," Bismarck complained, "and when the democrats among them find themselves supported by an equal number of their fellows from the provinces, they have almost a certain majority on the average attendance . . . exactly that kind of a majority which should not exist. That must be done away with. The German people have a right to demand that the Reichstag should not be Berlinised!"

Why was he up in arms? He well knew that the Reichstag could initiate no legislation, enforce nothing. What bothered him was the mere presence of the Reichstag in a city where liberal sentiment reigned. This created a potentially explosive situation.

"Away from the capital," Bismarck continued, "the members of the Reichstag need have no fear of the scandal-mongering press of Berlin. How many of them have the courage to despise the journalistic rabble? In revolutionary times, how many of them would have the courage to hold their ground? Such times may possibly return. In smaller towns it is much easier to protect them than there."

Another source of irritation to Bismarck was the fact that the Berliners were electing themselves liberal municipal governments. Bismarck called them "that democratic clique that rules Berlin," and complained that its members "noisily enforce the rights granted to them and act as if they could do whatever they liked."

At times, however, the Berliners' fierce allegiance to their city amused Bismarck. He liked to tell the story of the time he took a Berliner to see the famous Herrenhausen Palace garden in Hanover. Bismarck had praised its beautiful avenue of majestic trees.

"Nonsense," replied Bismarck's Berlin friend. "They're nothing at all compared to our Linden."

"A year later," Bismarck reported, "I walked down Unter den Linden with this same Berliner. It was summer and the linden trees had a particularly drab, miserable look about them. 'Well, what do you say?' I asked my friend. 'Are you thinking of those gorgeous trees at Herrenhausen?'

" 'Oh, for heaven's sake, leave me alone!' my companion replied. 'I can't tell you how furious I get when I see something that's better than we've got in Berlin!'

"There!" Bismarck concluded. "That's the Berliner for you!"

Bismarck was ruling unconstitutionally and was abhorred by everyone, as he himself admitted. In 1866, however, he became a national hero, for war against Austria had been engineered by him and had been won resoundingly at Königgrätz. When the Hapsburgs agreed to have no further say in the affairs of Germany, a North German Federation was established and Prussia became the dominant German power. Suddenly, two-thirds of Germany's 68 million people had become Prussians and the remainder allied to Prussia.

Even liberals cheered Bismarck now. He chose the moment to ask Parliament for an Act of Indemnity, excusing his four years of illegal rule. "Kind words," he murmured at the time, "cost nothing." When in response, Parliament overwhelmingly forgave him, it announced in effect that it would tolerate even illegality and would not even try for power. After this act, liberalism as a political force was dead in Prussia. Liberals and men of stature avoided politics; they entered industry instead. Industry grew enormously as a result and its power came to be married to imperial might, a development that served to crush most of the liberalism that was left.

The Berliners, however, tried to maintain a liberal stand. On February 12, 1867, they voted overwhelmingly for the liberal Progressive party and defeated all the conservative candidates, even those sacrosanct war heroes, Roon and Moltke, as well as Bismarck himself. Only briefly had they let victory parades bamboozle them. From this time on, the majority of Berliners voted liberal, democratic, and progressive. And it was just this voting record, writes Werner Vogel, a Berlin historian, that consistently created ill feeling not only between the Berliners and the royal court, but also between the Berliners and other Germans.

Despite this bloc of Berlin votes, the Government remained a military autocracy. The constitution, after all, was rigged from the start, for it established a three-class franchise which effectively denied any political power to the majority of the people. Those paying the two top categories of taxes received two-thirds of all votes, and therefore, two-thirds of all seats in Parliament; the overwhelming mass of the king's subjects received only one-third of the votes, and therefore, never were able to elect a majority to represent them. Further, the constitution was a masterpiece of cynical gobbledygook: It said the chancellor was "responsible," but did not deign to define to whom. It was understood, in any case, that he certainly wasn't responsible to Parliament or to the people; if anyone, then to the king. If Bismarck were defeated in an election, this didn't remove him from power, for he derived that only from the king. If Parliament tried to force him to resign, he simply dissolved that body. Nor could Parliament initiate any legislation at all. Its sole function was to approve the seven-year army budget—and this merely led Bismarck to create a war scare every seven years.

Parliament, in short, was mere window dressing for the military autocracy, at whose head marched the uniformed king—prodded, cajoled, flattered, bullied, and seduced by his uniformed, though civilian, prime minister; beside them clanked all the king's generals, officers, and officials, all effective power in their hands.

Bismarck's ambition to build a great and united German nation was realized in 1871, at the end of the successful war against France. Again Bismarck produced a new constitution, another reshuffle of the same marked deck. The three-class franchise was retained for the lower house, or Reichstag; he himself remained vaguely "responsible," and a new upper house, or Bundesrat, was created. This was supposed to represent the interests of individual states and actually govern the country, but in fact, it did neither and had only one meaningful power—to change (and perhaps liberalize) the constitution. But only fourteen votes were needed to block any change at all, and the Prussians, who liked to publicize the fact that they were in "a minority" here, had seventeen votes.

Like all Hohenzollerns, Wilhelm I didn't trust the Berliners, but he at least seemed to have more reason than most. There had been one assassination attempt against him shortly after he became king; now, in 1878, there were two more within three weeks. A demented apprentice fired four shots at him while he was driving down Unter den Linden, but missed each time. When, three weeks later, on the same avenue, a man named Nobiling hit Emperor Wilhelm with about thirty pieces of "grape shot," wounding him severely, his son was appointed to act for him. He recovered late that year, but for the first few days, all Berlin feared for the emperor's life. Thousands waited for palace bulletins. Then on the third day, they saw the big wooden bathtub arriving at the palace, as it did each week, regular as clockwork. If Wilhelm was well enough to take a bath he must be well indeed. This view was justified in a time when even the palace didn't have its own tub and bathing seemed a madcap enterprise at best. As late as 1896, a Berlin Association for Public Baths had to urge Berliners to try the experience. That year, it published its manifesto: "A weekly bath belongs to every German! Most people never bathe at all. It may take many decades before everyone can have his weekly bath. Only our descendants will regard as commonplace that for which we fight today!"

Those were fine stirring words: the type of demands Berliners were allowed to voice, since political demands were forbidden. In fact, political action became even more difficult now, for the two assassination attempts gave Bismarck a pretext for pushing through anti-Socialist laws. (Nobiling had been falsely "proven" a Socialist.)

These laws, however, suppressed more than the Social Democratic party itself. They crippled trade unions, killed the Socialist press, and made possible the subsequent persecution of all press critics, even from "bourgeois" newspapers; it started a witch hunt against all who might be harboring Socialist thoughts. The effect in Berlin, where vast numbers of citizens were Social Democrats, was dreadful. Countless Socialists were deported from Berlin without court hearings, even without being allowed to provide for their families. Georg Bernhard, editor-in-chief of the *Vossische Zeitung* during the 1920's, wrote that this resulted in "indescribable tragedies" in countless Berlin homes.

The two attempted assassinations mirrored the tensions in Berlin even though both assassins were deranged. The Hohenzollern palace sat in the middle of an exploding capital, for big boom years had come after the Reich was formed. The city had more elegant people than ever before, but it also had armies of industrial workers and these formed a potentially revolutionary proletariat.

In one ten-year span, 1880-90, the city's population had doubled, to more than two million. There was no provision to house all the new arrivals; the city could accommodate neither its workers nor its new industries. The city fathers began hurriedly to incorporate all surrounding suburbs. Still, countless people lived in Berlin without any fixed, permanent abode, kept on the move by the police. Others were jammed into the tenements that were then rising with amazing rapidity. Ultimately, even the Berliners admitted (perhaps even with a sense of achievement) that the city now had the worst industrial slums of all Europe. Bismarck called it "a desert of bricks and newspapers"; when he was once asked why he wore spectacles in the country and not in town, he answered that there wasn't anything worth looking at in Berlin.

He might have taken a look at the *Mietskasernen,* those "rental barracks" whose style is peculiar to Berlin. These consist of huge blocks of flats erected in the form of a hollow square, fronting on four streets. The large center court, however, wasn't meant to offer sun and air to residents. It was subdivided into smaller courtyards by putting up buildings which ran right through it, one behind the other. Thus small interior courts called *Hinterhöfe,* or "rear courtyards," resulted, often as many as five or six. One walked from the street through these inner courts by passing under arches which accentuated the gloom. At every turn, one faced another tenanted area; some of the inner buildings even contained small factories and workshops, which added to the dirt, din, and misery. This was a design without any decent standards whatever, but the law only stipulated that courtyards needed to provide outhouses and that each interior court could not be smaller than twenty-eight square meters. That restriction wasn't meant to give the residents elbowroom; it just so happened that Berlin's fire engines in those days needed twenty-eight square meters to turn around. One cannot help but come to the conclusion that the trucks managed this better than the residents could. In Meyers Hof on Wedding's Ackerstrasse, for example, one thousand people were jammed into verminous, dark flats facing *six* such inner courtyards. No wonder revolutionary talk went on in all this gloom. It needed constant repression, censorship, and arrests to keep these workers in their place. Prussian police spies infiltrated everywhere, even into apprentices' hostels, and kept tabs on everyone.

Few efforts were made to alleviate the misery. A decent workers' settlement was founded in Weissensee in 1872 and an early attempt at public housing was made in Moabit. In 1889, work began on District Spandau's Siemensstadt, this being the creation of Werner von Siemens, who helped build the largest electrical engineering enterprise in Germany as well as a city to house his employees. Yet such efforts remained unique. These were years of speculation, initiated with the billions in French gold Wilhelm I brought back as reparations in 1871. Within a year, 470 corporations were founded and the stock market was out of control. Twelve months later, the bubble burst, most of the corporations collapsed, and a suicidal wave swept from Berlin all the way to Vienna.

Widespread financial ruin led some Germans to blame the Jews who were already well-established bankers. Although they were fully emancipated in 1871, many nationalists wondered if Jews could ever "be real Germans." A rabble-rousing Protestant minister named Adolf Stöcker broke from the Social Democrats, formed a Christian Socialist Workers' party, and announced that liberalism, the free-market system, economic speculation of all kinds, and the stock market were all Jewish inventions. He even went so far as to campaign among Berlin's workers, most of whom voted Socialist, by telling them that socialism itself was a Jewish invention.

That sort of talk didn't sit well with the Berliners. When Stöcker offered his program to a vote in Berlin, he suffered a calamitous defeat, winning exactly 380 votes. Anti-Semitism, however, continued throughout Germany until 1880-81, until czarist pogroms finally shocked Europe into public opposition. Leading citizens of Berlin issued a manifesto denouncing anti-Semitism as a flagrant injustice, a blot on Germany, and a divisive element threatening the newly united nation. Among those who signed it were Max von Forckenbeck, a brilliant and progressive Berlin mayor, industrialist Siemens, Rudolf Virchow, the most famous German physician of the day, and Berlin author Theodor Mommsen, who in 1902 became the second man, and the first German, ever to win the Nobel Prize for Literature. Leading the protest movement and damning anti-Semitism as "a shame and a disgrace to Germany" was Crown Prince Friedrich Wilhelm, that unusual, liberal, and doomed Hohenzollern who later briefly graced the throne.

Much of the credit for the city's liberal and cultured air belongs to its press, which endured constant harassment. A law curbing press criticism had been passed in Bismarck's second year in office; newspapers which "endangered the public welfare" received two successive "warnings," and if they failed to heed these and cease offending the regime, they could be shut down temporarily or indefinitely, at Bismarck's discretion. Offending newsmen were brought to trial 175 times on such charges, in just Bismarck's second year in office.

It therefore took courage to stay in the newspaper business—and even more to enter it. One man who dared was a prominent Jewish Berlin merchant named Leopold Ullstein. In 1877, he bought an evening paper, and six months later, acquired a second and more important paper, the *Berliner Zeitung*. It introduced political cartoons. A typical one ridiculed the voting system by suggesting that a *fourth*-class franchise would soon be established —for those too poor to buy a third-class ticket. Nine months after Ullstein bought this paper, he announced its editorial position in words which perfectly described the aspirations and political realities of Berliners:

"The *Berliner Zeitung* calls for a constitutional government—no Chancellor Absolutism! It demands that the German people be set free and that they should no longer be treated like a conquered nation!"

The government considered words like these so inflammatory that the headquarters of the Corps of Guards (*Generalkommando des Gardekorps*) in Berlin issued an order forbidding all soldiers, on penalty of arrest, from reading liberal newspapers. The *Berliner Zeitung* was mentioned in particular.

Ullstein editors were brought to trial six months after the paper began publishing, and from then on, court actions never stopped. The persecution reached its height in 1894, during the so-called "monster trial" dealing with the "Rubber Hose Affair." The press had reported that unemployed Berlin workers who had protested their lot were beaten with rubber hoses after their peaceful demonstration had quietly dissolved. The police, on the other hand, denied that it had attacked these workers without provocation. All nine of the editors from nine Berlin papers on trial were convicted and sentenced to prison, despite the fact that every eyewitness in court had substantiated the press reports.

At one point in these proceedings, an angry defense attorney demanded that the police should have explained its actions. This remark astounded the judge, *Landgerichtsrat* Brausewetter.

"Explain?" he asked. "To whom?"

"The public, of course!"

86

"Oh, come!" Judge Brausewetter replied with annoyance. "The public doesn't exist!"

Shortly afterward Judge Brausewetter was removed from office on grounds of insanity. That didn't throw the proceedings into doubt, however, nor change the sentence. To enforce the laws in Berlin at the time, it helped to be a little mad.

Wilhelm II was emperor now, for his liberal father had died of cancer after reigning for only ninety-nine days as Friedrich III. Bismarck was expelled from office, for the vain young emperor believed he could rule alone. The departure of the chancellor didn't bring the Berliners any increase in their freedoms, though the new reign had begun with strange promises. Wilhelm II suggested radical social legislation, hoping to woo the Berlin workers to his side. On election day, when these workers were meant to show their trust in him, he showed his faith in them by alerting the Prussian army. When the votes were counted, his fears proved justified. The Socialists had tripled their mandate. One and a half million "red" ballots had been cast. The young Kaiser sulked and snarled that the workers had betrayed him. A year later, he addressed newly sworn Guards recruits as follows:

"You have surrendered yourselves, body and soul, to me; there is only one enemy for you, and that is my enemy. The socialist unrest of today could lead me to giving you an order to shoot down your own relatives, brothers—yes, even your parents, may God prevent it!—but, even then, you must obey my command without hesitation!"

On one occasion, Wilhelm was shown the house of an African king at a colonial exhibition. The skulls of his enemies, stuck on poles, fascinated the emperor. "If only I could see the Reichstag strung up like that!" he exclaimed. "The soldier and the army, not parliamentary majorities and decisions, have welded the German Empire together," he noted. "I put my trust in the army." As for the constitution, he remarked, "I have never read the constitution and know nothing about it."

Officers became more than ever the most important persons in Berlin. James Gerard, United States Ambassador there during part of Wilhelm's reign, was fascinated—and disconcerted—by the way society was structured in the city. "For years," he wrote, "officers of the army, both in the discharge of their duties and outside, have behaved in a very arrogant way toward the civil population. Time and again while I was in Germany waiting in line at some ticket office an officer shoved himself ahead of all others, without even a protest from those waiting. On one occasion I went to the races at Berlin with my brother-in-law and bought a box. While we were out looking at the horses between the races, a Prussian officer and his wife seated themselves in our box. I called the attention of one of the ushers to this, but the usher said he did not dare ask a Prussian officer to leave, and it was only after sending for the head usher and showing him my Jockey Club membership and my pass as an Ambassador that I was able to secure possession of my own box. . . ."

Although the existence of a militaristic autocracy was often stoutly denied, all the world got hilarious proof of it on October 10, 1906, after a handful of soldiers on duty in Wedding's Seestrasse were hailed by an army captain in uniform.

"You there!" he barked at them. "Come here! I am acting on the highest Cabinet orders. Follow me immediately!"

One of the soldiers summoned was Otto Möhler, today an octogenarian who lives in an old peoples' home in East Berlin's District Köpenick. He recalls that the captain "kept looking around all the while rather nervously," but that this aroused no suspicions. He marched the soldiers toward Köpenick Town Hall, collecting a few more along the way. When he arrived, he stationed some of his men to guard the outside and stepped into the building. There, he arrested the mayor and other officials and seized the *Stadtkasse* (the municipal funds). No one questioned his actions; quietly and obediently, they counted out 4,002 marks and 21 pfennigs. The captain took the funds and stepped outside, where he dismissed his men and departed alone. When the soldiers returned to their barracks, they learned they had helped a thief. They were court-martialed but of course were acquitted, for they had at least not disobeyed an officer's command.

Ultimately, the thief surrendered on his own. He turned out to be a Berlin shoemaker named Wilhelm Voigt, who had bought his uniform at a used-clothing shop. He'd never been after money, only freedom. Wanting a passport to leave Prussia, he had been denied one, and had hoped he could steal it. When he couldn't find one in the town hall, he had seized the funds instead. The story of the *Hauptmann von Köpenick* amused everyone except the embarrassed bureaucrats. Even the Kaiser thought it funny that anyone dressed as an officer could get away with literally anything in Berlin, even theft. In fact, as Ambassador Gerard noted with amazement, the officer class in Berlin headed a caste system so effective that it policed itself and needed little repression.

chapter nine

"I REGARD EVERY SOCIAL DEMOCRAT AS AN ENEMY OF THE EM-pire and Fatherland," Wilhelm II announced. Such people, he said, were "a breed of men who do not deserve the name of Germans" and, should they prevail, he would call upon the Guards "for protection against the gang of traitors . . ." This party, he said, "must be rooted out to the very last stump."

Nevertheless, the working class in Berlin made itself heard, not only in the votes it cast, but every March 18th, when Social Democrats commemorated the 1848 uprising by visiting the graves of the Berliners who had been its victims.

To get to the Freidrichshain cemetery, they had to walk through the outskirts of Berlin, for the authorities meant to keep this rabble out of the city proper, nor were the workers allowed to enter the cemetery until they had presented their wreaths for inspection to a police censor. He checked the inscriptions on the ribbons attached to each floral tribute. If he found "subversive" words, these would then be scissored away on the spot. Even the dead in Berlin were not allowed to be presented with dangerous democratic ideas. Yet few Social Democrats were actually dangerous radicals. Ferdinand Lasalle, one of the founders of German Socialism, who lived in a luxurious apartment at 13 Bellevuestrasse in Berlin, had cooperated with that arch-reactionary, Bismarck; many Socialists were later to follow his example. To be sure, they were committed to social reform, liberalism, and even democracy, but not to revolution or even significant social change. Most were moderates who would have been happy with a constitutional monarchy. Only a few sought a republic. Living and working conditions, rather than agitation, caused bloodshed in Berlin. During the early 1870's destitute workers resisted the razing of their clapboard shacks during a catastrophic housing shortage. The job of tearing down these unsightly barracks and of evicting their tenants had been assigned to the Berlin fire department, but mounted policemen formed a cordon to protect the wreckers. The tenants objected, and when hand fighting broke out, armed policemen charged in. That led to rioting and finally to barricades, hastily thrown up for street battles. At the Kottbus Gate, 159 Berliners were cut down with sabre blows. Later thirty-seven wounded men were arrested and sentenced to prison.

Prussian *Geheimrat* von Oldenburg-Januschau summed up the ruling class' view of the people and their Reichstag delegates by saying, "The job of dissolving the Reichstag wouldn't take more than ten men and one lieutenant." Those words outraged the city, shocked public opinion, and embarrassed the court—less because they showed a contempt for Parliament, but because everyone knew they were true.

This was all the more so after 1908, when Parliament lost another chance to achieve sovereignty. Wilhelm II had outraged Berlin (not to speak of foreign capitals) with intemperate anti-British remarks. The press printed cartoons by Heinrich Zille and others savagely mocking the Kaiser. So unrestrained were the denunciations, says Wilhelm's biographer, Emil Ludwig, that "the Germans might have been taken for a free and independent nation."

But the Reichstag took no action and Chancellor Bülow, who might have emerged a strong man, straddled the fence instead. It has been said that, from that day, Germany was administered, not governed. No wonder the Berliners no longer expected anything to change their situation.

They determined to enjoy themselves instead. This was easy, for they have always been interested in the art of living well, in being *"Lebenskünstler,"* those who can enjoy the times, no matter what they're like. It is a sign of a hedonistic streak in them, one which should not be underrated.

Whatever one might say against "Willem," as the Berliners called the Kaiser, he'd kept the peace; there were no wars from 1888 to 1914. Further, Berlin was more imposing and important than ever before, and never before had the Berliners as much reason to be proud of being Berliners. They were now the center of the nation and of everyone's attention. The city had attracted great numbers of the talented and industrious, even from abroad. All this made their city and—they were convinced—the Berliners themselves more cosmopolitan, more sophisticated and interesting. It was a time when even Americans came to Berlin, and by the thousands. Wilhelm II found them "amusing, charming" and made them welcome. They responded by forming the city's first American community, well before the turn of the century.

Because each one of the twenty-five German states sent a delegation to Berlin, the city contained more diplomats than any other capital in the world. Their presence contributed greatly to the city's glitter, as well as to its babel of languages and international flavor. The rich were everywhere to be seen, so long as one remained in the elegant sections of the city. So much were they evident that *Regierungsrat* Rudolf Martin annually published a directory of millionaires containing their names, addresses, annual income, and net worth. Not counting those who possessed a mere one or two million marks, he counted in 1913 forty-five men whose fortunes exceeded three million each, a figure that included *only* those who lived on the Kurfürstendamm.

That *Berliner Tempo,* the city's fast pace, was now accelerating; Berliners still speak of it with awe, despite the fact that other cities quickened their steps to match them. Not only did the population and the pace increase but so did the noise. Five thousand horse-drawn carriages, for hire as *Droschken,* or "hacks," were soon replaced by motorized cabs, *Kraftdroschken;* the first had appeared in 1901, introduced by a hackie named Thien. Four years later, there were thirty, and in six more years, three thousand seven hundred. The twelve hundred horses which pulled twenty-five million passengers in trolley cars also gradually gave way to power; the first electric trolley cars ran between Spandau Market and Pichelsdorf in the western suburbs, four years before the start of the 20th century. Eight years later, Mayor Rudolf Wilde launched work on Berlin's underground railway, then a span from the zoo to Potsdamer Platz. (Berlin got its subway two years before New York City did, but eighteen years after London; Berlin was eventually to have the second largest subway system in all Europe.)

When the Teltow Canal opened in 1906, it was only meant to be a waterway for transport between the Spree and Havel, and by extension, the Oder and Elbe. The Berliners, however, found respite from the booming city along its banks, and typically, discovered in it something good to eat: *Kanalforellen,* or "canal trout." Their need for recreation had grown, but was still easily satisfied. Diversions were simpler than they are today, more family-oriented. Berliners escaped to such areas as Tegel, then rural. (Like most such retreats, it is now a part of West Berlin proper, containing fifty thousand Berliners and an airport from which one can jet, nonstop, to New York in little more than the time that it then took Berliners to travel out there from the city.)

This was a time of solid virtues and old-fashioned tintype sentiments: One strolled in the Grunewald, walked *en famille* along the banks of the Havel, swam in Wannsee lake, or lunched *im Freien* (al fresco, picnic style), sipping the unpretentious wines produced in the modest vineyards which may be found around Berlin. A slightly more prosperous worker or petit bourgeois enjoyed these pleasures in one of those small gardens which Dr. Daniel Schreber had been urging city dwellers to cultivate for the good of their souls, those clusters of *"Laubenkolonieen"* filled with *"Schrebergärten,"* which sprang up in the 1870's and which ever since have provided Berlin families with bucolic retreats right in the middle of the teeming city. Sundays and holidays would be spent out in these allotments, pruning fruit trees and basking in the sun, enjoying a pleasure unknown to industrial workers of many other nations.

Berliners would also attend Circuses Renz and Schumann, go to a wide variety of theaters, even to see the new motion pictures. They strolled their ever more crowded avenues, observed the monocled Guards lieutenants airily lounging on that Café Kranzler terrace which they had staked out for themselves, or peered at the writers and artists in the café Berliners quickly nicknamed *Café Grössenwahn,* or "Café Egomania," after the conceits of its talented patrons. They bet on fleas at the Oktoberfest or on sweating athletes at the indoor bicycle races. They entertained each other at home over open-faced sandwiches or *Torten,* and washed them down, if they could afford it, with *Weinbrandt,* the German brandy, or with clear *Korn,* along with coffee. Patriotically, and as a matter of form, they toasted their Kaiser; particularly, and as a matter of pleasure, they toasted each other and their ladies, prosperity and achievement. They sang nostalgic and patriotic songs at fraternal evenings redolent with speeches, cigar smoke, beer, and *Schnaps*. They sat at their *Stammtische,* or "regular tables," in *Eckkneipen* or corner taverns and they congratulated themselves, as they always have done, on living in Berlin.

But affairs of state went on: The Prussian official who had sneered that it would take just ten soldiers and one lieutenant to create a total dictatorship overestimated the job. At five o'clock in the afternoon of Friday, July 31, 1914, one lieutenant and four drummers, leading the Guard of the elite Kaiser Alexander Grenadier Regiment, took up position in front of the statue of Frederick the Great, on Unter den Linden in Berlin. The drummers sounded a flourish and the lieutenant read an order signed by General von Kessel, then military commander in chief in the Mark Brandenburg. General von Kessel, he announced, was immediately assuming "complete power" in the city; officials could remain in office so long as they obeyed commands issued by him. Henceforth, house searches and arrests could be ordered by the general any time. The sale of weapons, explosives, and gunpowder to civilians was forbidden and no civilians could carry weapons without his authorization. Finally, all strangers who lacked good reason to be in the city were to leave Berlin within twenty-four hours. Ultimate power had been transferred to the military authorities.

Thousands of Americans in Berlin crowded the Wilhelmplatz in front of the United States Embassy. Many were without passports, funds, or "good reason" to be in the city. An emergency relief program was set up to help them leave. Those who could prove they were without funds got free tickets to the U.S.A.; the first Americans to sail left Berlin's Charlottenburg railway station on August 13. When a more determined program of aid proved necessary, a United States warship, the *Tennessee,* arrived in Germany with gold to finance a new relief operation that was headquartered in Berlin's Kaiserhof Hotel.

"A great number of the more ignorant Americans," noted United States Ambassador Gerard, thought the *Tennessee* and other United States warships would actually carry the stranded

94

Americans back home. Other more sophisticated citizens proved equally vexing to Gerard and his staff. One American woman, for example, told him she would agree to go home—but only if she was given a stateroom with a bath and Walker-Gordon milk for her children. Some Americans had no intention of leaving Berlin at all. Most of these, says Gerard, were "songbirds, piano players, and students"—just the sort of Americans who have always liked Berlin and the Berliners a great deal.

The news of war mobilization was on all lips. The people, frantic for the latest news, waited around newspaper kiosks throughout the city. Fear of a Russian invasion caused the city to tremble with war fever. Berliners outside the city raced home, among them Tilla Durieux, the star of Rudolf Bernauer's Strindberg plays at the Hebbel Theater. She found the city in a state of frantic excitement.

"Groups of people everywhere, and in addition, soldiers marching out of the city, showered with blossoms as they went," she noted. "Every face looks happy: We've got war! Bands in the cafés and restaurants play *"Heil dir im Siegerkrantz"* and *"Die Wacht am Rhein"* without stopping, and everybody has to listen to them standing up. One's food gets cold, one's beer gets warm: No matter—we've got war! Lines of people form, offering their motorcars for service . . . Soldiers at the railway stations are offered mountains of buttered sandwiches, sausages, and chocolate. There's a super-abundance of everything: of people, of food, and of enthusiasm!" Even the Social Democrats were swept along and voted for war credits. One young Socialist who broke with his party in protest established a clandestine newspaper; his name was Ernst Reuter.

Soon life became less fabulous, food became scarcer and enthusiasm dwindled. Meat, potatoes, milk, sugar, butter, and soap went on ration. No one over six years of age could buy milk without a doctor's certificate, which had the curious effect of guaranteeing a better supply of milk to the children of Berlin's poor than they had received before. Still, the poor got poorer and hungrier, while the rich, many of whom profited from war, ate as well as ever. This was because the expensive (and more exotic) foods which only the rich could then afford remained off ration for some time. The wealthy ate game, turkeys, ducks, fruits, and vegetables, while the poor simply ate less.

By the summer of 1915, the first protest demonstration in wartime Berlin took place. About five hundred Berlin *Hausfrauen* massed in front of the Reichstag building, but they were quickly dispersed and the Berlin press made no mention of the occurrence. They wanted their men home, were unhappy about the high price of food, and also angrily complained that the whipped cream wasn't as good as it had been before the war.

By winter there were more serious anti-war demonstrations, and a Socialist newspaper was suppressed. In December, 1915, placards called for a rally on Unter den Linden, but nothing came of it, as the Prussian police swooped down and made it impossible for a crowd to gather. That month, as copper roofs on Berlin's apartment houses were stripped off for war use, a prominent Berlin banker told Ambassador Gerard that most people he knew were fed up with the war, but that he doubted it would end soon. The banker said that Krupp and other industrialists were making huge fortunes from war production and that the Junker landowners were profiting just as much. Their lands were being cultivated free of charge by prisoners, and they were able to demand—and get— four or five times the peacetime price for their produce.

In December, 1915, nineteen members of the Social Democratic party announced in the Reichstag they would no longer support the majority S.P.D., which had backed the Kaiser's war. In March, 1916, these members were expelled from the S.P.D.'s Reichstag delegation and a month later formed the Independent Socialist party of Germany, or U.S.P.D. (for *Unabhängige Sozialistische Partei Deutschlands*). Among them were Karl Liebknecht and the man who, after World War II, would emerge as the president of East Germany, Wilhelm Pieck.

The demonstrations for peace and more food and the restiveness of the Berlin population interested the Kaiser very little. He had left Berlin on August 14, 1914, and from that day on practically abandoned the city, choosing either to live in Silesia, at Pless, or near the western front. There he was not surrounded by that restive population whom he had always distrusted; there he was surrounded by sycophantic officers and bathed in reported victories. ("You won't tell His Majesty anything but good news, will you?"

the emperor's aide-de-camp pleaded with a Reichstag delegate who came with urgent reports.)

Meanwhile, living conditions worsened in Berlin. By the time the war's third winter had been reached, not only were supplies exhausted, but so were the Berliners. Coal was extremely scarce and transport so difficult that the Berlin police issued an ordinance permitting oxen to draw wagons in the streets. Even stranger were the elephants recruited from Hagenbeck's show, which could now be seen pulling coal wagons from Berlin's railway stations. Shortages forced the authorities to cut light and fuel consumption and to darken the city. Soon only every other electric streetlight remained lit, and of the three bulbs in each, only one remained illuminated.

Women were recruited to do the city's work. They drove municipal vehicles, operated trolley cars, worked with pickaxes in construction gangs, and continued building the subway system. Even more unusual for the time, they staffed Government and military offices. By 1917, seven thousand Berlin women were also engaged in such social work as teaching other housewives how to cook without milk, eggs, or fat. The press helped out too. The *Vossische Zeitung,* for example, urged Berliners to try that "forgotten source of nutrition, the stinging nettle." Even the United States Embassy in Berlin pitched in until America entered the war, by opening a restaurant serving two hundred free meals a day to hungry Berlin workers. The Berlin breweries, attempting to slake thirsts despite the shortages, offered an *ersatz* beverage which they called a *leichtes Einfachbier,* a "simple, light beer," perhaps not unlike those popular in the United States today. Such a brew, however, could not be given away in Berlin gratis except in times of dire emergency, when the Berliners will drink anything; perhaps more than even a diet of stinging nettles, this thin beer underlined the fact that things were sliding from bad to worse. How could Berlin workers, who like their beer break as much as the British do their tea break, expect to continue working with this stuff in their bellies?

As defeat loomed large, two revolutions broke out in rapid succession in Berlin, one staged by a handful of generals and the other by the people of the city. Since 1916 the High Command had taken over complete control of both the war and civilian affairs. Paul von Hindenburg, and more specifically, the brains behind him,

Erich von Ludendorff, reduced the Kaiser to a figurehead. On September 29, 1918, Erich von Ludendorff declared that a true, democratic constitutional monarchy was to be set up—"overnight."

Suddenly, the imperial chancellor was no longer responsible to the Kaiser, but as in Britain, to a majority in Parliament. Prince Max von Baden, a popular, kindly, and liberal aristocrat (who always carried Emerson's *Essays* in his pocket) was named head of the Government and—*mirabile dictu!*—it even included two Socialists, Philipp Scheidemann and Friedrich Ebert. Even stranger, it was Ludendorff himself who had issued the order to establish a real constitutional monarchy. Ever since 1916, when he had assumed control with Hindenburg, he had used naked military force to crush the wave of strikes which swept Berlin, Leipzig, and other cities in the closing months of the war; he had imposed more restrictions, more censorship, more police terror to meet the mounting demands for peace, liberal reform, and universal suffrage.

The fact is that Ludendorff knew the war was lost and that the Allies were unwilling to negotiate terms of an armistice with his military dictatorship. It was for these reasons that he had bestowed on the Germans the kind of government they had never, even in five centuries, been able to win for themselves.

Democratically minded people were grateful, of course, for what had occurred, though it was noted that even this ultimate gift—parliamentary democracy—had been "granted" by leave of those in authority, by *die Obrigkeit.* The Reichstag had attained power not by struggling against autocracy, but by once again obeying a military command. What many of its delegates learned from this experience was that obedience always paid off best.

The leash that had been rotting had now been slipped. Soldiers, sailors, and hungry workers took to the streets, protesting against a continuation of the war. At the end of October, 1918, two battleship crews mutinied, and on November 3, the entire Kiel naval base had revolted, as indeed it had, though unsuccessfully, back in July, 1917. A few days later, the entire fleet was in revolutionary hands, and when word came that revolts had succeeded in Munich and Hamburg, hundreds of thousands of Berliners—aflame with these reports—surged into the streets and charged the center of the city on November 8 and 9. They chanted their defiance in the squares, overthrew vehicles, invaded and demolished Government offices, shot down army officers, and shouted revolutionary slogans under red banners. In their midst, Karl Liebknecht prepared to proclaim "a soviet republic." *

Entire military units, even such elite ones as the Czar Alexander Guards Regiment, joined the demonstrators. Hundreds of thousands of Berlin workers and their wives, as well as soldiers and sailors, streamed into the city center where Government offices clustered. Crack units such as the Naumburg Rifles, sent in to protect Government buildings, "went over to the people," and individual soldiers placed on guard by the Government either quit their posts or simply let the revolutionaries stream by. As one observer put it, they sat behind their machine-guns, "staring unseeing into space, refusing in any event to fire on the people."

As in every such uprising, many small dramas were being enacted everywhere. Typical of them is the story of the young army officer who watched this raging mob on November 9 from an upstairs window of the War Ministry and wondered how he'd get out alive. Some of his friends had taken the precaution of bringing civilian clothes to work; those who had slipped unscathed through the mob. Others ripped off their rank insignia, but even this did not always save them. Four majors were shot down in front of the Ministry's exit to the Leipziger Strasse, where overturned streetcars lay about amidst a mass of humanity. Finally, the young officer decided to risk escape. As he left the building, still dressed in uniform, a young Berliner rushed him, grabbed the ceremonial dagger that he had foolishly left attached to his belt, and tried to stab him with it. As the blade descended, a woman leaped in front of the officer and saved his life by shouting, "Can't you see? He's just a kid!"

---

* Liebknecht and his associate, "Red Rosa" Luxemburg, led the radical Left-Wing "Spartacus League," which they formed after breaking from the U.S.P.D. Independent Socialists, whom they had found not radical enough. With them went Pieck. Thus there were *three* "Socialist" parties at the time: the extreme Left-Wing Spartacists, the Left-Wing Independents, and the moderate S.P.D., or Social Democrats, who now called themselves "Majority Socialists" and who were led by Friedrich Ebert and Philipp Scheidemann. The "Majority" S.P.D. was prepared to leave the privileged classes undisturbed and to avoid a "social revolution," while both the other left-leaning groups wanted to dump the whole reactionary social system.

Some order had to be established before the city destroyed itself. When Liebknecht proclaimed a soviet republic from the palace balcony, Philipp Scheidemann of the Majority Socialists moved fast to nullify his action, by proclaiming a republic himself, from a window in the Reichstag. Friedrich Ebert was outraged, for the S.P.D. had settled for a constitutional monarchy, not a republic, but it was too late. Prince Max von Baden turned the Government over to Ebert. Thus a Socialist became the Kaiser's last imperial chancellor, a job he kept for twenty-four hours; the days of the Hohenzollerns in Berlin were finally ending.

At Spa, far from Berlin, the High Command moved fast to save itself and the officer corps by dumping the Kaiser and making a deal with the Socialists. Wilhelm II reminded them of their oath to him personally. "In such a situation," General Gröner replied, "the oath is a mere fiction." After that, the Kaiser agreed to leave the country altogether. The officer corps made a deal with Ebert, promising the army would protect the republic, if Ebert promised to prevent a social revolution. Ebert agreed. "The social revolution," he once said, "I hate it like sin!"

Now Ebert was chairman of a Council of People's Commissars that ruled Berlin for ninety days. Arno Scholz, a West Berlin newspaper publisher and long-time Socialist, says that sheer necessity forced Ebert's S.P.D. "not only to maintain the capitalist order, but even to shore it up wherever it was collapsing, just so some order would exist." No one but the old Prussian bureaucracy had any experience in government, as became abundantly clear when the revolutionaries formed their local councils. In Neukölln, the council members spent time bickering over whether to use round or square rubber stamps on documents. Such people, says Scholz, were *Krakeeler,* quarrelers, nothing more. Ebert felt compelled to turn to the old officials and conservative parties for help. He and other S.P.D. leaders lacked the charisma needed to capture the imagination of the Berlin masses. In fact, they were old and tired trade unionists, accustomed to compromise, happy with lofty resolutions, and so fearful of the extreme Left Wing and its "social revolution" that they gave the job of defeating it, along with all the guns and ammunition, to the extreme Right Wing.

It was this marriage of hesitant democrats and determined

100

generals which brought the Weimar Republic into being in Berlin. In finally achieving power, the Social Democrats resembled nothing so much as old maids, so delirious at finally reaching the altar that they did not care whom they were promising to love, honor, and obey. It made for a lovely wedding, but the marriage was a catastrophe.

A month later, in December, 1918, many of Berlin's street and public buildings still remained in the hands of the extreme Left Wing Spartacists and Independents. Mutinous sailors occupied the Berlin Palace grounds and even held Ebert's city commandant hostage. Ebert sent in Government troops, a "Free Corps" of mercenaries assembled hastily by the High Command with funds from industrialists. Eleven sailors were killed in the fight to free the city commandant; their funeral was attended by Liebknecht, who had just renamed his Spartacus League the Communist party of Germany, or K.P.D. Now the battle lines were drawn between the "reds" and "whites."

In January, 1919, the Free Corps defeated revolutionaries who had seized Berlin's newspaper quarter. "Someone must play the bloodhound," said Gustav Noske, the Socialist leading the troops. "I am not afraid of the responsibility." The fighting between the Left- and Right-Wing "socialists" left scars which continue to mar Berlin's political scene today. East Berlin's S.E.D., successor to the old K.P.D., still regards the Social Democrats of the West as traitors to the working class. One of the principal causes for this was the murder of Karl Liebknecht and Rosa Luxemburg.

The case against them was shaky. Both had moderated their stands and neither seemed bloody Bolsheviks. Liebknecht was an intellectual with a horror of bloodshed; tiny "Red Rosa" (who had taken part in the 1905 Russian uprising) had recently urged an end to violence. The two took refuge with a family in District Wilmersdorf, but were captured and brought to Berlin's fashionable Eden Hotel, which then served as staff headquarters for the elite Garde-Kavallerie-Schützen-Division. After he had interrogated them, the chief of staff, Captain Waldemar Pabst, told them they'd be transferred to Moabit Prison, but no sooner were they out of earshot than he issued orders for them to be killed. Liebknecht, he said, was to be "shot trying to escape," while Red Rosa "was to be shot by members of an excited mob"; afterward, their bodies were to be brought to the Berlin morgue and tagged "Persons Unknown."

The job was somewhat botched, which made the murders even uglier. When the prisoners reached the lobby, a certain Captain Petri demanded that they be killed right then and there. "Smash the pigs!" he shouted. An infantryman named Otto Runge, into whose hands Petri had pressed a one-hundred-mark bill, tried to oblige. He swung his rifle butt at both prisoners, injuring Liebknecht and severely wounding Rosa Luxemburg.

Both prisoners were then hustled into two waiting cars, Liebknecht into a vehicle containing four lieutenants and commanded by Navy Lieutenant Commander Horst von Pflugk-Harttung. He was driven to the Tiergarten, where the car came to a stop. *"Plötzlich Panne!"* the driver lied, claiming it had suddenly broken down. Liebknecht was ordered out and told to walk ahead. A moment later he was shot in the back. Seven bullets hit his body, each officer firing, though the second shot had already brought him down.

Rosa Luxemburg did not even get that far. She had been shoved into an automobile containing five soldiers and commanded by First Lieutenant Kurt Vogel. A short distance from the hotel (so close the shot could be heard there), a man leaped onto the running board, killed Rosa Luxemburg with one shot, and then jumped off again, vanishing in the dark street. Instead of delivering her to the morgue, Vogel's men dumped her body into the Landwehr Canal, from which her decomposed corpse was to issue later.

Back at the Eden Hotel, both groups of assassins reported "mission accomplished." Captain Pabst reprimanded them for not obeying his orders precisely, but agreed to enter Vogel's version of what had happened into the record: Rosa Luxemburg had "been dragged off by an outraged mob." He then assured his own superior that the two Spartacists had indeed been killed. This man reportedly was Gustav Noske, that respectable member of Ebert's government.

Courts-martial—and whitewash—were inevitable; predictably, all officers were acquitted. The principal embarrassment of the officer corps was Otto Runge. They tried to hide him by transferring him into the hussars and then declaring him as "missing" from his unit. When found by the Berlin police and brought up for court-martial, Runge was sentenced to two years imprisonment. The judges were satisfied when they discovered Runge was mentally retarded. Captain Petri was never called. As for the assassin who shot Rosa Luxemburg, the murder vehicle's driver identified him two years later as a naval lieutenant named Hermann Souchon. The public prosecutor summoned him for questioning, but he never showed up; Berlin's police registry office reported he had moved to Austria.

The courts-martial not only acquitted the officer corps of all blame, but the judges even congratulated the killers for making "prompt and complete" use of their weapons, assuring them they had no need to call Liebknecht to a halt before shooting. Such judges were later rewarded by the Nazis. In 1936, the "investigating judge" at this court-martial, Paul Jorns, who had made certain the murderers went free, became prosecutor at the notorious Nazi "People's Court."

The record of political justice during the Weimar Republic was wretched. Instead of finding new judges, Ebert had retained those reactionaries who had earlier enforced the Kaiser's autocratic laws. These men championed the militarists and Right-Wing "nationalists." They were opposed to the very democratic regime they were charged with defending.

chapter ten

THE BERLINERS' GOLDEN YEARS OF DEMOCRACY AND POLITICAL liberalism, their legendary 1920's, began more or less the way they would end. It was three in the morning of March 13, 1920, when Privy Councillor Arnold Brecht was awakened and ordered to an emergency Government meeting. When he got to the Reich Chancellery from his home in Berlin's District Steglitz, President Friedrich Ebert and Chancellor Gustav Bauer told him that an "Ehrhardt Brigade" was marching on the city to overthrow the constitutional government and reestablish an authoritarian regime.

No one could stop the soldiers advancing on Berlin, for the army refused to act. "Reichswehr does not shoot at Reichswehr," General Hans von Seeckt announced, so Ebert had no option but to flee and try to establish a government-in-exile outside Berlin. He still had one card left to play. If he could not count on his generals, he believed he could count on the Berliners. Brecht was handed a proclamation to give to the press; it was a call for a general strike.

After he had passed the proclamation on, Brecht thought of what else could be done before Wolfgang Kapp, a founder of the Right-Wing Fatherland Party, took over the Reich Chancellery at seven o'clock. First he sequestered 150,000 marks of Government funds for President Ebert's use. He then went from office to office, collecting all the Government's metal stamps used to make documents official. He slipped these into his overcoat pockets, to smuggle them out of the building. It was an action that might, of course, have occurred to any constitutional lawyer like Brecht, but it was also a form of resistance that could only have occurred to a German.

At 6:30, Brecht telephoned his brother in Steglitz. "Good morning, Gustav!" he said. "I'm at the Reich Chancellery. A *Putsch* is going to take place in a half-hour. The ministers have left Berlin in order to organize resistance from outside. A general strike has been called. What else would you do in the next thirty minutes, if you were in my shoes?"

Gustav Brecht responded in typical, practical Berlinese fashion. He realized that a general strike would mean an end to gas, light, and water services. "I have no idea what *you* might do," he said, "but I know what *I'm* going to do. I'm going to fill up the bathtub!"

Other Berliners also busied themselves for the arrival of the troops. One Socialist in the Landtag parliament building switched the nameplates on conference rooms belonging to the Social Democratic party and the Right-Wing German National party. "When the vandals come," he announced, "let them at least wreck someone else's furniture!"

Kapp arrived punctually at seven; he brought with him two companions, one of them a former Berlin police president. This was Traugott ("Trust God") von Jagow, who under the Kaiser could always be counted on to hound Socialists with a vengeance.* There followed an Alfons-and-Gaston routine, as one of Ebert's men frostily demanded that the trio remove their hats, which they did, apologizing that they had thought it wasn't necessary to do so in the lobby. Another tense moment arrived while everyone wondered "whether one should shake hands under such circumstances," Brecht recalls. A short while later, Brecht left the building, loaded with the Government stamps.

Back in his brother's flat, Brecht packed a bag, noting in passing that a maid who hadn't known better had rinsed dirty diapers in the tub, ruining the hoarded water supply. Then Arnold Brecht also left the city, to join President Ebert.

A week later, they were all back in Berlin, for the *Putsch* was over. Kapp had fled the country after Seeckt had withdrawn the army's support. The week he had spent in power had, in any

* Jagow was famous for an eight-word directive he had once used to ban Socialist demonstrations in Berlin, the wording still being considered the epitome of Prussian brusqueness: "The street serves traffic! I warn the curious!"

case, been an eerie one, for he had ruled over a silent, empty capital—its streets deserted, water and light provided only in hospitals,
and not a wheel turned. The strike had been complete; it was, says
author Walter Kiaulehn, "the only real general strike ever to take
place in Germany."

Unfortunately, it didn't save the democracy. Liberal reforms
failed to come. The regime was undermined, partly by economic
woes and partly by a national neurosis, the myth that Germany
had never been defeated in World War I, but "stabbed in the
back." The assassins ("the November criminals") were variously
described as members of a Catholic "Black International" or a
Social Democratic and Communist "Red International." Behind
both, or working with them, was a "Yellow International" of Jews.
Helping to propagate this nonsense was Ludendorff, who knew
better, for it had in fact been he who had urged an unconditional
armistice, later fleeing its consequences in Sweden.

Defeat hurt less than the Versailles Treaty, the terms of which
the Germans were not even allowed to discuss, much less negotiate,
with the Allies. Territorial losses and reparations were bad
enough; worse was the clause assigning all war guilt to the Germans. Inevitably, Berlin governments which tried to meet the terms
of this *Diktat* were tarred as traitors consenting to national disgrace. Moderates were vilified, democrats murdered or slandered,
and those extremists who shouted the most intemperate nationalist
slogans emerged as popular heroes. One of these was Adolf Hitler,
who had established himself in Munich, the center of Right-Wing
conspiracies. Thousands of unemployed army officers, noncommissioned officers and soldiers, as well as Free Corps mercenaries,
had come to Bavaria. They soon attracted thousands of the desperate, displaced, and dispossessed, for a ruinous inflation had
begun. The mark (worth 4.20 to the dollar before 1914) was
worth nothing. In November, 1923, one dollar bought four
trillion, two hundred billion German marks. Suitcases stuffed
with worthless paper money replaced pay envelopes. Lotte Lenya,
then playing Shakespeare and Molière, was at one point paid three
billion marks a week, which was then worth about five dollars and
wouldn't even pay her rent. Pensioners, retired people, and the
entire lower middle class were ruined, while landowners and busi-

106

nessmen used the inflated, worthless currency to pay off old mortgages, bank loans, and debts overnight.

As extremists inevitably prospered, Berlin remained the bulwark of democracy during the Weimar Republic. From 1920 onward, until illegally ousted, the Berliners maintained a stable, liberal Prussian state government of Braun and Severing. The fact that "Red Berlin" even had a Jewish deputy police president, Dr. Weiss, infuriated the anti-Semitic, anti-democratic "nationalists." By late 1923, Hitler hoped the Munich Government would "march on Berlin" to seize by force of arms a people whose loyalty he could not enlist.

That Berlin should have remained the major bulwark of the shaky democracy is all the more remarkable, because the city was filled with those most hurt by inflation: white-collar workers, members of the lower middle class, retired officials, students, and teachers. There were countless tragedies, among them that of the aged author, Maximilian Bern. He had become rich by means of an anthology, *The Tenth Muse,* but was wiped out by the inflation. Now he was too old and tired to fight fate. He withdrew all his savings (which ran into six figures) from the bank, spent them all on one subway ticket, took a last ride through Berlin, and then locked himself in his apartment. He was found later, dead of starvation.

Other Berliners speculated in the inflation, trying to use it to get rich quick. Clever fellows spent their days on the telephone, buying and selling commodities they never saw, briefly making fortunes by knowing the price of coal in every German city. Others sold cocaine instead of coke—or marketed desperate girls. By December, 1923, unemployment in Berlin had reached 235,000. Battles between "red" and "brown" *Rollkommandos* flared up, especially in the workers' districts of Wedding, Kreuzberg, Neukölln, Friedrichshain, and around the Alexanderplatz. Party meetings were disrupted, members beaten savagely, and passersby terrorized. In 1924, the Social Democrats established their own "defense force," the *Reichsbanner Schwarz-Rot-Gold* (named after the nation's flag). It made its first appearance on June 24, 1924, when thousands of *Reichsbanner* men in hundreds of trucks went on pilgrimage to the grave of Walter Rathenau, a victim of the Right Wing. Opposing them were the Communists' R.F.B., Red Front Fighters' League (*Rot-Front-Kämpfer-Bund*), and the Nazis' brown-shirted Storm Troopers, members of the S.A. or *Sturm-Abteilung.*

In the face of all this, however, the majority of the Berliners kept their heads. A new Reichsmark had stabilized the economy, and extremist fortunes were on the wane, for the time being. Now the Berliners could get on with their "golden years." These have been called "a dance on the volcano of the republic," but what a dance it was!

A somewhat raffish, almost "American," society—composed of entertainers and businessmen—had sprung up as the old one had collapsed. The only "school of manners" available to the Berliners now was the theater; actors and actresses formed their new aristocracy. Alongside them were speculators, wheelers-and-dealers, *nouveau-riche* businessmen, bankers, and merchants. Money was king in Berlin, it was said; every *piccolo* busboy played the market and every shopgirl dreamed of marrying wealth. The city developed into "a seething cauldron of lust, greed, and corruption . . . dreadful, doomed—and magnificent," as Martin Esslin put it. It was a social revolution of a kind, though not the sort that Ebert dreaded.

The new entertainment section that developed around the Kurfürstendamm, today the center of West Berlin, became young Berlin's Times Square and Broadway, existing alongside the more elegant Unter den Linden and the bawdier Friedrichstrasse as a center of amusement. Because movies more than anything else symbolized mass entertainment, huge and elaborate cinemas were built and every Berlin district crawled with *Flohkinos,* the "flea-cinemas," as Berliners called their new, small, neighborhood theaters. Frankfurter Allee, another entertainment center, offered the "Rose Theater," whose founder, Bernhard Rose, became the "Billy Rose of Berlin," specializing in *schmaltzy* live musicals glorifying princesses and dukes, which the Socialist press promptly condemned as "nationalist propaganda." Producers Max Reinhardt, Leopold Jessner, and Erwin Piscator elsewhere presented more stimulating drama and the Berliners flocked to see every offering everywhere. Brecht became famous in 1928 with *The Three-Penny Opera,* the success of which made him cocky, rich, and more Communist-oriented than ever. Walter Mehring, a founder of Berlin Dadaism, attempted to do in his "Political Cabaret" what Brecht and Piscator were doing on the legitimate stage: presenting "Agitprop" material "to mobilize the masses." For their part, however, the masses seemed to have been more enchanted by sheer amusement: by Rudolf Nelson's shows, in which Josephine Baker appeared nude, and by Lawrence Tilly's twenty-four British "Empire Girls" at the Admiralspalast, who could perform Rockette-like Prussian drill while looking leggy and pink-cheeked all the while. They flocked to the Metropol, to attend operettas starring Richard Tauber, whose premieres warranted an honor guard of Berlin police and even the attendance of Nobel laureates like playwright Luigi Pirandello and novelists like Heinrich Mann. Music set the pace and the craze was dancing. Vast and expensive "dance restaurants" like Ambassadeur and Barberina attracted thousands, while the annual Press Ball brought out every distinguished citizen, even Albert Einstein, one of the many Nobel winners then living in Berlin. For those not invited to this "royal ball of the republic," the zoo gardens offered five bands playing simultaneously, night and day, while at the *Ufa-Palast am Zoo,* the silent films weren't accompanied by the usual lone piano player, but by a symphony orchestra numbering seventy men. Those who wanted intimacy could find it in dozens of erotic *Tanzbars* like Königin or Rio Rita, or in the balalaika restaurants, tearooms, and bars such as Tary-Bary, which had been etablished in such numbers by Russian émigrés that the city was nicknamed "Berlinograd." Most such places seemed always to be jammed, for what was new was not just their availability. The emergence of the Berliner was just as new, for the average citizen had largely remained at home during the *Kaiserreich.*

A new Berlin girl was also emerging: She modeled herself after heroines in Vicki Baum's stories, after the independent office girl in the film *Die Privatsekretärin,* and after Hilde Hildebrandt of Rudolf Nelson's shows, the epitome of this new sardonic, sarcastic, Berlinese flapper. The impudent girls on Trude Hersterberg's "Wilde Bühne" (Wild Stage) proved they had *Schnauze*—the "big mouth" of Berlin's men—and that they could show off their wits as well as their bodies. *Schöhnheitstänze,* "dances of beauty," as nude dances were then called, could be seen everywhere—in cabarets, on the theatrical stage, and at many a private party as well. An American, Isadora Duncan, had introduced the Berliners to nude dancing back in 1905 when she establishd that Grunewald school of "free dance," quickly dubbed "the Barefoot Academy." While she teased with veils, Frau von Gross, who called herself Olga Desmond, quickly went further, and appeared stark naked before select audiences at her *Schöhnheitsabende,* or "beauty evenings," seeking to demonstrate the attractiveness of the female form to anyone entertaining doubts about the matter. It was not until the 1920's, however, that nude dancing came to be general and almost respectable. Beautiful, talented, Anita Berber became famous overnight. She was 21 when the decade began and the idol of all those tens of thousands of Berlin girls who then affected French and English names and called their boyfriends "Jimmy" or "Johnny" even if they were Ekkehardt and Traugott. She danced in the nude on stage at the White Mouse cabaret, used cocaine and morphine, was married and divorced, tried lesbian love, and could be seen at every night club, boxing match, bicycle race, bar, and party, usually leading an entourage of boxers, dancers, brawlers, and barflies who helped her create a disturbance wherever she went. She died at 28 of tuberculosis. She had burnt herself out, much as the city was doing. The final fitting touch in the symbolic tableau was presented by Willy Karzin, who read her eulogy. He was a Berlin cabarettist who later died insane.

Anita Berber's frankly erotic nudity was a sign of the "eroto-mania" of Berlin in those years. Everyone spoke of free love, trial marriages, and the sexual emancipation of women. Berlin became notorious for its army of pimps, prostitutes, transvestites, fetichists, and boy prostitutes, or *Strichjungen.* Yet much of the nudity was innocent fun, a "glorification of the body." Two dozen topless dancers in floral G-strings could be seen at the Apollo, in a tableau glorifying Brandenburg Gate. One group of Berlin nudists had their own private lake, on which they ice-skated in winter, dressed only in boots and earmuffs.

Mass entertainment meant mass sports as well, all new, for spectator sports had been unknown under the Kaiser. Football (soccer), racing, and boxing attracted hundreds of thousands, even prominent citizens like the Kaiser's son, Wilhelm, now nick-named "the Crown Prince of Sport" and affecting British tweed caps and knickers. Lakes came to be jammed with sailboats, and vast colonies of cabins were built. The "weekend" was discovered.

When Berliners look back on the twenties, they see the city swirling around one café: the Romanisches at the Kaiser Wilhelm Memorial Church. Herr Nietz, its tall, blond *Portier,* or doorman, barred all but the most famous; not even Max Schmeling was big enough to get in. "The air here had about it something like passive resistance," says one of its intellectual patrons; they loathed Nazism, but were no match for the emerging Storm Troopers.

Scandals rocked the administration of Mayor Gustav Böss and cast further disrepute on democratic government. Then, early in 1929, the economic barometer began to waver and dip. That spring, plans were afoot to film Heinrich Mann's novel, *Professor Unrat,* a book about an elderly schoolteacher, the incarnation of German respectability, who is led to ruin and degradation by a leggy songstress. A certain Fräulein Maria Magdalena von Losch was picked to play the part of the temptress, though she was a complete unknown; before appearing in the film (*The Blue Angel*), she shortened her Christian names to Marlene and then chose a new surname: Dietrich. The film turned out to be a perfect allegory of the times. On screen, as well as outside in the streets, the impotent old of Germany were reeling from their clash with new, surging, primitive, and revolutionary forces. That very spring, the disintegration of which the film spoke burst into Berlin's streets with renewed violence. Ernst ("Teddy") Thälmann, head of the Communist party, provoked a series of riots in working-class districts.

As the depression hardened into the winter of 1929-30, confidence in the currency and government plummeted. Unemployment rose, finally topping six million, and the resolute action proposed by the Nazis and their "nationalist" supporters seemed increasingly attractive. "We are," as Hitler was to say in 1933, "the results of the distress for which others are responsible."

Meanwhile, voices raised to warn of the Nazi danger went unheard or unheeded. Berlin in 1928 had 147 daily and weekly newspapers, the biggest of which was Ullstein's *Berliner Morgenpost,* with a readership of six million, but though the Social Democratic

111

party controlled in addition to its own news agency two hundred newspapers throughout the country, they could not stem the Nazi hysteria. The press in Berlin, says Peter de Mendelssohn in his great study of Berlin journalism, was "a blunt weapon on all fronts." Meanwhile, super-nationalist papers like those of Hugenberg's Scherl-chain screamed their attacks on the republic and boosted the Nazis, adding to the fires fanned by *Der Angriff* (*The Attack*), the paper Goebbels launched in Berlin in 1927. Unemployment and despair had radicalized the political climate.

There was good cause for despair. An Ullstein reporter wrote in 1931 that even the city's well-to-do districts were filled with dignified, well-dressed elderly people mutely begging for money.

In the face of this, it came as no surprise that thousands joined the Communists and Nazis. "Nationalists" were anxious for action as well as the small daily payment S.A. men got when no other work was available. Others, sincerely idealistic, believed Hitler would restore a sense of purpose to a floundering nation.

Democrats and liberals of the day were alarmed, but most underestimated the immediacy of the danger. Robert Neumann, one of Berlin's literati, admits that he told an interviewer in the late 1920's that "Hitler doesn't exist," because he'd never met a single Nazi among all his friends. Most Jews thought Nazism would blow over and joined the German Democratic party, one of the first to be blown away in the storm. There was actually a small Right-Wing Jewish group, the German Nationalist Jews (*Nationaldeutsche Juden*), who hoped for an authoritarian state and thought they might live with Nazism. Among those who recognized the danger was Albert Einstein, professor at Berlin University, director of the Kaiser Wilhelm Institute, and member of the Prussian Academy of Sciences. After nineteen years in Berlin, he prepared to leave for California in 1932. A few nights before he left the city, Robert Neumann spent an evening with him. "I have to go," Einstein told him. "If it turns out my theory of relativity is right, then the Germans will say I am a German and the French will say I am a Jew. Should it prove wrong, well, then the French will say I am a German and the Germans will say I am a Jew. That just shows you how much room there is left for me in Europe."

Although unemployment in Berlin zoomed to 636,000 by December, 1932, the Berliners, at least, refused to abandon themselves to the Nazis. The overwhelming majority of them recognized Hitler's strident appeals as irrational. "The greatest paradox," they said sardonically, "is that a teetotaler could get an entire country blind drunk." In the last Reichstag election before Hitler was named chancellor, almost three out of four Berliners voted against the Nazis and more than 1,500,000 Berlin votes out of a total of 2,666,073 went to those two parties most militantly anti-Nazi, the Social Democrats and the Communists. The Nazis received less than fifty percent of the combined K.P.D.-S.P.D. vote, while the balance of the votes were dispersed among the middle-of-the-road parties of the time. But the future, unfortunately, was not to be determined by free elections or by the Berliners.

Hindenburg appointed Hitler chancellor on January 30, 1933. The cabinet was overwhelmingly non-Nazi and Vice-Chancellor Papen said gleefully that Hitler was now so far shoved into a corner that "he squeaks." He did not realize it, but the conservatives had unleashed the Nazi terror. Overnight, the lakes and rivers of Berlin were dotted not with sailboats but with corpses smashed by hobnail boots or riddled with bullets. Walter Mehring's prophecy, written shortly after the end of World War I, was coming true. "Berlin," he had said, "your dancing partner is Death itself!"

chapter eleven

AT ONE POINT IN HIS CAREER, HITLER PLANNED TO RENAME Berlin "Germania"; neither he nor the other Nazis ever cared for the place. Not a single Berliner was among Hitler's circle of intimates when he became chancellor, and Hitler never really relaxed until he got back to his Bavarian hideaway. In Berlin, Hitler avoided public appearances: Major Nazi rallies were held in Nuremberg while meetings in Berlin were closed affairs, the tickets issued to party functionaries, many of them imported to Berlin for these events by special trains and buses. Berlin may have been *Reichshauptstadt,* the capital of the nation, but the *"Hauptstadt der Bewegung,"* or "capital of the Nazi movement," was Munich.

Two months after Hitler came to power, the Germans voted in their last "free" election, conducted under conditions of naked terror. A majority even then voted against the Nazis.* Seeing he could not achieve a parliamentary majority by means of elections, Hitler demanded an "Enabling Act," granting him dictatorial powers. Storm Troopers threatened democratic delegates with violence if they voted "No"; the Communists were banned from the Reichstag and only the S.P.D. mustered the courage to resist *en bloc.*

Once the dictatorship was official, Berlin Government offices quickly filled with thousands of Nazi functionaries, trooping in from all over the nation to replace Jews and all known democrats. A massive and corrupting "patronage" system began, largely based on outright theft; without it, says German historian Karl

---

* Berlin municipal elections, held a week later, showed an even stronger anti-Nazi vote. The outlawed K.P.D. won a half-million votes and the harassed S.P.D. got 565,943. Less than a million Berliners were swept along by the Nazi tide.

Dietrich Bracher, this regime could never have survived, for it "guiltily entangled" countless people who soon developed a criminal interest in maintaining the Nazis in power. Indeed, Nazism encouraged every kind of dirty, petty careerism, even in universities, for personal enmities prompted denunciations which now could lead to profitable positions in all fields. Tens of thousands of jobs opened up to those, qualified or not, who wore Nazi uniforms. S.A. officers told Berlin editors they were now on salary as overseers; publishers shelled out, hoping to stave off confiscation. Businesses, especially if Jewish-owned, were open to extortion and soon up for grabs; bankers and industrialists found they had to pay massive bribes to Nazi officials if they hoped to do business with the Government. Berlin, the richest city in the nation, was most vulnerable of all. Critics were told by Hitler that he could, alternatively, let his Storm Troopers "loose to loot in the streets."

On June 30, 1934, Hitler won the army's support by eliminating the competitive threat posed by the S.A. Storm Troopers. The bloody purge was later called the "night of the long knives." Firing squads in Berlin-Lichterfelde's S.S. barracks kept up their massacres for twenty-four hours, the command to fire being given in its courtyard more than one hundred times during that period. Even some of the S.S. men broke under the strain and were forced before the very firing squads they had just deserted. After this infamous night most of the opposition ended. Democrats, even conservatives like Papen's aides, were murdered during this night. All semblance of legality ended. The Reichstag became nothing more than an assembly of uniformed Nazi functionaries, charged with applauding Hitler and lustily singing the Nazi anthem. Observing this, the Berliners cynically referred to their Parliament as "Germany's most costly choral group."

The machinery of police control and terror was rapidly being perfected. Ultimately, forty-five thousand Gestapo officials, three million police, and one hundred thousand paid informers kept tabs on the loyalties of everyone. The very need for such a vast instrument of repression gave the lie to Goebbels' claim that the overwhelming majority of Germans enthusiastically supported the Nazi regime. "If that had been so," says Werner Steltzer of West Berlin's city government, "they wouldn't have needed so many spies, informers, Gestapo officials, and torture chambers."

Essential to the terror was the deliberate creation of an aura of horror, secrecy, and suspicion. Heinrich Himmler's deputy in the S.S., Reinhardt Heydrich, noted with satisfaction that "Gestapo and police are veiled in a web of rumors and whispered secrets, as in a political detective novel." The whispers concerned what went on in the Gestapo's cellars in Berlin, and later, in the concentration camps. The fear of unknown but suspected terrors was worst of all, though fear of the known was bad enough. Everywhere, Berliners saw people vanishing without a trace, and they all knew others whose opposition to Hitler before 1933 now made them unemployable. Ernst Reuter, mayor of Brandenburg since 1931, was arrested soon after the Nazis came to power and sent to the Lichtenburg concentration camp. He was twice released thanks to British pressure (the Nazis at that time still responding to foreign protests), but by January, 1935, Reuter was convinced he'd never survive a third term in a concentration camp. He fled to Holland just in time, for the day after he crossed the border, the Gestapo came to arrest him again. Other Social Democrats, like Arno Scholz, were forbidden to write or pursue other public careers. Arrested and interrogated countless times during the Nazi era, Scholz and many like him were compelled to report regularly (in some cases, daily) to police offices, never knowing for certain if they'd leave them alive.

Caught in this web, most Berliners sought anonymity, while others tried in varying degrees to profit as best they could. Some later hated themselves and endlessly repeated to their friends that they worked for the Nazis "only to prevent still worse." Some actually did do that, but only in a very limited sphere; ultimately, only those in powerful positions were powerful enough to resist the regime.

Anti-Semitic measures mounted slowly. Then on November 9, 1938, the storm broke. That night, twenty-three out of Berlin's twenty-nine synagogues were completely destroyed, tens of thousands of Jews were hauled off to concentration camps, and thousands of Jewish homes and shops were smashed. Because of all the broken glass left by the marauding Storm Troopers, the horror was later referred to as *Kristallnacht,* or "Crystal Night." Two days after it, my mother returned to Berlin from holiday and our janitor, Otto Ahrensdorf, came hurrying up to our flat. "Frau Konsul!"

he blurted out, "they must have emptied the insane asylums and penitentiaries to find people who'd do things like that!" His bewilderment and outrage were shared by many other non-Jewish Berliners who, like Ahrensdorf, had sheltered Jews from the Storm Troopers during the terror.

The morning after the *Kristallnacht,* Hans Werner Lobeck, today a Berlin official, passed the still-burning wreck of the Central Synagogue on Fasanenstrasse. A crowd of Berliners were watching outside a Jewish-Hungarian retaurant, the "Czardas," on Kurfürstendamm. Storm Troopers who had just demolished the place emerged with dozens of bottles of fine Tokay wine; on impulse, they suddenly decided to give these to "some of the old Berliners." As they proffered their loot, says Lobeck, a shudder went through the crowd and it fell back. The people dispersed, leaving the S.A. men alone on the sidewalk.

An hour later, Lobeck encountered another Kurfürstendamm crowd; this one behaved differently. It formed a circle around an old woman moaning next to a man who lay bleeding on the sidewalk. "My husband needs a doctor!" she cried, but the men around her just taunted and mocked her and even deliberately prevented her from reaching the phone booth on the corner.

Lobeck recognized the couple as Jewish owners of a corner shop. Evidently the man had been dragged out and beaten. Whether the mob around him consisted of "average Berliners," Lobeck could not tell; they might have been Storm Troopers in civilian clothes, for many S.A. men donned *"Räuberzivil"* (thieves' mufti) for the *Kristallnacht,* to attribute the destruction to *"Volkszorn,"* or "public fury."

Lobeck, who was then twenty, remembered the telephone number of a "half-Jewish" physician, and despite the ugly mood of the crowd, he pushed his way to the telephone booth to call for help. ("I was young then," he explains, "and had a lot of nerve.") He noticed an elderly man with a graying beard who was clearly horrified at what had happened.

"If only the Führer knew!" the old man wailed. "He'd put a stop to those bullies soon enough!"

Lobeck found this too much to bear. "You *Rindvieh,* you stupid ox!" he shouted at the old man. "Of course the Führer knows! What kind of an idiot are you?"

117

The old man was typical of countless Berliners who still hoped that responsibility would teach Hitler moderation. Few had the courage to face reality, and only the strongest went out of their way to help Jewish Berliners.

"It was a time for opportunists," says Professor Hans-Joachim Lieber, who was then a student in Berlin and a postwar rector of West Berlin's Free University. "It always seemed to be the mediocre and lazy ones at the university who were Nazis. Many hoped anti-Semitism would open up careers, as Jews were forced out of jobs. It struck me that none of the working-class students at the university were anti-Semitic. Like Jewish students, they had to work hard to overcome their social handicaps; if anything, they respected the Jews for working hard."

The same seemed to hold true outside the university. That non-"Aryan" one percent of the German population that had given Germany twenty-nine percent of its Nobel Prize laureates was being cut out of the life of the nation. Jewish businesses in Berlin were "Aryanized" (handed over to "deserving" Nazis), and many an inefficient, lazy shopowner was happy to see his Jewish competitors eliminated from the marketplace.

Even so more than one thousand Jews survived the entire Nazi terror in hiding in Berlin, right under the noses of the Gestapo. Being without ration cards, they were kept alive by their non-Jewish friends, who donated their own food. Thousands knew of their existence in Berlin, but the Gestapo didn't, because these thousands were steadfast and remained silent.

Because it was suicide to resist, many Berliners chose an inner disengagement, expressing their convictions and sympathies in small gestures that often required more than trifling commitment. "When Jews first had to wear yellow stars in public," says Arno Scholz, "every Berliner I knew felt ashamed. We tried to shield them from insults by Nazis if we encountered them in trolley cars or subway trains, by standing in front of them, so that no one could see the stars." A Jew who was a boy in Berlin during this time reports a similar gesture. He was stopped by a Berlin policeman for not having a reflector light on his bicycle, and was asked for his name. "Levy," the frightened boy replied. "Levy?" the *Schupo* repeated, clapping shut his notebook. "Run along. If your name's Levy, you've got enough troubles already." The raised-arm "German greeting," as the Nazis called the fascist salute, provided another small way of showing one's feelings. It was prudent to use it before party and Government officials, but Berliners elsewhere deliberately made a point of saying the traditional *Guten Tag* (Good day) to each other—and some even went so far as to say *Grüss Gott!* (Greet God!), which is South German and not even customary in Berlin.

When troops were mobilized in 1938 to march to the Czech border, the Berliners looked on in silence.

"I pictured the scenes I had read of in 1914," American correspondent William L. Shirer wrote in his *Berlin Diary,* "when the cheering throngs on this same street tossed flowers at the marching soldiers, and the girls ran up and kissed them. The hour was undoubtedly chosen today to catch the hundreds of thousands of Berliners pouring out of their offices at the end of the day's work. But they ducked into the subways, refused to look on, and the handful that did stood at the curb in utter silence unable to find a word of cheer for the flower of their youth going away to the glorious war. It was the most striking demonstration against war I've ever seen." Hitler, he wrote, was reported furious. A year later, when Britain declared war and Nazi armies rolled over Poland, it was much the same. Less than five hundred people out of a population of more than four million appeared before the chancellery. There was, wrote Shirer, "no excitement, no hurrahs, no cheering, no war fever, no war hysteria . . . not even hate for the French or British . . ." He wondered how a nation could go to war "with a population so dead against it."

Rationing was imposed, as well as a rule against listening to foreign broadcasts. "We know nothing," one Berliner complained to Shirer. "Why don't they tell us what's up?" In fact, they were told a great deal and that is just the point, for the Berliners had by then developed a strong skepticism towards the Nazi press.

When the Polish campaign began to claim its first casualties, half of the black-bordered notices in the Berlin newspapers omitted the expression, "Died for the Führer," announcing only "Died for the Fatherland." It represented a small and pitiful protest, but as Shirer noted at the time, "It is one of the few ways of showing your feelings toward Hitler."

Then, for a time, victories seemed cheap and Berlin women sported French hats, dresses, and shoes, or Norwegian silver fox-furs; every streetcar in Berlin smelled of French perfume. It was a way, says Arno Scholz, in which the population came to be implicated in this aggressive war. In this instance, as in all others, Nazism appealed mainly to the narrowest self-interest. Yet it was not long before the gifts stopped, the bad news started, and the mood turned. Soon the slightest expression of disaffection brought jail, then death. Roland Freisler's "People's Court" in Berlin was only one of several such special courts which meted out forty-five thousand death sentences. As these mounted in number, Berliners who doubted victory kept their mouths shut. A joke of the times tells of a Berliner who was asked if he still believed the Nazis would win the war.

"I'd rather believe in that," he replied, "than run around with my head chopped off!"

Later in the war, sensing Allied victory and revenge, Berliners wisecracked, "Better enjoy the war. The peace will be dreadful!"

Meanwhile, the bombs rained down on Berlin. Heavy raids began after the 1943 Casablanca conference, where it was decided to intensify bombing, both to destroy "military, industrial, and economic" capacity and to undermine "the morale of the German people to the point where their capacity for armed resistance is fatally weakened." The first major air raid on Berlin, March 1, 1943, followed; then, on June 10, the "combined bomber offensive" was launched—the R.A.F. bombing during daytime, the U.S.A.A.F. at night. Altogether, Berlin underwent more than 350 raids during the war; 35 of these were heavy attacks. About 75,-000 tons of bombs were dropped; ultimately much of what was left of the city was destroyed by means of 40,000 tons of Soviet artillery shells. By the time the Germans stopped counting the raids (March 3, 1945), the number had reached 352, and had lasted a combined total of 432 hours, 32 minutes, or the equivalent of one continuous alert lasting 18 full 24-hour days.

Yet these raids never fulfilled their purpose, if that was to destroy Berlin's industry or even to get the Berliners to call it quits. After the war, United States Strategic Bombing Survey reports revealed that Berlin's war-essential production dropped only twenty-five percent, while overall production was cut only fifty percent;

and this was mainly due to curtailed raw materials resources. Even after the war's worst raid on Berlin, its war-essential plants continued to produce at seventy percent of capacity. Water supply was never interrupted for long, for Berlin is surrounded by rivers, lakes, and canals; electric power breakdowns were repaired within forty-eight hours; and even the city's banking industry conducted business as usual to the very end.

As for undermining morale, the raids certainly did demoralize many Berliners, but the effect was not what the Allies expected. "Even those Berlin workers who hated Hitler," says Scholz, "joined the air defense system"—not to save Nazism, but their homes. They also worked hard to save their factories and to keep them running at near-capacity, because workers lost their draft-deferment status if the war-essential factories in which they worked were destroyed or crippled. Thus even those who had no wish to support a war they knew was lost, or which they opposed, needed to keep its supplies flowing, or risk being put into uniform.

What the raids mainly did was to leave 1,500,000 Berliners homeless. One million apartments were either totally destroyed or heavily damaged. Thirty thousand houses were completely destroyed, another 27,000 heavily damaged, and 167,927 left "partly habitable." In Charlottenburg, that centrally located district which reaches from the Kurfürstendamm to the Tiergarten and out to the Havel River, only 604 out of a total of 11,075 residential buildings were spared. Kreuzberg, a workers' district, lost 48 percent of its homes. Berlin-Mitte was 60.7 percent destroyed. One hundred million tons of rubble was left. "If 3,000 trucks with a capacity of 10 tons each were utilized," says the United States survey, "and each truck disposed of one load daily, about 3,333 days or 11 years would be needed to dispose of all the rubble."

Surprisingly, casualties were not as enormous as they might have been, thanks largely to the fact that air-raid shelters (mostly basements of apartment houses) were constantly strengthened throughout the raids. No one knows exactly how many Berliners were killed in the air raids, but most estimates place total casualty figures at 110,000 to 126,000, of whom 35,000 to 50,000 were killed, and the rest wounded.

Life in the shelters had the effect of drawing the Berliners closer together, as "cellar communities" (*Kellergemeindschaften*) fostered a degree of fraternity not seen in the city for years. Common danger created a community spirit and class differences disappeared among those who shared the expectation that they might be momentarily killed. Nazi rule had deliberately fragmented Berlin society, so as to control its several portions more easily, but this society was now being welded together in the cauterizing heat of the incendiary bombs.

The worst raid of the war was staged on Saturday morning, February 3, 1945, beginning at 11 A.M. About one thousand American bombers leveled much of the center of the city. Ernst Ross, who worked in an office building at the corner of Lindenstrasse and Markgrafenstrasse, fled to the basement with his brother, but the heat was so intense that he had to run out into the streets. Outside, the Lindenstrasse was a sea of flames, fires reaching so high that they leaped the buildings from rooftops on one side of the street to the other. Thousands of people had streamed out into the middle of the thoroughfare, fearful that their buildings might cave in on them; they soon had to flee, for it was clear that whoever remained behind in this street would be roasted alive. Ross set out on foot for his home in District Wilmersdorf, which he reached three hours later. His wife had given him up for dead, for she had watched the black clouds swirl up from the city center. The fires had caused such a strong wind that they blew charred paper all the way to Wilmersdorf.

Ursula von Kardoff experienced the raid in a deep shelter in the center of the city. She was a newspaper woman who by this time was deeply in trouble with the Gestapo, for she was a friend of almost every aristocrat involved in the July 20, 1944, plot to kill Hitler. No one was killed in her shelter, though women screamed that the end had come for all of them. When Fräulein von Kardoff emerged, she was swept along in a stream of people who had been bombed out, their faces gray or white with ash and their backs bent beneath what belongings they could salvage. "Why doesn't anyone go crazy?" she protested later, writing in her diary. "Why doesn't anybody go out into the streets and shout, 'I've had enough!' Why isn't there a revolution? . . ."

Heinz Wagner, living in Sebastianstrasse, was one Berliner whose family was bombed out. After he and his wife and daughter fled the area, he returned to his flaming apartment house to get

122

some milk out of its cellars. To his amazement, several old people remained seated in the shelters there. He pleaded with them, urging them to leave, but they shook their heads apathetically. What would they do without a home, they asked. Later, when Wagner returned once more, he found they had all suffocated to death.

As Wagner left the building, he heard someone scream for help; it was a woman standing inside a burning window frame on an upper floor. He shouted to her to wrap herself in a blanket and run down the cement stairs of the apartment house, but she couldn't hear him. On his return, he found her on the pavement outside, though he didn't recognize her at first. Her clothing had caught fire and she was a naked, shriveled black corpse. He covered her with a metal sign advertising cigarettes that lay nearby; a few hours later, he passed by again and saw a bunch of flowers lying on top of the sign, with a scrap of paper reading, "To my dear mother." Wagner spotted a policeman and told him there were seven old people dead in the cellar. The officer took out his notebook, didn't even ask their names, and jotted down, "House Number 36, batch of seven [*sieben Stück*]."

Countless others who died in cellars were buried and lost completely. One young Berlin woman who visited District Kreuzberg the day after the raid was horrified to find that entire sections were literally leveled to the ground and that entire blocks were sealed off by hastily constructed barriers. The houses were still smoldering and she was convinced that people might still be alive in the cellars underneath them, but the police were afraid of an epidemic, and anyway, didn't have enough personnel to dig them out. Many Berliners killed in this raid weren't found until years later, when old ruins were ripped down during the reconstruction of Berlin. When the ruins of Ritterstrasse 75 in Kreuzberg were cleared away in January, 1951, the authorities uncovered a pile of bones in the shelter beneath that building, which had once housed a printing company, the Firma Limpert. When they pieced the remains together, the carpet of bones made up more than eighty skeletons, accounting for almost everyone on the company payroll.

The bombs that day also hit the Prinz Albrecht Strasse headquarters of the Gestapo, but the prisons beneath it remained intact, still filled with prisoners rounded up after the July 20, 1944, plot to kill Hitler had failed. Those whose sentences were expected shortly were left inside these dungeons, now even more cheerless than ever without light, water, or heat.

Roland Freisler, the notorious Nazi judge at the Berlin People's Court, was just turning to the case of Fabian von Schlabrendorff, who had attempted to kill Hitler in 1943 and had also been in the July 20 plot. As the sirens wailed, Freisler ordered the court into the cellars. The building received a direct hit. When the dust settled, casualties were counted. Only one man was dead: Freisler himself, his skull crushed by a fallen beam.

The month had not passed before the city was once more hit by a massive air raid. On February 26, Districts Lichterfelde and Friedrichshain went up in flames, destroying the Alexanderplatz area and the Frankfurter Allee. Once again, vast residential districts roared with blast-furnace heat and tens of thousands of Berliners rushed out into the streets to escape suffocation. Clutching children or a few rescued possessions, they stumbled in search of safety, their clothing scorched or torn, hair singed or burned off their heads. A large crowd tried to find shelter near the central stockyards, but was halted by men suddenly shouting for them to get back. A moment later, a munitions train on nearby railway tracks exploded. On other streets people threw bedclothes out of windows. Some tried to lower furniture down on ropes, but no one bothered to try to put out fires any more. One wild-eyed man standing in front of a heap of household possessions kept repeating out loud, "This is the fourth home I've been burnt out of! What use is there in dragging all this crap to still another place?"

As the "Thousand Year Reich" thrashed about in its death agonies, the terror it unleashed reached countless homes. A forty-one-year-old doctor of law, Elisabeth Charlotte Gloeden, her architect husband Erich, and her mother, Elisabeth Kusnitzki, were all beheaded at Berlin's Plötzensee prison for having provided a refuge for General Fritz Lindemann, whom the Gestapo hunted after the July 20 plot. Elisabeth Gloeden's mother was executed despite her non-involvement; she merely happened to be visiting her daughter at the time, but was killed for not turning her in. The general's wife committed suicide. Elisabeth Gloeden also gave shelter to a Jewish refugee, Ruth Abraham, a woman who survived and who now lives in New York. Another Berliner, Maria Nickel, cared for Ruth Abraham's newborn daughter Reha for more than two years, while the mother and father went "underground." Maria Nickel was a complete stranger to Frau Abraham, sheltering the Jewish infant for reasons of sheer humanity—"prompted by her own good heart and never expecting any thanks for it," as Ruth Abraham says. Maria Nickel was not alone. Annedore Leber, widow of Julius Leber, a major resistance figure and herself a prisoner of the Gestapo, took note of the hundreds of Berlin office secretaries who worked for anti-Nazi conspirators in Berlin, who knew all but said nothing. One example is Admiral Canaris' secretary, Frau Schwarte, who remained steadfast though interrogated by the Gestapo from early morning until late at night for an entire week. Frau Leber also singled out a Frau Droste, who hid Jakob Kaiser and Elfriede Nebgen from the Gestapo, and Minna Amann, another Berlin woman, who brought food to the two anti-Nazi fugitives. Countless others remain anonymous; they are, in the words of Berlin's Jewish community, the "unsung heroes" of the time, who gave "no thought to what dangers they incurred for themselves" and who offered "significant help" to Jewish Berliners and other victims of Nazism.

The war entered its final phase. The great Red Army offensive began January 18, 1945; in eighteen days, the Russians crossed more than three hundred miles. In Berlin-Lichterfelde, sixty-four-year-old Reichsbank employee Albert Noack, who had fought the Russians in one of the Kaiser's elite Hussar regiments during World War I, told his wife and daughter, "It's all over now; once they start charging like that, there's no stopping them!"

Others knew it, too. Yet, while S.S. and Gestapo officials prepared their escape, assembling forged papers and depositing vast sums abroad to finance their "underground railway" to Spain and South America, Berliners who tried to do the same were summarily shot or hanged by roving executioners. The lampposts on District Steglitz's Schloss Strasse were festooned in grisly fashion, with bodies of soldiers and civilians executed for desertion or defeatism. Cardboard signs dangled from the swaying corpses. "I am a traitor!" they proclaimed to any passerby who had the stomach to look up.

The Berliners were subjected to a double-barreled assault—

from the Russians approaching the city from outside and from the Nazis smashing opponents and "defeatists" inside Berlin. By February 1, a few Red Army units penetrated the Oder River ice and Berlin was alerted to defend itself. The *Volkssturm* home guard was mobilized. Talk of escape and rumors that there might be a general evacuation were on everyone's lips. Gasoline prices on the black market soared, as anyone who had an automobile prepared to flee west or south. "People are herding together like deer in a storm," Ursula von Kardoff noted. "Everyone talks of forged passports, a *laissez-passez,* a bogus duty trip, foreign workers' identity cards, and certificates of one kind or another. Everyone has a different plan, each more idiotic than the last."

Like many another Berlin family, the Noacks decided to remain in Berlin-Lichterfelde. They had relatives only in the East, but couldn't go there because the Russians had already overrun the area; they feared their soldier son would never find them if they abandoned their home; Frau Noack was unwilling to leave behind her furniture and belongings, and anyway, Albert Noack still had his job. He remained working at the Reichsbank until ten days before the Russians entered Berlin and only quit then because he couldn't get to work any more, the S-Bahn trains having stopped running. Like many others, he stayed at his post, shifting papers that no longer had any meaning, scanning reports from offices already destroyed, and answering letters from officials no longer alive. "Duty is duty!" such conscientious Berlin burghers proclaimed in the midst of the chaos. *"Ordnung muss sein!"*—"There has to be order!"

In fact, however, there were fear and confusion. Horrible stories of what happened in territories overrun by the Soviet Army had begun to filter into Berlin, adding to the hysteria. Desperation was beginning to crowd the city's churches; aisles filled up and soldiers took Communion. No one spoke of that "Germanic," tribal Christianity with which the Nazis had hoped to arouse deep-seated stirrings. Deeper roots were being touched. And there were many pastors available, for throughout the Nazi era the churches had clandestinely trained seminarians in "underground" meeting places, so as to shield them from the Nazi ideology.

Fräulein von Kardoff resigned from the Deutscher Verlag (the former Ullstein Verlag) and prepared to leave Berlin. As she packed, a friend, a young army officer, came to visit and told her he was returning to the front. She pleaded with him not to go back, not to risk being killed in a war he knew was lost, but he shook his head. "I have to do my duty," he replied. "I can't leave my men in the lurch. I'm not a Prussian for nothing."

A defense of Berlin was mounted, mostly a ragtag army of old men and young boys, pitifully armed. Any Berliner not ready to enlist in the *Volkssturm* was in danger of being denounced by the Nazi overseer in his apartment house, and in any case, received no food ration stamps; one fought or starved. A Soviet force of 2,500,000 men armed with 41,600 pieces of artillery, 6,250 tanks and self-propelled batteries, and 7,500 fighter aircraft was supposed to be held back by 42,000 to 60,000 *Volkssturm* members and 44,000 to 60,000 ill-equipped and exhausted troops, armed with between 50 and 70 tanks. At the *Volkssturm* conscription office in District Schmargendorf, it was noted that the Storm Troopers doing the enrolling were strangers; as it turned out, Schmargendorf's local S.A. men had been sent elsewhere in the city, where their faces in turn were unknown. So it was throughout much of Berlin. The Storm Troopers during these last days didn't want to provide those who knew them with still more scores to settle when the Russians came.

The combat value of this defense force was virtually nil, despite the fact that some of its units did fight determinedly. They had no mobile kitchens, and if they happened to be fighting far from home, they simply went hungry. Exhortations took the place of nourishment. Berlin, they were told by a *Führerbefehl,* or decree of Hitler's, issued March 19, was to be defended "to the last man and the last round of ammunition." The idea that there might yet be a final Nazi victory, an *Endsieg,* still deluded the men in the *Führerbunker,* even if those Gestapo officials busily packing their bags with civilian clothes no longer believed it. Hans Leo Hardy, then fourteen and wearing the uniform of the Potsdam Military Orphanage, heard these words while on leave towards the end of the war in his mother's flat on Adalbertstrasse in Berlin-Kreuzberg. Couriers from the school arrived, asking him to return immediately. Leo's mother asked if his return was compulsory. As the boy picked up his gas mask and captured Belgian helmet, preparing to go, the couriers told her, "It's completely voluntary. But we must

127

warn you, if he didn't choose to go back, there might not be a place for him at the school after final victory."

Robert Heger, conductor of the Berlin Philharmonic, directed Strauss' *Death and Transfiguration* at Beethoven Hall on April 16, at 5 P.M. It proved an apt selection, for the massive Russian assault across the Oder had begun that morning. The city lay so close to the Red Army positions that a Russian tank could have covered the entire distance in half a day, but the Soviets took a week to do it. They overestimated Berlin's defenses, and furthermore, every Russian soldier knew the war was almost over. None wanted to get killed that close to victory.

On April 21, two days before the Russian soldiers entered the city suburbs, Berlin underwent its last Western air raid. From that day on, Soviet artillery pounded the city. During the last ten days of the war, forty thousand tons of artillery shells softened Berlin up. Soviet fighter aircraft strafed the streets. "This often happened while we stood in line in front of shops," says one Berlin *Hausfrau,* "simply because we had to spend so much time in queues to buy any food. When a fighter swooped down at us, we'd all dash into nearby apartment houses. Afterward, there'd be a mad scramble to get back in line, with each woman trying to better her position in the queue."

The first white flags greeting Russian troops fluttered from windows in the Kaubstrasse on April 23; street battles were fought in the northern and eastern suburbs of Districts Frohnau, Friedrichshain, Tegel, Pankow, and Köpenick. At the Potsdamer Platz, the only resistance was several stone barricades and a few rails jammed into the ground. The front was now so close that German soldiers bicycled to battle. East of Friedrichshagen and north of Müggelsee lake, Master Sergeant Gempel, and ten other regular soldiers were leading two hundred and fifty *Volkssturm* men; when the first Russians appeared, this force shriveled to twenty-five. Near Gatow Airfield, Major Komorowski, commanding a mixed *Volkssturm* and army unit, had the same experience. On the evening of his first encounter with the enemy, all *Volkssturm* men deserted and the gap had to be filled by recruiting stragglers. During the next two days of fighting, all of his men were either killed or captured. Closer to the town center, in Charlottenburg-West, *Volkssturm* Battalion Commander Heinrich Barth tried to protect three main

128

thoroughfares, though his unit had received only one hundred rifles. When the fighting began, only sixty of his men stayed at their posts. "The rest went home," says Barth. Whether the Führer knew it or not, these Berliners at least knew the fight was senseless.

But the Nazi regime was not yet through. On April 23, the last issue of the *Völkischer Beobachter* front-paged the final message from Hitler to the people of Berlin. He had not shown himself to them since Stalingrad in 1943; his message to them that day was no tender farewell. "Be warned!" he stated. "Anyone who undertakes actions that weaken our capacity to resist, or who propagates or even approves such actions, is a traitor! He is to be shot or hanged on the spot! . . ."

The day before, the S.S. had taken bloody revenge on a group of anti-Nazi Germans from District Moabit's Lehrterstrasse prison; in the dark of night, they were cut down by bursts of machine-pistol fire, while crossing a field of rubble in the heart of the city. When their bodies were found a week later, a handful of crumpled, rain-soaked poems fell from the dead hand of Albrecht Haushofer, forty-two, son of the geopolitician Karl Haushofer and a close collaborator of the Berlin resistance leaders. They had been written in captivity. One of them began, "Look well upon my comrades. They all had spirit, rank, and high repute . . . There are times when only madness reigns, and then it is the best that hang."

On April 25, Hans-Joachim Lieber and his fiancée took shelter in a large air-raid bunker near the Oberbaum Bridge. There they encountered the Russians for the first time. A Red Army unit captured the area and put an artillery battery beside it, with which they began to shell the city center. Then the first Russian soldiers entered the air-raid bunker itself. Pointing guns at the Berliners huddled there, they began stripping them of their watches. Afterward, they seized women and girls and dragged them off. Lieber hid his fiancée in a corner of the shelter's first-aid station. A few feet away from them, a woman lay moaning, shot through both legs. Suddenly a Russian soldier entered the first-aid station, saw the prone figure, threw himself on top of the woman and raped her. A few moments later, Lieber and his fiancée watched as the door burst open and a Russian political commissar stormed in, his face contorted with rage. He grabbed the soldier by the back of his jacket and dragged him off the wounded woman. Then he pulled him outside the bunker. When Lieber and his fiancée left the shelter, they saw the soldier sprawled dead in front of the door, shot in the back of the head.

Near Arno Scholz's apartment house on the Dillenburgerstrasse, *Volkssturm* men prepared a last-ditch defense, but were persuaded to abandon it by local residents. It was useless, they were told, and would only bring Russian revenge on all civilians in the block. When these defenders had left and only civilians remained behind, the Red Army tanks began to roll into the area. A man from a neighboring apartment house suggested to Scholz that they approach the Russians with hands held high, to advise them that no German soldiers were about. Scholz agreed to accompany him.

As they began walking towards the tanks, the man reached into his pocket and produced a Communist party membership card. "I've always remained a loyal Communist," he told Scholz with satisfaction. "Now I'm going to show my card to the Soviets."

"I don't think they'll be interested," Scholz warned him. "Better just tell them what matters, that the buildings contain only unarmed civilians."

A Soviet officer heard them out and then sent soldiers to check whether they were telling the truth. While they waited for them to return, Scholz's companion produced his K.P.D. membership card.

"I'm an old-time Communist, *Tovarich!*" he beamed—and had hardly uttered the word "comrade" before the Soviet officer smashed a fist into his face, sending him sprawling. Then he ordered soldiers to plunder the man's apartment and take him away. Scholz saw him next many years later, by which time he looked the worse for wear and was reluctant to talk. Scholz was let go after his claim that there were no defenders around had been confirmed. The Red Army unit moved on a few blocks. There, German anti-tank grenades knocked out three Soviet tanks, after which the Russians set all surrounding houses on fire by way of revenge.

By April 26, Zhukov and Konev had encircled the city. *Der Panzerbär,* a four-page news sheet that was the last Nazi newspaper to be printed in Berlin, headlined that day: "Bulwark Against Bolshevism! Berlin: A Mass-Grave for Soviet Tanks! Berlin Fights for the Reich and for Europe!"

Forty-eight hours later, even the men in Hitler's *Führerbunker*

130

beneath the Reich Chancellery had given up all hope that Berlin would be "rescued." Despite that, *Der Panzerbär* that day again exhorted the Berliners to fight to their death. ("Our task is clear," the paper's last issue proclaimed. "We stand and hold! The Führer is with us—and wherever the Führer is, there victory is also!")

The Führer, however, prepared to commit suicide. On April 30, at about 3:30 P.M., he put the barrel of a Walther pistol in his mouth and pulled the trigger. He was seated in front of a portrait of Frederick the Great. Four hours later, a gasoline fire consumed his body in the courtyard of the chancellery. On May 1, 1945, May Day for the Russian soldiers in the city, Berlin's *Gauleiter,* Josef Goebbels, and his wife ordered an S.S. orderly to shoot them, their children being already dead of poisoning. Then the surrender of Berlin was arranged for 6 A.M., May 2nd, but it took a while more for the last defenders to lay down their arms. Finally, General Weidling had to intervene personally to stop the shooting. When the last gun was put away, Berlin looked like the landscape of the moon, its streets a mere succession of craters, and along the edges of its boulevards, a few trembling walls, where houses had once stood. The air was sickly sweet from thousands of corpses lying about the streets, in the denuded parks, and under the ruins. Here and there, a few houses still stood, pockmarked with bullet holes, their windowpanes scattered about the streets. Their walls bore either Hitler's last call to ultimate resistance or the very first message posted by the Soviets: "Hitlers come and go, but the German people and the German state go on. Stalin."

chapter twelve

OF BERLIN'S 125,000 STREET LAMPS, NOT MORE THAN FOUR thousand were left standing on the day of surrender, May 2, 1945, and not one of these was lit. Seventy thousand prisoners of war seized by the Soviets trudged through the dark. Anyone in uniform, even subway guards, were sent away to camps. As these troops marched off, new German leaders arrived in the city headed by Walter Ulbricht. The youngest member of the team, twenty-three-year-old Wolfgang Leonhard, was returning to the city for the first time since boyhood. It looked like an inferno to him. All around were burning houses, ruins, and hungry people in ragged clothing. "Red Army soldiers singing, cheering, and often drunk," he noted afterward. "Groups of women clearing rubble away under Red Army guard. Long lines of people patiently standing in front of street pumps, waiting to fill a pail of water. All looked terribly tired, hungry, exhausted, and ragged." White flags and red ones (fashioned from Nazi banners) hung from windows; people walked about wearing white arm bands to indicate surrender, red ones to welcome the Soviets, or sometimes both.

In a Soviet Army command post in District Lichterfelde, Leonhard heard an officer angrily cursing the "outrageous" behavior of Russian soldiers. It was the first time he'd heard a Soviet officer speak about the looting and raping; he'd earlier heard about it from a German charwoman, but had hesitated to believe her.

That evening, Ulbricht split his men into five groups, taking Leonhard with him to Neukölln, where he first obtained the addresses of some local Communists from a Social Democrat. Then, together with Leonhard, he visited twelve Communist Party members meeting together in a tenement flat. They recognized him and were enormously excited, showering him with news of what the Berliners needed—food, water, light, coal, medicine, and a host of other supplies to prevent starvation, epidemics, chaos. Ulbricht, however, was more interested in laying down the political line. He questioned them about the behavior of Communists during the Nazi era, posing endless questions—"not, to be sure," says Leonhard, "as in a police interrogation, but also certainly not in the way one might expect an émigré to behave toward comrades who had lived in the midst of the Hitler terror for twelve years." All discussion of Berlin's real needs ended.

This became even clearer back at Soviet headquarters, when Ulbricht gathered his team to tell them their assignments. Broadly, they were to correct the inadequacies of Red Army appointments, for many Soviet commanders had hurriedly established Berlin district administrations as they swept through the city. Usually, they had installed anyone in office who came forward declaring himself a former concentration camp inmate, anti-fascist, or Communist. In one case, a commander had simply gone out into the street to grab the first passerby who struck him favorably. "You new mayor!" he told the flabbergasted civilian.

Ulbricht's men were given two weeks in which to staff each of Berlin's twenty districts with a mayor, a deputy mayor, and with men in charge of police, food supply, industry, social welfare, health, traffic, labor, education, finance, and church affairs. Ulbricht also spelled out the political requirements. Except in a couple of workers' districts, mayors were not to be Communists, but mostly Social Democrats; in bourgeois districts, they were to be recruited from bourgeois parties of the Weimar era. But in every single case, the first deputy mayor, the police chief, the head of personnel, and the department head in charge of education were to be Communists. "After all," Ulbricht concluded as the men set out to work, "it's perfectly clear. It's all got to look democratic—but we've got to have everything in our hands!"

The pattern of the future had been set, but not only by Ulbricht and his men. The Red Army left its mark, too.* In view of the fact

* When Milovan Djilas protested to Stalin about Red Army atrocities while the Russians were "liberating" Yugoslavia from the Germans, the Soviet leader shrugged off the complaint as though it were old-womanish. "Can't you understand it," he said to the Yugoslav Com-

that the Soviets wanted to consolidate their hold on the Berliners and even win them over to Communism, these Russian soldiers were throwing away the fruits of Russian victory.

The raping and looting that began when the first troops entered the city continued for several weeks. Very little of it seems to have been done in a spirit of revenge; most of it seems merely to have reflected their wish to taste what they regarded as the traditional spoils of the conqueror. There was about their actions something reminiscent of the sack of Rome or the rape of cities by the soldiers of Genghis Khan. Certain soldiers were unbelievably barbaric and cruel: Women were tortured, disfigured, or killed while being raped, or afterward, their breasts sliced off and their bellies cut open with bayonets. Innumerable Berlin men were forced to watch at gunpoint while their daughters, wives, and sometimes even aged mothers were raped, often by several soldiers and sometimes by a great many of them in succession. These horrors were for the most part the acts of individual brutes maddened by alcohol and victory, and in any case did not represent the kind of "national policy" that sent women in German-occupied countries to their deaths. Still, for two months, until British and American troops entered the city, Berlin's women hid and trembled, or as often as not, resigned themselves and endured. Watching it all, even many an old Berlin Communist who had secretly welcomed the Red Army invasion turned away in disgust.

Berlin's outer districts are parklike, filled with villas and small houses, often even with small farms; a lot of Berliners thought they'd be safer there than in the crowded districts closer to the city center. Those who fled learned they'd made a tragic mistake. They would have been safer in tenements and other multi-story apartment houses—and for a peculiar reason. Russian soldiers rarely ventured beyond the ground floor of any building and many women escaped them by hiding in attics, top storys, or on the roofs of apartment houses. Why this was so is anybody's guess; the Berliners' own opinion was that the Russians felt uneasy about these four- to six-story buildings, being accustomed to one-story structures in Soviet farms or villages.

There were other ways of escaping. Men were sometimes

---

munist, "if a soldier who has crossed thousands of kilometers through blood and fire has fun with a woman or takes a trifle?"

useful as lookouts, but small children and babies proved the best protection of all, for the Russian soldiers seemed not only fond of children but uncommonly respectful towards mothers—as long as they had babies in their arms. (Without children ready at hand, mothers were not spared. Both pregnant women and those who had just given birth were raped, even in hospital beds.) Thus any small child came to be a treasured possession to be shared among all female tenants in a building. Women who needed to go out shopping "borrowed" such children to take along into the streets; no case of a Russian ever molesting a woman with a small child seems to be known.

As it became known that Russians did not like women in slacks, most Berlin women affected the most shapeless, the dirtiest trousers they could find. Because Russians frequently entered houses or air-raid shelters to scan the faces of women huddled there until they found a young and pretty one, it became a cosmetic art to deface oneself as much as possible. Women smeared their hair, faces, and hands with dirt; they rubbed coal dust into their skin; they painted blemishes, wrinkles, warts, or splotches on their cheeks; they dressed outlandishly, wearing big straw shopping bags over their heads. Some Berlin women—more than are willing to admit it now—resigned themselves to the assaults, trying at least to minimize their brutality. Others sought the protection of a Soviet officer in return for their exclusive favors.

All these stratagems only succeeded some of the time because there was little consistency to the actions of Soviet soldiers and no one ever knew what to expect next. One soldier might seem bent on rape, then turn out to be friendly; another might be friendly for a few minutes, then turn vicious. The senselessness of many other actions also frightened the Berliners. Many Russian soldiers smashed everything in sight when they entered a house. Meissen china figurines flew out of windows, upholstery was slashed. Worst of all (because of the uncertain food supply) was the fact that they smashed glass jars containing preserved food, opened canned goods and dumped their contents out, threw other food in the yard, and then trampled it into the dirt.

It is easy to assume that these were acts of revenge, but many other countries overrun by the Red Army endured similar treatment, even those being liberated. Much of the destruction, then, seems to have been pure vandalism. All Berliners knew of better-educated Russian soldiers, usually from cities, and of Soviet officers who never acted like this at all. The U.S.S.R. in 1945 was not the industrial power it is today and the devastation wrought by the war had added to the backwardness of the country. Countless Soviet soldiers are reported to have ripped bathroom faucets out of the walls to take them along, since these "miraculously" provided running water. One Berliner watched as a Soviet soldier picked up an alarm clock that had suddenly startled him by going off in his hands, whereupon he dropped it like a hot potato, grabbed his gun, and blasted it to smithereens.

Richard Kleinmann, a thirty-seven-year-old city official supervising fruit and vegetable supplies in Berlin, had closed down his office when the Russians entered the city center, having determined that, as far as he could tell, the food reserves in the Westhafen and in Berlin's warehouses were enough to feed 3,500,000 Berliners for weeks, perhaps even months. He joined his wife in Staaken, on the outskirts of Berlin, and awaited further developments. These came a short while later, after the Soviet commandant of Berlin, Colonel General Bersarin, had put Dr. Andreas Hermes, a retired Reich minister, in charge of the city food supplies. Kleinmann was recalled to duty, to work with Dr. Hermes' aide, Dr. Franz Mendelson, former director of the Brandenburg Agricultural Chamber, whom the Nazis had fired in the 1930's.

"Take a bicycle," Dr. Mendelson told Kleinmann after he showed up for work in the bureau's new office on the Brandenburgische Strasse near the Fehrbelliner Platz in District Wilmersdorf. "See what food supplies the outlying farms still have, either in barns or still in the fields."

Kleinmann was amazed at the request. "But, Dr. Mendelson!" he protested. "There are plenty of warehouses full of food!"

Mendelson shook his head. "All gone . . . all gone!" he replied in a weary voice. "The Russians took everything. A few potatoes are left, nothing more!"

Trainloads of food supplies had in fact been rolling out of Berlin ever since the Red Army rolled in. While there were more than three million Berliners to feed inside the city, it was also a fact that there were more than two million Soviet soldiers to feed outside Berlin. In the days that followed, Kleinmann watched still more trains loaded with food, as well as all available livestock, driven out in herds by Red Army "cowboys." Hundreds upon hundreds of cows from Berlin's many dairies were being pushed eastward by soldiers on small ponies; Kleinmann noted with dismay that no one had bothered to milk them in days and that they now bellowed in pain as they were being herded through Berlin's streets.

Once all the city's food supplies had been taken out of Berlin, the Red Army became helpful in bringing new supplies in. They placed trucks at the disposal of Germans and even accompanied them into the countryside in search of produce. When these convoys, sometimes consisting of as many as twenty trucks, rolled up to a farm, a Soviet officer jumped out and simply ordered the farmers to load everything they had in their barns and fields onto the vehicles. Formalities such as payment were dispensed with, as far as Kleinmann could tell. After the trucks returned from scouring the countryside, the foodstuffs were dispatched to the various districts of the city.

Food rations had by now been established by order of the Soviet city commandant. Each Berlin adult was authorized a daily ration of fourteen ounces of potatoes, seven ounces of bread, .8 ounces of meat, .35 ounces of salt, and .07 ounces of coffee. Slightly higher rations were given to Berliners who worked in factories, municipal affairs, public supply, medicine, or certain other jobs. As was customary back home in the U.S.S.R., "intellectual workers" also got preferential diets; these included not only journalists but also most people in the arts, such as actors. But these daily rations existed all too often only on ration-cards and not in shops. Other means of feeding oneself and one's family had to be devised, or found.

One day during these times, Albert Noack's daughter, Edith, then in her twenties, looked out the window of her apartment house and saw a number of people scurrying across Unter den Eichen, through a hole in a fence, and into the Botanical Gardens across the avenue. Each carried a vessel of some kind: a pail, a large dishpan, or a bowl. Without hesitating a moment, Fräulein Noack grabbed a large wash basin from the kitchen and followed the others. When she got into the Gardens, she came across a small crowd staring fixedly at a horse tramping about. Edith Noack told the group to wait a minute; she'd get her father.

"There's a horse loose in the Botanical Garden!" she called to him as she ran back into the apartment and grabbed a large bread knife from a kitchen drawer. "Come on! Help slaughter it!"

Old Hussar Noack shrank back in horror. "Me? Slaughter a horse?" he blurted out in disgust. "Dear God—never!"

Edith ran off again. If her father balked, she'd do the job herself. All she could think of was that enough food was avilable out there to keep her family and several others alive for some time.

The horse had already been killed when she got back. A neighbor, who worked in a butcher shop, had cut its throat and skinned it. Now the carcass was being attacked by six people, using all kinds of kitchen knives. They worked feverishly, each to his own section. No one spoke. Great bloody hunks were tossed about, landing in pails, bowls, and other containers. The butcher helped Edith slice off the leg and thigh. She put it, rump down, into her large wash basin and staggered home. When she entered her flat, Albert Noack took one look and ran off into another room, clutching a hand over his mouth. Edith dumped the leg in the kitchen and ran back to get more, but in the few minutes she had been absent, the animal was stripped; nothing was left on the grass but its head, tail, and rib cage. It had taken seven people less than twenty minutes to get it down to that.

Getting enough to eat was not only the main concern of the day, but took up most of its hours as well. It was not just a matter of queueing up at a shop and having the endurance to wait; one had to be ready to walk, or if one were lucky, bicycle, across town for a small portion of fat, or out into the countryside to get potatoes. To get a bite to eat, it was a matter of being constantly on the go to follow up every slight rumor. Only the young and fit found the strength to keep this up for long; the sick or the old often starved to death in their rooms.

A physician in Berlin who watched these events estimates that the maximum calories any Berliner received during these days never amounted to more than one thousand five hundred per day, while the overwhelming majority lived on one thousand or less. Postwar privation, of course, tended to reduce the incidence of diseases associated with a high-calorie intake, such as heart ailments and diabetes, but ailments connected with inadequate diet soared. Dysentery claimed two thousand victims and three hundred deaths *every week*. Tuberculosis was the most common ailment in Berlin, the live birth rate had dropped from 15.7 per one thousand Berliners in 1939 to 8.6, while infant mortality had leaped from 5.9 per one hundred live births to thirty-six. Hans-Joachim Lieber's father was just one of thousands who succumbed in those days. Diabetes had led to complications; a foot had been amputated in May, and after two more months in the hospital, he died of blood poisoning and starvation. Food for the patients had consisted of two potatoes a day. In another hospital, an elderly woman from District Schöneberg received only raw carrots to eat; she finally died, weighing fifty pounds. Proteins were almost totally unavailable, and the only vitamin of which there was a reasonable supply was A. Because of the absence of virtually any Vitamin C, resistance to disease was low. There were children in Berlin who grew up without knowing what an orange, lemon, or banana looked like until they were old enough to try such "strange" fruit.

Poor nutrition continued to face the Berliners, even after food supplies became slightly more plentiful. It took all the inventiveness with which the Berliners are naturally endowed for them to scrape together meals that were at least filling. Artificial flavorings (such as banana) became available after a while and provided an endless variety of weird soups made basically out of water and a little flour; weeds grown in gardens provided soup greens and vegetables. The stinging nettle again came into its own, as it had during World War I; boiled, it was regarded as nutritious, though physicians warned that some people came down with a special ailment called "nettle-dysentery," probably the result of trying to exist almost exclusively on nettle broth.

One newspaper advised Berliners that it was best not to let hunger build up, and to take small portions of food four or five times a day. "The body, the intestines, and the stomach can slowly be accustomed," the paper concluded, "to demand far smaller quantities . . . Further, a nap can assuage hunger pains. Sleep can take the place of food!"

The months the Russians were in sole occupation of Berlin were to leave a number of permanent scars. When Konrad Adenauer met in Moscow with Bulganin and Khrushchev, Arno Scholz covered the meeting in his capacity as a Berlin newspaperman. He had occasion to speak privately with some high-ranking Soviet officers whom he had come to know immediately after the war. These officers admitted the Soviets had lost all chance of winning the political loyalty of the Berliners; they regretted it, for the city had, after all, one time been called "Red Berlin." Then the subject of the rape of Berlin's women came up. The Soviet officers were embarrassed and uncomfortable; they asked if Scholz would believe that they had nothing to do with such actions.

"I believe you," Scholz replied. "I know some Soviet officers tried to stop the raping. But most of them did far too little—if anything at all."

"How long do you think these memories will remain alive with the Berliners?" they asked.

Scholz thought for a moment, trying to formulate his reply.

"In Berlin," he said finally, "the children sing a song which goes like this: 'Ladybug fly, father is at war, mother is in Pomerania, but Pomerania has burned down! '"

The Soviet officers looked puzzled.

"What does that mean?"

"That song," Scholz explained, "dates from the Thirty Years' War. Berlin children still remember it three hundred years later."

chapter thirteen

ON JULY 4, 1945, RENEE SINTINIS, BERLIN'S LATE FAMED SCULP-tress, was watching a group of Russian soldiers ransack her apartment. When they had carried downstairs everything they could manage in their arms, two burly soldiers lifted up the large wardrobe in her living room, shoved the bulky piece of furniture down the flights of stairs, and laboriously hoisted it onto their truck. In her apartment, Renee Sintinis could hear them start the engine and prepare to drive off.

Suddenly there was another noise, a loud clatter that she remembered from the day the huge Soviet tanks first rolled into the city. She walked to the window to look out.

Just as the Russians were pulling away from the curb with her wardrobe teetering on top of their truck, they were stopped dead by a huge tank which had turned into the street. A moment later, soldiers clambered out of the tank and began shouting. Then, to her surprise, the Russians unloaded everything in their truck onto the sidewalk. She was even more amazed to see the same soldiers who had pillaged her flat lift up her wardrobe and lug it back upstairs. They made two trips, returning everything they'd taken. Their faces were surly and they worked quietly. Finally, one of them grinned sheepishly at her, muttered "Amerikanski!", and then hurried down the stairs again and climbed back into his truck. The tank pulled away and allowed the Russians to leave. Renee Sintinis watched as their truck drove off, empty. She sat and thought for awhile; then she began to put her things in place again. Suddenly, it seemed worth doing.

Fifty thousand soldiers from Britain's 7th Armored and the United States' 82nd Airborne Division had pulled into the city between July 2nd and 4th. As in Western movies, it looked as though "the cavalry had arrived." The impact was felt in various ways.

In her parents' apartment on Unter den Eichen, Edith Noack was alone with her dog when she heard the first United States vehicle clatter down her street. Looking out her window, she saw trucks filled with soldiers who looked to her like Russians. Because it was dangerous for a woman to be caught in an apartment alone, Fräulein Noack ran downstairs to her neighbor, Frau Zarnow, and the two women bolted the door, cautiously peeking out the windows.

A jeep driven by a single helmeted soldier wearing three chevrons on his sleeves had drawn up and stopped in front of their building. The soldier sauntered up to their front door, and a moment later, knocked on the door of their apartment.

"A Russian!" Frau Zarnow said anxiously. "What will we do?"

"Better open it a crack and see what he wants," Edith Noack replied when the soldier knocked a second time. "There are two of us and maybe he won't do anything, but he may have seen us looking out the window and know we're here."

Frau Zarnow kept the chain latch in place and opened the door a couple of inches. Edith Noack peered outside; the tall soldier stood in the hall, looking "threatening."

"Open up!" he said in what Fräulein Noack recognized as English.

"He's *not* a Russian!" she said to Frau Zarnow.

"I don't care!" the other woman replied, badly frightened. "You never know what they'll do!"

The soldier stuck an arm into the apartment. A paper bag hung from his fist.

"I been driving all day long," he said, "and I just want you to make me a cup of coffee."

Edith Noack took the bag and saw it was full of ground coffee. She convinced Frau Zarnow to open the door and boil some water. The sergeant stepped inside, sat down at the kitchen table, and rested his helmet on it. Frau Zarnow brewed the coffee; when she poured it out, her hand shook so much that the cup rattled in the saucer.

"Why are you so scared?" the sergeant asked, shaking his head in amazement as he watched the woman tremble. "I'm not going to hurt you. I told you, all I wanted was a cup of coffee!"

Summoning up what English she remembered from her school days, Fräulein Noack said, "We learned fear in the last two months." Then she told him about the Russians. The sergeant finished a second cup of coffee, listening in silence as she talked. Then he got up, picked up his helmet, and started for the door. Frau Zarnow nervously handed him the bag of coffee, but the soldier shook his head. Then he reached into his pocket and pulled out some chocolate.

"Keep it," he said. "And thanks for the coffee."

Frau Zarnow and Edith Noack watched him get back into his jeep and pull away. The older woman seemed to Fräulein Noack almost in a state of shock.

"He didn't touch us—or take anything!" she spluttered.

Edith Noack picked up the paper bag.

"There's more than half a pound of coffee here!" she blurted out. "It ought to last us for months! You realize what that means?"

"Yes!" Frau Zarnow said, collapsing in a chair. "It means they've finally come after all!"

It was easy for the Berliners to notice the difference between the Russians and the Western Allies. For one thing, the Western conquerors brought food into Berlin. Doing so was a massive operation. At times, as much as ninety percent of all rationed food in Berlin was of American origin. This meant that the food life-line to the city stretched more than three thousand miles to the Atlantic ports of the United States. Even bringing it from Western Germany wasn't easy, for the Americans had to carry it more than three hundred miles, of which the last one hundred were through the Soviet Zone, and there was then just one rail line and a single highway at United States' disposal. Finally, food was regarded by the Soviets as a political weapon, which meant they much preferred the United States sector of the city fed from faraway America than from the Soviet-controlled countryside around Berlin.

Public health posed another enormous problem. Hospitals had virtually no supplies and the number of beds had dropped from 38,000 in 1943 to 9,300. It was necessary at the beginning of 1946 to order the entire population of the city, without exception, to be immunized against typhus, there having been 13,000 cases of typhoid and para-typhoid fever during the first six months of the occupation. A rationing system boosted nutrition, giving five separate categories of Berliners 1,247 to 2,486 calories per day, depending on the nature of their work. This boosted resistance to disease, but an enormous polio epidemic in 1947 created another crisis situation. Almost 2,500 cases were registered that summer, 220 of which were fatal; the National Foundation for Infantile Paralysis of America flew a team of specialists and six iron lungs, as well as other supplies, to the city. The American Women's Club of Berlin donated thousands of cans of fruit juices, mineral oils, soaps, soups, and other items otherwise unavailable to hospitals.

A good deal of the imports weren't that altruistic. Individual soldiers brought in supplies on their own—to feed a huge new market in Berlin, the black market. It began as soon as the first British and American soldiers arrived (the French came a few weeks later), and rapidly increased into a major, if illegal, industry, continuing more or less unabated until the mid-1948 currency reform normalized the Berlin economy. It was a classic barter operation, based on supply and demand. What the Americans wanted and could afford to buy—and to a lesser extent, the British and French as well—were objects of permanent value, while the Berliners wanted mostly more food. Throughout this time, after all, the Red Army continued to requisition foodstuffs in large quantities from the Soviet Zone of Occupation, which surrounded and traditionally fed Berlin.

Another source of black-market goods stemmed from the tens of thousands of forced laborers and concentration-camp inmates who had been liberated and were now quartered in special camps, where they received an abundance of food and other provisions. Many of them bartered large quantities of food, cigarettes, soap, and other consumer goods for items of more permanently negotiable value: gold, silver, jewelry, furs, and the like. One center of this black market was the Alexanderplatz in the Soviet Sector. Just how busy a marketplace this became can be seen from a report concerning raids conducted there on just one day, October 23, 1945. The first *razzia* was staged at 11 A.M. and one thousand five hundred people were rounded up (among them about one hundred Allied soldiers); at 2:30 P.M., the police staged another raid, hauling away six hundred more black-market suspects; at 5 P.M., they swept down again, collecting another five hundred. Even Soviet troops became customers of the black market, for most of them had just received several months of back pay issued out of captured Reichsmark funds. They were less interested in what Berliners had to offer than in what the Americans owned. For a brief time after July, 1945, United States soldiers could exchange German Reichsmarks for American dollars and this sparked a brisk trade, principally in watches. Wheelers-and-dealers among the American forces cabled the folks back home and had cheap watches shipped over in vast quantities. One GI made a small fortune because he discovered there was *one* American watch no Russian soldier could resist and for which all of them seemed ready to pay almost any price. He had a small crate of them sent over. Each had Mickey Mouse on the dial.

Relationships between the GI's and the Berliners were initially guarded. An early ban on fraternization could bring a GI a sixty-four-dollar fine; still a good number of GI's went out with Berlin girls. Some older Berliners disapproved thoroughly. One former German Army colonel noted sourly at the time that Berlin girls were taking up "shamelessly intimate relationships" with the GI's.

"These little sluts sell their honor for miserable Judas money," he wrote in his diary. "Not even hunger can serve as an excuse for that!" The colonel wasn't typical, however. Most Berliners seemed to understand and many even approved. A pretty daughter in the family helped make life tolerable for many.

In fact, however, it wasn't only physical hunger which threw thousands of pretty Berlin girls into bed with British, French, American, and sometimes also Soviet soldiers. The prospect of comfort and fun also motivated them. The war had cost just the Western sectors of Berlin 170,000 military casualties and young Berlin men were hardly to be seen, the survivors being prisoners of war. Girls eighteen years old in 1947 had known little except war and privation since they were eleven years old; it was hardly surprising that the friendly Western soldiers attracted them as much as did their foodstuffs, cigarettes, nylons, cosmetics, and other gifts. After a time, there arose the exciting possibility of actually marrying one of these soldiers and of getting out of a country and city that seemed to have no future at all.

As for the Allied soldiers, they could hardly be blamed. "The Berlin girl," wrote Germany's famous author, Gerhard Hauptmann, "is the liveliest, gayest, noblest, cleverest, prettiest, most faithful, most piquant and tempting, and most understanding creature of the entire populated world."

Inevitably, intimacies led to an increase in venereal disease, although United States authorities reported with pride that the incidence of syphilis and gonorrhea among American personnel in Berlin was the lowest in the entire United States European Command. An attempt was made to register "VD contacts" among Berlin girls (GI's who contracted VD were asked to turn the girls in); as late as 1949, this file contained three thousand names and this was a mere fraction of the total, for many of the girls, said the United States Military Government, were "able to bribe their way clear with money or merchandise."

Relations between Berliners and the Western forces became so friendly that it seems odd today to note how sourly they were regarded by some in the West as late as the spring of 1948. Harry N. Sperber, for example, wrote an article for the April, 1948, issue of *Esquire* entitled "The Fräulein Wins the Peace" and bearing the subhead, "Homesick GI's are easy prey for German girls whose favors furnish a sugar coating for Nazi propaganda."

With the beginning of the blockade, attitudes in America changed. The Berliners no longer appeared as the defeated enemy, but rather as victims of Communist aggression.

The Cold War began while the Western Allies still hoped their great anti-Nazi alliance with the Soviet Union would endure. The United States and British forces which entered Berlin in July, 1945, closed their eyes to the fact that the Red Army had stripped all Berlin, the Western sectors included, of virtually all its industry, small workshops, museums, and anything else which seemed valuable at all.

Ulbricht's hurriedly constructed administration, including a Red-run police force, was presented to the U.S. and British as a *fait accompli*. When the Interallied Military Kommandatura issued its Order Number One on July 11, 1945, it maintained all these officials in power, including the Red-run police. The United States

Army also evacuated those areas in the Soviet Zone of Germany that the latter had overrun during its advance. The division of the country into Zones of Occupation had been agreed upon in 1943; a European Advisory Commission, set up after the Moscow foreign ministers' conference, worked out the details. The commission split Germany into Soviet, United States, and British Zones and divided Berlin into three parts, the northeastern of which was to be occupied by the Red Army. In November, 1943, an amendment determined that the British would occupy the northwestern sections of Berlin, while United States forces would occupy the south of the city. (As no one at the time regarded France as a "major power"—one which had made a major contribution to the winning of the war—there was no talk then of Four Powers; it was not until the Yalta Conference in early 1945 that France was invited to accede to the occupation agreements, and ultimately, it was the British who gave the French two of their Berlin districts to occupy, Reinickendorf and Wedding.)

While a one-party dictatorship was being erected in the Soviet-occupied sector of the city, the Berliners in the Western sectors also continued to have trouble with the Russians and the German Communists. Ulbricht had appointed Red *Obleute* to supervise the Berliners in their houses, streets, and neighborhoods. They operated in much the same way as the Nazis, until they were finally banned in the Western sectors as undemocratic elements. The Communist-controlled police force, however, remained in charge in all sectors of the city until 1948.

Red Army soldiers also continued exercising their right to enter the Western sectors. An example of what happened to many hundreds of Berliners is provided by Berlin merchant Konietzny, whom three Russian military policemen kidnapped from the British sector, drove into the Tiergarten, beat up, and robbed. After they had left, the merchant limped over to a British MP station in nearby Moabit, a part of District Tiergarten and told his tale. He had been dragged off in full view of hundreds of Berlin bystanders, including a policeman who refused to intervene.

As Konietzny prepared to go home, one of the British officers said, "Nasty that it happened in our sector, but you might at least take comfort in one thing."

"What's that?" Konietzny asked dubiously.

"Well, I mean, it wasn't anything personal," the officer replied. "We get reports like that from at least ten people every day, just at this one station here."

Many Berliners were kidnapped by the Communist-controlled police; most of the victims were either anti-Communists or opponents of the Socialist Unity party, or S.E.D. (*Sozialistische Einheitspartei Deutschlands*). This had been formed throughout the Soviet Zone of Occupation, including East Berlin, in March, 1946, when Soviet pressure forced members of the Social Democratic party into a shotgun wedding with the Communist K.P.D. A few S.P.D. members were willing to form such a "united working-class party," remembering that its lack helped bring Hitler to power, but the overwhelming majority of Socialists were against it. They knew that formation of this S.E.D. meant a one-party dictatorship would be established. This became clear in March, 1946, for no vote on the merger was permitted in the Soviet Zone; when the East Berlin districts of Friedrichshain and Prenzlauer Berg defied that ban on March 31, Red Army soldiers raided S.P.D. offices there and confiscated the ballots.

In West Berlin, however, the Socialists did poll their members on March 31, and although this election was limited to the S.P.D., it nevertheless was the first free election to be held anywhere in Berlin since March, 1933. The decision was equally historic: Seventy-one percent voted against being absorbed into the S.E.D.

In October, 1946, *all* Berliners were given the right to cast their first free vote in thirteen years. The choice lay between the S.E.D., which Berliners were already calling *die Russenpartei* (the Russians' party) and the Social Democrats, Christian Democrats, and Liberal Democrats. "This was a crucial election," says Berlin newspaper editor Frank E. W. Drexler. "The times seemed to provide the textbook seedbed for Communism. This cold, hungry, unemployed, and ragged industrial proletariat were without any real hope for the future. Furthermore, they had always leaned left. Theoretically, the Communists should have won."

Instead, the S.E.D. received only 19.8 percent of the city-wide vote, while the Social Democrats emerged strongest, with 48.7. An unprecedented 92.3 percent of eligible voters had gone to the polls, guided, says Drexler, by the Berliner's "famous political nose." They sniffed the air and decided they couldn't trust the S.E.D. The S.E.D. responded in like fashion. This free election was the last ever held in East Berlin. The Communists had learned their lesson.

chapter fourteen

ERNST REUTER RETURNED TO BERLIN ON NOVEMBER 30, 1946, ending an eleven-year Nazi-era exile; he toured the city's streets on his first evening there, driving through them in a Volkswagen owned by the *Telegraf,* that new Social Democratic newspaper that Arno Scholz had launched in March. Watching the moonscape of ruined Berlin and the exhausted, shabby population, Reuter murmured, "It's enough to stop your heart beating!"

Soon it would be worse. By June, 1948, all pretense at Four-Power cooperation was collapsing. The Western Allies prepared to create the Federal Republic of Germany and to introduce a new currency, the Deutsche Mark or D-Mark, and the Soviet Military Administration in Berlin warned that the city was part of the Soviet Zone and that the British, French, and American troops in the Western sectors no longer had any place in it. There was briefly talk of introducing a special currency for all of Berlin, to be called a *Bärenmark,* after the city's symbol, the Berlin bear; then the Soviets ordered Berlin's mayor to accept their own new East German mark as the currency for the entire city. The deadline for acceptance was 6 A.M. on June 23. That morning the Western military commandants countered the move by advising the city government that Soviet orders did not apply to the Western sectors of Berlin. The *Magistrat,* Berlin's "City Hall," was to put the issue to a vote before the city parliament at 4 P.M.

The meeting was delayed two hours. Columns of Communist toughs pressed on the Parliament Building and invaded its chambers, demanding *one* currency only and that the Western currency be banned from the city.

Unlike 1933, the delegates stood firm and outvoted the S.E.D., knowing much more was at stake than mere money. Communist thugs afterward beat up several delegates. Heinz Kessler, later commanding general of East Germany's Air Force and today a lieutenant general and chief of staff of the East German Armed Forces, directed the toughs against sixty-year-old Jeannette Wolff, who had spent six years in a Nazi concentration camp. A Jew was again being beaten in the streets of Berlin, as in the Nazi era.

When the vote was taken, Ernst Reuter said its consequences "may prove difficult and complicated, but we shall bear them!" In fact, neither he nor any other delegate realized what they would be.

That night, June 23-24, 1948, marked the beginning of the Berlin blockade. Soviet Zone power plants, pleading "lack of coal," switched off all electricity to the Western sectors. At the same time, "technical difficulties" halted passenger and freight traffic along railways and roads to West Berlin. The city was completely cut off from the West, except by air. Worried city officials checked its supplies; they found to their dismay that there was food for only a month and enough coal for ten days. Ernst Reuter addressed a crowd of Berliners at a football field in Gesundbrunnen.

"We shall fight with everything we have," he called out, "and to the very end, against this armed threat that aims to make us the slaves of a one-party system. We lived in such slavery during Adolf Hitler's Reich! We've had enough of it! We don't want a return to it!"

Seventy thousand Berliners roared their approval. In Heidelberg, General Lucius D. Clay responded by launching plans for the Berlin Air Lift, stating that only war would drive the Americans from Berlin. But whether this air lift would continue depended on the continuing steadfastness of the Berliners. Clay came to the city on June 25 to assess the situation for himself. He spoke directly to Reuter, then one of several *Stadträte* or city councillors, asking whether Reuter felt the Berliners were prepared to stand fast.

"Herr General," Reuter said with firmness, "there can be no question at all about where the Berliners stand. The Berliners will commit themselves to the defense of their freedoms and they will accept any help offered to them in a spirit of gratitude."

Clay then telephoned Washington. He admitted there was risk of war, but predicted it was unlikely. He urged that not the slightest suggestion be made that United States forces might be withdrawn from Berlin. America, he said, should overcome the blockade. President Harry S Truman, overriding several close advisors, then chose the irrevocable course suggested by Clay and Reuter. That day, the first three C-54 Skymasters flew nine tons of cargo into the city, the Royal Air Force joined in, and General Wedemeyer arrived to supervise the unprecedented effort at supplying what was now truly a beleaguered city.

The same day, S.E.D. leader Hermann Matern addressed the People's Police in East Berlin, warning them to get ready to prevent "a mass flight of Berliners once the Western occupying powers withdraw from the city." But he was in error, for both the Allies and the Berliners stood fast. A letter written by poet-physician Gottfried Benn to the publisher of *Merkur,* in faraway Baden-Baden, seems to sum up the feelings of most Berliners.

"And so I now say farewell and ask you to accept these greetings from darkened, blockaded Berlin, and from a part of it, moreover, which is close to starvation," he concluded. "This is being written in a room filled with shadows, in which the electric light has burned for only two out of the past twenty-four hours, for our gloomy and rain-filled summer has even robbed the city of its last chance at any luck and settled autumn over our ruins, ever since our spring began.

"Yet this remains the city whose lustre I love; whose misery I now choose to bear with civic pride; whose second, third, and now fourth Reich I have experienced, and from which nothing could now tempt me into leaving . . ."

By the time the air lift was one month old, more than twenty thousand flights had been completed, bringing in one hundred thousand tons of supplies. Within three months new runways had been built at Tempelhof and Gatow airfields and a third airport, Tegel in the French sector, had been completed. Planes landed every forty-five seconds. Even amphibian aircraft were used and landed on the Havel River. In July, the Russians ceased attending meetings of the Interallied Military Kommandatura altogether.

In September, Berlin's three non-Communist political parties (the Social Democrats, Christian Democrats, and Liberal Democrats) called a mass meeting in front of the ruined Reichstag Building, a few yards from the Soviet sector and its Brandenburg Gate.

More than three hundred thousand Berliners came to the Platz der Republik from all four sectors of the city. At the end of the rally, Ernst Reuter addressed the conscience of the world.

"People of America, England, France, Italy!" he shouted. "Look upon this city and know that you must not abandon it or its people—that you cannot abandon them! The people of Berlin have spoken: We have done our duty and we shall continue to do our duty!

"Peoples of the earth—do *your* duty as well! Help us during this time that confronts us, not just with the roar of airplanes . . . but with your steadfast, indestructible commitment on behalf of those ideals that alone can guarantee our future or indeed secure your own ideals as well! Peoples of the earth! Look upon this Berlin and upon the people of Berlin! Be certain of this: We intend to win this battle and we shall win this battle!"

When the rally broke up, tens of thousands of West Berliners followed the S.P.D., C.D.U., and L.D.P. leaders to the Allied Control Council Building, to present a documentation of Soviet and East German terror. Meanwhile, the East Berliners who had attended the rally turned to go home. The People's Police waited for them at the Brandenburg Gate with guns, determined to prevent them from entering. The crowd pressed on and began to shove its way through the police cordon, onto Pariser Platz and Unter den Linden. Then the police began firing. Wolfgang Scheunemann, fifteen, tried to shield a nurse and was shot dead. He was the first Berliner to be killed at the Soviet sector boundary. Twelve others were wounded that day.

When the gunfire began, hundreds flattened themselves onto the pavement, but one young man climbed to the top of the Brandenburg Gate and ripped down its red flag. The People's Police responded by arresting demonstrators. A British officer raced to the Soviet War Memorial and posted British military policemen there, to protect the Russian honor guard from the fury of the Berlin demonstrators.

Later that night, the Voice of America beamed a broadcast to Germany, "We have heard your voice, Berliners!"

With the beginning of the blockade, the Western conquerors came to be regarded as *Schutzmächte,* Berlin's "protective pow-

153

ers." Yet it was not their air lift alone which broke the Soviet stranglehold. The spirit of the city never wavered. Most of the two million West Berliners were women and children; despite deprivation, they were never cowed. The air lift prevented starvation, but not malnutrition; rations at one point were as scant as in the days immediately following surrender. Only very small quantities of meat, butter, fats, and sugar were allocated. Dehydrated potatoes became a staple. Powdered milk was flown in for Berlin's children, and as winter began, an issue of twenty-five pounds of coal was made to each household in the Western sectors; an additional fifty pounds were allocated to homes supporting children below school age or persons who were sick, incapacitated, or blind. Electric power was available in homes for only a couple of hours a day, and as these often came in the middle of the night, hundreds of thousands of *Hausfrauen* needed to set their alarm clocks for the small hours of the morning, to do their ironing and whatever work needed to be done under electric light. Some parts of the city intermittently received little or no gas and light at all; because darkness that winter fell at about four in the afternoon, homes and apartments remained cold and gloomy for much of the time and thousands of families had to go without warm meals.

If the Berlin women who managed under these conditions were the heroines of the air lift, the heroes were its pilots. The lift cost seventy-nine lives—nine German, thirty-one American, thirty-nine British. When the blockade began, pilots were so moved by the Berliners' determination to resist Soviet pressure that many of them volunteered to fly five or six flights a day into the city, and upon landing, even helped German airport personnel unload their planes. A real camaraderie developed. The pilots may still have had reservations about Germans, but these men were Berliners; that seemed to make them different. Bill Fish was one of a good many pilots who felt Berlin was special. He bombed it during the war, he brought it supplies during the air lift, and then shuttled to and from Berlin as a Pan American flight captain during the 1960's. Ten years short of retirement, he had his choice of Pan Am runs; he chose the Berlin-West Germany flight, so that he could bring his wife and children to Berlin to live. He hadn't expected it, but Berlin over the years had become part of his life.

154

There were countless private efforts to help West Berlin during the blockade. The one which most touched the Berliners was mounted by the pilots themselves. Most pilots dropped dozens of chocolate bars, attached to tiny parachutes, just before landing. The youngsters who waited with outstretched hands still talk of these *Schokoladenflieger* (chocolate pilots) a generation later. The efforts of the pilots were backed by those of Allied civilian and military personnel in the city, who also launched private relief operations, donating food and clothing to schools, hospitals, and Berlin welfare agencies. Coupled with this was a massive effort launched by charitable, private, and religious organizations throughout the world. During 1948 and the first eight months of 1949, relief supplies totaled more than 26 million pounds and were worth more than 10.5 million dollars. The record day of the lift was April 16, 1949, when 12,849 short tons of supplies arrived in 1,383 flights. That day, a plane landed in Berlin every sixty-three seconds.

In the midst of the cold, dark, hungry winter of the blockade, hundreds of thousands of Berliners queued up patiently to cast their votes in the municipal election of December 7, 1948, to choose a mayor for West Berlin. An astounding eighty-six percent of eligible voters went to the polls that day. General Clay watched them wait, shivering, in the streets. The aged or bedridden were often carried by relatives or friends. Clay was impressed; such people, he said later, understood the power of the polling booth. It was also clear they were determined to continue resisting Soviet pressure, for 64.5 percent of them had voted for the symbol of their defiance, the S.P.D.'s Ernst Reuter. (The Christian Democrats received 19.4 percent of the vote and the Liberal Democrats 16.1. West Berlin's own S.E.D. organization, invited to participate, declined as usual to take its chances at the polls.)

As their mayor, Ernst Reuter embodied their courage and increased their resolution. Armed with cane and beret, he was for the Berliners what Churchill had been for Londoners during the Blitz.

There was another vote which showed even more the average person's steadfastness. Every West Berliner could have accepted higher food rations from the S.E.D. in East Berlin, just by visiting the Soviet sector and picking them up. Only four percent chose to take this bribe.* The rest preferred to remain cold and hungry.

Today, many Berliners look back on these days of the blockade with nostalgia. It had been during this time, when others thought their fortunes were at their lowest ebb, that the Berliners attained a kind of exaltation. They knew this had been their finest hour.

In the autumn of 1949, a Berliner whose works embodied his own strong commitment against tyranny arrived from Zurich, Switzerland, to make his new home in Berlin. He moved not into democratic West Berlin, but into the Soviet sector, where he was to become "artistic advisor" to a theater, the Berliner Ensemble, now headed by his wife. The shabbily dressed man settling down in East Berlin was playwright Bertolt Brecht, that long-time Communist sympathizer, coming home after a Nazi-era exile. He had vague hopes his reputation might allow him to influence events for the better in East Berlin, though he had enough doubts to take precautions for himself. Before moving, he took out Austrian citizenship to make it impossible for the East German Government to restrict his travel; he also protected himself against censorship by placing the copyright to all his works in the hands of a West German publisher. Thus prepared, Brecht moved into a flat in the back of an old building on Berlin's Chausseestrasse, overlooking Hegel's grave in the Huguenot cemetery. His move outraged many people; asked why he made the choice, Brecht is reported to have said that West Germany with its former Nazis in powerful positions reminded him of a degenerate, dirty old roué, while East Germany's Communist state looked like a syphilitic old whore. But there was a difference, he claimed, for "the whore is *pregnant*."

Earlier that year, Wolfgang Leonhard, the youngest of the original Ulbricht group, made an equally decisive move—in the other direction. On March 12, 1949, he left East Berlin for Yugoslavia. His absence was first noticed three days after he left East Berlin, when he failed to give a lecture at the S.E.D. school in which he taught. The police, however, did not know where he was until April 22, because there was no mention in the Western press that

* This four percent includes all Communist functionaries in West Berlin and all those West Berliners who then happened to have their jobs in the Soviet sector.

he had crossed the border. Then Leonhard's statement was broadcast over the "heretical" Yugoslavs' radio. Four days later, the S.E.D. expelled Leonhard from its ranks, dissolved the class he had been teaching, reversed every policy he had ever set, and scattered all the students he had "infected" to other schools.

Commitments were clearly defined at the end of the blockade. Not only was Berlin officially split, but the country, too. In 1949 the S.E.D. regime formed the German Democratic Republic, or G.D.R., of which East Berlin was to become the capital, while in the west three Zones of Occupation were merged to form the Federal Republic of Germany.

Watching these moves, Ernst Reuter announced, "If *I* were Federal chancellor, I would go to Berlin and establish the Federal Government there!" But the Berliners had no say in the matter and bucolic Bonn became the seat of government while West Berlin, retaining its special status under the supreme authority of its Allied military commandants, was eventually compensated by being allowed to assume the rank of a state (or *Land*) in the West German federation.

The end of the blockade didn't solve all problems; a third of the West Berlin labor force remained out of work for several years. But a measure of prosperity was attained gradually, as the Marshall Plan and other aid flowed in. Eventually, the economy was healthy enough for the Western sectors to be called "the show-window of democracy." Those making the comparisons were East Berliners, who worked in and visited the Western sectors in those years. Consumer goods were only one attraction; West Berlin's uncensored publications, provocative theaters and cabarets, as well as its lending libraries, were others. Tens of thousands of East Berliners came over each evening. It buoyed up their morale as well as their courage, for they could not only seek relief from their regime on brief visits, but still needed only to walk a few blocks, take the S-Bahn or U-Bahn trains, and leave Communism altogether. Many did just that, coming from all over East Germany by way of East Berlin—in 1949, 129,245; in 1950, 197,788; in 1951, 165,648; and in 1952, 182,393. They sought not only political freedom, but also freedom from economic exploitation. The G.D.R. was pursuing a policy of limiting consumer goods in favor of building up heavy industry. A successful policy, it has made East Germany the second-largest industrial power in the Soviet bloc and the seventh in all Europe. The benefits this policy brought its people, however, remained small for many years, for the products of its heavy industry flowed east to Russia on confiscatory terms.

The battle for Berlin was never allowed to slacken during these years. The city remained the prize the Soviets wanted, for withdrawal of the Western forces from the city would allow the East German regime to consolidate its territory and eliminate not only a free and democratic bastion but also an outpost of Western intelligence activity, this being a time when an estimated seventy or more Western cloak-and-dagger agencies operated in West Berlin. After the failure of the blockade, the Soviets briefly decided to give Ulbricht's chief rival, Gerhard Eisler, a free hand. Eisler was an ambitious, fanatically anti-American adventurer. In 1950, Eisler planned a coup against West Berlin for the Whitsun spring holidays. More than one hundred thousand uniformed members of F.D.J., or "Free German Youth," the S.E.D.-run youth organization in East Germany, were to be unleashed onto West Berlin. These child crusaders were to capture all public buildings in the Western sectors, chase out all West Berlin city officials, and then provoke so many incidents that the G.D.R. would "be compelled" to send armed People's Police units into West Berlin "to rescue the children." *

The Soviets, however, thought better of this plan after noting the Western military commandants' reaction: They had warned that the F.D.J. "army" would not be allowed to invade the Western sectors of the city. United States troops were put on the alert and began intensive maneuvers in street fighting; the latest United States' jet fighters flew into Tempelhof to augment the American garrison. In Bonn there was talk of war breaking out over Berlin. The Soviets defused the crisis by ordering the People's Police to

* The People's Police had already been made into a quasi-military force in 1948, when its *Bereitschaftspolizei,* or "emergency police force," was established. (This was in 1952 equipped with military arms and uniforms and renamed *Kasernierte Volkspolizei,* or "Barrack-Housed People's Police." In 1956, these units became part of the regular G.D.R. armed forces then established.)

158

seal off the sector boundaries into West Berlin, so as to stop the F.D.J. The Western commandants then did an about-face and welcomed the youngsters. After the parade of 220,000 youngsters ended in East Berlin, thousands of them trooped into the Western sectors in uniform, but peaceably. Western loudspeaker trucks at sector crossing points even invited them to come on over and see the "showcase of democracy" for themselves. Since the East Berlin authorities had not made adequate provision to feed this enormous army of youngsters, West Berlin provided thousands of meals. The result was a disaster for Eisler, who never recovered his prestige. He was demoted and later appointed chief of the G.D.R.'s radio-broadcasting committee, a job he held until his recent death. Ulbricht, who had never liked Eisler, and who had predicted the children's crusade would never work, consolidated his power.

After the 1950 Whitsun youth rally, pressure on West Berlin was maintained in different ways. In April, 1952, a Soviet jet fighter fired upon an Air France passenger plane flying in the Berlin Air Corridor; in the five months that followed, Ulbricht sealed off 200 of the 277 streets leading from East to West Berlin. Then all properties belonging to West Berliners in the outskirts of the city were expropriated. In the main, this robbed West Berlin's workers of their small garden allotments and what graves they had in out-lying cemeteries. All bank accounts, businesses, land, or other property owned by West Berliners in East Berlin were seized. Repeatedly, the Soviets demanded the shutdown of West Berlin's anti-Communist newspapers and of R.I.A.S. (Radio in the American Sector), an American facility.

Then on March 5, 1953, Stalin died and everything suddenly seemed possible, even a relaxation of Stalinist terror in the G.D.R. In the midst of it all, however, the regime blundered badly. On June 16, 1953, its newspapers called upon East Berliners to raise their "work norms" voluntarily by ten percent, meaning they were to do that much more work for the amount of pay they were previously receiving. This was being asked of them at a time when an East Berlin construction worker earned 1.21 marks per hour and when a pound of margarine or butter cost four and ten marks respectively in the state-owned "HO" shops of the Soviet sector.

Berlin's construction workers were understandably outraged.

All hope that conditions might get better ended. The workers on Block Number 40 of Stalinallee refused to begin work; they sat or stood about at the construction site, discussing the newspaper articles among themselves. Their overseers telephoned the G.D.R. trade unions for help, but when a functionary arrived and ordered the workers to drop their papers and pick up their trowels, they paid no attention to him. "Shove off!" they told him. "It's too late for that!" Then they grabbed a banner which functionaries had prepared in advance and crossed out its slogan, "Block 40 raises its norms ten percent!" Instead, they scrawled a new slogan on the reverse: "We demand a lowering of work norms!" Holding it aloft, the men from Block 40 marched down Stalinallee, intending to confront the Government leaders and protest not only the new measures, but high prices and poor food supplies as well. They numbered eighty men. They did not know it yet, but they were the nucleus of a nationwide East German uprising.

The eighty demonstrators marched slowly, for everywhere along their route they collected more members. Other construction workers on Stalinallee dropped their tools, left their jobs and joined them; passersby on the streets left the sidewalks and entered their ranks; housewives and youngsters left apartments and swelled the demonstration. People's Police at Strausberger Platz tried to halt them, but were overrun. The marchers crossed the Alexanderplatz and the Lustgarten (Marx-Engels Platz today), paraded down Unter den Linden and past the Soviet Embassy, moved toward the Wilhelmstrasse and then toward the Leipzigerstrasse, collecting more and more people. They chanted a call to other Berliners to join their ranks and to refuse enslavement.* It took them four hours, until one in the afternoon, to reach their destination, the G.D.R.'s House of the Ministries, formerly Hermann Göring's Luftwaffe Building. By this time, the original eighty marchers had grown to eight thousand. As they approached the Government building, each window closed and its metal gate clattered shut. The building was as silent in the face of this demonstration as was the Government of East Berlin itself. The marchers stood in front of it, chanting their demands and insisting that they speak with Party Boss Ulbricht and with Otto Grotewohl, that former Social Democrat who had become S.E.D. co-chairman and Prime Minister of

* *"Berliner, reiht euch ein, wir wollen keine Sklaven sein!"*

the G.D.R. Finally, three officials stepped out to talk with the workers. Minister of Mines Selbmann pleaded with them, but they just shouted him down as a traitor. He offered to do what he could to get the norms lowered, but was shoved aside by a worker who shouted, "We're no longer interested in that! This isn't just a demonstration against high norms and we don't just come from the Stalinallee. We represent all Berlin! This is a popular uprising! We want to be free!"

Singing an old German workers' song of freedom (*"Brüder, zur Sonne, zur Freiheit!"*) and calling for a general strike on the following day, June 17, the demonstrators marched back to the Stalinallee. They tore down S.E.D. placards and banners, removed posters belonging to the German-Soviet Friendship Society and ripped up pictures of Walter Ulbricht. That afternoon, Grotewohl announced that the increases in the work norms had been canceled and asked the demonstrators to go home peacefully. The People's Police remained in its barracks; it readied its armored cars for action, but did not use them yet.

Ernst Reuter, attending a congress in Vienna, meanwhile tried desperately to get a plane back to Berlin. But there was no seat available on any commercial airline, and when he asked the United States forces to fly him back to Berlin in a military plane, he was turned down.

When the news reached West Berlin that the demonstrators were calling for a general strike for the following day, June 17, R.I.A.S. newsmen tried frantically to obtain approval from United States headquarters to let them broadcast this to East Germany at large. Headquarters temporized, and when a policy decision on this failed to arrive by 5 A.M. on June 17, R.I.A.S. executives acted on their own and put the general strike call on the air. The news struck like a bombshell. Between 300,000 and 372,000 workers in East Germany went on strike and demonstrated in more than 250 cities and towns. Steel workers in Hennigsdorf, outside East Berlin, formed themselves into a column numbering 12,000 men and women and marched onto the city to support their Berlin colleagues. By 7 A.M., about 100,000 East Berliners had collected in the streets and began to move to the center of the city. Handbills were passed about, calling for guarantees of freedom of speech and of the press, free elections, an end to zonal borders, withdrawal

161

of all occupation forces, an end to the militarized police units, freedom for all political prisoners, repatriation of all remaining prisoners of war in the U.S.S.R., and lower prices.

They were united in their aims, but that was all. They still had no leaders, and furthermore, they had no arms. They did not know it yet, but Soviet armored columns were moving from the East German countryside toward East Berlin, slowly, as they had to take the long way round to bypass the United States sector.

When the enormous mass of demonstrators reached the Government buildings, confusion in these offices was complete. Not a word had been heard from Ulbricht or Grotewohl (who had, in fact, asked for help from the Red Army). One official collapsed, fearing a heart attack, when he saw what was going on. He was Bruno Leuschner, chairman of the G.D.R.'s state-planning commission, an old-time Communist and a veteran of Nazi concentration camps. A colleague, Fritz Schenk, and a secretary helped Leuschner onto a couch. He regained his breath a few moments later.

"Those are the people about whom we've kidded ourselves for years," Leuschner gasped, "thinking we represent their interests! Have we done *everything* wrong?"

A minute or two later, he recaptured his equanimity. "Ah well," he told Schenk, "after all, it's only a few thousand people and not the whole population. Anyway, you can't take Berlin as a yardstick. The atmosphere here is contaminated by West Berlin. All this is due only to that damn hornets' nest!"

Toward late morning, the troops finally appeared. When the first tanks arrived at Leipzigerstrasse, they were surrounded by such an impenetrable mass of Berliners that they had to come to a complete halt. Workers even chalked slogans onto them: "Freedom!" and "The goatee must go!" (a reference to Ulbricht). A short while later, Soviet infantry and People's Policemen pressed forward, so as to free the tanks from the crowd. The Berliners howled defiance, shouted "Shame!" at the soldiers and policemen, many of whom began to waver, clearly unwilling to use brute force. Then a loudspeaker truck behind the police and Red Army infantrymen blared out a command from Major General Pavel T. Dibrova, the newly arrived Soviet commandant in the city. It announced that martial law had been declared, that all gatherings of more than three people were forbidden, and that violators would be tried by military courts. One demonstrator who recognized General Dibrova in one of the hemmed-in tanks reports that he saw him, not being able to make his voice heard over the roar of the crowd, give a hand signal to the Soviet troops to push on through. The signal warned the Russian soldiers and German policemen what would happen if they hesitated or wavered in the face of this uprising, for the general slowly drew his index finger across his throat.

The troops moved forward, the tanks began slowly to roll, the crowd fell back, and then the first shots were fired, whether by Russians or People's Policemen is unclear. Women and children in the mass scattered into surrounding buildings, but hundreds of Berlin youths defied the Soviet armor with their bare hands and with hurled bricks. This happened in full sight of West Berliners, standing horrified at the Western boundary of Potsdamer Platz, where the tanks had pushed the demonstrators, meaning to seal off access to the Western sectors. Violence raged through many other streets and squares in East Berlin. Shots were exchanged on Stresemannstrasse as late as seven in the evening (a West Berliner was mortally wounded there); in Bernauerstrasse, a People's Policeman shot and killed a nine-year-old boy.

By evening, the Soviets were in complete control. Then began the revenge. Willy Göttling, thirty-five, a West Berliner who just happened to be passing through East Berlin on his way from the French to the United States sector, was arrested by the Red Army and summarily executed by a Soviet firing squad. Eighteen Soviet soldiers and 116 People's Policemen and regime functionaries lost their lives in this uprising, and 267 demonstrators were killed. After it was over, 92 people were summarily shot and 14 sentenced to death; 1,200 others were sentenced to 6,000 years imprisonment.

The epitaph was given by Bertolt Brecht after his death three years later, in a poem called "The Solution":

> After the rising of the 17th June
> The secretary of the Writers' Union
> Had leaflets distributed in the Stalinallee
> In which you could read that the people

Had lost the Government's confidence
Which it could only regain
By redoubled efforts. Would it in that case
Not be simpler if the Government
Dissolved the people
And elected another?

After the uprising, the Berliners awakened to the fact that the Western Allies were referring to West Berlin only when they stated that they meant to defend the freedom of the city. Despite the fact that all of Berlin was to be ruled jointly by the four military commandants, the three Western commandants had clearly received instructions that their responsibilities ended at the Soviet sector border. Reuter, who telephoned the United States commandant as soon as he returned from Vienna on the 18th, was turned down when he asked that United States troops at least be deployed at the Soviet sector boundaries, so as to demonstrate Western force. It was almost as though a deal had been made behind the backs of the Berliners. Both West and East would leave each other's portions of Berlin alone—and the Berliners to their separate fates.

The most striking monument to the uprising is a simple stone in District Zehlendorf. It bears these words: "In memory of those Russian officers and soldiers who had to die because they refused to fire on the freedom fighters of June 17th."

Another who died, a little more than three months afterward, was Ernst Reuter, exhausted by his long fight against the despotisms of the Right and of the Left. He was buried in Berlin and is today commemorated by a number of buildings and a major square, the former Charlottenburg "Knee." A bronze sculpture representing a flame was placed there ten years after Reuter's death, bearing his warning, "Peace can only endure in freedom," but Reuter's real shrine is in the hearts of his Berliners. He seemed the greatest of them all, for he had briefly made all of them seem great.

chapter fifteen

FOR A TIME AFTER THE WAR, THE SOVIETS AND THEIR EAST GER-
man satraps made use of the very concentration camps which the
Nazis had built. Though these were afterward abandoned in favor
of more modern structures, they led to a bitter Berlin joke about
one prisoner who found himself back again in the camp from which
he'd earlier been liberated.

"Excuse me," he said to a Communist guard upon arriving. "Is
the old number tattooed on my arm still valid?"

In the face of such oppression, the lure of the West increased.
West Berlin, its gateway for East Berliners and East Germans in
general, infuriated the Soviets and became for them "a bone in the
throat," as Khrushchev called it. The Berlin Ultimatums followed;
then came the Berlin Wall, turning all of East Berlin and the G.D.R.
into one vast concentration camp.

The wall is different from almost any wall one can recall or imagine. The Great Wall of China kept out nomadic hordes and
Roman walls protected civilization against barbarian tribes. In
Germany, medieval cities built walls to protect their burghers and
their gold against the marauding armies of robber barons and
enemy states, but the Great Wall of Ulbricht can only be compared
with the wall Hitler built around the Warsaw Ghetto, for it is meant
to keep people prisoners inside. No one, not even the border
guards, believes the official statement that its purpose is to prevent Western spies, saboteurs, kidnappers, and *agents provocateurs*
from entering the G.D.R.: even the barbed-wire atop the wall
refutes this, being tilted so as to prevent East Berliners from
climbing up and over. On May Day, when the G.D.R. parks its
armored cars at the wall's checkpoints, these vehicles and the heavy

machine-guns mounted on top of them do not face toward the West, as though securing the frontier, but unabashedly East, so as to discourage any escapes by the massed citizens. They make a mockery out of that article in the G.D.R. Constitution that proclaims, "Every citizen has the right to emigrate."

Too many availed themselves of that "right," however, as far as Ulbricht was concerned. From 1949 through August 12, 1961 (the day before the border was sealed), 2,800,000 East Germans fled the G.D.R., as many citizens as populate East Germany's twelve largest cities, or about one out of every five of its citizens. The Federal Republic estimates that another 430,000 East Germans escaped since 1945 without registering in the West. The G.D.R. tried to halt this flow by making *"Republikflucht"*—literally "flight from the Republic"—a crime punishable by three years imprisonment, but this statute didn't help. From 1950 through the first half of 1961, an average 19,000 East Germans escaped into West Berlin *each month*. The G.D.R. denounced this steady flood as "slave trading" and "pirating of individuals." What bothered the party most was that it was losing much of its top talent and the productive element in its society.

Scientists are a good example. More than 1,600 of them fled the G.D.R. from 1958 to 1961. The effect was devastating. Of this number, 513 belonged to the faculty of *just one* university.

Three-fourths of those leaving were under forty-five years of age; half of them between twenty-five and forty-five, and every fourth refugee less than twenty-five years old. The G.D.R. was being left with a disproportionate number of old people. On the collectivized farms old women picked through potato fields, looking like black crows, while their men, equally aged, rode tractors, or more often, horse-drawn plows. The departure of the young had a big effect on East Berlin as well. The number of its apprentices was cut in half, for example, from more than thirty thousand in 1955 to less than fifteen thousand in 1962, adding to the industrial woes of a country already ravaged by confiscatory Soviet trade "agreements." Thirty thousand students fled the country, often just after getting their diplomas at East Berlin's Humboldt University, the former Friedrich-Wilhelm University on Unter den Linden. About eight hundred engineers and technicians also fled their East German jobs, along with an equal number of judges, state attorneys, and notaries employed by the S.E.D. regime. Nearly all of them left via the open border in Berlin.

All this cost East Germany a great deal. *Pravda* in 1961 quoted Walter Ulbricht as saying it cost the G.D.R. more than thirty billion marks just to prepare a labor force, only to have it "then recruited by West Germany," but in subsequent interviews Ulbricht bandied other figures about, making them all suspect. A London paper quoted him two weeks before the wall went up as saying, "This is no political emigration, but filthy man trade . . . carried out with large sums of money invested by Bonn authorities, West Germany monopoly capital and the United States in West Berlin."

Easy access to West Berlin's free atmosphere bothered Ulbricht even when it involved those not settling in the West to stay, for the number of people crossing between East and West Berlin came to a half a million *a day;* of these, about sixty thousand actually had jobs in West Berlin industry or homes; these were called *Grenzgänger,* or "border crossers." The rest came to West Berlin to refresh themselves at its libraries or entertainments. So many came to read books not available at home that, when the border was sealed, the American Memorial Library noted the loss of thousands of volumes that East Berliners were then unable to return. (Needless to say, these books have been written off and the library is happy that they are probably circulating clandestinely in East Berlin.) Hundreds of other East Germans rushed to West Berlin's theaters, cinemas, and cabarets, thirsting for entertainment that wasn't larded with propaganda; they were allowed to buy their tickets with East marks exchanged at a 1:1 rate by the West Berlin city government, and in the twelve months before the border was sealed, the number of such tickets sold to East Berliners came to a staggering ten million.

In mid-June, 1961, Walter Ulbricht told a press conference that "nobody has the intention of building a wall." Practiced in reading between the lines, East Germans concluded that the border might well be sealed or at any rate made more impassable. These fears were heightened when the East German press launched a hysterical daily campaign against "slave trading." The *Grenzgänger* suddenly found themselves sharply harassed by People's Policemen whose ranks at the border had been strengthened sixfold. Some

Germans were even compelled to surrender their identity papers to these *Vopos,* and between July 29 and August 4, it was estimated that every second East German traveling to Berlin was intercepted by the People's Police, for anyone making that journey might well complete it in the Western sectors. Some official and semi-official West German agencies believe Ulbricht deliberately stampeded East Germans into a panic during these weeks, so that he could use the mounting flood of escapees to justify closing the border. A West German Government information bureau says flatly that Ulbricht built the wall to perpetuate the division of Germany and reinforce the G.D.R., deliberately creating "an eleventh-hour panic" and doing it so successfully that he duped the West into believing the wall was built for economic rather than political reasons.

Certainly there were those in the West who aided him. West Berlin's sensational Springer-owned newspapers have been accused of being prime culprits. Perhaps unwittingly, but it is often claimed deliberately, they fanned the panic in the weeks before the wall with headlines almost as hysterical as those which appeared in the S.E.D.-controlled press—"Mass Escapes!" . . . "The Flood Reaches Avalanche Proportions!" . . . "Escape Stream Doubles!" . . . "Alarm Atmosphere in the Zone!"

Whether or not Ulbricht deliberately fanned the panic to justify the wall, most observers became convinced that it was the flood of refugees that specifically prompted him to seal the border. In any event there was nothing the West would do to stop him. President John F. Kennedy, says Arthur M. Schlesinger Jr., discussed the matter with Walt Rostow while walking through the White House Rose Garden early in August. Kennedy "observed that Khrushchev would have to do something internally to reestablish control over the situation—and that, if he did, we would not be able to do a thing about it." Schlesinger indicates that Kennedy's view was quietly realistic, based on power politics and a recognition of spheres of interest. Eastern Europe, including the G.D.R., "was a vital interest for Khrushchev, and he could not stand by and let it trickle away," Schlesinger writes, citing Kennedy's view. "But it was not a vital interest for the United States."

"I can get the alliance to move if he tries to do anything about

West Berlin," he quotes the President as saying about NATO, "but not if he does something about East Berlin."

What Ulbricht did caught everyone in the West by surprise, the State Department and the C.I.A. in Washington included. The move was even kept secret from Ulbricht's own troops until midnight between Saturday, August 12, and Sunday, August 13.

At one minute past midnight, the alarm siren at Border Checkpoint Number 4 awakened Sergeant Rudi Thurow, an East German platoon commander assigned to border patrol at Röntgental, about twenty miles north of Berlin. Thurow hurried into his clothes, and went to make sure his men were getting dressed. Some were cursing, others were still lying in bed; several had just come from twelve hours duty at 10 P.M. Thurow walked past their beds, yanked their blankets off, and told them to hurry. Then he joined the other noncoms and officers of the company in the office of First Lieutenant Witz, the company commander.

Lieutenant Witz, who had received his information from Soviet officers just a half hour earlier, addressed the men. "A bolt is being slammed in the door," he said, to stop the "eighty-three espionage and terror centers in West Berlin" from draining the G.D.R. of its best manpower. If it hurt some citizens, Witz said, that couldn't be helped; it would protect the vast majority of East Germans. Then Witz read aloud from several typewritten sheets of paper he pulled from a "Strictly Secret" envelope; this was a long denunciation of Western Allied aggressive intent, the NATO alliance, West Germany, and West Berlin. Then he stated that the border leading to East Berlin would be sealed.

In the shocked silence that followed his announcement, Witz assured his men that no military conflict would result; further, all Soviet Army units around Berlin were standing at the alert. Border guards would be supported by soldiers of the National People's Army (the N.V.A., or *Nationale Volksarmee*), by the Emergency Police (*Bereitschaftspolizei*), and by the "Factory Fighting Groups" that at this very moment were occupying all strategically important positions in East Berlin. The man next to Thurow muttered, "Will the Allies stand for this?"

Shortly after 2 A.M., forty thousand East German soldiers and police, equipped with tanks, cars, personnel carriers, trucks, and other vehicles, rolled up to the border and closed it off, some laying down barbed wire. U-Bahn and S-Bahn travel was similarly cut and all East Berliners were forbidden to step into the Western sectors. For the time being, West Berliners with "valid papers" could still enter East Berlin.

By 4 A.M., Sergeant Thurow and his men had moved to Bahnhof Bernau, a border crossing point between the G.D.R. and West Berlin, in the north of the city. The first East Germans arrived a few minutes later on their way to work in West Berlin. Almost none had heard the news. When Thurow told them to turn back, one called out, *"Sei doch ein Mensch!"*—"Act like a human being, will you!" Thurow avoided his eyes. He felt uncomfortable, but followed orders. He refused to let anyone pass through, with the exception of one woman whom he had known throughout three years of service at this railway station. He was afraid to take chances on any of the others; any one of them might be an informer and his actions were very likely under observation. Over and over again, he told the workers who now began to pour into the station, "Read the newspapers! They'll tell you all you need to know!" Some of them went to the kiosks, bought papers, but came back nevertheless. The crowd got bigger and bigger; everyone was in an ugly mood. At 5:30 A.M., Thurow reported to company headquarters, "There's unrest here and people are soured off. Otherwise, everything's rolling normally."

At 6 A.M., thirty men and women arrived to help Sergeant Thurow's border guards; most of them wore the uniforms of "Factory Fighting Groups." Thurow recognized one of the men as an officer in the State Security Service who at one time had questioned suspects at this station. The girls all wore the blue blouses of the Free German Youth. These thirty newcomers mingled among the outraged workers. Thurow heard one worker say, "Now no one can expect me to do a thing more for the state! I refuse to recognize this frontier, if they're going to bar my way to my own mother!"

A party functionary approached Thurow and accused his men of not being strict enough. "Why don't you tell these people that this sealed border around West Berlin is an anti-fascist protective wall?" the functionary demanded. Thurow and his soldiers had

170

already been instructed in that phrase but had so far avoided using it; none of them wanted to invite ridicule.

"We do our duty," Thurow replied, keeping his voice down, "and we don't need any instructions from people like you!"

Many of the people now coming to the Bernau Station found their way to Thurow's guard room, trying to get a special pass. Several of them knew he'd shut his eyes over the past three years to many an irregularity, just to help people in need. Today, however, he remained firm. Over and over again, he told them, "I've got my orders; I can't let you go through!" As he repeated that throughout the day, he more and more felt that the order was unjust.

He wasn't alone. That afternoon, Pfc. Gottfried Herrmann came into Sergeant Thurow's office, walked over to the sink, scrubbed his hands like Pontius Pilate, and then walked up to Thurow's desk. "I'm ashamed of myself," he said bitterly.

Gottfried Herrmann would be the first of Thurow's company to flee to West Berlin. Within the next twelve months, sixteen out of the ninety-six soldiers would have fled, too, Rudi Thurow among them.

The border had been sealed so fast that even Joachim Lipschitz, then West Berlin's interior senator in charge of security, had been caught unawares. When he opened his office mail on Monday morning, the day after it was all over, he found it contained a report advising him "nothing unusual" was expected to happen in Berlin. An official had written it before leaving for the weekend and had posted it routinely on Friday.

Heinrich Albertz, former mayor of West Berlin, was then head of the city's *Senatskanzlei,* or "chancellery." On August 13 at 2:30 in the morning he queried what action the Allied commandants would take. He soon learned that the Western Governments would not act at all.

"Only this explains," says Albertz, "why the Allied soldiers remained in their barracks and why, so far as I know, not even their free time that Sunday was canceled."

No one, however, ever asked the Western Allies to intervene, not Mayor Willy Brandt nor West German Chancellor Konrad Adenauer. Brandt talked with the Allied generals at 11 A.M. that morning; all he asked was that Allied patrols be sent to the border, to reassure the people and to underscore Allied readiness to defend the Western sectors. He urged that protests be delivered to Moscow and all other capitals of Warsaw Pact nations "this very day." It took more than two days for the Western Allied commandants to protest to their Soviet counterparts in East Berlin and it took even longer for a protest to reach Moscow.

The West Berliners were outraged—and alarmed. Willy Brandt wrote Kennedy on August 16, asking for a stronger Western response. The President replied by sending Vice President Lyndon B. Johnson to the city, to carry a letter from Kennedy to Mayor Brandt and also to demonstrate by his presence that West Berlin was still "an ultimate American commitment." A battle group was also dispatched from West Germany.

Although the President's letter impressed many Berliners, the Springer-owned newspapers weren't satisfied. *Bild* carried huge headlines reading, "The West Does Nothing!" and "Is Germany Being Sold Out?" In fact, there was nothing the West could do. "Theoretically, it might have been possible," says former Mayor Albertz, "but practically, not."

"What could we have done?" one United States Army staff officer in West Berlin told me years later. "Imagine what might have happened if we had sent in tanks to flatten the barbed wire. Suppose that the *Vopos* then built a second barbed wire barrier ten yards farther east. Should we have flattened that, too? What about a third barrier, put up fifty yards inside East Berlin? The Soviets would no more countenance our invasion of their sector than we would stand for their rolling into West Berlin. It might have meant war."

Hans Kroll, then West German Ambassador to the Soviet Union, was instructed to tell Khrushchev how much the wall aggravated tensions in Berlin and that all Germans, in Berlin and elsewhere, regarded this barrier "in their old capital city as a provocation." Kroll reports that Khrushchev could understand these feelings.

"I know the wall is an ugly thing," Khrushchev told Kroll, "and one day it will disappear. But only when the reasons for its construction have disappeared."

Kroll, whose report of this conversation appeared in his memoirs, says Khrushchev continued by saying, "What was I supposed to do? More than thirty thousand people—and, mind you, among them the best and most capable people from the G.D.R.—left their country in the month of July. It isn't hard to figure out how soon the East German economy would have collapsed had we not taken steps against this mass flight.

"There were only two kinds of countermeasures possible. For us to block air transport, or the wall. The first named would have brought us into serious conflict with the United States, which might possibly have led to war. I neither could nor wanted to risk that. So there was nothing left but the wall.

"I also do not want to conceal from you that it was I who in the final analysis gave the order. It is true that Ulbricht had been pressuring me for a long time, and more than ever in the last months, but I do not want to hide behind his back. He's much too narrow for me."

Kroll urged Khrushchev to get Ulbricht to liberalize his regime, saying people would then stop fleeing the G.D.R. Khrushchev ignored the question. First, West Germany must sign a peace treaty with the U.S.S.R. "Why is it that your Government refuses so stubbornly to talk with Ulbricht about this?" he asked. "I often speak to people I don't like. One doesn't have to start by kissing one another right away!"

Far from kissing, West and East Germany remain at loggerheads even today, despite recent low-level talks about trade between the countries. The Cold War, which elsewhere has been thawing for years (but which in 1968 seemed reborn after the invasion of Czechoslovakia), has always remained in force in Berlin. The wall is its symbol, not only its expression. Since 1961, this wall has been greatly strengthened and its guards increased. Fourteen thousand N.V.A. soldiers now man the border between East and West Berlin. Those among them whose aim seems poor are in deep trouble; Ralf Gängelbach, accused of "missing" an escapee on purpose, was sentenced to three years in prison. Others have received similar prison terms for the same crime. The official N.V.A. regulations order guards first to call out a warning and then to fire a warning shot if suspected escapees fail to respond; the next shots must be on target. In actuality, few warning shouts are ever given, for a new N.V.A. regulation allows guards to shoot without warning "if the situation requires." The guards are painfully aware that their jobs make them unpopular, not only in

West Berlin, but among their own people, and the G.D.R. has taken this into account by eliminating from their uniforms all insignia which previously identified their function. The East German Army, West Berliners note with satisfaction, is an army of deserters, just as East Germany for many years had the dubious distinction of being the only known country to have *both* a rising birth rate and a steadily declining population.

The result of the wall in terms of human tragedy is well-known. For a few days after August 13, some East Berliners managed to get through the border, leaping over the barbed wire, or swimming the Spree River and other waterways; ultimately, most such possibilities were cut off. While escapes in Berlin itself seem virtually impossible today, it remains an amazing fact that almost twenty-seven thousand Germans have managed to flee to the West since the wall was built, most crossing the mined frontier to the Federal Republic. Sixty-three refugees were killed and more than two thousand arrested at the Berlin Wall during the first seven years of its existence; another seventy-two died at the G.D.R. frontier with West Germany.

One of the most disturbing results of the wall is that almost all contact between the Germans in the West and in the East has been cut, along with all contact between the East Berliners and the Berliners in the West. Seven out of every ten Berliners in both sections of the city have ties to Berliners in the other section that they are unable to maintain.

The fact that they are walled in has meant that the East Berliners have had to come to terms with Ulbricht and his regime. This, says Rudolf Merker of the S.P.D.'s Eastern Bureau, has led the people there "to walk about with two faces" and the Government to begin actively competing with West Germany both politically and economically. It has finally developed a sense of itself (*Selbstbewusstsein*) as a state, says Merker, and ever since the wall, has tried to increase its international prestige and industrial power.

"There are really two ways of looking at that wall," a State Department officer attached to the United States Mission in West Berlin told me, "and one is obvious: It is a cruel, inhuman monstrosity. Those people who see it only in this way feel a moral necessity to do whatever they can to help people escape.

"The other is more difficult," this official commented, "but very

174

realistic. The wall, let's face it, has helped the East Germans to some extent. Before it went up, there were thousands of university graduates who escaped to the West just as soon as they had their degrees. As a matter of fact, the influx of these people increased sharply during the summer, right after graduation. This, of course, infuriated the Ulbricht regime, for it had spent tens of thousands of marks educating and training every one of these people, giving them hospitalization, free student housing, and what-not. These students would take advantage of this, and abhorring the system, would take off for the West as soon as they could. Today, the students have to remain after graduation, and because they don't see any likelihood of escaping, they cooperate. Many—maybe most—continue to loathe the regime and its ideology, but the necessity of earning a living day by day and the sheer pleasure of working in a field that interests them captures their energy. They've made a big contribution. Anyone who saw East Berlin ten years ago and contrasts it with the East Berlin of today can see the enormous strides they've made. They may be, and they are, way behind the West Germans, but there's no question that the East Berliners now live much better. One reason for this is that loathsome wall. It has forced young university graduates to work in the East and make their economic contribution there.

"At the same time, the East German Government has learned to relax just a little. It used to regard all these students with great suspicion, because it knew many would leave after graduation. As a result, repressive measures were considerable. Today the regime knows they'll have to stay; consequently, it has relaxed at least some of its controls.

"Finally, it's no use denying that the wall has helped the West. The fact of the matter is that all these hundreds of thousands of East German refugees were an unsettling influence on West Berlin, as well as a constant international irritant. The wall's changed all that."

Arthur M. Schlesinger Jr., reporting the views of the Kennedy Administration, said much the same thing. The wall, he wrote, "represented a solution, at considerable political cost, of the problem that, more than anything else, had led Khrushchev to reopen the Berlin question earlier in the year."

It ended the Berlin crisis sparked by Khrushchev's "Berlin

Ultimatum," which had warned that the Soviets might call for an end to United States, British, and French occupation of the Western sectors.

"By stanching the blood flow from East Germany," Schlesinger writes, "the wall secured the most immediate Soviet interest in Berlin. Kennedy's determination to rebuild the military power of the West had shown Khrushchev that he could not obtain his maximum objectives by bluff. Now the wall, by achieving his minimum objective, released him from the necessity of forcing the issue to a showdown."

Such views, understandably, are not popular with the Berliners, but that does not change the fact that they determine policy. No matter how the Berliners feel about it, the Western Allies welcome the relaxation of tensions which the wall unexpectedly brought in its wake; ever since they started compromising with the Soviets, their concern has never been to defend the East Berliners nor all of Berlin, but only the Western sectors.

The wall sharpened commitments. A boycott of the G.D.R.-run S-Bahn trains in West Berlin followed; some of the S-Bahn trains seem almost ghostly today, rattling empty throughout the Western sectors. The wall also shook out the timid. Werner Crome of the *Tagesspiegel* met a Berlin businessman who was of sterner stuff. Before the wall went up, he had planned to leave West Berlin for West Germany. "Now it's out of the question," he announced. "Now one remains in Berlin no matter what!" A few days later, Crome heard the same in East Berlin, from a taxi driver. "I might have packed off for the West, too," the cabbie said. "But now— never! Now that Berlin's up against it, I'm staying!"

This Berlinese cockiness has become more defensive of late. Professor Lieber says the Berliner is no longer as willing to accept criticism of Berlin as he once had been. "He can still laugh at himself and his city," Lieber said, "but now he sets limits. The wall has led to a certain provincialization."

Cabarettist Rolf Ulrich of *Die Stachelschweine* noted the same. "That wall is altering the Berliners, slowly and subtly," he claims. "They're hemmed in and this makes them nervous and hypersensitive. We kidded the Berliners in one skit, and though our reference to Berlin was ironic, the whole audience cheered at the very word. Now, that's not just civic pride."

Slowly and subtly, the wall is changing the Berliners. What was an outrage has become a cancer of the spirit. Edgy, jumpy, and suffering from claustrophobia, the West Berliners for the first time in their history now periodically lose their coolness under fire. Their students, who are questioning some of the black-and-white Cold War commitments held by the mass of citizens, have become the target of a neurotic over-response. "You look for that famous Berlin tolerance in vain today," says Ralf Weber, a student at the Technical University. "Berlin has lost the air of a cosmopolitan city," he adds. The wall and the other barriers surrounding the Western sectors have in fact acted like a noose which each year tightens a little bit more. Berlin, which ever since the unification of Germany in 1871, provided the cultural and political impetus for the entire nation, has been denied its traditional centrical role, not only since 1961, when the wall was built, but ever since 1945, when Germany was effectively sundered. Other cities, like Munich, have become international communities as well, evolving from their role as regional capitals into competitors. They have no wall; their citizens are not hemmed in on all sides; they have a higher standard of living than does Berlin; they make for a peaceful way of life, in which the depressing reality that is East Germany may be forgotten or at least ignored. The main function of Berlin, according to the *Tagesspiegel*'s Dr. Wolfgang Wagner, has been to keep alive the memory of Germany divided. Events have made it impossible for the West to abandon either West Berlin or the East Germans themselves, he says. The biggest contribution of the city is regarded in Bonn as being this: "Berlin makes the status quo in Germany intolerable for everyone."

Yet such a role is not a natural role for a city or its population. As other West German cities continue to grow and prosper, the Berliners are supposed to satisfy themselves with being symbols. The status quo is more intolerable for them than any others.

"I don't have much patience with those good people who believe a special task, function, or mission must be created for Berlin," wrote one champion of the city, Sebastian Haffner. "If there is a single city with more tasks, functions, or missions than it can quickly digest, that is Berlin . . . the toughest city I know," for it survived bombings, the last days of the war, hunger, a blockade, and even a great depression. "Now it's supposed to begin to think about dying?" Haffner asks scornfully. "It won't even consider it!"

There are other Berliners who remain equally optimistic. Always, they proclaim, *"Berlin bleibt doch Berlin!"* They will once again be citizens of the capital of a free, united Germany. One questions this in West Berlin at one's own risk. It is a hopeful and courageous stance and typically Berlinese, but it is not held by everyone any more. Haffner, however, expresses the view of those who regard the future with confidence; referring to Berlin after the unification of Germany takes place, he says:

"Maybe it will once again be rather an ugly, vulgar, loud capital, more controversial than loved. Berlin's manners are everywhere notorious and the city never had much good luck. But, ye Gods, how well bad luck suited it! The years from 1945 until today, and those which stretch yet a little into the future, will always be Berlin's greatest, a time of which one will speak a couple of thousand years hence, a period no one can ever take away from the city. And how proud those Berliners who lived through these times will be a few years or decades from now! Even the fools among them—and make no mistake, they exist—will look like heroic figures in fifty years."

In saying so, he makes the assumption that in fifty years Germany and Berlin will have been reunited. Perhaps they will, but much will have to change for that to happen. The Soviet Union at present is firmly opposed to any reunification that would threaten the "socialistic order" in East Berlin or the G.D.R. There are twenty Russian divisions in East Germany to make sure that does not happen, and most of them are encamped in a ring of iron around Berlin.

chapter sixteen

AFTER THE WALL HAD SUNDERED THEIR CITY, THE BERLINERS longed to roar their defiance of the monstrous barrier. They were given an opportunity to do so, as well as a much-needed boost to their morale, when President John F. Kennedy visited West Berlin in 1963, 149 days before he would be assassinated.

When the Presidential Boeing 707 touched down at Tegel Airfield to a twenty-one-gun salute, Kennedy was accorded an unprecedented reception. Berlin had never seen anything like it before—or has since. No Hitler, no Bismarck, no Kaiser or king had ever received so passionate an outburst of affection from so many. Three-fourths of the population of the Western sectors were out on the streets, cheering, waving, shouting themselves hoarse. A mass delusion had seized them all; they hoped, even believed, that Kennedy would deliver them, not merely give them words to bolster their courage.

"We come to a city," Kennedy said on arriving, "which is three thousand five hundred miles from the United States but we come to a city which we feel to be a part of us." The words were the first expression of a relationship between the Berliners and John F. Kennedy that came to be symbiotic, for the Berliners that day buoyed up his spirits as much as he lifted theirs.

He encountered the Berlin Wall at both Brandenburg Gate and at "Checkpoint Charlie" on the Friedrichstrasse. For reasons best known to themselves, the East Berlin authorities had marked his visit by making this the first time in the history of Berlin that it was even impossible *to see* through the Brandenburg Gate's Doric columns. Five red banners hung between each row, blocking off sight of Unter den Linden. What instead faced Kennedy was a huge yellow sign with large red lettering. The words accused West Germany of violating the 1945 Potsdam pledges against militarism and Nazism. "These pledges have been fulfilled in the German Democratic Republic," the poster shouted. "When will these pledges be fulfilled in West Germany and West Berlin, President Kennedy?"

Similar words greeted Kennedy at Checkpoint Charlie; they decorated the barbed-wire entanglements and the death strip, where the President could see the armed East German N.V.A. guards, and past them, East Berlin itself. Standing atop a platform, he looked two hundred yards east and saw a crowd of people at the Eastern end of the closed border area filling the sidewalk and overflowing into the Friedrichstrasse itself. They didn't cheer or wave as did the West Berliners; their salute to Kennedy was to stand there in the face of the *Vopos'* guns, still and silent, keeping their vigil at the death strip, where many like them had died.

The President left the wooden platform and walked the block back to his motorcade at the Kochstrasse intersection. Hundreds of jubilant, almost hysterical, West Berliners crowded around him; he mingled among them and shook their eager outstretched hands. A hand-lettered sign held on a stick danced above him, calling out, "John—you our best friend!" Confetti and torn pages of telephone books were thrown out of the windows and showered down upon him; a handful hit a German reporter in the face as he was running down the sidewalk, sending him sprawling with his camera.

From Checkpoint Charlie, the Kennedy motorcade moved through streets lined with hundreds of thousands of more Berliners, to visit the Air Lift Memorial at Tempelhof and from there to Rathaus Schöneberg, where the President was to deliver the major address of the day. In the White House press bus, which had the lead position in the motorcade, a Free University student serving as an interpreter turned to the reporter who had fallen down in the crowd, Edwin Roth of the *Tagesspiegel,* who'd flown with Kennedy to Berlin from Wiesbaden that morning.

"There's a first-aid station at the Rathaus," he said. "You can have that wrist looked after the minute we arrive."

Roth nodded, but he knew first aid wouldn't help. He needed an X-ray and then a cast; he'd broken his wrist. At Rudolf Wilde Platz, the Red Cross aid station behind the Rathaus looked like a front-line field hospital. Long rows of unconscious men, women, and children lay around, having fainted after waiting hours in the heat.

Kennedy, meanwhile, had stepped into the Rathaus and asked Mayor Brandt if he could use his office for a few minutes. The reception he'd received, the sight of the wall, and the memory of those East Berliners standing silently watching him at the Friedrichstrasse had moved him deeply. Now he wanted to make some changes in the speech he and Theodore C. Sorensen had prepared in advance. Then he stepped out onto the balcony of the Rathaus. As far as his eyes could see, the square in front of him and the streets leading towards it were packed shoulder-to-shoulder with a solid mass of Berliners.

After introductory speeches by Otto Bach, president of the Berlin House of Representatives, and Chancellor Adenauer, Kennedy addressed the crowd:

"There are some people in the world who really don't understand, or say they don't, what is the great issue between the free world and the Communist world.

"Let them come to Berlin!

"There are some who say that Communism is the wave of the future. Let them come to Berlin!

"And there are some who say in Europe and elsewhere we can work with the Communists.

"Let them come to Berlin!

"And there are even a few who say that it is true that Communism is an evil system, but it permits us to make economic progress.

"*Lass sie nach Berlin kommen!* Let them come to Berlin!"

The crowd, says Schlesinger, "shook itself and rose and roared like an animal" at these remarks.

"I know of no town, no city," Kennedy continued after it had quieted down, "that has been besieged for eighteen years, that still lives with the vitality and the force and the determination of the city of West Berlin . . .

"When all are free . . . the people of West Berlin can take sober satisfaction in the fact that they were in the front lines for almost two decades."

181

Then Kennedy concluded with words no Berliner could ever forget.

"All free men," he said, "wherever they may live, are citizens of Berlin. And, therefore, as a free man, I take pride in the words: *'Ich bin ein Berliner.'* "

When he uttered those words, the men and women in the square below him went wild. Kennedy, who considered most crowds irrational, was at first exhilarated, then troubled by the Berliners' response; on his return, he told his aides in Washington that if he had said "March to the wall and tear it down!", these Berliners would have marched.

Anxious to rectify some of the impressions made at the Rathaus, Kennedy later that day delivered a more restrained address at the Free University, where he stated that "no easy course" to re-unification existed and that only Western strength and unity might bring it about. Again, he received a great ovation, for his presence in the city seemed to symbolize the resolve of which he spoke. When he left at 5:45 P.M., after just eight hours in Berlin, his visit had done more to restore the spirit of the Berliners than any event since the wall went up almost two years earlier.

West Berlin, more than any other European city, was stunned and horrified at the news of his assassination. Without being summoned, tens of thousands of West Berliners that night came to Rathaus Square where he had spoken; plays and films were broken off; night clubs closed; all the neon lights in the city were extinguished. The next day, a carpet of flowers covered the square, all small bouquets brought by Berliners. Mayor Willy Brandt flew to Washington for the funeral and broke down in tears when he met Jacqueline Kennedy; among the heads of state attending, Brandt was a special Kennedy guest, for the President's widow realized John Kennedy had meant it when he said, *"Ich bin ein Berliner."*

If Kennedy's visit helped for a time to dispel much of the fear which Ulbricht's wall had created, the passage of time has done so even more. Most West Berliners now go about their daily affairs trying to ignore its existence as best they can. In District Neukölln, for example, there is a small recreation field where the Landwehr Canal swings northeast into the Spree; here, West Berliners relax, watching the reflection of the trees in the water, the grass and the flowers, apparently oblivious of the skeletal scaffolding of an East Berlin guard tower which looms nearby.

In Neukölln, the fortifications between it and East Berlin's District Treptow run for about ten miles. The district has another six miles of fortified frontier facing not East Berlin but the surrounding countryside of the G.D.R. At Lohmühlen Platz, across the canal from the small Western park, the Berlin Wall juts out like an armored bastion toward Neukölln, swinging about almost full circle to take in the square and then veering off at a right angle to run three blocks along one side of Harzer Strasse. This zigzagging is a reflection of the erratic course Berlin's district lines took when they were established in 1920. Because those were democratic Weimar Republic days, every Berlin property owner made sure he had his say in determining the district boundaries; no one wanted the city to place a factory, block of apartment houses, or vegetable farm half in one district and half in the next, especially as taxes varied from one district to another. The city planners generously obliged and did their best not to sever a man's property; they snaked their boundaries tortuously about the districts, never imagining, of course, that anyone would be so mad as to petrify these border lines into stone. It is for this reason that people unfamiliar with every turning of the wall are forever running smack into it. Touring along this boundary is a little like walking back and forth through a complicated maze, for its path seems to veer in and out continually, fooling you occasionally by running straight for a block or two, only to come around almost full circle to encompass a few buildings. It's been a massive undertaking; the barbed wire tangled around West Berlin would stretch almost long enough to reach from Berlin to San Francisco.

The wall has changed over the years and is now being prettified with flowers and modernized with electronic devices. Soon Ulbricht intends to replace it entirely with a "modern national boundary." On August 13, 1961, it consisted only of barbed wire strung knee-high; then it was made more impassable as this was heightened and the guards were strengthened in number. On August 16th, the first stones were dropped in place. The fact that much of it was being run through city streets made the job easier. The East German authorities were able to brick up the windows of their buildings along the demarcation line, making the houses themselves serve as a barrier. Wherever there was a gap between buildings, of course, they had to erect a stone barrier, but the total length of the Berlin Wall they actually had *to build* runs about nine miles, or about a third the distance. West Berlin statisticians are kept busy compiling data about this border, and the way they have it figured, the cost of materials *alone* comes to about $1,875,000 for the wall and at least $1,625,000 for the barbed wire. Towers, bunkers, searchlights, and construction of a "death strip" comes to another $2,000,000, making for an investment in sterility of $5,500,000; this does *not* count wages paid to construction and demolition workers, the value of the property either bricked up, torn down, or the loss of income from the stores, workshops, and factories affected.

"It was," wrote Pierre Galante and Jack Miller in their book about the wall, "like splitting Manhattan down the middle of Fifth Avenue from the Battery to the Bronx; like splitting London with a zigzag line from Barnet to Croydon. If your home lay one side and your offices the other, you could not go to work. If your mother lived one side and you the other, you could not visit her. The wall might run across your garden and you couldn't go to the toolshed at the bottom."

In fact, few people actually live within one hundred yards of "the other side" of the wall. The reality of the barrier is far more ghastly than one can imagine. It has cut a wide swath through Berlin, leaving everything dead along its Eastern side, as though some defoliated, poisoned ground had been slashed through this urban jungle, allowing nothing to grow but gun emplacements. This stretch is wider where West Berlin faces not the Eastern sectors of the city but the countryside of the G.D.R.; there the "forbidden zone" (*Sperrgebiet*) reaches further into East Germany. Of this, the last ten yards, those closest to West Berlin, constitute the *Todesstreifen,* or "death-strip," and anyone caught on it is shot on sight. Ulbricht's troops have cleared a "forbidden zone" around West Berlin that covers an approximate area of five hundred thousand square yards. Much of this area had to be cleared not only of trees and houses, but also of people, before the N.V.A. could erect its gun emplacements. This required the forcible relocation of many East Berliners, all of them hauled off without warning in early morning hours and brought under heavy guard to temporary East Berlin quarters. Many of their houses were later either bulldozed completely or only the fronts of them were left standing so as to become part of the wall, windows bricked up behind their panes in such a hurry that curtains still fluttered from some of the sealed-up spaces. Later, the fronts of these houses were ripped down to a height of about ten feet, leaving only the ground-floor windows showing.

The Western side of the fortified boundary varies in appearance, depending on whether it runs through a thickly populated residential neighborhood, as it does for about twenty miles, through factory areas, as it does for about ten, or through countryside, as it does for about sixty. In central downtown areas, the Western side of the Berlin Wall tends to look almost as dead as the Eastern side. Because the barrier has created so many dead-end streets, few people want to build along them. Vast stretches of West Berlin along or near the wall remain almost as they looked after the bombing ended, except that all the ruins have been torn down and the rubble either leveled or carted away. The empty fields here contain a few old buildings left over from before the war; looking lonely and somewhat grotesque in these deserted neighborhoods, they await the unification of the city, for urban planners have zoned much of this area of Berlin to reserve it for a brilliant, bright, and modern city center they plan to build some day.

Where the wall cuts through a residential street like Bernauer Strasse, this means that only the Western side continues to have stores, workshops, inhabitants, and a general air of normal life; the houses directly across the street are all empty, the shops deserted, and the rooftops snarled with barbed wire. Recently, they were reduced to house fronts, one story high. Coca-Cola signs stare up at the N.V.A. guard towers and models on advertising posters display the latest in Western girdles and bras to the East German troops. They, for their part, tend to watch impassively as West Berliners pursue business and pleasure in the shade of their wall; very occasionally, if one of their superiors is about, they will gesture their contempt at you, or if no one is watching them, will smile and wave a greeting.

Elsewhere along the wall, Western souvenir shops have sprung up, selling *Dias* transparencies of what has become West Berlin's biggest tourist attraction, post cards, scarves, ashtrays, souvenir

Berlin bears, and such other *Kitsch* as models of Berlin's Eiffel-like *Funkturm,* or radio tower. Touring the wall with a city official one day, I stopped in to buy a roll of film for my camera. He looked the crowded counters over disapprovingly, shaking his head. "We don't like these little souvenir and junk shops one bit!" he announced. "They capitalize on misery and make their money on the outrage of the people who come to the wall."

Every guided tour takes Western visitors to certain sections of the wall such as the Bernauer Strasse and the streets which approach it often seem crowded with shiny, gaily painted excursion buses. Customers clamber up the wooden platforms to peer fixedly across into the death strip, hoping for the thrill of receiving a sinister look from one of the eighteen-year-olds guarding it in East Berlin. Elderly street cleaners patrol the Western sidewalks, searching for tourist litter: empty film boxes, chewing-gum wrappers, cigarette butts, *Schultheiss* beer bottles, and those small, mustard-smeared pieces of cardboard on which the nearby *Wurstläden* hand out their steaming frankfurters. The other side of the wall tends to be neater, for litter presupposes the presence of normal life.

On one of the occasions I visited Lohmühlen Platz, I spoke with a bored middle-aged West Berlin policeman, standing atop a small platform overlooking the wall and the square in which the East Berlin guard tower stands. He rested the submachine gun he had never yet used against his portly frame and watched the equally bored youngsters of East Germany's National People's Army, or N.V.A., who stood no more than twenty feet away from us. One of them tinkered with a motorcycle parked beside the wooden stairs that zigzagged their way up sixty feet to the observation hut; others stood inside the hut itself, their collars open and overseas caps casually shoved to the backs of their heads. One of them swung his binoculars over to get a closer look at us. Another N.V.A. soldier inside the hut leaned against a window, watching the West Berliners sunbathing in the sports field across the canal.

"Those boys exchange a greeting with us sometimes," the Western policeman explained, "if there's no officer around over there. I toss them a pack of cigarettes every now and then; we get a special ration for that purpose, since we want them to be friendly and not consider us enemies. Most of those kids are all right, you know."

Some of the guards throw the cigarettes back over the wall at their Western donors; the policeman said these were true believers —"or maybe they want the others to think they are."

"Most of them are from small towns in Saxony or places like that, or right off the farms," the policeman explained. "Ulbricht tried using East Berlin guard detachments at first, but he soon had to shift them to other places, bringing these farm boys here instead. He found out Berliners can't be trusted to kill Berliners!"

The West German Government regards the killing of people who try to escape the G.D.R. as murder and the border is studded with huge Western placards, held aloft on high wooden frames, which advise the N.V.A. soldiers of that fact. One shows a photograph of a sinister N.V.A. officer and proclaims, "He who orders murders is doubly guilty!", while another is directed at the soldiers themselves, telling them, "Even he who murders on orders is responsible!" The latter seems to be a lesson learned over more than twenty years of war-crimes trials but, while the parallel with Nazi genocide is tempting, many thoughtful Germans question its validity and believe these N.V.A. soldiers cannot legitimately be regarded as murderers so long as other soldiers, representing regimes equally in disfavor, can obey their orders with impunity. Still, the silent accusatory "dialogue" continues over the Berlin Wall, sometimes in tones more seductive than ominous. "Also for you—free elections!" one Western poster advises the guards, while another appeals to them as fellow countrymen, calling out, "We belong together—nothing can separate us!" Ulbricht's posters answer back with charge and countercharge, often pleading for "normal relations" between West and East Germany, which means recognition of Ulbricht's G.D.R. as a sovereign, independent, "second" Germany.

At Harzer Strasse in Neukölln, where the apartment houses on one side have all been evacuated and bricked up, West Berlin children have knocked out portions of the wall between the buildings, making peepholes through which they can look east. What they see on the other side is a field of rubble almost covered with barbed wire, not strung across but simply dumped there in rolls and bales.

I followed this stretch of the Berlin Wall one day, after many a visit to more dramatic sections of the barrier, such as the Brandenburg Gate and Potsdamer Platz, wanting to see the wall within the Berlin neighborhood, as it cut through families and friends living on one side or the other of a residential street. The wall continued down Harzer Strasse until it reached Bouché Strasse, where it made a ninety-degree turn.

Bouché Strasse's boundary with District Treptow is 755 feet long. The apartment houses on its northwest side, the street itself, and both sidewalks, all belong to East Berlin; West Berlin has only the block of flats on the southeast side of this street, a strip of greenery in front of its houses, and a thin walkway between this greenery and the doorways leading to apartments in this block. The wall here was built six feet back from the actual sector border, giving the West Berliners another six feet of elbowroom. Technically speaking—and fine points like this are discussed endlessly in Berlin—the passersby, the residents, and the United States Army Jeeps that patrol this portion of the wall actually trespass on East German territory as they drive down the sidewalk.

The wall on Bouché Strasse is made of two rows of concrete blocks. Passing along the street, you can see nothing below the second-story level of apartment houses in the East; the day I walked here, the only sign of life was an East Berlin boy shining his shoes on a balcony. Some American GI's drove by and waved to him as though they saw him there every day, but it was impossible to tell whether the slight movement of his head was a nod in response. Not many East Berlin families are allowed to live in apartments directly beside the wall, and those who do are for the most part a special, select breed; in any case, a wave westward is *verboten* in East Berlin.

Bouché Strasse's stretch of wall ends at the corner of Heidelberger Strasse, where the barrier again veers off along the latter street. I walked along it until I reached the corner of Sülzhayner and Wildenbruch streets, a few blocks on, where a small colony of gardens, one of Berlin's *Laubenkolonieen,* used to flourish, each of its plots having its own small wooden shack set in amongst the flower and fruit trees. When the border between West and East Berlin was sealed, the barbed wire cut right across these workers' garden plots, and as most of them were located across the district boundary line, in East Berlin's territory, the N.V.A. soldiers soon arrived to raze the entire colony.

As I picked through the undergrowth walking along the very edge of the wall, a retired West Berlin street cleaner, Erich Kops, approached me and told me what had happened. Ulbricht's gray-uniformed gardeners had come, pruning and weeding with bayonets, as Kops and his friends watched. Kops and his wife had always lived in the Western districts of Berlin; now they are separated from Kops' two brothers and their families, all of whom live in East Berlin, a separation shared by seventy percent of all Berliners. Those Neuköllners who here lost their small garden plots represent only a small fraction of the other West Berlin amateur gardeners who lost similar patches because of the division of the city.

At this spot on the border, there are not only guards, but dogs as well, as there are at about 185 other places along the frontier around West Berlin. The dog at this intersection patrols a trench several hundred yards long that the N.V.A. had dug parallel to the wall. Still another dog is stationed about one hundred yards behind this trench at the small East Berlin playground here to keep the children from straying too far west. The dogs are usually hooked onto a dog run, a three-hundred-foot cable stretched between two upright posts, and they patrol their stretch of ground by running back and forth, summer and winter, day and night. One can watch as the N.V.A. soldiers throw them their meat from a safe distance; the dogs, one is informed, are a cross between German shepherds and wolves and many of them are so ferocious that even the East German guards don't wish to approach them.

"When I first heard them howl," a West Berlin policeman stationed at the wall told me, "I shuddered. I was in Russia during the war and those dogs remind me of what the wolves sounded like out there. It's only after awhile, when you watch those dogs every day, that you get to feel sorry for them, especially in winter. They're chained to that cable for the rest of their lives and aren't any more free than anyone else is over there."

At the intersection of Harzer and Onckenstrasse, a few blocks away, a thirteen-year-old West Berlin girl named Inge stood atop a wooden observation platform and peered through the barbed wire into East Berlin. Hair cropped short, slight for her age, and very serious, she stood there silent, just watching. An East Berliner a few feet away was washing his motor scooter in the late afternoon sunlight; two N.V.A. border guards, *Grepos,* patrolled the length of the street, one on each sidewalk, carrying machine pistols.

"Have you ever been over there?" I asked her and she brightened. "Certainly," she replied. "When I was very little. My mother says there's a park, just over there a little bit, in which I used to play. Now we go to the Grunewald." The park she referred to is Treptower Park, which houses the Soviet Army Cemetery. It also has Spree River excursion boats and swimming facilities, as well as the Restaurant Zenner, since 1822 a favorite place for Berliners to eat and sun themselves.

The new "modern frontier" with which Ulbricht is replacing the Berlin Wall is, inevitably, more deadly yet. The first barrier an escapee encounters is an eight-foot wire-mesh or Cyclone-type fence. If he gets past that, he comes upon another "contact fence" a few yards farther on, containing thin wires electrified to set off alarms at the slightest touch. High-intensity searchlights illuminate these barriers and dogs prowl the shadows behind them. The next barrier is a series of trip wires, set to fire off flares. Then comes a ditch filled with barbed wire, and beyond that, a strip of cement along which N.V.A. guards can patrol. Past the walkway and just east of the eight-foot wire-mesh fence between the death strip and West Berlin, the N.V.A. plans to have a strip of carefully raked sand meant to show footprints, and finally, a strip of grass. Presumably this latter is a cosmetic device.

Soldiers from N.V.A. guard units who have escaped to West Berlin (and more than five hundred have done so, with another 1,568 crossing to West Germany) report that every single obstacle along the "modern frontier" was first tested by the G.D.R.'s star athletes. The barriers were heightened, deepened, and broadened until each finally proved impassable, even for the swiftest and most agile East German decathlon champions. Only after being subjected to these gruelling tests were they regarded as good enough to pass.

In the future, even the guards, who know every step of the course, will have a hard time escaping. They have long been forced to operate in pairs and are never permitted to know their partner beforehand. Still some make the break. One guard who did reach safety turned around to see one of the N.V.A.'s guards setting a dog after him. The fierce beast raced through the death strip into West Berlin and charged up to a West Berlin policeman on patrol, who was holding a submachine gun. Seeing the armed man—and possibly mistaking him for one of its own trainers—the dog stopped, sat down, raised its right front leg, and gently offered its paw. The policeman cautiously shook hands and the dog was granted political asylum with the soldier it had pursued.

Like most Europeans, Germans don't easily strike up conversations with strangers, but there are times when they will speak out spontaneously. People caught in a crowd watching a fire or an accident feel a need to share their impressions; people peering through the Berlin Wall seem to feel the same way. This unnatural barrier dissolves formalities and seems to create a kind of kinship.

There are two places in West Berlin where I experienced this often. One was at the Brandenburg Gate and the other at the Potsdamer Platz. Large wooden observation platforms allow a look across into East Berlin at both these points, just as smaller platforms, accommodating only three or four people, dot the Western side of the wall along its entire course. I often came to Potsdamer Platz because, although I was allowed freely to enter and leave East Berlin through the Friedrichstrasse checkpoint reserved for non-Germans, it was impossible for me to approach Potsdamer Platz from the East. What once had the reputation of being Europe's busiest circle is now part of the death strip itself.

"I lived here for forty years!" an old man muttered to me in amazement, one day as I stood atop the platform there. "I live in West Germany now, but I lived near here for forty years! This is the first time I've been back since the wall went up. Just look at that! How it's all changed!"

Over there, where he was pointing for my benefit, once stood the biggest department store in all of Germany, Berlin's famous "Wertheim," founded by Adolf Wertheim and forcibly "Aryanized" into the "AWAG" store under Hitler; it was a palace once, with bronze statues, marble, a "Hall of Onyx," a popular restaurant, and so many fine things to please the eye that the oriental carpet department alone ran to three floors. Walking from it, along the Leipziger Strasse to Dönhoffer Platz, one came to another huge department store, founded by Hermann Tietz in 1912 and later called "Hertie." There were the Hotel and Café Fürstenhof, the Excelsior Hotel, the Palast-Hotel, the Café Josty, the Pschorr-bräuhaus, and the "Haus Vaterland."

Of Wertheim, all that remained at the end of the war was a tiny shop in the cellar, where one could buy paper napkins and painted tiles. Potsdamer Platz then became a center of black-market trading. Since the wall went up, it has become the center of nothing. It is a huge, razed field, as neat and barren as an airport runway, studded only with anti-tank barriers and barbed wire. In the middle of this, there is the old subway entrance, marked *Bahnhof Potsdamer Platz,* sealed up, but with its sign still visible, standing like the marker on a grave.

As I looked at this enormous square, what struck me most about it was the total absence of life. Not even a *Grepo* border guard could be seen patrolling its expanse, although a West Berlin police-man assured me that soldiers were hiding in the square, watching us watch. Still, everything was hushed. Even the hares and rabbits which have recently invaded this cement field, even the rats which I learned infest the ruins nearby, were not in sight. I pictured Potsdamer Platz as I had seen it a few days earlier in an exhibit of paintings by Otto Antoine, a favorite and gifted painter of Berlin's street scenes, and I thought of the hundreds of thousands milling about this square; of the buses, taxis, and trolley cars that snarled themselves hopelessly here, of the tumult and vibrancy of life on all these streets. The silence, emptiness, and desolation seemed dreamlike, as though the place were entranced. Berlin, like the inhabitants of the Sleeping Beauty's palace, is waiting for a prince to hack away the thorny thicket surrounding them; for a time, the Berliners thought the prince was John F. Kennedy.

chapter seventeen

NO ONE, LEAST OF ALL THEIR RUSSIAN OVERLORDS, TRUSTS THE East German border guards on duty around West Berlin. Despite every effort at picking only politically reliable men for this duty, only a minority of the G.D.R.'s guards are convinced supporters of the S.E.D. regime. In fact, even the most politically reliable become unreliable when they come near that frontier. Before Sergeant Thurow escaped to the West, his political commissar, Lieutenant Grunewald, complained to him about just that problem. Not only were trusted guards escaping, he said, but no one in the unit even seemed to care.

"It's come to this," Grunewald groaned, "when Pfc. Liebig deserted today along with the other soldier on patrol with him, not a single person here cared enough to take the name of that traitor down from our honor roll! He's still got his name up there as one of our best and most reliable men!"

All the N.V.A. guards who attempt to escape across the border that they are meant to seal risk death, just as do all other escapees. A good many guards have paid with their lives. One morning at 4:55 A.M., for example, West Berlin customs guards stationed at Brandenburg Gate watched one N.V.A. guard attempt to flee. Some time before, another guard had vaulted the wall under the amazed eyes of dozens of Western tourists, but the barrier at the gate had since been reinforced. This new attempt failed. Three bursts of submachine-gun fire cut the man down across the border near West Berlin's Reichstag Building; he either died instantly or was mortally wounded, for he collapsed in a heap and lay motionless. The soldiers who killed him let him lie there for a full half-hour before they brought a stretcher. Afterward, they dumped him into a truck at Brandenburg Gate and he was driven off down Unter den Linden.

Four months later, two more soldiers, both sergeants, stationed at nearby Stahnsdorf, tried to escape at the Kohlhasen Bridge. One of them was a *Waffenmeister,* or "armorer" charged with maintaining his unit's weapons. The sergeants chose a duty-free day, armed themselves with pistols and submachine guns, and left before dawn, circling through the woods south of Berlin. Three miles before they got to the Kohlhasen Bridge frontier, they encountered their first guard dog and had to kill it to stop its barking. By 6:30 A.M., they had reached the road that connects West Berlin with the village of Steinstücken, one of the two "Berlin exclaves" not contiguous to the city but nevertheless part of West Berlin, and guarded by a token force of American soldiers. The frontier here seemed too heavily guarded and the escapees backed off into the woods and tried to reach the death strip elsewhere, coming upon it close to an N.V.A. guard hut. Here, they ran into another dog, this one chained to a cable. This dog also began to bark noisily and also was killed. The shot, however, had alerted all the guards in the area. Frantic now, the two sergeants began to run backward across the frontier, firing from their submachine guns at the guards now shooting back. They reached a row of six-foot-high tank traps covered with barbed wire; it was here that the older sergeant, the twenty-four-year-old armorer, was hit by five bullets and collapsed, apparently lifeless. His companion tossed away his gun and clambered over the tank barrier, managing to get through three more rows of barbed-wire barriers without being hit. Then he stumbled into a water-filled trench which he thought was part of the G.D.R.'s border fortifications; actually, it was part of a testing area maintained there by West Berlin's Technical University. He had reached freedom. His companion still hung limply in the barbed wire, bleeding to death. A few minutes later, the guards ran to where he lay entangled, grabbed him by the feet, dragged him head down through the sand, and threw him into a truck.

One *Waffenmeister* who was successful was a sergeant who escaped west of the city, at Staaken, near the Berlin district of Spandau. He'd celebrated New Year's Eve with his fiancée, who spent the evening trying to argue him into fleeing, for she wanted to leave, but the sergeant wasn't eager; he thought it too difficult and felt life in the G.D.R. wasn't all that intolerable yet. His views changed by chance. He missed the train back to his unit and his fiancée telephoned the company commander, to explain why he was late. She received a furious tirade over the telephone, coupled with threats that both she and her sergeant would be arrested if he didn't get back immediately. "That does it!" the sergeant snapped. "I've had enough! We're going!" Although unarmed, he took his girl to the border. They managed to flee successfully, in what West Berlin policemen said was "a hail of bullets."

A month later, in February, a hurricane roared through Germany, killing and injuring scores of people, damaging 313 East Berlin buildings—and destroying six G.D.R. watchtowers as well as ripping up many border barriers. The winds also swept a twenty-two-year-old border guard to freedom. The month after that, during March, another young sergeant and a private clambered over the wall at the Bernauer Strasse in broad daylight, apparently unobserved. Another guard, stationed at the wall at Rudower Strasse, disabled the submachine guns of the two other soldiers in his watchtower and fled successfully while they watched, unable to do anything about it; another sergeant at the Sandkrug Bridge ordered the private on patrol with him to "check over there," and while his back was turned, dashed across the frontier. Even more dramatic was the escape of two guards one Sunday afternoon the following November, near the Tutzinger Strasse. Seeing two policemen on the West Berlin side of the frontier, the guards unobtrusively indicated to them with hand signals that they were about to make a dash for the border. The policemen immediately took cover, aimed their weapons, and prepared to return fire if any shots entered West Berlin territory. The two guards then dashed for the barbed-wire entanglements, hacked at them with their submachine guns, and climbed over them, ripping clothes and skin. Soldiers in a watchtower three hundred yards away spotted them and fired eight bursts of thirty to forty rounds, some of which hit West Berlin. The Western policemen opened up with their own submachine guns, shooting warning bursts past the tower. In the midst of all this, the two escapees managed to flee, under fire crossing them from both directions. Seventeen days later, after several other guards had escaped elsewhere in Berlin, two more climbed down from a watchtower near West Berlin's district Zehlendorf and not only turned themselves but a surprising amount of equipment over to the West Berlin policemen, getting through with side-arms, submachine guns, flare pistols, a considerable supply of ammunition, and even a light Soviet-made machine gun recently issued to border guard units. Shortly after that, the G.D.R. ordered two-man patrols abandoned wherever possible in favor of three-man patrols. It wasn't enough for one guard to watch his companion on duty; now a third was assigned to watch them both.

The number of East German soldiers, including border guards, who have fled for the West is staggering. In the first ten years of the existence of the National People's Army, twenty thousand soldiers fled west: two thousand every year, 166 every month, eleven every two days—or about one soldier every four and one-half hours! All these guards were interrogated in the West and asked their motive for fleeing. Of 546, four admitted they fled because they were about to be punished, eight because they wanted an economically better life, eleven for family reasons, thirty-one for political motives, and thirty-three for sundry other causes. But an overwhelming 459 said their duties, specifically shooting refugees, proved intolerable.

Aware of the way his people feel about the sealed frontier and the order to kill escapees, the East Berlin regime continually tries to justify both. "Every nation," says Alfons Steiniger, professor of international law at East Berlin's Humboldt University, "has the right to prohibit its citizens to travel into certain other countries." Whether nations do indeed have such a *right* is something about which jurists are not yet satisfied. The G.D.R.'s legal journal, *Neue Justiz,* calls an unauthorized attempt to leave the country "an act of terror," punishable by up to fifteen years imprisonment. The defense minister, General Karl-Heinz Hoffmann, told S.E.D. delegates from a border-guard unit that "class-conscious" reasoning demands that weapons be used against "all enemies who touch our border—and anyone who tries to break through our frontier is our enemy." His deputy, Admiral Waldemar Verner, says, "Our socialistic order is more worth defending than any other; the use of weapons to do so is not only just, but also humane!" As for the idea that his Germans kill their "fellow countrymen," Ulbricht answered that bitter accusation by saying, "some of our citizens were of the opinion that crossing the border between the G.D.R. and West Germany meant exchanging one part of Germany for the other, while actually they exchanged the socialist camp for the imperialist camp . . ."

The press in East Berlin is also kept busy drumming up statements of support for those who kill escapees. *Neues Deutschland,* the official S.E.D. organ, quoted Hellmuth Hermann, identified as living near the border at the Heinrich-Heine-Strasse crossing point, and thus presumably a trusted East Berlin functionary, as saying, "The West would like to seduce us with the argument that the border ought to be open for everyone. Those words don't impress any of us who live in the border area itself. We have wonderful ties of friendship with our border guards. They use their guns to protect the fruits of our work." Major Günter Engmann, appearing on an East Berlin TV program entitled "Shots from the Neighbor" (*"Schüsse vom Nachbarn"*), was equally enthusiastic. The truth, he said, has finally come out: The wall not only prevents the plundering of the G.D.R. and an aggressive war, but the whole world now knows that shots at the frontier are arranged by the West whenever it feels that tensions have eased too much!

The order to shoot escapees does not actually exist, according to Ulbricht. He claimed in an address before the 12th plenary meeting of the S.E.D.'s central committee in April, 1966, that no "alleged command to shoot" exists, only "certain rules regulating the use of weapons, especially of firearms." This semantic exercise fools none of the guards, of course, for they all have orders to shoot anyone "attacking installations belonging to the armed forces." Anyone trying to force his way through their barriers is regarded as doing just that.*

Many guards deliberately score low at target practice so that they can have an excuse to miss at the frontier. In one unit, train-

* There are secret regulations which have never been published in East Germany and which unit commanders must keep locked up, that specifically order guards to shoot. The first is Service Regulation III/2 of the Frontier Police, superseded in 1962 by the N.V.A.'s Regulation DV-30/10 and 30/9. Paragraph 210 of Regulation 30/10 specifically refers to the course of action soldiers are to take after killing in the line of duty. One of the rules is to let the dead (or presumed dead) "lie on the spot, without any change" until company headquarters are notified.

ing at Mühlhausen, every single man missed the bull's eye and all got reprimands. They call these their *Fahrkarte* (ticket) to West Berlin, if they ever decide to escape.

A great effort is made through para-military and youth organizations to improve the scores at target practice. All youngsters who score well discover later that, if they miss an escapee at the frontier, they are sent to prison for complicity in that escape. *"Schiess-sport ist Volkssport!"* ("The people's sport is shooting!") Ulbricht's propagandists proclaim.

The border guards are also inundated with political instruction, which aims at reducing the rate of defection. Much of it seems of questionable value, according to the escaped guards. Sergeant Thurow's own experience at one political lecture provides an example.

Asked to speak about the Moscow 22nd party congress, Thurow restricted himself to reading out the report *Neues Deutschland* devoted to the subject, an exercise he delivered in a monotone for over an hour. After this, there was a political discussion. Thurow at one point referred to "progress the G.D.R. had made under socialism" when a soldier from the back of the room interrupted him to ask, "Why isn't there any pepper in the G.D.R.?"

"We had to spend a lot of money for the barbed wire, cement posts, and other measures taken on August 13th," Thurow replied. "That had its effect on our economy. The barbed wire had to be bought from Czechoslovakia with foreign exchange . . ."

"Not so!" shouted Party Secretary Wilcke who had just entered the room. "The equipment for securing the border didn't cost much at all! The barbed wire was already here. The blame for poor food supplies here can be charged to those lying Western broadcasts. Whenever RIAS broadcasts a false report that salt is in short supply, then uninformed people begin to hoard it, and even the strongest economy couldn't survive that!" Having said this, Wilcke ordered the question-and-answer period ended and sent the soldiers out of the hall.

On another occasion, a soldier in that company had rashly blurted out, *"I'd* never shoot at my brother!", meaning a fellow German; he was hounded by S.S.D. secret policemen and political officers until he retracted that statement.

Political discussions and a good deal of assigned political study tend to stretch the border guards' days out beyond the hours they're supposed to be on duty, and help make life pretty unpleasant for them. What with the informers who infest the barracks, the S.S.D. officers who interrogate them to ferret out the disaffected, and the constant political supervision, it is difficult for officers and noncoms to keep morale up in the border-guard companies, despite somewhat preferential treatment.

Regulations are severe, voluminous, and cover every eventuality. Rules regarding the use of their weapons are especially detailed. Former regulations against shooting into West Berlin have been relaxed and guards are now permitted to fire at escapees even after they've reached Western soil, so long as a hill or similar obstruction behind the defector exists to stop the bullets. The procedure whereby a warning shout is followed by a warning shot before the escapee is actually fired upon has also been relaxed. Guards are now told to fire directly any time they feel a warning would be a waste of time. If their shots attract West Berlin civilians or officials to the scene, the guards have orders to cease firing toward the West, but there remain some instances when N.V.A. regulations allow them to shoot at even West Berliners. These arise when such people try to aid a refugee, possibly a wounded one, who lies entangled in the barbed wire just east of the border line. Should a Red Cross official or anyone else try to cut the refugee loose, the guards have orders to fire on them to prevent such an "attack on the G.D.R. frontier." The only Westerners whom the guards are never under any circumstances allowed to fire upon are United States, British, or French soldiers. A deliberate fear of West Berlin's police is also inculcated into the guards; they are falsely told such policemen will shoot at them to provide cover for escapees, and are ordered in such cases to fire above the policemen's heads so as to force them to take cover. They aren't told that the police are actually under orders to provide cover only for escapees who have actually reached West Berlin soil.

They are forbidden to have the slightest contact with anyone across the border. Thurow provides the story of a drunken American soldier who came up to the barbed wire across from where Thurow and a slow-witted private were patrolling and who whistled at them to come closer. This happened just after Thurow's unit had been warned that GI's would throw stones and bricks, trying "to provoke" the border guards. Sure enough, this tipsy soldier was indeed heaving things over at Thurow, yelling, "Hey, is that your idea of a democratic Germany?" Thurow saw what it was that he was throwing and immediately told his companion to take cover. The GI had been pelting him with cigarettes. Thurow picked them up, shoved them in his pocket, and then threw some stones at a small East German building behind him, breaking a windowpane and frightening his companion half to death. At reveille next morning, Thurow was surprised to be called before the entire company and cited for heroism in standing his ground while "American gangsters" had attacked with stones.

Seven other border guards were not so lucky. Suspected of fraternizing across the frontier, they were surrounded and arrested on the spot, some of them caught red-handed with Western chocolates and cigarettes, two noncommissioned officers among them. They were tried, convicted, and sentenced to from four to eight years each. In another case, reported by *Volksarmee,* the G.D.R. army newspaper, a sergeant and three soldiers had accepted cigarettes and bottles of beer. In tones of outrage, *Volksarmee* reported that one of them had tried to excuse his contact with the Western guards by saying, "I thought those fellows were just doing their jobs, like we were doing ours!" All seven were convicted and sent to jail.

If considerable punishment awaits those who act human, the rewards given to those who act inhuman are also impressive. Soldiers who refuse to be seduced by Western smiles or cigarettes and who are willing to shoot to kill receive bonuses and gifts. In Thurow's company, cash prizes and extra furloughs were handed out. One young border guard who escaped, Peter Hagens, tells of promotions and other rewards as well. Speaking at a West Berlin press conference organized by Dr. Rainer Hildebrandt's "Thirteenth August Working Association," Hagens said that he was the only one, except for the killers, who watched on December 13, 1963, as two border guards brutally murdered twenty-four-year-old Dieter Berger near the Teltow Canal in Berlin. Berger, he said, had stopped after the first warning shot was fired; he had even turned back, obviously to surrender. Despite this, two guards named Reiner Schäfer and Dantz continued shooting at him, even after he had crawled back East, wounded, for more than thirty feet. Berger died on the way to the hospital. The two guards, members of the 42nd border regiment, were summoned to East Berlin's city commandant, General Poppe, who promoted them and gave them each a *Leistungsmedaille,* a medal for "meritorious achievement." Schäfer was more meaningfully rewarded in that his request for transfer away from the border guards was granted.

Civilians also receive ample rewards for giving information about escapes. Such informers are called *Grenzhelfer,* or "border aides," and receive $37.50 for each escapee successfully betrayed, plus an electric razor or a woman's handbag, depending on their sex. (Informed sources say they also receive additional monthly pension, once retired.) The number of youngsters, most enrolled in the S.E.D.'s "Ernst Thälmann Pioneers," who have denounced escapees has so far come to about twenty. A Berlin schoolboy, fifteen years old, was one of these. He had spotted a man lurking about some ruins near the Berlin Wall and had called a People's Policeman; he was given a bicycle by way of reward, plus a certificate suitable for framing. In another case, which aroused the outrage of West Berliners even more, a "Thälmann Pioneer" named Jutta Baum turned in three men who'd asked her about the lay of the frontier; all three were seized and imprisoned. The G.D.R.'s press showered Jutta with praise for her patriotic act; in West Berlin, the *Berliner Morgenpost,* hardly noted for restraint in describing such people, chose in this case to pity rather than condemn the girl. It summed up her well-meaning, if tragic, action in an editorial headlined, "Poor Child," and noted that Jutta Baum was only eleven years old.

It isn't only members of S.E.D. mass organizations who are dragooned into this kind of work; anyone in a position to ferret out a potential escapee is forced to cooperate in preventing "flights from the republic." The "stewardesses," for example, aboard the G.D.R.'s holiday ship *Fritz Heckert* are under orders to spy on passengers and search their luggage for items which might point to escape plans. The ship's master, Captain Eckholz, and its political officer, a functionary named Thomas, told the girls to look for inflatable life belts and swim vests, food preserves, clotheslines, and flashlights, any or all of which would indicate an attempt to leave the G.D.R.'s holiday cruise at some foreign port. They were also warned that they'd be regarded as "accomplices" in the escape, if passengers occupying cabins assigned to their care did manage to flee.

One of East Berlin's most famous escape attempts occurred in the early afternoon hours of August 17, 1962. At 2:12 P.M. that day, two eighteen-year-olds tried to reach West Berlin over the wall two blocks away from Checkpoint Charlie. East Berlin guards spotted the two young men and fired at them. One got into West Berlin safely, but the other was hit. His name was Peter Fechter.

This boy, whose last-known address was Behamstrasse 11 in the East Berlin district of Weissensee, lay severely wounded between the barbed wire and the wall, in full view of both East Berlin guards and a crowd of angry, despairing West Berliners who had quickly gathered. He lay there, slowly bleeding to death. The border guards, among them at least one officer, didn't budge; they didn't examine the extent of his wounds, didn't give him medical aid, nor call an ambulance. As the minutes ticked by, Fechter called out repeatedly for help in a voice racked with pain. With each cry, the West Berlin onlookers grew more horrified. Some ran to the American Military Police station at Checkpoint Charlie, urging, pleading—even demanding—that a military ambulance come to rescue the boy. West Berlin policemen threw bandages over the wall to Fechter, but he was too weak to make use of them; he lay crumpled, legs pulled up, on his right side, with his back pressed against the wall.

At about 3:10 P.M., or 58 minutes after he'd been hit, the East Berlin guards went into action. They tried to throw a smoke screen around Fechter, presumably to hide themselves while they retrieved his body; in the course of this action, they also heaved ten tear gas grenades into the West Berlin crowd on the other side of the wall. An American MP Jeep, which had earlier driven up beside the police, now pulled away as the fumes began to spread. Overhead, a United States Army helicopter circled the area, keeping headquarters informed. West Berlin policemen responded to the gas attack by throwing ten tear-gas canisters of their own back at the East Berlin guards, but none of these actions of course could help Fechter any more. By the time two steel-helmeted N.V.A. soldiers and a People's Policeman retrieved Fechter's limp body, they didn't even bother using a stretcher. If Fechter wasn't dead, he was dying. The entire incident, taking about one hour, had been played out not only in front of the Berliners, but also in front of news photographers; the tense and apprehensive faces of those N.V.A. guards concerned in the affair were captured for all posterity and splashed all over the West Berlin (and the world) press the next day. These pictures and the minute-by-minute account of Fechter's hour-long unattended agony sparked five days of tumultuous mass-protest demonstrations in West Berlin. On the third day, these became so violent that West Berlin police needed to use force against the rampaging mobs of Berliners and had to seal off the entire West Berlin area around Checkpoint Charlie, where the killing had taken place. A wave of outrage washed over the Americans in West Berlin as well. The failure of the United States Army to send an ambulance to aid Fechter infuriated the Berliners. "Coming on top of our inability to stop the construction of the wall in 1961," an American State Department officer told me, "the Fechter incident sent United States prestige down to a new low."

One question highlighted by the Fechter incident was whether or not the Eastern border guards involved were liable to murder charges in the West. In fact, the *Schiessbefehl*—the G.D.R.'s secret order to shoot escapees—has resulted in more oratory in the West than trials. Only one border guard, a slow-witted twenty-two-year-old named Fritz Hanke, has actually stood trial and been imprisoned for killing an escapee. A member of the 42nd border regiment, Hanke was stationed at West Berlin's Teltow Canal and there killed Max Sahmland, thirty-seven, a farmer from Wildau, who had slipped into icy January waters to swim to West Berlin. The body was recovered two months later with seven bullets in it. Hanke's responsibility came to light afterward. Apprehended after he himself had escaped, Hanke was sentenced to fifteen months' imprisonment, less as punishment, the court indicated, than to let him "repent" his sins.

Only one other East German border guard has even been summoned for trial. This was Fritz Lange, charged with forcing two refugees who had already crossed into the West to turn back at gunpoint; Lange, however, never showed up for his trial in Lüneburg on August 31, 1965, and it was recessed after two hours;

a few days later, he sent the court word that he'd returned to East Germany.

Those two cases neatly sum up the dilemma: Almost none of those who killed escapees are caught or can be brought to trial, while those who are tried often seem to be more trouble than they're worth. It simply hasn't been resolved yet whether soldiers following military orders can honestly be tried for "murder," though it should be noted that the general public and the more sensational papers have no doubts about the matter. They echo the simplistic formulation of C.D.U. politician Reiner Barzel: "Murder is murder and murderers remain murderers!"

Just in case the issue is ever settled, the Germans are ready, having for years painstakingly kept detailed records and files. Like the office at Ludwigsburg that compiles records of Nazi war crimes, they have established an office at Salzgitter for the G.D.R. In addition, West Berlin's district attorney maintains records of his own, as he is regarded by the West Berlin Government as being responsible for *all* Berlin, the Eastern sector included.

The ultimate responsibility may never be determined. It's easy enough to say it lies with Walter Ulbricht; it may lie with the Soviets instead—or with something as impossible to try as the Cold War. Dr. Hans Dichgans, an eminent West German jurist, wrote in the *Neue Juristische Wochenschrift* (*New Legal Weekly*) that he believes Western courts can't claim jurisdiction over border guards, no matter what they do, simply because whatever sovereignty may exist in the G.D.R., it is not German. Ulbricht's Government, he says, must be regarded as a modified form of an occupation regime, and just as German courts cannot try cases involving arbitrary commands issued by Western occupation authorities, they can't claim jurisdiction over the Soviet-imposed Ulbricht regime either.

After the trial of Hanke, Dichgans noted that no new border guards who had anything on their conscience escaped to the West; indeed, guards are told that "revenge-thirsty" West Germans regularly imprisoned soldiers who flee the G.D.R. Any visitor to the wall in West Berlin can note the guards' apprehensiveness. Watch one even through binoculars and he'll face you unflinchingly; let him see you train a camera lens at him and he'll either turn his back or slip a hand casually over his face, as though to scratch his cheek or rub his jaw. The guards are camera-shy; none of them want Salzgitter or the West Berlin district attorney to have snapshots of them on file.

It is vital that they be better informed, says a West Berlin association of former N.V.A. border guards, and it has called upon the city's radio and TV stations to assure them they'll be well-received. City officials agree, for the Berliners by and large have a clearer picture of the guards' dilemma than do politicians outside Berlin, expressing outrage from the safety of distant Rhineland offices. To be sure, the mass-circulation newspapers in West Berlin for the most part denounce the guards furiously and many West Berliners find it absolutely impossible to see the guards as anything but their deadly enemies. The more thoughtful among them, however, try to approach the problem with understanding. When Willy Brandt was mayor, he urged West Berliners who had received G.D.R. passes to enter East Berlin to develop friendly relations with any guards they met. "Let's not build any additional artificial walls of our own," he pleaded over the radio.

Heinrich Albertz, his successor for a time, broadcast an appeal directly to the border guards a few days after West Berliners were particularly horrified by new deaths at the wall.

"Especially in the light of recent events," Albertz said, "it's become even more difficult for me to defend you soldiers of the border brigades in and around Berlin against being characterized as devils, against all form of generalizations and accusations. For years, I've refused to see every one of you as a murderer, criminal, or enemy. For me, you were, are, and remain my fellow countrymen, burdened by a heavy conflict of conscience and unable to evade pressures put on you . . .

"In the name of the Berliners, in the name, therefore, of your fellow countrymen, I appeal to you to prepare an end to these murders! I call upon the functionaries to lift the order to shoot and I ask my own fellow citizens in Berlin—despite all their bitter experiences and no matter how hard they may find it to do so—to regard you, the soldiers of the border brigades, as their fellow Germans."

It is clear to many thoughtful Berliners that the question of responsibility may never be solved legally, but only politically. In 1966, when an exchange of speakers between the West's

205

S.P.D. and the East's S.E.D. was considered, many West Germans said that if Ulbricht came to West Germany to speak he ought to be arrested for murder the moment he stepped across the frontier. It was around this time that *Der Spiegel* ran a Rudolf Augstein editorial that had some sharp comments about the issue.

"Ulbricht's border guards," Augstein wrote, "are no more murderers than are Johnson's soldiers in Viet Nam." Then he asked in heavy irony why so much fuss was being made just because these particular Germans shot straight and didn't miss their targets. "I have seldom heard of Germans deliberately missing the target if, for example, they're to stop someone smuggling coffee across the border or shoot innocent Belgian hostages, charged with crimes they never committed.

"As we are great at collecting files, we in West Germany have put together criminal charges against several hundred People's Policemen, have even legally sentenced one such poor fish, but when it comes to their chief, whom the Federal Supreme Court says is directly responsible, we'll allow him to come here if he will to address a mass rally. Can this still be called normal?"

The last question posed poses the problem. Nothing's "normal" when it comes to the sealed border—and the position of the West Berliners sealed *inside* a box made of barbed wire, is least normal of all. "We are split and schizoid," a West Berliner told me. "No wonder so much of what happens here seems mad."

No people, not even the Berliners, can maintain a steady state of moral outrage at the same level of intensity over many years, yet whenever some of them begin to feel inured to the killings, something happens to arouse their indignation again. Some deaths are reported as dryly as battlefield casualties, especially if the precise details are unknown, and these, of course, don't infuriate Berliners as much as do the more "dramatic" killings, such as Fechter's. Reading about them in brief news items in their morning papers, under headlines announcing "Another Killing at the Wall," they are left feeling somewhat sick over their breakfasts of bread and jam, but not so that it spoils their day. So long as the killings are "routine," they can even entertain thoughts about coming to terms some day with Ulbricht's regime, but then a more dramatic incident always occurs.

206

Two killings that particularly outraged the Berliners took place on March 14, 1966, at the Kiefholzstrasse section of the wall, between District Treptow and West Berlin's Kreuzberg. At about 7:10 P.M., border guards fired at two East Berliners trying to cross the death strip near S-Bahn station Planterwald. A few minutes afterward, an East Berlin ambulance came to the scene. Two days later, information reached the West that the two East Berliners who tried to escape had been brought to a hospital severely wounded and that they died shortly afterward. Both victims were children, one thirteen and the other ten years of age.

Again in January, 1967, Berlin tempers passed the boiling point because two escapees were killed *after* they had already reached West Berlin territory safely. This, says *Der Tagesspiegel,* was "one of the worst incidents since the construction of the wall." The stretch of Teltow Canal near the Wrede Bridge where these killings took place belongs entirely to West Berlin, as do both banks of the channel, yet the border guards pursued the escapees through the barrier, onto West Berlin's narrow, grassy "towing path" that runs along the Eastern bank of the canal between the barbed-wire frontier and the water, seized one of the escapees, and killed two others. One man had swum across the 150-foot-wide canal to within about nine feet of the Western bank when he was killed, just a moment after he had called out to three West Berlin workers from the nearby Eternit Plant for help. They held out a long pole for the man to grab, but it was at this moment that the guards fired across the channel at the escapee in the canal and at his would-be rescuers. They took cover; when they emerged, the refugee had vanished under the water. The third man, who had not been seized, was observed by the West Berliners to slip into the water, from which he never emerged. All this happened at 2:20 A.M. and, by the time the West Berlin police *Einsatzkommando* had arrived, it was all over. They shone searchlights across the river at the border guards and ordered them off the eastern bank; after the command was repeated once more, the guards finally withdrew through their barbed wire. Then the West Berlin policemen went across and found a trail of blood leading from the barbed wire over the grass to the water's edge. It was clear that the second man to enter the canal had been hit before he ever reached it.

Other attempts to cross the waterways surrounding West Berlin occur when least expected, in the bitter cold of winter. Such an exercise takes stamina and a good many who succeed are young and vigorous. Because these escapees swam through almost-freezing water, they all had to be taken to the hospital. One young man who was fired upon told police afterward that he'd made no advance plans to flee.

"I just suddenly decided to chance it," he said. "I guess sometimes someone just has to have luck!" Asked why he fled, he said he found life intolerable under the S.E.D.'s rule, as did many of his friends. "But my particular problem," he explained, "was that I just couldn't keep my mouth shut about it!"

It isn't often that Berliners can experience a sense of triumph over Ulbricht's guards, but it does happen occasionally. A dramatic recent case concerned a pretty, twenty-five-year-old stenographer named Ursula who had fallen in love with a Frenchman visiting her hometown, Leipzig. The Frenchman wanted to marry her and tried to get her a G.D.R. exit visa. Not only was this denied but, as soon as the application was made, Ursula was placed under close surveillance. Anxious to join her lover, she decided to try to escape. On September 21, 1965, near the Friedrichsbrücke, she slipped unobserved onto an East German barge loaded with G.D.R. sand meant for West Berlin and hid under a tarpaulin weighted down with coal briquettes. A few hours later, an East German tug, the *Johannes,* pulled the 120-foot barge through East Berlin's border inspection; despite a close check of its cargo, Ursula's presence wasn't discovered. A little while later, the stowaway peeked out and, seeing West Berlin's Reichstag and Congress Hall buildings, knew she'd reached the Spree's West bank. At that moment, the tug's captain and his wife spotted the girl, immediately released their towlines, swung the tug around, sped over to where she was, and jumped aboard the barge to grab her. A few West Berlin fishermen, dangling their lines into the Spree, saw the girl struggling to free herself and called nearby customs guards. As these hurried over, the girl managed to wrest herself loose from her captors and leap into the water. She reached safety, "her whole body trembling," as the customs guards said, and was taken to their office and wrapped in a blanket. Meanwhile, West Berlin's "Political Police" had arrived. They arrested the captain and his wife on charges of attempted kidnapping.

"What do you mean?" the tug's captain protested. "I was just trying to stop her from jumping in the water. After all, I had no idea whether she could swim!"

Like all successful escapes, this one served to tighten security measures. Seven weeks later, two men and a woman tried the same means, hiding under a load of East German gravel. They were discovered and arrested. The guards had learned their lesson.

The waterways connecting West Berlin with West Germany are reserved for goods traffic; passengers take either road, rail, or air routes (all of which carry freight as well). The West has pledged itself to maintain free access along these routes, for each is an umbilical cord nourishing the city. Almost fifty percent of all those who travel to and from West Berlin use the *Autobahn* highways to Hamburg, Hanover, Frankfurt am Main, and Munich. These annually carry 2,800,000 travelers in almost 860,000 vehicles, or more people than live in all the Western sectors. Private cars are augmented by the almost fifty bus companies that compete in the tourist traffic to and from West Berlin, running 250 buses a day during the peak holiday season. Commodities and industrial products also roll in and out of West Berlin, and are as sharply controlled by the East German border guards as are passengers. Much of this traffic earns the G.D.R. a great deal of valuable Western currency, for shippers on the waterways and anyone using the roads in and out of West Berlin pay tolls and taxes. The "road-use tax" alone has earned Ulbricht more than 400 million West German marks, and while it is said to be for "road maintenance," Western agencies believe these funds actually finance espionage, propaganda, and subversion in West Germany. This is just one of the reasons why Bonn insists that its officials and their families always travel to West Berlin by air. They don't want them to finance subversive activities, much less risk possible harassment, detention, or arrest; furthermore, Bonn rejects Ulbricht's claim that the G.D.R. is a legitimate state and insists it doesn't want its officials' passports inspected, much less stamped, by Ulbricht's men. The G.D.R. earns even more money today, for in 1968 it began treating West Germans as it does all foreigners, in that it charges them a transit visa fee; new levies of goods and public transport were also added. Estimates of how much the G.D.R. may earn by means of the new regulations vary up to about $50 million each year.

Travelers grumble about the new charges, but still millions travel to and from West Berlin on the three *Autobahn* routes leading through the G.D.R. The experienced traveler is sanguine; those making the trip for the first time are often filled with trepidation. Incidents do occur en route, but they are rare. As a matter of fact, the only advice Western authorities feel compelled to give you before you enter the G.D.R.'s stretch of *Autobahn* is that you later report any incident you may have observed (so as to warn and aid future travelers); they also offer the unofficial suggestion that you "fill-'er-up" in West Germany rather than in the G.D.R., if you value your car's engine.

Those who come at night to the Marienborn checkpoint on the *Autobahn* from Hanover to West Berlin and who have never been there before are likely to discover that the border area here is particularly beautiful, for a string of glittering lights rises and falls over the hills in the countryside. In daytime, this proves to be an illusion created by the searchlights along the border's death strip. It is not the only bizarre aspect of the frontier here. The signs, as you speed through the Western checkpoint read, "Welcome to the German Democratic Republic"; they are gaily flanked by huge G.D.R. national flags and by red banners, but also by barbed-wire fortifications and watchtowers. Passing them, you come upon your first East German soldier, who politely waves you to a building where you present your passport for control. This guard barracks has segregated entrances for Germans and foreigners. Ulbricht's regime likes to harrass the West Berliners and West Germans and sometimes keeps them in queues for hours, but tends to process non-Germans with courtesy and dispatch. Inside the barrack, your passport is slipped through a small slit in the wall and afterward slipped back by some unseen and unknown official who made sure your name isn't on the black list. You declare all currency and such valuables as cameras, binoculars, and radios, and then pay the road tax. The guards then stamp your passport with a G.D.R. transit visa, using up an entire page each time. The whole procedure often takes less than half an hour for non-Germans, allowing you time in the waiting room to leaf through the literature advertising holidays at East German health resorts, visits to the Leipzig Fair, all filled with photos of happy, productive citizens of "democratic Germany."

There are still two or three more passport checks as you drive in a slalom course through the border area, but all except the last of these are perfunctory. Just before you finally get through the border and onto the G.D.R.'s *Autobahn,* your passport is given another of those mysterious inspections. You pass it through a slot in a small wooden shack, large enough only for one man to be seated inside. The shack has no windows that are visible to a driver and you suspect the guard inside must roast on a hot summer day. If, indeed, there *is* someone inside, for no words are exchanged between the guard next to your car and this Mysterious Presence, nor can you see even a hand returning the passport; it just slides out silently, as though by itself.

The entire enclave containing the passport-control sheds and guardrooms is about one hundred yards long and seems to be hollowed out of the solid barbed wire surrounding it; every driver experiences a sense of relief getting through it, even though it leads into East Germany proper. A slip of paper the border guard hands you and which you are later to surrender shows the time you left this checkpoint and allows the guards at the other end to know when you should have reached them. Any undue delay on the journey must be accounted for to their satisfaction, perhaps by presenting to them a receipt from one of the *Autobahn*'s *Mitropa* restaurants, proving you stopped for an expensive bite to eat in the G.D.R. Few people, however, do.

Aside from Western cars, traffic is light through the G.D.R. You see few East German vehicles on the road, except perhaps a few antiquated trucks, one or two agricultural vehicles, and perhaps a half-dozen Wartburg passenger cars. As all cars in Europe carry a nationality plaque above their rear license plates ("D" for Deutschland, "GB" for Great Britain, and so on), our own car carried a "USA" plaque. It elicited smiles and waves from East Germans on every trip through the G.D.R., usually making us feel oddly unhappy, as though we should apologize to these people for not having helped them in any way.

The signs "Berliner Ring" become more numerous after an hour and a half and presently you approach the tightly sealed border between East Germany and West Berlin. Again your papers are all checked and another invisible presence examines your passport. Here, however, you are asked to leave your car, open up the trunk, the engine compartment, and even the glove compartment. You lift up the seats of your car to show there is no secret compartment underneath in which an escapee might hide. If, as in our case, a tarpaulin covers luggage on the roof rack, it needs to be removed, to show there are only suitcases and no human beings under that. You drive past a mirror shoved under your car to make sure you're not transporting an escapee tied down there. The border guard who does the inspecting is friendly, at least to non-German travelers, and sometimes even smiles a bit sheepishly as he thanks you for your cooperation.

I spoke about this one day in West Berlin with a Swiss novelist who told me of his own first experience on the *Autobahn*. Unfamiliar with procedures and wanting only to hurry for a day's visit to Brunswick across the West German border, he hadn't expected he would need a permit for the brief trip. When he got to the G.D.R. checkpoint outside West Berlin, a border-guard officer insisted he should have obtained a visa to enter East Germany, these being obtainable in East Berlin's Ministry for Foreign Affairs, behind Unter den Linden's *Zeughaus,* that old Prussian armory. The young Swiss blew up and demanded not to be kept waiting; he insisted that the guard get authorization to let him through by telephoning "East Berlin."

"You mean," the guard officer corrected him sternly, "the Capital of the German Democratic Republic!"

The Swiss nodded to get this nonsense over with, but ultimately lost his patience and told the officer to stop the *Scheissdreck* ("all this shit").

"I'm sorry," the officer replied. "Just between us, I think all these permits are *Scheissdreck* also, but I've got my orders."

"For heaven's sake," the Swiss author demanded, "can't you trust me?"

"You know, my friend," the officer replied with a sly smile, "faith is good; trust is also good. But *Kontrolle* [controls]—that's best of all!"

There used to be eighteen Berlin trains each day just to Frankfurt am Main; today, there are two trains only and the trip, what with all the inspections, takes twice the time. Berlin, once the rail hub of central Europe, has become a siding. As expected, the big postwar increase has been in highway and air travel. Flights are popular not just because the trip is short but because air passengers aren't checked by any Eastern border guards. They're also cheap, fares into (but not out of) West Berlin being partly subsidized by the city government to encourage immigration and tourism.

Even seasoned travelers are particularly impressed by Tempelhof Airport. Like so many other aspects of Berlin and Berlin life, this field is unique and usually surprises newcomers. Its enormous terminal building was designed to resemble a flying eagle, the curve of the main building representing its wings; these embrace the runways and provide an overhang under which passengers can walk in comfort even in the worst weather, the planes never more than a few yards from the main building, while the field itself is located in the very center of town. Jets roar in over the rooftops of Neukölln, dropping down suddenly onto the runways at the edge of the apartment houses; yet, despite this, the United States Air Force officers in charge of air safety boast it is the safest airport in the world. It certainly was the most advanced when it was conceived in 1922 and developed in the 1930's. "It was so much ahead of its time that we never had trouble fitting jet clippers into it," says a U.S.A.F. officer stationed there. As might be expected, the field saw a lot of action during the war. The Luftwaffe colonel commanding the field, Adolf Boettger, defied last-ditch Nazi orders to destroy it rather than surrender in late April, 1945; instead, he only destroyed some documents and then killed himself. When the Russians prepared to relinquish it to their American allies after holding it for sixty days, they tried to do what Hitler hadn't managed. They set its buildings on fire, as well as opened up the entire complex of buildings to desperate and destitute citizens, who rushed in to plunder and pillage. The American Air Force had little to work with when they took charge on July 2, 1945, but have enormously modernized the field since, at a cost shared by the West Germans in recent years. The Air Safety Center control system, which the U.S.A.F. operates at this field, to guide planes through the air corridors, is so accurate that Poland's *Aeroflot* pilots, heading from Western Europe to East Berlin's Schöneberg Airport, prefer to use this American system even though they have to restrict themselves to the air corridors to do so.

Tempelhof won't be able to handle the four million passengers flying in and out of West Berlin by 1970; much of this traffic will be centered at Tegel, which already handles direct flights to New York and elsewhere. Plans to rebuild Tegel at a cost of $30 million are supposed to make it "the world's most modern airport." It's also farther out of the city center. The citizens of District Neukölln will be happy when many of the jets switch over to the expanded Tegel facility. The noise at Tempelhof drives everyone who lives near it crazy.

The access routes keep West Berlin alive, but it is an odd fact that daily passage through the wall without controls, checks, or harassments of any kind is allowed only to West Berlin's sewage. For more than a million Western marks a year, Ulbricht allows this to be pumped into his huge *Rieselfelder,* or "sewage fields." The only other exception is the cremated dead. A West Berlin church official periodically carries several urns of West Berlin ashes to the Berlin Wall's Heinrich-Heine-Strasse crossing point and turns them over to the border guards for delivery to the Stahnsdorf Cemetery outside Berlin.

Stahnsdorf is one of two Protestant cemeteries still "owned" by the Evangelical Church in West Berlin, though they lie in East Germany, having been placed outside the Berlin city limits in 1910. Because Stahnsdorf was established to serve Protestant Berliners residing in the Western portions of the city, all of its graves, about seventy thousand in number, belong to West Berliners, none of whom are now permitted to visit them. These are only a few of the 250,000 West Berliners who owned property or land in East Berlin or in the G.D.R. countryside around the city. One plump, balding West Berliner has four plots at Stahnsdorf Cemetery. Because his wife wanted to be buried there, beside her mother and grandmother, Max Werner (as I shall call him) bought two graves for himself and his wife back in 1942, gambling, as he puts it, "that we wouldn't be blown to bits in an air raid." Visits to the family graves were restricted in the 1950's, first to immediate family members and then to only one person once a month; they were eased in 1956, to permit others to come also, on three annual

214

occasions. To obtain permits for these extra visits, Werner had to travel from District Zehlendorf to a remote workers' section in East Berlin, queueing up eight abreast, sometimes for six hours, in front of the small store where S.E.D. functionaries processed applications. All visits of any kind ended, of course, in 1961, when the border was sealed around West Berlin. A year later, doctors advised Werner that his wife didn't have much time to live. Trying in vain to get a permit for her to be buried at Stahnsdorf if she died, he finally was advised by West Berlin church authorities that her only hope of getting to that cemetery was via the method previously described: cremation.

"I refused," Werner says, "mostly because they wouldn't let anyone accompany the ashes, so there was no way to be sure they'd ever get there."

As it turned out, Frau Werner survived her illness and still lives today, though as an invalid. When she does pass away, Werner plans to bury her in West Berlin, her coffin encased in steel.

"Someday," he explains, "it may be possible to move her, to rest beside her mother and grandmother, after all."

Meanwhile, Ulbricht's regime earns valuable foreign exchange, even from the cemetery. Werner pays a monthly fee to a West Berlin church authority to see to it that his occupied graves at Stahnsdorf are well-tended. This Western organization turns over about fifty thousand dollars a year to the G.D.R., all of it collected from West Berliners who care about the graves they may not even occasionally visit. In fact, the only way a West Berliner can get into East Berlin anytime and without any trouble is to travel there either as human waste or as human remains.

chapter eighteen

AMONG THE MORE NOTORIOUS CHARACTERS IN IRON CURTAIN escape stories are the *Fluchthelfer* (escape helpers) who charge money to smuggle people out of East Berlin. They are often regarded as questionable, even sordid, men, and their business is said to be a cold-blooded exploitation of human misery. This portrait finds favor with West Berlin's city authorities and the Allied forces, but that doesn't make it entirely true. Like so many other ideas people entertain about Berlin, both East and West, the simplistic picture of the *Fluchthelfer* as a bad guy bleeding the innocents isn't quite realistic.

However, if the issue is complex, at least one fact is plain. Getting an escapee out of East Berlin has become a "military exercise," and most escapes cost money. Freedom, it appears, cannot be obtained at a cut price.

A tunnel which was dug between two Berlin basement apartments on either side of the wall is a case in point. It brought twenty-seven escapees to freedom; each paid $250—part of the sum going to the apartment owners who had made their flats available for this purpose, the rest going to four West Berliners who'd dug the tunnel at considerable expense and all of whom were later maligned for their "ignoble" motives. Even West Berlin students, whose efforts have often been hailed as idealistic, are today condemned if they charge money. The high cost of such an operation is often ignored when the condemnations are issued. The most successful tunnel ever built under the wall is an example; this cost between ten and fifteen thousand dollars. Those who condemn the fact that escapees pay their way claim to do so from high moral principles, but in fact an enormous amount of official hypocrisy is involved. It has led many West Berliners to the conclusion that the Allies and their own city government have, in this respect at least, sold out many of those who still want to flee to West Berlin.

A sensational trial of three professional *Fluchthelfer* in 1966 brought some of the real facts into the open for the first time. The men involved were Albert Schütz, Gerhard Schramm, and Karl-Heinz Bley. They were in business for profit and admitted it. Their expenses, they explained, were heavy: a forged passport had cost them $250 until they were able to buy them wholesale from Spain; couriers whom they employed for risky trips into the G.D.R demanded over $100 for each journey. Accordingly, they themselves charged each escapee between $750 and $1,000 but only, they claimed, after an escape succeeded and not in advance. (Some *Fluchthelfer* charge as much as $2,500, and demand half the money ahead of time.)

The incident which brought these *Fluchthelfer* to public attention began in November, 1965, with two American soldiers, a sergeant and a Pfc. They were seated in a bar in Wedding when a man approached them, introduced himself as "Gerd" and offered them $80 for portions of their uniforms. The two soldiers accepted. The next act occurred on December 19, when a German car bearing United States Army license plates approached East Berlin's Friedrichstrasse crossing point and was flagged routinely through the frontier towards Checkpoint Charlie in West Berlin. This car contained two bogus "American soldiers." One of them wore only a GI raincoat and cap over his German civilian clothes; the guards failed to notice that the other man had sewn his sergeant's chevrons on "upside down," British style. Because East Berlin guards are not allowed to stop or search vehicles bearing Allied plates, nor demand the credentials of Allied soldiers, the car had no trouble getting through, nor did the guards spot the two East German girls hidden inside the vehicle, one of them in its trunk.

The *Fluchthelfer* also had no trouble in the West—that is, until *Bild Zeitung* published a story about the escape nine days later, along with a photograph showing the bogus sergeant cockily posing in front of a poster advertising a James Bond film and another picture of him helping one of the girls out of the car's trunk. The latter photograph clearly showed that the car carried United States Army license plates.

That blew it as far as the West Berlin and United States authorities were concerned. *Bild*'s report was confirmed by the United States Army, and two days later, the West Berlin police clapped the *Fluchthelfer* into jail. "We cannot condone the theft and fraudulent use of Allied uniforms and insignia," a United States spokesman stated; the Army promptly arrested the two GI's involved and ultimately court-martialled them. They were sentenced to three and four months hard labor, fined, and reduced to privates. They had violated standing orders which forbid any member of the American Armed Forces from aiding "the unauthorized departure" of anyone in the G.D.R.

A West Berlin court in Moabit tried the three Germans, fined them, and sentenced them to prison terms ranging from six weeks to five months. Immediately, there was a howl of protest from West Berlin's Association of Victims of Stalinism, which charged that "political realities forcing Germans today to use illegal means had been completely ignored." Indeed, the association raised a central and moral question: Should all means be countenanced to rescue people wanting to escape to the West, or is the West actually prepared to abandon such people?

Meanwhile the *Fluchthelfer,* outraged by the sentences they had received, called a press conference and announced that their activities not only had been known to several official agencies but had also been supported by them. In fact, they said, they had acted on behalf of the West Berlin city government (the *Senat*), of West Berlin's S.P.D., of the "Eastern Bureau" of West Berlin's Christian Democratic Party, and also on behalf of "other influential German agencies." They said that all these agencies promised them help if they ever were arrested. Now they felt they had been doublecrossed and therefore wanted to tell all.

The West Berlin police, they said, had known for years that Schütz and Bley owned "great numbers" of forged passports, forged "official" rubber stamps, bogus license plates—even weapons. As a matter of fact, they said, the police had a year earlier confiscated a large trunk belonging to them, which contained pistols and forged

218

passports, yet they were never charged with illegal possession. Furthermore, just before they were arrested, they'd been told by West Berlin's Political Police that they had nothing to fear; then, just as they were about to fly to West Germany to meet a new batch of escapees whom they'd smuggled through the frontier, they had been picked up.

"If this sentence remains in force," said Karl-Heinz Bley, "it'll mean that all aid to escapees in the future will be impossible."

A State Department officer attached to the United States Mission in Berlin had a different view. "We don't sympathize with them," this official told me. "None of them deserve any consideration. These people are just in business." That, however, was said *before* the three Germans held their press conference. Everyone ran for cover after that. Mayor Albertz huddled with leading city officials for hours after the accusations were made. When he emerged, he didn't do much to refute the suspicion that they were substantially true. The only statement his city government could offer after hours of deliberation was the comment, "It is obvious that the interests of Berlin have not been served by the irresponsible chatter of *Fluchthelfer* Schütz and Bley."

Many idealistically motivated and "non-profit" *Fluchthelfer* were disgusted. One of them is Paul Norden (as I shall call him), today a West Berlin welfare worker.

"It's been known for a long time," he said, "that official United States diplomatic and Army vehicles or their plates have been used to get people out of East Berlin. Nor has it ever been hard to convince American soldiers to 'lose' their identity papers or uniforms for a few days in return for a few hundred marks. One American officer was shipped out of West Berlin altogether because he made thousands of dollars helping this trade at the frontier. All this had been kept nice and quiet until Schütz and Bley brought it into the open. Of course, these men made unauthorized use of United States license plates and uniforms, but they were not punished because of that. They were made scapegoats because what they did had become public knowledge. Furthermore, what is ignored in all this is the fact that professionals like these three men are just the types who very often *do* succeed in bringing people to safety in the West. Yet they are maligned and condemned. If you condemn them for their success, you also condemn a lot of East Berliners who want to escape to continued imprisonment in the G.D.R."

The trial of these three *Fluchthelfer,* according to informed West Berlin sources, was a demonstration of the fact that there is a growing desire on the part of West Berlin and Allied authorities to curb, if not to stop, all clandestine actions aimed at helping people escape from Ulbricht's regime. "The reasons for this," says Norden, "are political and completely disregard humanitarian considerations."

Even the *Tagesspiegel,* not usually given to intemperate language, was outraged by the official hypocrisy. An editorial said that first official reactions lent credence to the *Fluchthelfers'* charges that city agencies and other organizations had indeed been the real "employers." These official agencies, it pointed out, had countenanced previous violations of the law and had persecuted the *Fluchthelfer* only for political reasons. (Their use of Allied uniforms, said the *Tagesspiegel,* was regarded as giving the G.D.R. an opportunity to threaten Allied access rights into East Berlin.)

"All of a sudden," it said of the authorities, "these gentlemen got cold feet. Not one of them . . . admitted his responsibility or found a word of exoneration that might have eased the lot of the accused. What scandalous moral cowardice they demonstrated by this behavior! Those who employ *Fluchthelfer*—and, considering the pressure of the wall, there are good reasons to do so—must also be willing to admit to the consequences and not back off, leaving the others in the soup by themselves. Those who now speak of 'irresponsible talk' and of 'avoiding this matter in public' only show they have a bad conscience . . ."

Certainly many of the people involved quietly modified their stands. Major General John F. Franklin, then United States commandant in Berlin, took into account the youth, previous records, and good prison behavior of the soldiers, reduced their sentences, and shipped them out of Berlin. Then on May 18 a German appeals court cut the sentences of the three Germans. Much of the condemnation now looked like self-righteous hypocrisy, but that isn't surprising. There doesn't seem any way to deal with that wall without coming out a little dirty.

A physics student who calls himself "Jens Jacob" is a "non-profit" *Fluchthelfer*. Tall, slim, in his late twenties, he was fined by a West Berlin court for unauthorized possession of weapons in connection with the tunnel through which fifty-seven people reached freedom in October, 1964. One East Berlin border guard was killed in that action, but the students who built the tunnel insist that they were not responsible. He was killed accidentally in a hail of bullets fired by other guards when the tunnel was discovered and surrounded. The G.D.R. afterward demanded prosecution for murder, but West Berlin only slapped the students' wrists. Jens Jacob was furious at even that.

"The police now have internal directives to stop all attempts at aiding escapees," he says. "It's a filthy business. When Lipschitz was alive and in office as senator for the interior, help such as we provide to escapees was encouraged, even supported. Now they have no courage left at all! My defense attorney said, 'Twenty years from now we'll feel ashamed that we ever conducted any trials like these.' "

Jens came to West Berlin in autumn, 1962, after studying in Munich and Kiel, drawn by the city's musical and theatrical life, for he plays both the violin and trumpet and is also a passionate theatergoer. He was able to go to the theater in East Berlin, being allowed to pass through the frontier with his West German passport. Six months after his first visit, he came to know a young married couple in East Berlin, both medical students who wanted to escape. Jens promised to help, though he had no idea how.

For six months, he toured West Berlin bars, hoping to meet a *Fluchthelfer*. In autumn, 1963, he finally encountered a student who admitted he was a *Tunnelgräber*, or tunnel digger. They talked cautiously for two hours in Jens Jacob's furnished room near the Fehrbellinerplatz, and after the student decided he could trust Jens, he took him to a place near the ruins of the old Anhalter Railway Station in West Berlin. There he showed him the start of a tunnel into the nearby Eastern sector. Jens decided to help dig it. It was to be his first tunnel. Since then, he's dug others and, altogether, has helped more than 150 people to escape from East Berlin. What bothers him is that his friends were prevented from risking the trip because the wife was about to give birth. He has hopes of bringing them across some time in the future.

221

"It now costs about eight thousand marks ($2,000) to prepare a safe plan of escape," Jens says. "It also takes a lot of time to work out all the details, though it's possible even now to get someone out of East Berlin within a day, if there's a real emergency. Such crash programs, however, always risk the loss of life."

Every second one of his assistants, Jens says, is a former escapee and all are motivated as he is.

"One simply can't do otherwise," Jens says. "I've decided a hundred times to quit but, whenever I hear of someone else who has to get out of East Berlin, I decide I'll help just once more. After awhile, it gets to be a habit. If there's no action for a few months, we sort of drift together and say, 'Isn't it about time we got somebody else out again?' "

Jens has sacrificed a good deal to aid the escapees. The time he put into this operation has interfered with his studies and caused him to fail a crucial examination. He quit school altogether for six months after that and went to work as a laborer, taxi-driver, and as a beer-truck driver to earn enough money to start another tunnel. As expenses mounted for one of these, he began borrowing and at one point owed as much as three thousand marks, a debt he ultimately worked off by driving a taxi, again at the cost of his studies and future career.

One night at the Berlin Wall, Jens' men were about to signal an East Berliner preparing to escape with their help, but were ordered away by a nearby West Berlin policeman. Finally, Jens tried a diversionary tactic. One of his men ran some distance away and smeared anti-Communist slogans on the Berlin Wall. While the West Berlin policeman chased him, the others helped the escapee across. The entire action, Jens Jacob says, had been prepared over a five-month period. It took exactly 9.5 seconds.

"No sooner had the escape succeeded," says Jens, "than we heard a terrific roar of cheers from nearby apartment houses. Apparently dozens of people had watched it from their windows. A few minutes later, a police car roared up. That was quite a spectacle: Those bulls stood there red-faced and infuriated, looking as though they were chasing the world's worst criminals while, all around them, people cheered wildly. It summed up the attitudes of the Berliners—and of their police."

But even the police accept the idealism of many of the student *Fluchthelfer;* they reproach the students because they rock the boat. As for the "criminal" type of *Fluchthelfer,* he is not the one who accepts payment but *does* deliver the goods; he is the kind who promises an escapee he will help him, but afterward fails to do so.

"Such people usually accept a few thousand marks in advance payment," says Fred Brandt, a West Berliner who was a political prisoner in the G.D.R. before he fled West. "Then they claim the plan's fallen through or that their agent was arrested while carrying the money. That might be true sometimes, but usually you can suspect fraud.

"About fifty forged passports were once delivered at East Germany's Leipzig Fair, at about three thousand marks each. These were all foreign passports, enabling those carrying them to pass unhindered through the Friedrichstrasse checkpoint in East Berlin. But the forgeries were so crude that all but two of the fifty were nabbed by the border guards and arrested. I don't know how it was that two managed to get through the checkpoint. Perhaps the guards were asleep or maybe they were bribed. But that's typical of the way some criminals prey on misery."

There is a type of *Fluchthelfer* with whom the Allies sympathize without reservation. He not only charges no money at all, but is also not involved in any large-scale action likely to embarrass them. One example is twenty-seven-year-old Heinz Schöneberger, who at Christmas, 1965, tried to free his brother Horst and two girls, Christel Reszke and Monika Proppe. He drove his Ford through the Heinrich-Heine-Strasse crossing point. The car tore around the slalom barriers, in a barrage of gunfire; it finally crashed into the candy-striped steel barrier, the last before West Berlin. That stopped the vehicle, the hood of which crumpled as though it had hit a tree. The guards kept firing. Heinz Schöneberger leaped out and started to run, but was hit five yards east of the border. Mortally wounded, he dragged himself across and collapsed in West Berlin. He was rushed to a hospital but died of his wounds. His twenty-four-year-old brother, despite his wounds, was hurried to a court in Potsdam where he was quickly sentenced to fifteen years' imprisonment; the ultimate fate of the two wounded girls, also captured, is unknown. One of them, Christel, was only seventeen.

The three Western commandants in West Berlin all protested sharply to the Soviet Ambassador in East Berlin but the reaction, as expected, was nil. Schöneberger, the G.D.R. said, was an American intelligence agent and in the employ of "ultras," meaning anti-Communists in West Berlin. In fact, he was just a courageous individual who was trying to save his brother and two young girls. The effectiveness of such foolhardy, individual actions is questionable, but they're about the only ones of which official agencies approve. They make for "heroics," the very kind the more effective (and professional) *Fluchthelfer*, as well as the organized students, eschew.

One *Fluchthelfer* who remains convinced of the need to aid escapees today is "Paul Norden," whom I came to know well during my stay in West Berlin. Born in Saxony in 1933, Paul's commitment dates back to the Nazi era.

Paul's maternal grandfather was Jewish, leading his mother to be branded a half-Jew, and Paul himself "of mixed parentage." The Red Army entered his home town just in time for him, because his mother was in constant danger of arrest. He even learned a new phrase in Russian to shout at the soldiers. "Welcome!" the then twelve-year-old Paul yelled. "We're glad you've come. My mother's a Jew!"

His experience under Nazism made him a passionate supporter of those who destroyed it; he became a devoted Communist and remained one until he was 17, when an acquaintance in the East German secret police admitted to him that "the terror is true." Paul, who had earlier regarded talk of East German injustice as slander, found this admission shattering. He soon decided to act and began by distributing anti-regime leaflets.

In 1951, at the age of 18, he visited West Berlin. The border between West and East Berlin was open and Paul says he sauntered through it, "smiling innocently" at the People's Policemen stationed there, wearing his F.D.J. uniform and carrying a book by Lenin.

He returned home that night with a can of berries, which contained phosphorus and a time fuse (the latter, he says, labeled

224

"Made in U.S.A."); with it, he set on fire a pavilion built to commemorate Stalin's birthday. "Maybe it wasn't much," Paul says, "but it was the talk of the area and proved there was resistance after all."

Just before Paul's nineteenth birthday, he was arrested by the East German State Security Service, the S.S.D., and interrogated for almost forty hours before being bound over for trial.

"This was the usual farce," Paul Norden says. "I spoke with my lawyer no more than five minutes before it began and then I had to listen to him attacking me instead of presenting my defense. I'd already been told, just before I entered the courtroom, that I'd be given fifteen years, so I knew what to expect. At the end of the trial, I was told that cooperation with the State Security Service would get me a public sentence of only eight years and that I would actually be released after three. But I refused flatly and was kept in jail for almost ten years, the first of them in solitary confinement. That was the worst: I spent twelve months trying not to go crazy."

As a direct result of Norden's trial, regulations were issued forbidding anyone to bring tinned, canned, or otherwise sealed goods into East Berlin or the G.D.R. These are still in force; those wishing to bring food to an East Berliner today have to use jars with screw-type lids so that they can be opened at the border and inspected.

Norden was released when he was twenty-seven. His sentence had failed to "cure" him; he was more determined than ever to work against Ulbricht's police state.

"They let me out of prison just in time," he says. "It enabled me to reach West Berlin just before the border was sealed. I stayed there awhile, then went to South Germany, where I was offered a job."

He became a machinist, content to adjust himself to what he calls "a richer and more fluid society than I'd ever known." His experience in West Germany wasn't a happy one, however, and he soon returned to Berlin.

"The atmosphere in West Germany," he told me, "disillusioned me rather quickly. It seemed false, hypocritical, and too materialistic. For one thing, educated West Germans refused to consider me their social equal, because I was 'only a worker,' but what bothered me most was that West Germans seemed only interested in improving their lives materially. They cared little about the future of Germany and nothing at all about their brothers in the G.D.R. When I recognized this, I knew there was only one place for me—Berlin.

"Berlin is really unlike either West or East Germany: a blend of traits from all over the world, a kind of *third* Germany. It's also a place where refugees from the failure of Communism, like myself, can find an identity, a role to play, a contribution to make, and a serious future to build.

"I learned I could have confidence in the Berliners. For one thing, I never forget I am half-Jewish and never let anyone else forget it either—and I am proud of the Berliners who hid Jews during the Nazi era. I'm just as proud of the way they are today determined to defend their city. I consider myself 'a Berliner' now and I am accepted as such. This is a town you can trust."

Determined, as he puts it, to repay that trust, Paul Norden fought the Berlin Wall as a *Fluchthelfer*. He is a gentle and soft-spoken humanist—but one with a streak of steel. He is a passionate liberal and, along with many other young Berliners, has worked on a kibbutz in Israel.

Another former political prisoner of the G.D.R. authorities who fought the Berlin Wall is a young man I shall call Ernst. One of the first men he wanted to get out of the G.D.R. was Friedrich Hager, who had served a ten-year sentence in the same East German prison in which Ernst had been jailed.

"Former prisoners maintain contact," Ernst explains, "though there is no organized underground movement as such. But there are always ways one hears about in which one can help."

Ultimately, Ernst was put in touch with a Herr H., a professional *Fluchthelfer* who wanted $1,500 to arrange the escape but who agreed to deliver Hager first. Ernst accepted the terms; they were the going rate at the time.

"This Herr H. had me do a lot of the arranging," Ernst says. "It was a weird business. I telephoned people I'd never heard of, whose names I never knew, and whom I never met. The only one with whom I kept in constant touch and whom I'd actually met was H. He was about thirty-six, had a family in East Germany, and claimed to be a medical student in Berlin."

226

The route chosen for the escape was the *Autobahn* from West Berlin to Hanover.

"All these roads are, of course, heavily traveled by trucks," Ernst says, "and at that time, one particular group of truckdrivers were in business on the side, smuggling people out of East Germany."

The procedure involved still others. A certain Herr W. who lived in a small East German town near the *Autobahn* also hoped to escape, so as to join his wife in West Germany. He in turn had a friend who worked in a filling station directly on the East German *Autobahn*. Herr W. had already helped several people, receiving secret messages, hiding them in his home, and finally leading them to the highway near the service station, where he helped them onto the trucks used in these operations. After his cooperation was assured, Hager needed to be notified of the exact escape plans, but the courier who was to brief him in East Berlin took sick and Ernst's political record kept him from going himself.

Just as the plan seemed to fall through, an American girl, Lynne Mann, whom Ernst had met in West Berlin, volunteered for the job. She memorized all the pertinent information and then entered East Berlin with her American passport. Hager had already received a telegram signed "Father," asking him to come to East Berlin, and she met him in a public square near Unter den Linden. He pulled an East German atlas out of his briefcase and she pointed to the place near the *Autobahn* where he was to go. Then she returned to West Berlin.

Hager then traveled to the village in which Herr W. lived and waited. As he was on vacation from his job, no one was looking for him as yet. Herr W. made him feel welcome, but tension mounted as the days passed without news, for his vacation was almost over. Finally, just before it ended, a telegram arrived. Decoded it read, "Go to the appointed spot, midnight tonight."

There were four escapees in all when the truck pulled up by the side of the road and stopped for a few seconds. The drivers locked the men into secret compartments and roared off. They were armed with pistols and late model guns which fired smoke bombs, all of them United States issue, and Ernst believes, either stolen or bought from American GI's.

The guards at the Marienborn checkpoint never examined the trucks and they rolled into West Germany without trouble. Hager caught a plane back to West Berlin, flying across the very same stretch he had just traversed in secret, and both Herr H. and Ernst met him at the airport. H. collected his money; he had already agreed to reduce his fee. Afterward, H. took them to an apartment where Ernst was handed what he calls "an official-looking piece of paper." This warned him never to talk of the escape, on pain of trial in West Berlin. Ernst signed. Hager was taken to American and West Berlin intelligence officers to be interrogated, was placed in a refugee camp for clearance, and soon allowed to resume a normal life. Ernst went back to work. Two months later, however, the West Berlin police summoned him and questioned him about Karl-Heinz Bley, against whom they were then preparing proceedings and with whom Ernst had once negotiated before choosing Herr H. While Ernst was at police headquarters, he was shown the "private" document he'd signed for H. "I was amazed to see it in the police files," Ernst says.

The story of Hager's escape can be told because there is no longer any need to keep it secret. Some time ago, someone trying to use this escape route panicked and revealed the facts to the G.D.R.'s State Security Service. From that day on, it became impossible for escapes to be managed within those large trucks rolling along the *Autobahn*. The N.V.A. guards know all about them.*

Still, there are other escape routes which remain open even today. These, of course, cannot be reported; the day they can, they'll have been closed. Meanwhile, despite all attempts to curb or stop the *Fluchthelfer,* they continue their activities—and continue to exacerbate feelings in Berlin. Those who deplore the activities of "escape helpers" today point out that the G.D.R. "has all the leverage in and around Berlin" and is able to harass the West. Officials charge that East-West negotiations over the release of political prisoners in the G.D.R. (whose freedom on several occasions was purchased by the Bonn Government) are jeopardized by private *Fluchthelfer* initiatives.

* Even in telling this story today, it has been necessary for me to alter certain details and all the names involved. The G.D.R. regime is fully capable of taking revenge on relatives of the participants.

"We're willing to meet with you to discuss these matters," the East Germans tell Bonn's representatives, "but not if you violate our borders, shoot our men, or use criminal elements against us."

The *Fluchthelfer* are pragmatists with few illusions. They approve of the barter between the two Germanies, whereby human lives are traded for groceries and cash. Some even go further and support a *de facto* recognition of the G.D.R. as "administrating" East Germany, if that would facilitate negotiations over political prisoners. *Die Zeit* published a letter signed "A West Berlin *Fluchthelfer* group" that suggested just that but that also made the point that "help to escapees will continue to be necessary" until the group's "humanitarian demands" are fulfilled in the G.D.R.

"The wall is a violation of human rights," says a *Fluchthelfer* leaflet addressed to the G.D.R.'s border guards. "Aiding escapes represents a restoration of a human right . . . He who helps to unite Germans in this way unites Germany—and he who helps unite Germans helps remove the biggest obstacle on the road to a united Europe!"

Those are to some extent "German motives," but the Berlin Wall and what it represents in terms of broken families has come as such a shock to non-Germans that it has led many of them to enlist in the fight against it. Several have even been imprisoned in the G.D.R. for trying to do so.

"We warn all Americans we can reach who plan to enter East Berlin not to get involved in any aid to escapees," the chief of the Eastern Affairs Section, Political Affairs Division, United States Mission, told me. "Every now and then, of course, one of them does. When and if Americans are arrested by the G.D.R., trying to get them out becomes a responsibility of this section."

The Eastern Affairs Section functions like an unofficial "United States Embassy" to East Germany in the sense that it performs the tasks normally assigned a diplomatic mission. Yet the fact that the United States Government (along with Bonn) maintains the fiction that the G.D.R. does not exist hampers its effectiveness, for it can never deal with any official in East Berlin and has to operate through channels which purport to be "private." These have been conveniently provided by the G.D.R. in the person of a "private lawyer" living at the end of Karl-Marx-Allee, at Alt Friedrichsfelde

115, in East Berlin's District Friedrichsfelde. He is Wilhelm Vogel, the man involved in the Gary Powers-Colonel Abel exchange. When an American is arrested in East Berlin, a member of the United States Mission's Eastern Affairs Section gets into a car with State Department plates, drives through Checkpoint Charlie, flashes his diplomatic passport at the *Vopos* at the Friedrichstrasse checkpoint, and talks with Vogel. Sometimes a private American attorney is brought into the act. One of these is Maxwell M. Rabb, a New York attorney who is president of the United States Committee for Refugees and who has made eleven trips overseas, at his own expense, to obtain the release of seven prisoners. "In each instance," says Rabb, "I was called in only after all avenues had been exhausted and no release of the prisoners had been obtained."

In March of 1966, such negotiations secured the release of John Van Altena of Milton Junction, Wisconsin, a twenty-two-year-old University of Wisconsin student who was arrested and sentenced to eight years for trying to smuggle a woman and her five-year-old daughter out of East Berlin in the trunk of an American-built Ford. Van Altena spent twelve months in solitary but was not otherwise mistreated; after another five months, he was released, six years and seven months ahead of time. Asked at a press conference in West Berlin why he'd endangered himself, he replied without hesitation that it was simply to help people.

"I'd do it again," he added defiantly. "Only next time I'd be more careful."

Four other young Americans who were released shortly afterward were Moses Reese Herrin, of Akron, Ohio; Frederick Matthews, of Elwood City, Pennsylvania; Mary Helen Battle, of Oakridge, Tennessee; and William Lovett of San Francisco, California.

Herrin and Matthews had been engaged by a West Berlin *Fluchthelfer* group to bring a thirteen-year-old girl to West Berlin, so that she could join her parents who had escaped some time earlier. The attempt failed and both men were sentenced to eight years in prison. They had a hard time of it, especially as they were Negroes. "The guards wouldn't let me bathe for the first three weeks," Herrin reports, "because they said dirt wouldn't show on my skin."

Negotiations finally freed these two Americans. The last word they hurled at the G.D.R. guards as they crossed Sandkrug Bridge to West Berlin (after six months in jail) was "Freedom!" A few days later, at a press conference, they showed themselves as defiant as Van Altena had been. "We brought out five refugees before they ever arrested us!" Matthews announced with satisfaction. He also said he intended to stay in West Berlin since the city seemed like "a second home." Van Altena had said much the same; he planned to enroll at the Free University. The Berliners will welcome such people. The way they see it, they *proved* they were Berliners, no matter where they come from or what color skin they have.

Britain's Arthur Wilbraham, a geophysical engineer and student of philology, is another who has an emotional commitment to West Berlin. The G.D.R. sentenced him to five years for acting as courier for a group of West Berlin *Fluchthelfer*. Anton van As, a twenty-four-year-old Hollander, was jailed for the same reason. So were two Iranian students, Iradi Saedsamii and Esmail Rahnoma. All these, and many others, paid or are still paying for their convictions and all symbolize the dilemma presented by *Fluchthelfer* activities. While all these men may fall into the bin labeled "Cold War heroes," as do Heinz Schöneberger, "Jens Jacob," "Paul Norden," and the members of Reiner Hildebrandt's "Thirteenth August Working Association," it is difficult to sort others out that neatly. What of men like Bley, that professional smuggler working for profit, and of Schütz, that "underworld character" sentenced twelve times for criminal activities before becoming a *Fluchthelfer?* Such people do not make pretty heroes, are not "showpieces" of the Free World, and no one wants to hand them a medal or even pat them on the back. The fact remains, however, that it is just such questionable characters who bring many people to freedom. Whatever their motives, whatever price they may charge, it is impossible to deny that their sheer professionalism and expertise has often reunited children with parents, husbands with wives, and has brought passionate opponents of tyranny out of danger. Such men pose a real dilemma, one which the authorities apparently refuse to face. If it is true that anyone who helps reunite Germans works for a united Germany, and maybe, even for a united Europe, then this also holds true for former criminals engaged in such activities. It goes to show how hard it is to sort out the good guys from the villains in Berlin with complete accuracy.

There are, however, some villains about whom no Berliner has any doubt whatever. They're not only those who leave escapees in the lurch; they even include those who do help escapees into West Berlin but in ways so conscienceless as to outrage everyone.

Three of these were professionals engaged in 1965 to smuggle Angelika Probst into the West, on behalf of her West Berlin fiancé, Klaus Schulp. The leader of the *Fluchthelfer* group was Kurt ("The Shark") Wordel; his two assistants were Joachim Podelski and Klaus Lindner, who was assigned to do most of the dirty work. Lindner knew a pretty, dark-haired eighteen-year-old girl named Gisela, from Hildesheim, who'd been in trouble for prostitution; he argued her into helping him for a fee. Despite the fact that she suffered from an inflamed appendix at the time, Gisela accompanied Lindner to a café in East Berlin and there allowed him to take her overcoat and the West German passport inside it. Angelika Probst was switched for Gisela and brought safely to West Berlin, while Gisela was left in East Berlin without papers. "Don't worry about it," Lindner told Gisela. "Just tell the guards at the border that your overcoat and all your papers were stolen. The longest they'll hold you is twenty-four hours, if that much."

The inexperienced girl did as she'd been told; the guards, of course, immediately suspected the truth. She was arrested, hurriedly operated on for appendicitis at a *Vopo* hospital, then quickly sentenced to eighteen months in prison—though she was released in spring, 1966, after serving a little more than four months.

The case caused an uproar, especially as it was at first thought Gisela was an innocent victim of a *Frauentausch* (an exchange of women), rather than an accomplice. Further, the gang seemed particularly sordid. "Shark" Wordel, a former taxi driver, had earned $375,000 in just the previous year "off the partition of Germany." Further, the group was careless: *Stern,* Germany's largest-circulation magazine, claimed that seventy-five percent of all its escapes (money paid in advance) had failed. With heavy irony, *Stern* published a photo of Wordel receiving a medal from a United States officer (for pulling an American pilot out of a burning plane); while he may have saved the pilot's life, he had sacrificed the lives of fifty escapees withhin one year, *Stern* charged.

A real *Frauentausch,* in which an innocent girl was duped,

took place when Peter Selle, twenty-six, lured seventeen-year-old Dorothea Voss into East Berlin, and while seated with her in a café, stole her papers and left, leaving her in the lurch in East Germany. He used the documents to bring his own wife to the West and was later sentenced to a year in jail by a West Berlin court for abandoning Dorothea Voss. He might have received a stiffer sentence had the court not taken into account the tragic consequences of the Berlin Wall. Peter Selle, it pointed out, was driven out of his mind with longing for his wife. Much the same could be said of the other West Berliners who have members of their families across that wall. More than one million of them do.

chapter nineteen

THE EAST BERLIN REGIME IS OFTEN WILLING TO OBLIGE THOSE who wish to interview its functionaries, but it is less cooperative if one wants to meet a worker. Yet it is possible to meet such people privately. A middle-aged East Berlin invalid is a case in point. I shall give him a pseudonym, because he's had troubles enough already.

"Karl Bauer" looks ten years older than he is, mostly because of wartime injuries that have now made it impossible for him to keep working. Yet his hands are those of someone who's labored hard all his life, as indeed he has. Before the war, he was an artisan's apprentice; then he was drafted into the *Wehrmacht* and served six years. He was severely wounded four times and returned home to Berlin a broken man; today he limps and is in pain if he has to stand or walk for any length of time. Despite his injuries, postwar conditions were such that he had to work; this finally stopped when his leg condition worsened so much that the G.D.R. Government put him on "half pension," giving him 123 marks a month, plus twenty more for "extra care," since he cannot even bend down to tie his own shoelaces. His wife's earnings boost the income of the family to almost double his pension and they also received some additional money to help support their children. "It's not much," he says, "but we manage if we're careful."

No matter how much Berliners have gone through, they rarely show self-pity or catalog their sorrows to enlist your sympathy; Bauer told me of his ruined health and difficult readjustment to postwar life without seeming to feel sorry for himself. In fact, he displayed another Berlinese characteristic: he is rather proud of everything he's had to endure. Like the British, the Berliners also feel most comfortable when they have their backs against the wall. Bauer didn't want my sympathy—he wouldn't have known what to do with it except let it embarrass him—but what he wanted was my total interest.

"If you're going to write about us," he said to me in his slow, quiet, but intense way, "I hope you won't write about Berlin like it was Paris. And if you're going to say anything about us in East Berlin, I hope you'll tell what terrible conditions people here have to put up with! If you're willing to do that, then I'll talk with you, but if you're just interested in what Ulbricht says, then leave me out!"

I mentioned several Western books and articles which reported progress in the G.D.R. and asked him about them.

"There are two sides to it," he said after thinking quietly for a while. "First of all, those figures don't tell you everything, even if they haven't been exaggerated. It comes to this: when you interview *Bonzen,* you've got to expect to get the official line those big shots give you. Every one of them either is a trustworthy party member or acts like one. The fact remains that, no matter what those figures say, life for the little people here is different—and pretty hard.

"The other side," he continued, "is that this progress isn't due to Comrade Ulbricht or his Russian friends, but in spite of them! There's been improvement and none of us like to see it belittled or enjoy the West Germans sneering at us like we're poor relations. Because, of course, it's *we* who've done it—not *they!* Not our fancy leaders in their villas, not the big-mouth functionaries with their speeches, not the *Spitzel* who sneak around listening to conversations. Ordinary people built this part of the country up and they did it without all that Marshall Plan aid the West received! What we got instead were five-year plans that gave the Russians most of the things we produced. Yet despite all that, we did build up this country! We spat in our hands like good, honest German workingmen and we said to ourselves, 'Well, if we can't get out any more, if we've got to stay in this workers' paradise, then let's at least try and make it liveable!' Only the *Bonzen* won't tell you that. They'll claim it's due to Marx or Engels or something . . ."

Bauer paused and took another of the West German cigarettes I offered him. He held it for a moment between his fingers, feeling its paper appreciatively. I knew the gesture; virtually everyone I encountered in East Berlin did the same thing.

"You never know over here what you're likely to smoke," Bauer explained. "Sure we get our cigarettes for the same price you get them in West Berlin, but even the same brand hardly ever tastes the same from pack to pack. Sometimes they got damp during storage or while being shipped; sometimes we get decent tobacco, other times rotten stuff. At least you in the West get a good quality product for your money. That's the whole problem of living over here: You can't really rely on anything. Maybe heavy industry is doing fine, but when it comes to consumer goods, everything's slipshod. Nothing seems to work the way it should. That makes life very difficult."

Bauer produced a photograph of his family and showed it to me. His youngsters seemed to be happy, normal pre-schoolers, no different in appearance from any you'd see elsewhere in Europe; they looked well-fed and nicely dressed. His wife was a neatly groomed woman with a Slavic cast to her cheerful face and it was clear from the way Bauer's eyes lit up while I looked at the picture that he was very fond of his family.

"She's a happy little woman, my wife is," Bauer said, "and if she's no beauty, then a cripple like me has to face the fact that he's no movie star either. She's good to me and the children and can work just as hard as someone twice her size. She's at her job every morning at five and works straight through until 2:30 in the afternoon when she comes home to take care of the children and of me. I do what I can, but I'm not much help, you know. She's very good with money and that's especially important because it isn't easy to budget here. To do that properly, you have to be able to plan when you're going to buy what things. We never know when anything's likely to be available. Maybe my wife would like to cook liver and plan to serve it on a special day, but we have to face the fact that liver's only going to be available now and then. We have to order it in advance and also make sure we're at the shop in time to get it. Chances are one is out of luck. So we never know from one day to the next just what we'll be eating—or buying. And when shopping is as disorganized as that, it gets more expensive.

"Now I won't say everything's bad over here; transportation and rents are cheaper than in the West, for example. But some

236

things are very expensive. I bought my little girl a wool coat with a hood; that cost me 120 marks, while you in the West can buy it for less than half the price!"

I asked Bauer what he was doing for his wounded leg and he told me that he gets a mild painkiller and also undergoes massage.

"They tell you over here that social welfare and medical care are so much better than in West Berlin," he says, "but you know, there's a big difference between theory and practice! Take me for example: I need a specialist for my leg. Now, there used to be one in my district of Berlin, but ever since he died two years ago, I have to travel to another district, where they still have two such specialists. All their offices are terribly overcrowded and one has to wait for hours to get examined.

"My little girl's another example. Her eyes are all right except that now and then they tend to cross. Now that's not nice for a pretty girl, especially when she grows older, so we wanted to do something for her. The only eye doctor we could go to was located quite a way from where we live, yet my wife had to take our little girl there four times without even getting to see him once! One time, when she took her down there, his office was closed because the waiting room was already too crowded. The next time, there was a sign that the doctor had been called away. And so it went— until I finally took my daughter down the fifth time and got her examined, after we'd been waiting five hours. He prescribed eyeglasses for her and we got them all right, but recently, she's been complaining they hurt her. If we take her down to the eye doctor again, it'll be the same story once more. It takes us one hour to get to the doctor's office by streetcar and another hour back. Added to that, there's a wait of maybe four or five hours, so it means a whole day is lost and it's hard on the girl, too, because children can't sit still that long."

"You seem to be pretty well-informed about what's happening in the West," I told Bauer. "Do you have relatives there who come over on visits?"

"Most everything I know comes from watching Western television," Bauer replied. "We're allowed to turn on Western TV and radio stations, you know, so long as we're alone. Naturally, it's discouraged, but everybody does it. The only law against it is about disseminating Western propaganda. What they mean by that is that you can't watch Western TV or listen to Western radio if you have a guest in your house.

"I wouldn't do it, anyway," he continued. "We have to be careful. Suppose I have a friend over and he asks me to turn on Western TV and then afterward he tells his friends he watched a terrific movie on television while visiting me. Now if that got around, they could accuse me of spreading Western propaganda, so when anyone visits us, we only turn on our own stations. Naturally, none of us believe what they tell us, but then we've gotten to the point where we don't believe the West either. We figure they're both lying."

Bauer's voice suddenly took on a note of outrage.

"People over here live like they're in a prison!" he said angrily. "They've got barbed wire and guns all around us—and for what crime? It's like the war's still on. They tell us how wonderful the world is now—they can get a man to the moon even—but they can't arrange it so men can live decently, like they're supposed to, over here! It gets you depressed! You know we Berliners are well-known for our sense of humor and we even like to laugh when things get especially tough, but over here in the East, we're getting a little worn out from that. There's this heavy feeling everyone carries around with him and it makes everyone irritable. You have no idea how people treat each other! In the West, if you asked a trolley-car conductor for directions, you'd probably get a decent enough answer; here, if you get any answer at all, it's a surly one. And you can't blame him either! Chances are, he's had to work sixteen hours that day because his relief didn't show up. It's like that in everything; all life seems so very disorganized. I know one woman whose job makes her work four hours on and three hours off; after that, she works four more hours. But she lives an hour from work, and if she went home during her break to catch a nap, she'd manage to get only an hour's sleep, spending the other two traveling. So, instead, she goes to the canteen where she works and tries to catch a few winks resting her head on the table. If she's irritable when she gets home, you can't blame her! And so it goes. There's a shortage of help and workers: nothing seems to function properly or get repaired right; even the things one buys fall apart or sometimes don't work properly right from the start. Then they have those mass rallies, and everything's disrupted. Streets are blocked off, streetcars and subway trains are rerouted, and you can't get anywhere. Everybody grumbles, but it isn't just ordinary complaining, because we Berliners don't really like constant fault-finders. It's just that we get sick and tired of them calling this a workers' and farmers' state in which everything belongs to the people, when we know different. Look what happened when our construction workers demonstrated in 1953! They brought in Russian tanks to shoot us down!"

I asked him if he didn't know any convinced Communists or Germans who supported the Socialist Unity party. Bauer shrugged his shoulders and admitted those existed.

"But you never know what they *really* believe," he said. "Most of them just talk that way to keep their jobs or get better ones. It isn't that they think Ulbricht's going to bring us a better future; it's that they want to make sure *they've* got a better future! Ask any ordinary person over here what he thinks and he'll tell you that all those characters would switch sides at the drop of a hat if things changed! As for ordinary people like myself, the West saw what we think of all this right enough! The June 17 uprising in 1953 showed them—and then there were all those millions who crossed the border. The rest of us are caught here now, but we have a saying that if that wall ever came down, those guards had better climb the first trees they see or they'd get trampled to death by all those rushing into West Berlin! I worked in a repair shop for a while before I got pensioned and I had plenty of chances to talk with plain Berlin workers. Those fellows there didn't think this workers' state represented their interests; not one of them! It's just like it was under the Nazis—only with one difference! Under Hitler, there were enough Germans who were pretty damn enthusiastic about the Nazis, but nowadays over here, I've never found any ordinary East Berliner who's enthusiastic about Communism."

The difficulties Karl Bauer and his wife encounter in budgeting and shopping are general through East Berlin. In terms of *real* wages (those which take into account inflationary prices), workers in the East have a standard of living at least forty percent below that of West German workers. While it is true that rents, books, transport, and food staples (such as potatoes) are very cheap in East Berlin, the savings vanish in the face of vastly higher prices for other goods and considerably higher taxes. Ironically, the tax system in the G.D.R.'s "workers' state" hits lower-paid industrial workers far worse than these are hit in "capitalistic" West Germany. On a monthly income of 625 marks, an unmarried worker in the East would pay one hundred marks each month in taxes, versus sixty-four in the West, while the difference widens even more sharply if he is married and has children. On the same salary, a married worker with one child pays nineteen marks in taxes in the West, while he pays about sixty-nine in the East. If he has two children or more he would pay no taxes at all in the West, while he would continue to pay them in the G.D.R.: 55.80 if he had two children, 43.80 if he had three, 32.80 if he had four, and 22.80 if he had five.

West Berlin industrial workers average about $50 a week, white-collar workers can make somewhat more than that, and executives, of course, earn higher salaries, those commencing at about $250 a month. Pay scales in East Berlin are somewhat lower. Industrial and white-collar workers earn between $126 and $163 a month. After the taxes an East Berlin worker pays, how much has he got left? The only way to understand true costs in the G.D.R. is to compare the amount of time it takes a worker to earn the price of an item, in both West and East Germany.

A table-top television set costs a West German worker 215 hours and 37 minutes of working time; it costs an East German worker 812 hours and 30 minutes. A small Volkswagen costs a West German 1,167 hours and 58 minutes, a small East German car costs 6,166 hours and 40 minutes. A refrigerator costs 88 hours and one minute in the West, as against 541 hours and 40 minutes in the East. A vacuum-cleaner costs 53 hours and eight minutes' working-time in West Germany, versus 147 hours and 55 minutes in the East.

The relationship between the cost of clothing in West Germany and the G.D.R. is equally devastating. It costs a West German worker four hours and 23 minutes to buy a pair of leather shoes, while it costs his East German counterpart nine hours and 42 minutes. To buy his wife a dress made of 50 per cent wool, the West German worker invests 17 hours and 13 minutes, while it would cost him 33 hours if he lived in the G.D.R. It takes an East German worker twice as much time to earn enough to buy a pound of flour, almost three times as much for butter or eggs, and six times as much for either coffee or tobacco. Furthermore, these items aren't always available. It is true that the G.D.R. abolished ration cards but a form of rationing persists on many items. In butcher-shops, for example, each customer is assigned a number and can only buy the available cuts when his turn comes. In the case of liver, one's number is called out about once every three months. This system, of course, also makes it impossible for an East Berliner to buy liver in several shops, for he is registered at only one. Liver is mentioned here because it is extraordinarily scarce in East Berlin—so much so that East Berliners joke that progressive, Marxist methods will soon revolutionize animal husbandry, by developing a breed of cattle and pigs that will actually each contain a liver.

A simple shopping expedition in *KaDeWe* (*Kaufhaus des Westens*) or any other of West Berlin's glittering department stores is enough to show you where the difference in living standards lies. Mass production of consumer goods, intense competition among manufacturers and retailers, and modern merchandising techniques offer a West Berliner an overwhelming variety of high-quality goods at reasonable and often low prices. In East Berlin the worker is robbed blind by manufacturers of schlock merchandise priced sky-high. Welles Hangen, the United States journalist whose tour of the G.D.R. resulted in a book called *The Muted Revolution,* was equally shocked at the high prices he encountered at East Berlin's big Alexanderplatz department store as were my wife and I, noting that medium-quality women's knit dresses cost one hundred dollars.

"These prices," says Hangen, "explain why unsalable dry-goods inventories worth $187,500,000 accumulated in East German warehouses one year. There are other warehouses crammed with useless typewriters, unwanted toys, and accordions equally offensive to eye and ear. East Germany is short of everything except shoddy, overpriced merchandise. It is enough to cause the death of any salesman."

Although East Berliners will admit that consumer goods are more available than they were in the past and that they are of a better quality, they know that it might take the G.D.R. many, many years to catch up with Western standards. They have a joke which sums up both the present situation and their attitude towards it. It tells of an American aircraft company that encounters problems with a new jet plane and so far has failed to find any solution. Each time they test the jet, its wings rip off, always tearing at the same place. Finally, they call in an East German, having tried everyone else. He studies the plane's wings, notes exactly where they always tear off, and then to their amazement, drills a series of holes, one right next to the other, along just that line. To their even greater amazement, the jet plane survives every test and even pulls out of the most murderous power-dives without losing its wings. "We never had any idea East Germany had an aircraft industry," they tell the specialist who solved their problem. "Aircraft industry?" he exclaims in reply. "*I* work in the paper mill that makes all the toilet paper used in the G.D.R. The one place our paper *never* tears is where it's perforated!"

That's a joke, of course; or is it? Until the wall went up, the S.E.D.'s TV propagandist, Karl-Eduard von Schnitzler, bought all his toilet tissue in West Berlin.

One time I visited East Berlin was during the Christmas shopping season; I arrived on a chilly and rainy December morning, parked my car near the Alexanderplatz, East Berlin's traffic and shopping hub, and walked toward its railway station, looking for a restaurant in which to get a hot cup of coffee. On the way there, I did some window-shopping and walked through some of the stores. A state-owned "HO" vegetable and fruit shop offered a mountain of gnarled, small apples and very little else; ten or twelve housewives waited at the counter, attended by salesladies who resembled dental assistants or nurses in their starched white caps and uniforms. The window of the HO food shop was decorated with glass jars containing preserved food (no canned goods were visible anywhere); goulash, stuffed cabbage, navy and green beans floated in these jars in an unappetizing scummy fluid with a thick layer of solidified grease under their gray metal caps. A little farther on, I passed the windows of the HO "gift shop," bearing the usual admonition to shop early for Christmas; this had a dime-store quality about it, offering a hill of wooden kitchen spoons on one counter, a pile of plastic trays and boxes on another, some knicknacks, and little else. I didn't count the items the store carried, to be sure, but gained the impression it couldn't have offered more than fifty different things that day, none of them particularly interesting and all priced much higher than in West Berlin. An East Berlin HO liquor store was nearby, with a large display of bottles in its windows. It offered German whiskey for $5.50 a bottle, while in West Berlin it was then being sold at seven marks or $1.75 a bottle (and worth not a penny more). Vodka and German brandy completed the display, each priced between $2.50 and $3.75, then about twice what you'd pay in West Berlin.

The large central department store on the Alexanderplatz— large only in comparison to other shops in East Berlin—claims twenty-one hundred East Berliners buy there every hour, or 15 million a year. Much of it is being turned into a self-service operation, for the G.D.R. is chronically short of workers, a problem aggravated in mid-1967 when it finally caught up with the West in offering a five-day week. Yet, even here, goods are available only periodically, a mad dash and scramble developing when the news gets around that it suddenly has some item for which East Berlin housewives have been waiting.

Even the chronically optimistic East Berlin press betrays the frequent existence of minor shortages. One recent hot summer day, for example, East Berlin's *BZ am Mittag* hailed the fact that almost seven tons of ice a day were being provided "despite the heat," then added that "supplies of alcohol-free drinks unfortunately remain insufficient." Its evening edition, *BZ am Abend,* explained that East Berlin breweries, charged with producing cola- and citrus-flavored soft drinks along with beer, couldn't manage. Not only were bottles in short supply, but so were workers. "Again Berliners are under the impression," the paper clucked, "that their summertime thirst just isn't being taken seriously." Not so, said the city's chief brewer, for the breweries could meet their quota in barrels and East Berliners could get plenty of beer and soft drinks from the tap. The problem with milk, *Berliner Zeitung* indicated, was more serious. The dairies had run out of bottles, because an estimated 307,000 empties were standing around in East Berlin homes. This means that an East Berliner does not only have to cope with shortages in his home, but is also asked to make up the state's own shortages and to rectify the errors of its planners, producers, and suppliers.

Another example was the shortage of fruit East Berliners underwent one recent summer, watching in outrage as hundreds of tons of fruit spoiled by the side of the city's roads. The official explanation, that not enough workers were available to pick the fruit from the trees, didn't satisfy them; they were infuriated that the fruit had to rot because they themselves were forbidden to pick it for their private consumption.

Even if East Berlin doesn't offer any real value for money, *some* of its shops at least offer good merchandise—at surprising prices. Strolling along what was once the Frankfurter Allee, then the Stalin Allee, and now the Marx-Engels-Allee, one is startled to find several elegant shops. The average East Berliner can't afford to patronize these any more than an average London dock worker can afford to shop on New Bond Street or a New York taxi driver at Cartier's; the East Berliner calls these shops *Uwubus,* a word he stitches together from the first letters of *Ulbricht's Wunderbuden,* meaning "Ulbricht's Miracle Booths." They offer branded, imported Scotch whisky for twenty dollars a bottle, as well as most major United States brands of cigarettes; several *Uwubus* (officially called "exquisit stores") offer luxury items for ladies. One of these is "Madeleine," a high-fashion dress shop on the Marx-Engels-Allee whose windows at times become a bizarre mixture of elegance and hard-fisted propaganda. Once during the celebrations attending the twentieth anniversary of the Socialist Unity party, I found the chic mannequins in its windows elbowed aside by S.E.D. banners and posters hailing working-class solidarity. Inside the small shop, prices strike one as staggering: A "Western-style" dress costing about thirty dollars in the U.S.A. sells for $150 to $200 in East Berlin. It didn't surprise me that more women were ogling the dresses than were trying them on.

Not far away is another "exquisit" shop, the *"Parfumerie* Babette," offering a small, unattractive bottle of G.D.R.-produced cologne plus a bar of soap, gift boxed, for what many a worker earns in three hours. Many of these are produced by the state-run cosmetics industry, VEB Berlin Kosmetik, which East Berlin's *National-Zeitung* calls the "House of Service to Beauty" (*Haus im Dienste der Schönheit*) and which, it claims, exports to Moscow, Budapest, Warsaw, and Oslo. Some products are produced by partly nationalized G.D.R. companies such as the Exquisit KG (or Exquisit Limited), which produces among other items a line of bath oils and perfumes bearing the seductive brand name "Q" and an anti-dandruff shampoo called "Poo-Exquisit."

These luxury-shops are in such radical contrast to everything else in East Berlin that one is flabbergasted when one first encounters them. It is only later that one learns that East Berlin has its own "capitalist class," a stratum of society that isn't only well off, but one that is very rich indeed.

The existence of this class is no secret to the East Berliners, but its actual way of life is certainly treated as one of the greatest state secrets of the German Democratic Republic. Not even second-echelon party functionaries, themselves well-to-do, have any idea of the luxuries which Walter Ulbricht and his immediate aides enjoy.

North of Berlin, near the town called Gross Dölln, Hermann Göring used to entertain at his vast Karinhall estate; it is in this section of the Mark Brandenburg, called the Schorfheide, for "scurfy meadow," that Walter Ulbricht has built his own *dacha,* right beside the ruins of Karinhall, blasted in 1945. Ulbricht's own estate includes sixteen buildings, elaborate security precautions, and sporting facilities. On the banks of Lake Döllner, it has boathouses, a volleyball court, a shooting range, a gymnasium, underground oil tanks, its own heating plant and electric-power station, a special guard detachment complete with watchtowers and a building for the State Security Service, a kennel, a greenhouse, and a home for the resident estate manager. The main building, lying beside the lake itself, is equipped with heated marble floors, custom-built furniture of rare African woods, crystal chandeliers (themselves worth an estimated million East marks), bulletproof windows, and a special underground *Führerbunker* containing rose-colored walls and a bar. The security of the luxurious complex is so tight that not even the chimney has been overlooked. Were anyone to get through the exterior security arrangements and try to slip down into Ulbricht's lair like Santa Claus, he'd hit electrified wire-mesh barriers, setting off an alarm and bringing on the helmeted N.V.A. soldiers and the estate's S.S.D. detachment.

Another heavily guarded complex of buildings is in East Berlin's suburb of Wandlitz; this is the walled-in ghetto of the S.E.D. aristocracy, those the East Berliners call *Super-Genossen,* or "Super-Comrades." One of the homes here belongs to Erich Honecker, security adviser and personnel chief of the S.E.D. Politburo and the man in effective control of the G.D.R.'s army, police, S.S.D. secret police, as well as the party apparatus. Honecker has emerged as Ulbricht's chief aide and is considered the S.E.D.'s "crown prince," Ulbricht's heir-presumptive. He lives in a two-story mansion consisting of a living room, dining room, kitchen, and toilet on the ground floor, and above, a master bedroom, a dressing room, a maid's room, two workrooms or studies, two baths, and a guest room for his father, Wilhelm, who lives in West Germany, as do all Erich Honecker's relatives. This latter fact, says *Der Spiegel,* is as much of a state secret in the G.D.R. as is the knowledge that East Berlin's former mayor, Friedrich Ebert (son of President Ebert) was a heavy drinker, and that the G.D.R. Council of Ministers maintains a special counter where the aristocracy of Communism not only can buy the very best that is produced within their country but can as well order from elsewhere goods such as costly West German cars and equally expensive ladies' clothes from Paris.

The rich in East Berlin are not, however, restricted to this very top level. They also include top scientists, artists, and performers. The G.D.R. pays them princely salaries and even permits them such benefits as relative freedom to travel in the West. Generalmusikdirektor Suitner, in charge of all East Berlin's music, makes an estimated ninety thousand dollars a year at the official rate of exchange. Then there is a yet broader class of leading intellectuals who earn two or three times what workers make. One of the greatest benefits all these people enjoy is that they will eventually receive the *Intelligenzrente,* the "intellectuals' pension," of between sixty and eighty percent of their incomes. Certain physicians who are *arrivistes* in the allegedly egalitarian society also make small fortunes, as do select journalists, authors, and some professors. They may not live with Honecker in the ghetto at Wandlitz, but they maintain elegant villas or live in luxury apartment houses in the city. Not only are they able to afford what capitalists elsewhere can buy, but they can do so at preferential prices, in special shops and commissaries which are strictly off-limits to hoi polloi. It is people like these who patronize East Berlin's night clubs, expensive restaurants, and theaters.

Aside from those whose high salaries raise them into a new

East Berlin aristocracy, there are a few other groups who are also quite well off. Some own shops and small enterprises that either continue to remain in private hands or have only been partly nationalized; others are elderly widows who were rich before Communism and who now live off the gradual sale of jewelry and other valuables; others are property owners and landlords who continue to be independent because the state is content to watch them and their buildings fall into ruin. A great many East Berliners live in privately owned, old tenement buildings that have not been renovated or improved in thirty years simply because there isn't any money for repairs. An apartment consisting of a kitchen and three rooms (heated by coal stoves) still costs only fifteen dollars a month in rent, as it did thirty years ago, in one of those buildings. The landlord isn't allowed to raise these rents, so he cannot afford to make any improvements, and he becomes in this case at least an *un*willing slum landlord. He doesn't want his property to deteriorate each year and depreciate in value, but there's nothing he can do about it. The state won't take it off his hands, though he might be happy if it did, because the state doesn't want to incur the expense of renovation. He at least manages to live well—the rents are being paid—though the same cannot be said of his tenants.

Life in East Berlin is, of course, toughest for people like the invalided Bauer and those too old to work, which is an observation holding true elsewhere as well. Here there is one compensation, however, for upon reaching the age of sixty-five, East Germans are allowed out of the G.D.R., to spend four weeks each year in the West, so long as they have a relative to visit. Most of them seem to be able to find at least *some* relative, and even if these cannot put them up, West Berlin (which welcomes such pensioners with fifty marks pocket money) provides facilities. Ulbricht hopes these unproductive oldsters will like the West so much that they'll leave altogether, for their pensions are, of course, a drain, but in fact few take advantage of that offer. These are unusual tourists, unique because they are traveling westward through the Berlin Wall. Most of the emigrants to the Federal Republic or West Berlin have immediate family willing to take them in. Others are satisfied with an annual visit and hesitate to embark on an unsettled future. In East Berlin they have old friends and old neighborhoods, and it often seems too much trouble for elderly folk to embark on the tiring, difficult and time-consuming business of obtaining a permanent exit visa.

As they are unproductive and can hardly be called the wave of the future, Ulbricht's S.E.D. leaves them alone, particularly if they live alone; they are not bothered by functionaries trying to reeducate them. They live peaceful lives—if extremely modest ones. Most of them need to manage on about three marks a day, but as they point out, old people don't eat as much as the young. Despite their low pensions, they certainly are not starving. West Germany, on the other hand, spends a good deal more for each of its older citizens.

In terms of certain other benefits, the East is ahead of West Germany in providing completely free education and medical care, as well as in offering possibilities of more rapid promotion to its people. Karl Bauer's experience with free medical care, however, shows its benefits are often difficult to obtain, while both higher education and quicker success are generally geared to political reliability.

Social welfare has been a feature of German life ever since Bismarck launched a nationwide system of reforms to take the wind out of the sails of the Social Democrats of his day and it should be noted that the old, in both the West and the East of Berlin, as well as in "both Germanies," receive old-age pensions and free medical care to an extent that exceeds many other countries. To be sure, Ulbricht's minimum pension of 150 marks a month amounts to only $37.50 at the official (G.D.R.-imposed) rate of exchange, but such basic necessities of life as rent and food staples can be bought for that amount. In both East and West Berlin, then, the old "manage to manage," in the West somewhat better due to the wide variety of relatively inexpensive consumer goods.

The aid-to-the-aged program was radically reformed in West Berlin in 1957, when annual pensions rose from 3.3 to 23.3 billion marks. Some Government officials (and Wehrmacht career officers) retire with extremely handsome pensions; one former lieutenant colonel with almost forty years' service receives almost four hundred dollars a month, a sum equivalent to twice that much in the U.S.A. in terms of purchasing power. The average pensioner, however, gets much less: $100 a month. This, while very modest, is not inadequate.

Most of the West Berlin pensioners live at home and a number of them even get meals brought to their homes, an effort financed jointly by a respectable Berlin foundation and the somewhat less respectable, though legal, Berlin lottery. On both sides of Berlin's Wall, then, there are those who worry about this population of more than six hundred thousand old people, about how to care for them and make their lives reasonably satisfying or even productive. The answers found in the West are various, ranging from education and inexpensive theater tickets to outings and basket weaving, while in the East they tend to take on a somewhat more political note. East Berlin today has a number of "Peoples' Solidarity Clubs," which aim at integrating pensioners who live alone at home with the community at large. The first to be established, in 1959, the *Klub der Volkssolidarität* in the Bützowstrasse in the Prenzlauer Berg District has been followed by seventeen more. "Many-sided entertainments are offered in its tastefully arranged clubrooms," East Berlin's *Berliner Zeitung* says of the pioneering club, explaining afterward what is meant. "Slide-film lectures and musical afternoons arouse the interest and attention of these veterans just as much as do discussions of the day's political questions. In the past four years alone, about seventeen thousand cultural-political entertainments were arranged for 1,800,000 visitors." Some other efforts made by the clubs strike one as probably more popular among the East Berliners, few of whom are likely to be enthralled by a talk on S.E.D. philosophy. Thus the *Veteranenklub* in Boxhagenerstrasse in the Friedrichshain District arranges outings to East Berlin's zoo and excursions to Köpenick or Birkenwerder, while that district's thirteen thousand pensioners are also invited to a number of Christmas parties arranged for their benefit.

About 350 East Berlin pensioners are employed part-time maintaining East Berlin's public telephone booths; they report any damage and sweep them out with dustpan and brush, for which services they are paid a modest sum. Such makeshift employment is not needed in West Berlin, which hums with efficiency for the most part, but elderly women still perform some very odd jobs indeed. No one who has visited the city is likely ever to forget the sight of those women who work in West Berlin's Tiergarten as park laborers. All seem of indeterminate age (or vaguely in their sixties), and all trudge around in their own special homespun uniforms: faded-blue, full-length sweatsuits of that baggy variety in which German athletes trot about, knee-high men's socks crumpled up over the pale-blue trousers, above which they wear shapeless, tentlike, printed housedresses and sometimes even huge aprons on top of these, with ragged old sweaters completing the bizarre ensemble. Even more unforgettable to visitors from outside Germany are those old, tattered women who maintain Berlin's incredibly malodorous *Aborte,* the public conveniences. One quickly reconciles oneself to seeing them sit in the dank, tiled passageways separating the men's and women's toilets at railway stations and the like, but it takes a while longer to adjust to seeing them mop away about the feet of men using the urinals. They mutely collect the ten or thirty pfennigs one pays, depending on which facility one has used (the lettering on the urinal wall reads, "P.P. 10 Pfg.") and they seem indifferent to their underground existence. Nevertheless, it strikes one at first that this is hardly what one imagines as a dignified old age for even the simplest of women.

Enforced idleness and lack of money plague old people everywhere, of course, but the Berlin Wall aggravates the problem for West Berliners, for it means most of them cannot afford to travel out of their city at all. They may not be in old-age homes, for the most part, but they remain locked up nevertheless. The West Berlin *Tagesspiegel* noted with dismay that "only 8,200 out of almost 400,000 old people, or two percent," take advantage of facilities aimed at filling their hours with some form of productive work or study. In general, the paper admits, the living standard of West Berlin's old people is decent enough, but it points to the fact that more than 100,000 of them, or one-fourth, live on less than $60 a month, 240 marks. "No one," the *Tagesspiegel* editorialized, "ought to be smug enough to regard that as being sufficient."

Many of those locked in West Berlin are, in fact, in despair. The more sensational newspapers wallow in righteous indignation at this misery and feed their readers a steady diet of reports about it. Willi Rogge, eighty, pushes his wife Alma, also eighty, into the

Neukölln Ship Canal and jumps in after her; Charlotte W., seventy-four, not otherwise identified by the *Kriminalpolizei,* plunges from her apartment at Gartenstrasse 51 in Wedding, distraught because her old house is to be replaced. One senses that many of those others who live out their lives hover on the brink of desperation.

Countess Jutta von Schlieffen, whose bureau in West Berlin offers counsel to those desperate enough to plan suicide, is kept busy. In one year, more than 5,680 people dialed its telephone number, *32 01 55,* and another 1,610 came to her office to plead for help, while 900 succeeded in killing themselves, and another 2,200 attempted to do so. West Berlin is in so many ways an attractive and fascinating city in which to live, but it has always had the highest suicide rate in the world. Predictably, Countess Schlieffen's organization was the first of its kind in all Germany. A physician and theologian named Dr. Klaus Thomas founded it in 1956, then three years later set up a rival organization of his own in Steglitz. Obviously there is plenty of work for two. The Evangelical (Protestant) Church—and West Berlin's helpful lottery—supply some funds for the countess' group, but most of the money is donated, as are the services of its forty-five volunteers and those emergency pastors who race off to rescue would-be suicides in their own neighborhoods. The office, in the Jebenstrasse behind the zoo station, is in the center of West Berlin's lively amusement district; its name is one of those Germanic tongue twisters that aim at precise definition; translated literally, it means, "Telephone Soul Ministry Berlin: Care of Tired of Living." * It provides not only spiritual counseling but psychotherapy. The countess is no United States or British-style society matron genteelly devoting time to charity work. "My branch of the Schlieffen family," she says, "never had any money. We were poor as beggars and had little contact with the aristocracy. That's helped me win the confidence of those who turn to us and I at least never had any difficulties adjusting to new conditions after the war."

The isolation of West Berlin, coupled with the irresistible magnetic pull of prosperous West Germany, has encouraged a constant emigration over the last twenty years. The result may be seen in the Western residential districts where villa after villa, for-

* *Telefonseelsorge Berlin* (*Lebensbemüdenbetreuung*).

merly the homes of wealthy bankers and manufacturers, of well-established physicians, scientists, and professors, and of rich publishers, merchant kings, and prominent lawyers, have been divided up into small and medium-size apartments, none of whose tenants set the elegant tone of the city in the way the former tenants did.

Today's newly prosperous workers have become petits bourgeois, polishing Opels and Volkswagens, watching quiz shows on TV, being herded in group flights to Majorca and Italian resorts, and losing that rowdy, almost Rabelaisian air that used to characterize the working-class districts of the city. They have become burghers—and many have taken on the characteristics of those they always despised. As most of the very rich have deserted the city, the middle and lower middle classes now set the dominant note, transforming much of Berlin into a city of stolid *Hausfrauen* and cautious middle-class shopkeepers. What is gone, says *Der Spiegel,* is "the cosmopolitan type [*der Grossbürger*], the bankers and privy councillors, the aristocracy of money and intellect, the Jewish elite . . .

"The expulsion of the non-Aryans had already maimed Berlin's interior life," the magazine continued, "well before its exterior world was destroyed. The bizarre many-sidedness of its people and their talents, which this city knew so brilliantly how to absorb, has all vanished. What was left was the middle class and the petit bourgeoisie . . ."

These, said *Der Spiegel,* always constituted the solid backbone of the city and were never much different from other bourgeois living elsewhere in Germany, both in their virtues and their shortcomings, but what is so different now is that they determine much of the tone of West Berlin, something they could never have done before. Berlin, it says, is now dominated by a *Kleinbürgertum*—by which it means an intolerant, punctilious, narrowminded, prudish, and pedantic German small-town class.

Yet any visitor to West Berlin knows a different city and a different people: elegant, open-minded, tolerant, worldly, still Berlinese. He believes that this Berlin is the real Berlin today, but he is as wrong as those who see mainly the middle-class Berlin of the Steglitz and Spandau districts or the "bourgeois" workers of Wedding and Neukölln. Both of these are partial portraits, distortions of reality. The fact is that West Berlin continues to embrace a host of different Berliners and many of them are not only well-to-do and elegant but brilliant and cultured. Germans who are pessimistic about West Berlin's changing society are like that reader of the *Morgenpost* who complained that "an elite" no longer existed to set an example for the rest of the Berliners. This is certainly true, but it is not due entirely to the war or to emigration. West Berlin today is an essentially fluid and amorphous society, just as are other Western cities; many critics of West Berlin haven't yet accustomed themselves to the change. Those who used to dictate Berlin's manners, morals, mores, and tastes are gone, along with its other dictators. No postwar lectures on democracy did this. What made the change in Berlin is the changing state of society throughout the world, as well as a prosperity such as Germans have never experienced before. This has not only leveled the upper classes downward, but it has leveled the lower classes upward, as well, until the gulf between has narrowed significantly. What remains may no longer be as sparkling as under Wilhelm II, nor as brilliant as Berlin was during the Weimar Republic, when great differences in income separated the city's classes and created an aristocracy of wealth, position, and culture, but it is nevertheless something rather special, particularly for the Berliners and the Germans.

It's something Europeans from stiffly structured societies perhaps understand less readily than Americans. It strikes one that Berlin—at least West Berlin—for the very first time has more than just a democratic government and constitution: It has what Americans know as a "meritocracy." As class differences become meaningless, as material well-being raises the living standards of the workers and shopkeepers to the point where they attain dignity within their society, West Berlin becomes more egalitarian than ever. If it's lost some of its glitter in the bargain, then that seems to be part of the price one pays for democracy. The glitter, perhaps, can be added, but once the Berliners get the taste of democratic egalitarianism they are unlikely to return to the despotism of old.

chapter twenty

I MET HARRY HANDWEIN TWO DAYS AFTER I ARRIVED IN BERLIN
to research this book. Harry was playing a grand piano which was
covered with an old Persian rug; the place was a small, intimate
lounge called Inge und Ich ("Inge and I"), on the corner of
Lietzenburger and Uhland, near the Kurfürstendamm. I'd pushed
back the heavy red curtain inside the door and stepped over to the
bar to order a Courvoisier. Harry played in that soft, seductive
style Germans never master unless they've worked abroad and
learned to stop thumping the keyboard; after awhile, I went over
to talk to him—leaning on the piano as he played "Moon River."
Three or four heavyset businessmen with girls twenty-five years
their junior sat at small tables nearby. Behind the bar, the manageress, a brassy blonde in her thirties, polished champagne glasses.
She was new; the real "Inge" had been bought out by some "syndicate," which was then opening another cocktail lounge and
restaurant in Berlin, the La Perla, to which Harry was being moved.
I followed him there and got to know him well. Harry is a Berlin
musician who was on tour of South America with a big band in the
early 1930's; he stayed on in Argentina when the Nazis began per-
secuting the Jews. He married a local girl, had children, and remained in Buenos Aires for twenty-five years, but never really
felt right there. In the 1960's, he moved back to Berlin. The fact
that he was Jewish didn't matter; people like Harry Handwein may
be born as Jews, but they remain Berliners by choice and conviction.
He was happy to be back. He still played the old songs like
"Let's Face the Music and Dance." In a way, nothing had changed,
he said. The old songs remained the best, the old melodies brought

back the city as he'd always known it. *"Berlin bleibt doch Berlin,"* he grinned, repeating the slogan. It was almost as though Harry were back at the Romanisches he'd known as a young man.

Across the wall, three or four East Berlin couples pushed themselves about the dance floor of the Moscow Restaurant's nightspot, moving slowly to a fox trot that also recalled Harry's era. A woman bartender rocked a shiny cocktail shaker in a rhythmic beat between her hands. The bar offered wines, beer, vodkas, and something called "Jolly Mix," a blend of whisky and "Mandarin-ginger" liqueur. The lights went out and a spot illuminated the opening bill in the Moscow's salute to "Spring, Women, Fantasy." Three girl dancers undulated to a Benny Goodman recording of "Goody, Goody."

The Moscow isn't the only nightspot in East Berlin. Some of them, as in West Berlin, offer Germanic-style Beatles and the big beat. A good many of these East Berlin restaurants, bars, and nightspots sound like a roll call from Warsaw Pact nations: the "Budapest," "Bucharest," "Warsaw," and so on, plus the "Neva Bar," the "Tokay Cellar," and others with an Eastern flair. The new "Linden-Corso" recently opened at the historic corner of Unter den Linden and Friedrichstrasse, where the Café Bauer used to stand, close by the old Café Kranzler. It's got a "concert café," a wine restaurant, an upstairs dance bar and an espresso café, plus tables outside where one can watch humanity flow by as of old. Next to it is the *Nachtbar,* or "night bar," where 245 East Berliners, most of them functionaries, sip Russian vodka, Slavic wines, and the products of the G.D.R.'s own "People's-Owned" distilleries. There are still others. There's the *Tanzcafé* "Nord" or dance café "North," the "Wine ABC," the Ratskeller, a fish restaurant called "Lukullus," and the Friedrichstrasse's Press Café, which, like the Press Club, is a favorite of actors, writers, propagandists, and their hangers-on. These and a few others just about complete the picture. It's not a lavish one compared to either the size of the East Berlin population or to what West Berlin offers, but it's all the planners will allot. The tourist trade, whose foreign money they help collect, isn't all that big. Most of these places are new and all are centrally located. As soon as you travel out of the hub of East Berlin and into its neighborhoods, it seems impossible to

255

get a bite to eat or something to drink. That feature of almost every West Berlin intersection, the *Eckkneipe* or street-corner tavern, seems absent. New ones haven't been built; many that survived the air raids have been closed. Only a few old places remain in the Eastern sector. The Café Zenner and the "Historical Wine Rooms" are two famous ones; another is the "Letzte Instanz," which means in English "final appeal," something like the American "Last Chance Saloon."

The big bars, nightspots, and restaurants mentioned above are the ones the G.D.R. publicizes in its bi-weekly guide, *Wohin in Berlin?* ("Where to in Berlin?") a title shared by a similar West Berlin weekly publication. There are also supposed to be about four hundred other places in East Berlin where one can grab a snack, but I dare you to find them. The total figure reported in the S.E.D. press must include every little snack bar and quick-lunch counter in East Berlin's 402.8 square kilometers. A typical such facility is the one located opposite the entrance to the Soviet Military Cemetery in Treptow Park. It's a wooden shack where one can buy beer, soft drinks, hot sausages, and slides showing the Red Army graves. It's no restaurant, but consists of just a small counter perhaps three feet long, in front of which you queue. You drink your beer and eat your *Würstchen* at stand-up tables outside.

In addition, there are some cafeteria-style restaurants. We've visited several; most of them are small, shabby, and provide indescribably unappetizing food. Stale cakes and limp "salads" compete for shelf space at their counters; one is best off with just a bottled drink, saving one's appetite for the downtown area. The fact of the matter is that not much effort is put into places that don't bring in foreign currency. Ulbricht expects his workers to eat at home or in factory canteens. This doesn't sit well with the Berliners; no matter what their income may be, they like to eat out.

East Berlin functionaries and others who can afford the better restaurants patronize them heavily. According to *Neue Zeit,* an East Berlin journal, forty thousand visited the Linden-Corso in its first month, "among them many from abroad," the paper stated with satisfaction. "Of the 130 dishes on its menu," it added, "eight hundred are sold each day, substantially exceeding the norm." *Neue Zeit* also reported that "Lukullus" fed six to seven hundred people a day. There's little doubt such places are popular. East Berliners, after all, have done without decent restaurants for so many years that they can't help but succeed, especially as there's so little competition. Further, the food has improved, and the only difficulty now is the high prices. Even today, though, the East Berlin press finds it newsworthy that a new dish is being offered in some restaurant or café. "Two tons of mushrooms were supplied to Berlin hotels in the past three months," said *B.Z. am Abend*, almost as though the writers had good reason to shout hurrah.

"The new Salad Bar at Berliner Strasse 98 now offers twenty-five different salads," according to an enthusiastic report provided by another East Berlin paper, *Der Morgen*. It also reported that, among the many self-service restaurants opened in East Berlin (to counter the G.D.R.'s chronic shortage of workers), the one at Bahnhof Friedrichstrasse "offers a new treat to customers: They can now fish out their own bockwurst from the steam tables." The fish restaurant, Lukullus, says *Berliner Zeitung*, newly offers an *Edelfisch-Fondue*, or fondue of "noble fish," while the Budapest recently introduced "veal-and-rice-Benkö, named after Istvän Benkö, the restaurant's Hungarian chef.

He is one of fifteen Hungarians employed at the Budapest. There are also an Hungarian manager, baker, and cook, as well as two waiters and a nine-man orchestra from Budapest. The G.D.R. and Hungary have swapped restaurant personnel every six months for several years, East Berlin trusting this will bring an international flavor to its cooking. International here doesn't, however, include French *haute cuisine* nor any French, Italian, Rhine, or Mosel wines. The restaurateurs are all oriented solely to the "people's democracies" and the U.S.S.R., since they are all state employees working for the "HO" *Handels* (or trade) organization. The effort made does, of course relieve the relatively monotonous Central European cuisine and is a step forward. Knowing East Berlin's past twenty years, one can't but applaud the four thousand pounds of mushrooms. There may be something melancholy about so much fuss being made over a new dish, but there's also something touching about it. It's clear that many East Berliners are trying very hard, considering the limitations, to take the "D" for "Drab" out of the G.D.R.

It's still a world removed from West Berlin, however, even in the first-rank places. The menus may include dozens of dishes and the wine list a lot of East European wines, but one usually finds that many of these are not available. More important, while the prices aren't higher than in West Berlin, the amount one gets for one's money is a lot less.

Wanting a quick bite on the Karl-Marx-Allee, I visited the Moscow one day and chose the filet steak. I told the waiter I didn't want a full-size meal, only a small steak without any vegetables.

"We don't have any small steaks on the menu," he replied. "We have just one kind of steak, a regular-size portion."

I said I hoped I'd manage. As it turned out, it was no problem. The steak wasn't much larger than a pack of cigarettes and couldn't have weighed more than a quarter of a pound.

It was tasty enough, but I could have bought a steak three times that size for the same number of marks in West Berlin. If one calculates the *real* market value of the East German mark and ignores the exchange rate Ulbricht sets, the price of this hamburger-size steak would buy five pounds of beef in West Berlin.

It isn't just the food or décor that differ in East Berlin restaurants. It's also the diners and the atmosphere they create. I visited the "Bucharest" on one of those December weeks when West Berliners were allowed to cross through the wall to visit relatives in East Berlin. The place was a good deal more crowded and much more animated than I'd found it on normal occasions. It was easy to spot the visitors not only by their appearance, but by the parcels and leather or string bags they carried with them, all overflowing with citrus fruits, bananas, and other gifts. The place was so crowded that day that it was difficult to find a table. Presently, however, two men rose from their chairs and my wife and I hurried over to occupy them. The two East Berliners who were leaving both wore small lapel pins showing S.E.D. membership. One of them also wore a medal next to his buttonhole. A third man remained seated with us at our table, smoking a cigarette and finishing a glass of wine. He filled out a four- or five-page questionnaire of some kind and then addressed some Christmas cards.

A waitress came and we ordered a portion of "breakfast goulash and eggs" and a portion of "Moscow salad and Romanian salami." Both proved tasty, far more so than the coffee substitute. The man

258

at our table never looked up once. His middle-aged, bespectacled face remained utterly expressionless. It's a point worth mentioning only because it's the custom throughout West Germany for those occupying a table to nod or smile a greeting to those joining them. Certainly it's customary to glance with curiosity at anyone who unexpectedly begins speaking in a foreign language. If the English my wife and I spoke in any way startled this man, or if he even noticed it, he never showed it. Like most others in East Berlin, he kept his counsel. One never knows the real identity of strangers and it's well-known in East Berlin that there are *Spitzel* (informers) in every public place. Nor is a Westerner tempted to begin a friendly chat with a strange East Berliner; say a wrong thing to the wrong man and you can get yourself charged with spreading propaganda. This also keeps Westerners from responding too freely should any East Berliner voluntarily address them; such people might be *Spitzel* trying to provoke rash statements. In such an atmosphere, not only communication breaks down, but all cordiality. The only friendly smile of welcome we got in the Bucharest came from Walter Ulbricht, whose large portrait beamed at us benignly from the wall, as though he were the founder.

Aside from this picture, the only other decoration in the room was a mural of Romanian peasants in folk costumes, some of them dancing; it was amateurish, like those Neapolitan scenes one sees in United States pizza restaurants. An empty bandstand waited, perhaps for the supper crowd. Large cone-shaped chandeliers formed of neon tubing lit the room brightly. A Christmas tree stood to one side, looking naked with only twelve ornaments in red and gold. Our table was decorated with a small potted plant peeking out from a bed of moss; we encountered the same plant on tables in several other East Berlin restaurants. One gathers this model was ordered in the thousands.

Later, we visited the Opera Café, next to the Opera on Unter den Linden. Its windows overlook the only place in all Berlin where you can watch a scene right out of the past: German soldiers goose-stepping while changing guard. As a matter of fact, since Four Power agreements prohibit the presence of any German soldiers in Berlin, those honor guards at the "Monument to the Victims of Fascism and Militarism"—Karl Schinkel's "Neue Wache," built between 1816 and 1818—violate Inter-Allied agreements.

Still, so many others have been violated with impunity that only an occasional routine protest results from the Western commanders. These soldiers are quite a sight and few tourists miss the display. The only new thing about the goose-stepping *Landsers* is their Russian helmets; the rest of the *tableau* is as it always was.

The Opera Café, like the Linden-Corso, consists of several restaurants on different floors. The basement has a night club that features French *chanteuses* and is open from 10 P.M. to 5 A.M. The building has a uniformed doorman and the atmosphere is posh by East Berlin standards, which means it has carpets and waiters in full dress. The latter are as professional as any in West Berlin. They're also grateful if you treat them as waiters and not as comrades by ignoring the menu's admonition against tipping "our fellow workers."

We went to the upstairs restaurant overlooking Unter den Linden; the headwaiter seated us at a table together with two young men and a young woman. They sat across from us on an upholstered bench along the wall and spoke quietly. Judging from their conversation, the man on the left was an East Berlin student. The others were visiting him from West Berlin. The Western girl was a dumpy little creature with those Slavic features one sees so often on German farm girls; her Western husband looked like a worker in his Sunday best. Both seemed bored, even ill at ease; it appeared that their visit to this East Berlin friend or relative was undertaken as a duty and that they were anxious to be home again. They shared a bottle of white wine and spoke like old acquaintances who find to their discomfort that they have little in common any longer.

As usual in East Berlin, we ordered steaks. It isn't that the G.D.R. is cattle country; it's just that it resembles many a section of the U.S.A. in that the only thing that you can safely eat if you dislike bad cooking is a steak. We'd had our experience with East Berlin beer, so we didn't order any; even the waiters had apologized to us about it. My wife asked if there were French wine; after all, the Opera Café is one of the three or four best restaurants in the capital of the G.D.R., a nation that has the highest living standard of all the Soviet Union's East bloc states. The waiter seemed amazed.

"French?" he said. "I can offer you a good Romanian wine, but that's all we have today."

"Is it dry?" I asked.

"It's the wine we have. I can't say if it's sweet or dry. It's what you might call strong."

We took a chance. It turned out dry enough and quite delightful.

In the corner to our left, three men vacated a small table. Like those we'd seen leaving the Bucharest, these had party buttons in their lapels. One of them also wore several medals. No sooner were they gone than the headwaiter deferentially led two other men to their seats. They also wore party buttons. The short, thin, sharp-nosed man in his thirties deferred to his companion, who might have been sixty years old but was built powerfully. His head was shaved clean, giving him the look of a Mongol. He wore a dark blue suit and a dark blue wool shirt with a red tie and snapped his fingers for the waiter in a manner that didn't seem too comradely. Once they had seated themselves, the East Berlin student across from us lowered his voice even more. That's one thing you've got to say for East Berlin: It's a place where you can have a meal in peace and quiet.

The presence of the two men at the corner table had an effect that I'd noticed elsewhere. One summer day, after visiting the Soviet Military Cemetery, I stopped for a beer at the small *Imbiss* or snack bar mentioned earlier. I took my beer bottle and paper cup to one of the chest-high stand-up tables out front and watched the people in line. Three young boys, none of them taller than five foot three, came over. They looked at me quietly for a few minutes. Finally, the smallest of them, about five foot even, mustered the courage to talk.

"From over there, *wa?*" he said in a thick Berlinese dialect.

I nodded and said in German that I was an American. The boys exchanged wide-eyed glances as though they'd hit the jackpot.

"Tell me," the leader of the trio said. "What do you think of this war in Viet Nam?"

"I'm against all wars," I replied.

"What I tell you?" he said to his friends and then turned back to me. "They tell us a lot of things over here, you know, but I know better! I got an uncle over there!"

He asked if I had some cigarettes, and when all three reached for my pack, I told them to help themselves. There followed that unfailing ritual of appreciation. I asked them how old they were and whether they were still in school. As it turned out, the smallest in the group was the senior in age, seventeen, while the others were fifteen and sixteen; none were in school. All were apprentice automobile mechanics. We talked for about ten minutes, never once touching on politics. The question about Viet Nam had been the only brush with that subject and my answer had apparently satisfied them.

Suddenly, one of them muttered the comment *"Schnauze!"*—short for *Schnauze halten!* or "Shut your trap!" A trio of East German soldiers had pulled up in an open jeeplike vehicle and were sauntering over. The three boys leaned against their tables nonchalantly, not watching them directly. It was a hot day and the soldiers had stopped for a beer. They didn't bother with the queue, but just stepped to the head of the line, the eight or ten people waiting there giving way to them without those howls of outraged protest a similar action would set off in West Berlin. Once they collected their bottles and drove off, the seventeen-year-old regained his courage and made a face for my benefit.

"Diese Kerle!" he sneered, meaning, "Those characters!"

"Always best to keep your trap shut," said one of the others. "At least when you see a uniform."

After a few more minutes, we parted. I left them the cigarettes and walked across the parking field behind the shack, trying to avoid the muddy potholes, wondering why better facilities weren't offered across from East Berlin's "holy of holies," the Soviet Army grave site. When I drove off, down Pushkin Allee towards the Spree River's Stralau Bridge, I caught sight of the three boys cycling behind my car, waving a farewell to me. Again I had the feeling that usually comes over me when I leave East Berlin, the sinking sensation of having said a final good-bye. Every day you come to East Berlin seems like visitor's day in an institution. Those you leave behind, like these three boys, still haven't finished serving their full sentence.

Ordinary East Berliners who aren't well-heeled enough to patronize night clubs can afford tickets to entertainments such as theater, opera, concerts, ballet, and the cinema. The stages of East Berlin are heavily subsidized and first-rate. As for the cinema, there are five big movie houses in the downtown area and about forty in the neighborhoods. Most of them show G.D.R. or East European films, but some from the Western world are also presented if judged harmless. During one recent month, neighborhood theaters showed four American films, *High Noon, Journey to the Center of the Earth, The Old Man and the Sea,* and *The Thief of Baghdad,* while the classic film theater in Unter den Linden's German History Museum showed *Mrs. Miniver, Dodsworth,* and *The Best Years of Our Lives.* Aside from the stage and movies, there aren't too many popular entertainments. Propagandistic lectures go on all the time and draw their allotted share of persons enrolled in the mass organizations or workers from factories; in addition, there are the East Berlin historical museums, which are excellent, and the exhibitions of Eastern European arts and crafts, provided in special downtown buildings such as the House of Polish Culture.

I saw one exhibit of collages at the House of Czechoslovak Culture; there was also a guest book in which an anonymous East Berliner had written, "How wonderful it is to be able to laugh again for once." The show wasn't only funny, however; it was brilliantly satirical, lampooning bureaucratic pomposity and all the other woes with which so much of East Europe is saddled. This was before the invasion of Czechoslovakia; after Dubcek's liberal era began, visits to this center were discouraged.

The heavy touch of the functionary can be felt on almost all activities except perhaps swimming, which East Berliners can enjoy at more than fifteen pools and beaches. Even spectator sports are regarded as political weapons, either to upgrade the G.D.R. "national image" or to drum home some propagandistic theme. Races are usually run "for peace" and competitions are held "against American aggression." Until 1949, only local sports were permitted in what was then just the Soviet Zone of Occupation, but when the G.D.R. came into being, national sports came to be desirable. Today, the G.D.R. reports that 72,500 East Berliners are "active sportsmen." Inevitably, Ulbricht's functionaries chose team-names copying those of Soviet sports associations: "Locomotive," for railway workers; "Turbine," for the fuel-and-power industry;

"Science," for students; "Dynamo," for police and other control organizations; "Forwards," for athletes in the armed forces. Bonuses, special privileges, and even salaries are paid favored "amateurs," many of whom competed with West German athletes for the very first time at the 1968 Olympic Games. The success of the G.D.R. Olympic team, which returned from Mexico in triumph, with many more medals than the West German team was able to win, was celebrated by the regime so enthusiastically that one would have thought the G.D.R. had won a seat in the United Nations. Seventeen medals were won by East Berliners. International competitions have proved headaches in the past, for the G.D.R. lost many an athlete at such events. One who escaped recently was Jürgen May, one of the G.D.R.'s most honored light athletes. A West Berlin student *Fluchthelfer* group brought him and his fiancée to the West via Hungary, which they were visiting. Jochen Döll, heavyweight boxing champion of the G.D.R., is another who fled. His club, called "Dynamo Berlin," was visiting Helsinki, Finland, at the time. Ralph Borghard, champion iceskater, is another; he defected at Davos, Switzerland. There are many others. One of the most famous is Harry Seidel, champion cyclist of the G.D.R. Seidel fled to West Berlin shortly after the wall went up in 1961 and then became a one-man army against the barrier. He repeatedly entered East Berlin to bring others out of it, including his wife and four-month-old baby. His attempt to save his mother failed; she was caught and sentenced to eighteen months in prison. This infuriated Seidel and made him even more active. He helped dig more than half a dozen tunnels and helped forty-two people escape, fearlessly risking his own life in daring "Scarlet Pimpernel" forays into East Berlin. When he was finally caught on November 14, 1962, he was sentenced to penal servitude for the rest of his life. Then, four years later, the Ulbricht regime suddenly set him free and "expelled" him to West Berlin. Seidel rejoined not only his wife and child, but also his mother, who had also been allowed to leave the G.D.R. after her release from prison as she had reached pensioner's age.

Whether it's sport or entertainment, there's small chance of an East Berliner withdrawing from the drumfire of propaganda. Such harmless amusements as the "People's-Owned" Circus Busch at the Büschingplatz provide a forum for slogans and appeals, and even the traditional carnival-like *Weihnachtsmarkt,* or "Christmas Market," in recent years featured "Viet Nam Bazaars" and other S.E.D. run benefits.

For the average East Berliner, this endless assault isn't merely an attack on the nerves. It also breeds resentment. Almost every ticket he buys is, in effect, made into an endorsement of the S.E.D. regime, a vote for Communism. Even if he's out only for a good time, that isn't how the S.E.D. sees it. The fact that he attended a dance, "incidentally" hailing Soviet friendship, is said to "prove" he backs Soviet policies. His attendance at a concert doesn't always mean he's gone only to hear the music, but is interpreted as his endorsement of whatever propaganda theme that concert celebrated. Most East Berliners, of course, put up with this as an unavoidable by-product of being entertained. Sometimes, however, they've had enough. We saw an example of this during the annual May Day parade in East Berlin, which in 1966 also celebrated the twentieth anniversary of the founding of the Socialist Unity party.

The military part of the parade was already over when my two teen-age sons and I cleared East Berlin's customs and passport controls. We got to Unter den Linden in time to watch the tens of thousands of worker delegates march by under red flags. They swung down the avenue from the Friedrichstrasse and flowed in two streams towards Marx-Engels-Platz. The boys and I kept up with them by walking along the tree-lined center lane of Unter den Linden, between the two columns of marchers. Suddenly, the two columns merged; a moment later, we were engulfed by them. We tried to get through them and off the avenue, but white-jacketed People's Policemen lined the curbs, barring access to the sidewalks. Swept along, we had no choice but to continue down toward the two tribunals, together with these thousands of marchers. The boys looked at me nonplussed; through a fluke, we weren't only watching the parade past Walter Ulbricht, but had become part of it.

It wasn't a proper parade, however. Even as we passed Ulbricht, between the two tribunals on East Berlin's "Red Square," the tens of thousands of Berliners marching never stopped chattering privately to each other; they were simply enjoying the warm sun, the walk, and the talk. Some of them held babies in their arms, some munched apples, several tipped beer bottles to their mouths—even while

265

Ulbricht saluted them, waving his white Panama hat at the crowd. As we passed him, I looked around to gauge the reaction of the marchers; not more than half a dozen were waving back at their leader. The only really orthodox enthusiasm came from the several hundred sweating functionaries who were broiling on the steps of those two tribunals. As each group passed, the public-address system called out its name and its achievements.

"People's-Owned Factory Such-and-Such," the unseen announcer shouted. "Norm Exceeded 150 percent! *Es lebe die V.E.B. . . .*"—meaning "Long live the People's-Owned Enterprise," or simply, "Three cheers."

The functionaries on the stands responded dutifully, though they seemed hoarse and even lackluster by the time we passed. *"Hoch! Hoch! Hoch!"* they were shouting in unison—a German chant that follows such a call for three cheers. Meanwhile, the workers being celebrated ambled on, guzzling beer or lemonade from bottles, fanning their sweating faces with hats, wiping the noses of their children, or laughing among each other at some private joke.

No sooner had we passed through Marx-Engels-Platz than the next delegation trooped past Ulbricht. Our group continued over the Rathaus Bridge, swung down the Poststrasse, and started filing to the Molkenmarkt. The sidewalks were free of policemen, and we were out of sight of the Marx-Engels-Platz. All of a sudden, the demonstration simply ceased! The parade vanished. Our entire column dissolved to nothing within minutes; all those hundreds of people around us, all those hundreds ahead of us, were nowhere to be seen.

We could still hear the faint sound of the loudspeaker on the big square. No more than a handful of streets away from where we now stood, Ulbricht and the other S.E.D. dignitaries continued to wave happily at the marching throng. Where had all these thousands gone? A few hundred could be seen along the Rathaus-strasse, walking towards Alexanderplatz; the curbs here were lined with canvas-covered wooden booths selling beer, lemonade, and the G.D.R.'s "Club-Cola," as well as snacks. A few hundred more were in the area's few taverns, wine rooms and restaurants; that tavern called the "Historical Wine Rooms" was jammed when we looked in. Yet those who could be seen accounted for only a fraction of those who had marched through Marx-Engels-Platz, and downtown East Berlin seemed amazingly empty. Those whom we saw (and we searched the area for much of the afternoon) never remotely approximated the number of those in the line of march. We concluded that thousands must have drifted into S-Bahn and U-Bahn stations the moment they left the parade and gone home.

This seemed especially surprising when one considers how many free entertainments were offered that day. Amusements in East Berlin are so scarce that one would assume the people would flock to any available entertainment. Certainly this day was crammed with events. A pink, eight-page leaflet advertising the program for that day's *Volksfest,* or "national festival," was being distributed everywhere, and loudspeakers announced each new event. Lieutenant Colonel Gerhard Baumann was to lead an army orchestra in front of the International Cinema, while the Post Office employees' brass band was to play at the House of Teachers; the public was invited to join painters, weavers, potters, and others in a "Street of Folk Art" set up on the Berolinastrasse; judo and boxing exhibitions were on the agenda; and finally a major review entitled *"Frieden, Leben, Freundschaft"* ("Peace, Life, Friendship") would be staged, followed by an *Abschlussball,* or "Final Ball."

But first, the day's festivities were to be kicked off by two major bicycle races, consisting of twelve and twenty-four laps each around the Karl-Marx-Allee. These were scheduled for 1:30 P.M. and we decided to go. Since most Berliners love nothing more than a bicycle race, we fully expected to find the sidewalks jammed with excited spectators.

No one was watching! We stayed to observe the puzzling spectacle of athletes outdoing themselves in an arena empty of spectators for more than an hour. There couldn't have been more than twenty people on either sidewalk who paid the remotest attention to the race. As a matter of fact, the sidewalks were also almost deserted, though the race had been well-publicized in advance. A dozen East Berlin workingmen, identifiable in their visored workers' caps, stood about a booth that sold beer and soft drinks. Although it is just such industrial workers who are most enthusiastic about bicycle races, these men chattered among themselves, their backs to the race. They recognized us as coming from "over there" in the West, and raised their beer bottles to us in a friendly greeting.

We saw the same thing happen elsewhere that day. Soldiers oom-pah-pahed away in front of the International Cinema, the postal clerks' brass band blared with enthusiasm before the House of Teachers, but both groups of musicians were serenading the wind. Berliners weren't there, despite their love of bands and music.

An hour or so after the last marchers had filed past Ulbricht in Marx-Engels-Square, downtown East Berlin seemed even less crowded on this national festival than it is on an ordinary working day. It seemed to be a boycott of sorts, as though these East Berliners had turned down all the entertainment because it had been staged to celebrate the twentieth anniversary of the S.E.D. It was an ostentatious display of disaffection, conducted in that cool, calm, manner which is so typically Berlinese.

Some of the East Berliners did not go home, however, but drifted over to the *Tierpark* in Friedrichsfelde, at the far end of Frankfurter Allee. Just as the *Autobahn* highway network survived Nazism, this "animal park" or zoo, established in 1955, is likely to remain in future decades the S.E.D. dictatorship's most popular and lasting gift to the Berliners. Its director, Professor Dr. Heinrich Dathe, has created a spacious animal preserve unique in the freedom that it allows the animals within their specially built enclosures so like their natural habitats. When its present three hundred acres are finally extended to 395, Dathe's *Tierpark* may actually be the world's largest in size, but what is most remarkable about it is its sheer beauty. It is a flower-filled wildlife preserve with streams filled with exotic fish, banks of these streams crowded with rare water birds, and a span of trees and bushes filled with other birds of all kinds. A major excursion retreat for the East Berliners, it provides them not only with its natural delights, but also with a respite from propaganda.

It is not only the excellence of Dathe's *Tierpark* that draws the Berliners to this bucolic retreat in their city. What draws them most is their love of animals and greenery. There are limits to this, of course, because the Berliners are urban types. They enjoy nothing so much as a day in the country—but a day will do. It refreshes them and it helps them appreciate their pavements more. They don't really want prolonged contact with the country; they'd go crazy out there, because there's nothing *"los,"* nothing "going on"—except nature's processes. Parks and zoos are therefore just exactly right for them in that they permit a light bucolic baptism without requiring total immersion. As for the animals, they have their favorites in the zoos, visit and feed them regularly, delight in their growth, read about them in the feature pages of their papers, and have a real affection for them all.

More than affection, however, is lavished on their dogs; these get real love. Berliners often treat them better than they do their husbands, wives, or children. They're not mad for cats, but any breed of dog will do, though first and second place go to German shepherds and dachshunds. The latter are the special favorites of those thousands of lonely widows in West Berlin. Most of these shiny, brown *Dackels* grow grotesquely fat under such loving care. They are stuffed with cakes and candies in *Konditoreien* or fed under restaurant tables with the better cuts of meat or bread sopped in thick gravies. They can hardly walk, are carried about, nuzzled, pampered, babied, and coddled.

Horses, on the other hand, have to work for a living. Most any Berliner today can afford a small pickup truck if he's in business, but quite a few horse-drawn carts can still be seen and one suspects their owners simply cannot part with the nags. Still other horses are used by the big breweries, who deliver a good deal of their beer in huge, barrel-laden wagons drawn by majestic cart horses. They've learned it makes for good public relations.

For a major city, West Berlin has a surprising barnyard population—and much of it is housed within the interior courtyards, or *Hinterhöfe,* of old Berlin apartment blocks. In addition to the horses stabled in West Berlin, there are still almost 800 calves, 213 cattle bred for slaughter, 1,700 cows for milking, 39 heifers, nine bulls, and about 16,000 pigs, sows, and swine. Crowded alongside them are almost 1,100 sheep, 230 goats, and 200,000 chickens. Some of these animals have never seen the countryside once in their entire lives, but spend them just as the Berliners do, inside apartment blocks, surrounded by asphalt.

The walled-in condition of West Berlin—combined with the Berliners' fondness for animals and love of greenery—has made West Berlin's own zoo immensely popular, more than ever before. The number of entry tickets sold each year almost equals the total population. More than two million people a year wander through this green refuge near the downtown "Kudamm" entertainment center. Since West Berlin can't spread out, its zoo also has no room in which to grow; the result is that its animals are just as overcrowded as are the rest of the West Berliners. It may be true that Dathe's *Tierpark* will soon be the world's most spacious zoo, but Dr. Heinz-Georg Klös' West Berlin zoo threatens soon to become the most populated one. It is already the largest in Europe in terms of population and the second largest in the world. The same thing can be said for the aquarium in West Berlin as well. Only the San Diego Zoo in California and the Florida Oceanarium have more to show than West Berlin.

This is quite an achievement, considering the fact that World War II utterly destroyed the work of one hundred years. Three air raids in 1943 and 1944 sent much of the zoo up in flames. Those animals that weren't killed in the raids later died of starvation or were killed in artillery duels during the last weeks of the war. As if this weren't enough, the zoo terrain became a battlefield in the last days. Of its four thousand animals, only ninety-one survived the war. (Rather surprisingly, these included two "heavyweights": "Siam," an Indian elephant, and "Knautschke," a hippo.) No sooner had a postwar zoo been created than the blockade began. The city was forced to kill several large carnivores as well as some animals needing a special diet. The air lift simply couldn't feed them along with all the other Berliners. Since then, so many specimens have been added that the zoo is now "bursting its seams"; Dr. Klös is in the unusual position of having to sell off many new-born animals just to give the others elbowroom.

The zoo's shady paths are just one retreat for the West Berliners on a warm day; they head for the parks as well. "To most humans," says *Time* magazine, "walking is the pedestrian business of putting one foot in front of the other. Not so in Germany. There it is a cherished tradition, a cure for ills mental and physical, and the kinetic tie that binds family and society together."

This may still be true in West Germany, but Berlin's somewhat different. True, thousands of Berliners continue to parade through parks on any mild Sunday and holiday, but most of them are elderly or middle-aged. Berlin's youth has, by and large, abandoned perambulation as a way of pursuing pleasure. Still walking continues to be a family hobby. Everyone dresses in their best clothes. They are weighed down with great bulky overcoats, the men with fedoras clamped securely on their heads, scarves wrapped about their necks, the women in "felt helmets," squat in fur-collared coats that hang straight down from ample bosoms, looking like shapeless robots whose moving parts consist only of heads that nod demurely and feet that tread ever on, obeying some unspoken command.

They say they're out for an outing, but that doesn't explain the motivation. One concludes that the *Spaziergang* is an activity as inexplicably compulsive as the primal urge that sends Americans out driving on Sundays. Only the young lovers in the parks, lightheartedly sauntering, arms about each other or holding hands, seem to enjoy themselves; their elders are reminiscent of gray penguins as they promenade up and down the paths.

There are almost 490,000 West Berliners between twenty-one and thirty years of age, and if their leisure hours do not bring them onto the lanes in Berlin's parks, they tend on pleasant days to head for lakes and beaches, sailing, canoeing, or swimming. So crowded is the Halensee Beach, or *Strandbad,* with pretty, young Berlin girls that it's referred to irreverently in Berlin as *das Nutenaquarium,* "the whores' aquarium." It is wrong, however, to conclude that all the skimpy bikinis at this downtown lake conceal even skimpier morals. The name given the beach is half-affectionate, reflecting again the fact that Berliners deride what they like most.

Even if Berlin beaches aren't big by the standards of cities on the ocean, Halensee on a peak day can look as crowded as Coney Island. Much the same can be said of the other pools and beaches available to West Berliners, and it might be noted (as *Der Spiegel* did) that no other city offers as much opportunity for sailing, swimming, or fishing as Berlin. Mention this to a Berliner and he'll take it for granted, just as he takes for granted that his zoo would be the largest in Europe; he expects Berlin to have the most of everything, both good and bad. He hails its virtues, but complains that they've declined; he uses superlatives to condemn and praise everything about Berlin. He'll boast of the 80 to 100 million trees of West Berlin, but complain they're far too few. Most of all, however, he complains about the weather (when he isn't complaining about the G.D.R. or Russians). He'll exalt the virtues of Berlin's

271

air—that *Berliner Luft*—and condemn in equal terms the fact that the weather is God-awful. Actually, Berlin temperatures are quite mild in summer, mostly hovering in the seventies and rarely ever going up to eighty-five or ninety. If the weather pushes beyond seventy-five, Berliners say with what almost seems stoic pleasure that it's unendurable, unbearable, intolerable, and their papers proclaim "a tropical heat wave." Such exaggerations send Berliners out by the thousands, gasping for breath and fanning themselves with newspapers. (A typical *Bild* headline: "Berlin a hothouse!")

It's no good arguing with them. Visitors are best advised to go along with these Berlinese attitudes, grab a newspaper and a towel, and head out to the beaches along with the rest. Those who point out that, compared to other cities, Berlin has it easy, are dismissed with a shrug—and with a special Berlinese expletive.

Like Chinese mandarins who contemptuously dismissed Westerners as "barbarians," the Berliners airily dismiss all critical non-Berliners as *doof*. It means "dimwitted," and aptly, rhymes with "oaf." Berliners, however, deliver it without arrogance; there's no "Prussian sneer" attached to the term. They call you *doof* in tones of understanding, almost of sympathy, as though they suddenly realized you simply couldn't be blamed for the things you said. Stupidity such as yours, they imply, is almost majestic. It doesn't only explain a great deal about you, but excuses it as well. Sadly, they'll note that Berliners, not being *doof,* have no such "easy out." Almost as though in envy, they'll mutter, "You've got it good—you're *doof!*"

Thoughts in this city turn easily to pleasure, rather than to politics, during the summer months. On a warm day, Berliners line up several hundred strong before the gates of any of their more than twenty-five public pools, some driving from home ready for action, already wearing swimming clothes, others carrying them in rolled towels along with wrapped *Wurst* sandwiches, folded newspapers, and transistor radios. Except for the young, Berliners today do not on the whole look any more attractive at poolside than do Americans who are past thirty-five: Their diets lead them to run to fat as they get older; they tend to look dumpy, square, and lackluster, for prosperity has brought them what they call "manager diseases" such as obesity and cardiac conditions, as

272

though these were somehow the fruits of democracy denied their friends and relatives across the wall. Here, at the pools, they baste themselves with Nivea cream and stretch along grassy banks to tan, and everywhere and all the time, to eat, while others splash about shoulder to shoulder in the water, queue up to careen down wet slides into the pools, or do genteel breaststrokes for exercise.

Even more than parks and pools, however, the Berliners love a festival, no matter how artificial its motivation may seem. Steglitz, for example, celebrated the *Steglitzer Woche,* or "Week of Steglitz," with forty concerts and four fireworks displays, all under the motto "The Tirol Greets Berlin!" A few bands and folk dancers had been brought from Innsbruck; these were enough to lure so many other attractions to the festival site at the Teltow Canal that the "Week" of Steglitz lasted more than two. A quarter of a million Berliners attended and even the United States Army got into the act on closing day, parking some military vehicles nearby for inspection by the curious. Local fairs like these are set up all the time and everywhere, apparently just because Berliners like them.

While local district fairs are organized without anyone even bothering to find an excuse for them, others do celebrate a legitimate event. Thus Kladow, a part of District Spandau, celebrated its seven hundredth anniversary with four days of carnival merry-making, beer-drinking inside huge tents set up by breweries, and by devouring tens of thousands of sausages and rotisserie chickens. "May in Neukölln" was celebrated with fireworks, British and French Army band concerts, and countless glasses of *Mai-Bowle,* a punch made of May wine. It might as well have been "April in Neukölln," or for that matter, "October 7 to 14 in Neukölln," for any date will do. Berliners do not celebrate the things festivals stand for; they celebrate the festivals themselves. Having a celebration is a good reason for a celebration in Berlin. When the weather gets to be good enough, one is hard put to avoid them.

Three festivals in particular are most popular with the West Berliners, which means they're the biggest and offer the most in terms of food and drink. They're the Christmas Market, the October Festival, and the "Green Week of Berlin."

"Green Week" is really an international agricultural show, but Berlin doesn't handle trade shows in a business-only manner. Although the fair attracts seven hundred foreign and five hundred German exhibitors, nearly five hundred thousand Berliners also attend. And while the exhibitors and buyers work, the visitors look, admire, and above all, eat. In one typical week, the Berliners consumed incredible amounts of apples, potato fritters, glasses of wine, French oysters, barbecued halves of Danish chickens, quarts of British beer, portions of apple cake, and took home with them ten tons of Dutch cheese, twelve tons of Belgian meat, and fifteen thousand jars of British marmalade. A great many companies find this "Green Week" a major food promotion and don't hesitate to come a considerable distance to Berlin to attend it. The head of the Israeli pavilion claims it's the most significant agricultural fair in the world for Israeli produce. With its thousands of flowers and plants from many countries, its crowded boardwalk atmosphere, and its oceans of food and drink, it combines much of what Berliners hold most dear: food for the body and for the spirit, as well as plenty of crowds.

Exactly the same things draw West Berliners to the October Festival. In one recent year, more than a million of them downed five hundred thousand quarts of beer and consumed 217 miles of sausages. Let us not forget the half-chickens from dozens of rotisseries, the chocolates and other candies, and the tons of potato salad. The *Oktoberfest* in Berlin isn't as beer oriented as its counterpart in Munich; it's more of an amusement park with glittering pavilions, tens of thousands of bright lights, flea circuses, gambling booths, and dance orchestras. It celebrates nothing in particular except the month of October, which is good enough for a Berliner.

The Christmas Market, on the other hand, is aimed at boosting sales. About a dozen large halls near the West Berlin *Funkturm,* the same halls that housed "Green Week" exhibits, are filled with things to buy, with entertainments to prompt one to buy, and with enough religious window dressing to encourage giving. The Berliners stroll through all this like children in a toy department, eyes wide with delight and mouths open for traditional Christmas cakes and goodies.

As long as there is good food to eat, good beer, and *Schnaps* with which to wash it down, and lots of people around him, he is happy. The *Grüne Woche* is as crowded as Berlin's beaches in the summer, but the Berliner doesn't complain about being jostled. One

West Berlin newspaper explained this feature of the Berlinese psychology this way:

"Other people may want solitude in order to relax," it wrote; "they may look for lands as yet unpopulated by man, for cliffs untouched by people—we, however, have a horror of solitude that is deep-seated in our hearts. And why is this? Simply because there's nothing going on in those kind of places.

"Something *always* has to be going on, as far as we're concerned!

"Before we'll even go to any public entertainment, we first ask if it's sure to be nice and crowded. Even a masterpiece bores us if the gallery is half empty. How often have we not turned back, almost in horror, after discovering that our favorite, cosy tavern only has one customer inside?

"No Berliner," the paper concluded, "has ever become a hermit!"

Department-store chains like Karstadt spend a lot of time and money assessing the Berliners' temperament, likes, and aversions, and they usually know how to treat him right. When Karstadt opened another of its branches at Tempelhof, it staged a festival, with music, snacks—and all the free beer one could drink. It was almost too successful. Berliners crowded into the store in such numbers that the store had to shut its doors just a short while after it first opened them.

When Schultheiss marked its 125th anniversary recently, it invited all West Berlin to get free beer from twelve district *Bierbrunnen,* or "beer fountains." The Berliners queued up in lines hundreds of yards long and nine hundred civic dignitaries came out to hail the brewery as a major civic institution. Yet Berliners aren't freeloaders; it isn't a glass of free beer that prompts them to line up in the hot sun, jammed behind police barriers in orderly queues. It's the festival, the occasion, and the crowds around them that draw the Berliners out of the comfort of their flats or even out of their taverns. They'd rather die than miss the action.

Anyone over the age of sixteen may drink beer in Berlin taverns and it would seem that they all do, for beer consumption in West Berlin comes to 108 liters per person, counting every man, woman, child, and infant in the Western sectors. That's more than two quarts a day, but if this seems a lot, let it be noted that the West Germans put away 124 liters per capita each year. Schultheiss and

Bärenbier are just two of the breweries that join with the city in supporting Professor Bruno Drews' special brewing and distilling research institute at the Technical University, hoping, in the words of Director Drews, "to make Berlin beer even healthier, tastier, and more stable than it is." Fifty of his scientists are hard at work on sundry projects, all dear to the heart of the Berliners. They are doing what they can to prevent beer from going flat in bottles, to build a better head of foam on each glass, and are even attempting to take the pain out of over-indulgence by trying to find out just what ingredient gives a man a headache when he's had a few quarts of beer too many.

The best of that summer beer called *Berliner Weisse* used to be so explosive in the old days that tavern owners, to lower the pressure, kept it buried in the fine, white sandy soil under their establishments. The really good *Weisse* therefore came to be called *Sandweisse* and the very best *Champagnerweisse*. It used to be decanted like fine wine and cost as much as a mark, whereas plain *Weisse* then cost fifteen to twenty-five pfennig, depending on the size of the glass. It does resemble champagne in that it is just about as bubbly, though it's a good deal lighter, since it only contains 2.8 percent alcohol. Berliners drink it with a shot of *Kornschnaps,* their *Strippe.* They also like to add a shot of raspberry juice, turning the *Weisse* red and sweet, or a jigger of *Waldmeister,* a European herb called "woodruff" that is outlawed today. (Berliners now turn their *Weisse* green with imitation *Waldmeister,* much as Pernod is used to imitate absinthe.) These are summertime drinks, however, preferably consumed under chestnut trees in the *Hinterhöfe* of old Kneipen; in winter, Berliners drink a stronger beer, some of it very strong indeed.

In addition to the beer, Berliners drink almost twenty liters of wine each, a great deal more today than earlier, a tribute to both growing sophistication and wealth. The wine restaurants in Berlin are many and much frequented, and any restaurant at all which takes pride in its kitchen has an excellent and international wine list. Berliners who are fond of wine go to special *Weinstuben* like the delightful Habel near the Roseneck, the Historical Wine Cellar on Alt Pichelsdorf, Lutter and Wegner, or Hardy's near the Opera, which specializes in wines from Baden and serves them with a platter of twenty French cheeses. As for average Berlin workers, or, for that matter, average burghers, they still stick to their *Molle und Klaren,* their beer and clear corn *Schnaps,* a sort of German gin without a juniper taste. It's a Berlinese boilermaker, as powerful as one with whiskey.

"When it comes to tippling," says *Time,* "nobody out-topes the West Berliners"; it went on to report they downed eighteen fifths of hard liquor a year each. The explanation was simple: Liquor in West Berlin was so cheap through 1965 that anyone abstaining was *doof.* Local whiskey cost $1.25 a fifth and *Korn-schnaps* often only 75 cents. People came on pilgrimages from all over, just to tie one on in West Berlin. Swedish businessmen and students, who love to drink but hate the price of Aquavit back home, drove all the way to the Kurfürstendamm and never sobered up once while there. All this is over. The preferential liquor tax structure the Berliners enjoyed for fifteen years was canceled January 1, 1966, as West German inflation rose. Why it was ever granted isn't certain; no one wants officially to confirm the rumor that cheap liquor was an incentive to induce West German workers into the embattled city, the theory being that they'd need more than their normal quota after seeing the Berlin Wall. Prices have since climbed fifty to one hundred percent; the days before the tax boost saw a mad scramble for remaining inexpensive stocks. People queued up for cases of Vat-69 at less than four dollars a fifth. When it was clear that the Berliners could no longer call their city a *Schnapsparadies,* Willi Kinnigkeit of Munich's *Süddeutsche Zeitung* noted sadly that it no longer paid to travel there just for a cheap *Sause,* as Berliners call a drinking spree. Even beer went up five to ten pfennigs (or 1¼-2½ cents) a glass and bottle respectively. Berliners howled, threatened a beer-drinkers' strike, but soon went back to drowning these new sorrows. The only ones who saw the silver lining were reformers trying to do something about the rate of alcoholism in West Berlin, which in ten years had climbed five-fold.

A city that puts away 163 million liters of beer and 30 million quarts of hard liquor a year, of course, would have to have its share of drunks. Not even the 22 million pounds of coffee West Berliners consume annually sober all of them up all the time. Some of these drunks tend to get into trouble, and since the worst trouble they can get into is connected with the border, it's inevitable that the more daring among them run into the wall. Every now and then some West Berliner tries to scale the wall to get into East Berlin. Some get shot at as aggressors; others are simply dragged down by West Berlin policemen. Occasionally, one of them gets over and is hauled away by East Berlin guards. It usually turns out that these drunks had relatives in East Berlin and simply decided to pay them a visit.

Berliners have always had quite a reputation for brawling among themselves but a great deal of verbal abuse comes first, for the Berlinese argot provides an amazing number of insults and threats. Wilhelm Franke, author of a compendium of such epithets, says they demonstrate the Berliner's "love of and inclination toward grotesque exaggerations," some of which have a decided poetic flair.

"One blow," the Berliner warns, "and your nose will stick out the back of your head. The second blow would be desecration of a corpse!" His opponent isn't nonplussed, if he's a Berliner. "I'll clobber you so you can look out from inside your rib cage, like a monkey in a zoo!"

"I'll spit in your eye so hard you'll have to swim away!"

"Oh, yeah? I'll hit you so hard your features will run off your face!"

That kind of an exchange, of course, often escalates into a fist fight. But even when they fight the brawl maintains a Berlinese flavor. Every nation, perhaps even every major city, seems to have its specialty: Parisians toss acid or slash, Italians ram stilettos, Americans use guns. The Berliner, like the Irishman, uses his fists or chairs and beer steins. And often even the losers emerge victorious.

Take, for example, a fight that erupted at 11:30 P.M. on an October evening outside the Big Apple, a young people's discotheque on the Bundesallee in West Berlin. Two policemen saw a crowd burst out of the night club and a free-for-all begin on the sidewalk. The police naturally raced over to intervene.

Now it so happens that Berliners regard fights as private affairs. When the two policemen charged in with their billy clubs, three young workers grabbed their night sticks and turned them against the cops. Their wives tried to restrain them, but this only seemed

278

to infuriate them more. Anyway, it was too late. The cops were flat on the sidewalk. When one of them drew his revolver and shouted, "I'll shoot!", the three young men just laughed and one of them spat out, "You wouldn't dare!" The cop didn't, but the other one had by this time crawled to his patrol car and radioed for help. Spectators had thought of doing the same thing; two of them had already telephoned police headquarters.

"Three fellows here are beating two of your men to death!" one of them reported. "Send three cars right away—or, better yet, five!"

"No cars available now," headquarters said. "Ask them to hold it."

Just then, that perennial stalwart, the Berlin taxi driver, happened by and charged in with a metal stop sign he'd found in the patrol car at the curb—one of those round disks on a pole policemen use in Berlin. He joined the cops, flailing away at the attackers. A few moments later, reinforcements did arrive: not five, but eight, patrol cars loaded with cops and one *Einsatzkommando* unit, or riot squad. Together they managed to subude the three workers. At the station house the workers were proven drunk but refused to say anything in their own defense, though the police threatened to start proceedings against them later, since both cops had to be hospitalized. The workers left the station triumphant. It had taken eight patrol cars full of policemen, one riot-squad unit, and one taxi driver to subdue the three of them. All in all, it wasn't a bad evening's work.

While such brawls aren't confined to Berlin, these young men did exemplify certain local characteristics. Berliners like their beer and feel no embarrassment about being intoxicated. They're not mortified the next day if they were loud and unruly, and furthermore, they object to interference from any busybody, cops included.

A similar incident concerned a man brought to trial on charges of hitting a police sergeant in the face when the officer interfered in a quarrel he'd had with a barmaid. Arguing his own case in heavy Berlinese, he at first denied everything, then accused the *Hauptwachtmeister* of acting officious. When he was finally sentenced to sixty days in jail instead of the six months the prosecution had demanded, he addressed the judge in tones of heavily ironic gratitude. "In that case, Herr Amtsrat," he said, "I'll do you a favor, too! I'll pass up an appeal. That'll cut short your paperwork." He walked out of court triumphant. He'd had the last word, which all Berliners feel they must have. He hadn't "humbly" accepted judicial clemency; by returning the favor, he'd made himself the equal of the judge. He'd canceled the debt. Furthermore, it had been all worthwhile. The officer had been guilty of *Wichtigmacherei,* of making himself important, a sin no Berliner likes to see go unpunished; hitting him was meant to cut him down to size. One can, after all, push Berliners only so far and then they hit back. Later, they may well concede your point, for they pride themselves on being reasonable, sensible, and peaceable folk.

The story that there are four corner bars facing each other at *every* West Berlin intersection isn't really true. There are only about five thousand bars, restaurants, cafés, beer halls, night clubs, and neighborhood taverns in West Berlin, scattered along its 554,-200 acres of streets, squares, and avenues. Still, they certainly seem to be everywhere in West Berlin, especially downtown.

Berliners like it that way. In his *Berlin,* Walther Kiaulehn refers to a kind of primordial hunger at the bottom of the Berlin soul; it is, he says, a constant hunger for food. At every hour of the day or night, the Berliner is tortured by the thought of possible hunger pangs; he assuages them before they ever arise. He arms himself against the onslaught of hunger with *Stullen.* These are slices of dark bread with something—anything, even just butter—in between, wrapped tightly in paper and placed either in a briefcase, pocketbook, or overcoat. Whenever Kiaulehn's father pocketed his *Stullen,* he'd always announce, "Just in case of mobilization!" Indeed, that's what they're for: as emergency rations, just in case traffic, business, a friend, or war delayed one's search for a meal. They're not always eaten, says Kiaulehn, but they're always at hand.

"As long as I live," he writes, "I'll never forget the sight of a man who collapsed on the Schlossbrücke in 1911. A small crowd gathered. One Good Samaritan straightened up and announced, "I got a feeling he's hungry. Anybody got a *Stulle* on him?" Immediately fifteen wrapped *Stullen* packages shot forward toward the stranger.

The *Stulle* is not the only defense against the threat of incipient hunger pangs. Booths selling hot sausages and rolls stand at almost every West Berlin intersection, winter and summer, rain and shine. Avenues and streets are peppered with *Schnell-Imbiss,* or quick-snack counters, and every department store not only has a restaurant, but usually several corner counters at which shoppers can grab a quick quarter-chicken, pork chop, small fish fillet, or sausage, standing up. Even the most elegant Berlin theater, even the Opera, has such quick-snack counters. When intermission comes, droves of well-dressed, upper-class Berliners mob the stands like famished Indians, to get a sandwich or a steaming *Bockwurst.* The sight boggles most foreigners. When a group of French university students who had come to West Berlin on a guided tour were asked what they would most remember about the beleaguered city, one Parisian replied, "The sight of ladies at the Opera, standing about eating hot sausages with their fingers!" The emotions aroused by strong drama, Kiaulehn explains, simply make Berliners hungry; not even the most distinguished ladies can endure sitting through *Hamlet* unless they fortify themselves between the acts. Those who can't afford more than their tickets come armed with *Stullen.*

Restaurants are all over West Berlin and every *Kneipe* sells the Berliners' favorite tavern food: sausages, roast chicken, potato salad, herring, and *Bouletten,* the mealy hamburgers served cold and dunked in mustard. Usually, they also offer hard-boiled eggs, sour pickles, and *Brathering,* roast herring. Put them all together and they're enough to make Berliners fight for them, as Americans were once supposed to fight for Mom's apple pie. The *Stulle,* as a matter of fact, contains enormous emotional content, for it reminds every single Berliner of his mother, who never let him venture out to school (or anywhere at all) without placing one in his hand.

If there's something about the Berlin mother that reminds one of a Jewish mother ("Sh, first you eat!"), oddly enough it's not the only thing about Berlin that's vaguely Yiddish. Even some common Berlinese words—*meschugge, mies, Mischpoke,* and others—are based on it. Until the mid-1930's, the city had a lot of popular

Jewish restaurants; the best known of them, Berg's on the Markgrafenstrasse, attracted great numbers of non-Jews as well. Today, there's just one kosher restaurant in West Berlin, the restaurant in the Jewish Community Center on the Fasanenstrasse, and none at all in East Berlin.

A great many international restaurants feature Italian, French, Syrian, Turkish, Balkan, Danish, Czechoslovakian, Bavarian, Viennese, Romanian, Japanese, and Chinese cuisine. (One of the latter serves egg rolls stuffed with sauerkraut.) So many restaurants of all kinds exist, as a matter of fact, that *Berlin in a Hurry,* a guide published by Eugene Cotton, an emigré American in Berlin, and by his wife Hilda lists ninety-one, as well as eighty-three night clubs in the downtown area alone.

Probably the most Berlinese of all is Aschinger's near the *Bahnhof Zoo.* Open until the early morning hours, it's a haunt of students, travelers, and those needing a late-night snack after the theater, a party, or a night club. The snack they consume is invariably Aschinger's specialty, a yellow-bean soup on which generations of Berlin students lived almost exclusively. It costs just pennies, and until recently, was handed out with as many free rolls as anyone might wish to eat and pocket. (The average customer here took five a day.) Recently, the hand-out was cut because some crank called the health authorities. He didn't like the fact that the rolls were out in the open in a self-service bin, and the officials agreed. Customers rummaging with their hands among the rolls might spread germs. "It's something we've imported from America since the war," a student told me. "A hygiene-*Fimmel,*" meaning a nutty idea. Henceforth, the city decreed, counter girls had to hand out the rolls neatly and hygienically, using sanitary tongs, two with each bowl. The manager, Herr Hintz, was horrified. Aschinger's had made its fortune by giving away free rolls; not only was a tradition threatened, but the entire enterprise. No one was returning for second helpings of rolls, though they were offered. It was one thing to grab them, but Berliners have their pride and don't like to have to ask. "No one wants to look greedy in front of others," Hintz explained, deciding to satisfy the fusspots and the students at the same time, by installing an automatic roll-dispensing machine. This let the rolls drop down hygenically and allowed customers to grab as many as they liked, one by one.

Just twenty years after Aschinger's first opened in 1892, it had fifty outlets throughout Berlin; later on, it had as many as eighty. The secret of this success was simple: The restaurant provided better food cheaper than any place else. The cooks used mass-cooking techniques and always stuck to a few tried and true dishes. It then took twelve thousand pigs, ten thousand head of cattle, and nine thousand sheep a year to supply its kitchens, but now there remains of this vast Berlin institution only the one outlet at the zoo station; those which weren't bombed out in West Berlin during the war were nationalized in the East afterward. Yet this Aschinger outlet at the zoo at least keeps up the tradition of the *Berliner Küche* it always served, its cuisine consisting of the afore-mentioned soup, bockwurst and salad, Kassler smoked pork, pigs' knuckles with sauerkraut and puréed peas, and a variety of other dishes, all of them low in price, high in calories, and best en-joyed washed down with a *Molle,* or glass of beer.

Another famous old restaurant that is still flourishing is the Alter Krug ("Old Jug") in the heart of Dahlem, that elegant, resi-dential villa section near the Free University. Unpretentious out-side, it is a former farmhouse dating back three hundred years, bearing no advertising signs, no neon lights. As a matter of fact, even if the owner, Heinz Hüser, wanted to modernize its exterior, he wouldn't be allowed to do so, for the building is under city protec-tion, like a church. Hüser's cooking, which has won several interna-tional gastronomical prizes, attracts diplomats, famous actors, local dignitaries, and bishops, as well as such public figures as Willy Brandt and Prince Louis Ferdinand of Prussia, the Kaiser's grand-son and today's head of the House of Hohenzollern. What is most unusual but typical for Berlin is that every evening the Alter Krug transforms itself into a Berliner *Kneipe,* filled with local residents and students sitting over their *Molle und Klaren,* alongside the dig-nitaries eating venison in cream sauce (currently $1.90) or beef Stroganov ($1.75). It's as though Le Voisin in New York were each evening overrun by youngsters in sweaters.

"In the old days," says Hüser, "the Hohenzollerns used to have their breakfast here before they went hunting. The atmosphere was different. The students, for example, today sit over beer or even Coca-Cola, discussing politics endlessly. In the old days, they were serious about drinking and less serious about talking.

They used to get drunk, charge out of the place with their steins, and heave them into the village pond outside. It was said that the owner used to fish his steins out after closing time—and that the ducks were never sober. That sort of thing doesn't happen any more," Hüser concludes, and one is not certain whether he says it in relief or with regret.

Atmosphere and excitement are always important to the Berliners. Certainly their predilection for crowds never deserts them even while they eat, and so Berlin restaurants are often very crowded and frequently enormous in size, resembling huge beer halls, except that the tables are covered with linen and the waiters are in evening dress. *"Haupstache is Stimmung!"* the Berliner says, meaning "Main thing is there's atmosphere"—something going on, something *"los."* Because he demands this, there's almost always something *"los"* in Berlin restaurants, bars, night clubs, and corner taverns. Maybe there's just a crowd, enjoying themselves peaceably: no matter, the Berliner is happy just to see the crowd and to await developments. Maybe there's some action: a dance, an overflowing beer hall, or any one of a number of those beat-music clubs that open and fold as rapidly as their platters are flipped, the Blow-up, High Speed, Closed Eye, Liverpool Hoop among them. Of these, Rolf Eden's Old Eden Saloon is one of the few that have endured. Arthur Frommer helped popularize it among five-dollar-a-day tourists, calling it "the swingingest, hippest, looniest, and most surrealistic night club in Berlin . . . packed not only with happy young people, but also with every conceivable type of whiz-bang invention and entertainment device . . ." It's open till five in the morning, is deafening to the ear, and so jammed with customers that they can't even find a place to stand and dance, much less sit down. That's the kind of place Berliners like. For those who enjoy a mix of modern beat rhythms, an occasional Bavarian dance, and a lot of big-band noise, there is the equally crowded and enormous Neue Welt (for "New World") on Neukölln's Hasenheide, which even includes an undulating slide on which customers can careen from the second story down to the dance floor, an activity that seems to make more sense to them with each stein of beer they drink.

There are a great many such clubs and dance halls in Berlin, not to speak of the tourist-type night clubs. There's the Badewanne (for "Bathtub"), Walterchens Ballhaus ("Little Walter's"), the Eierschale (the "Eggshell") and several others. All overflow with *Stimmung,* which means "with people," for the Berliners and their inexhaustible appetite for entertaining themselves in herds create the atmosphere.

Should a Berliner want *Gemütlichkeit,* he goes to his *Kneipe* (pronounced *Kneyepuh*). He goes there even if he doesn't want it; in fact, he goes there as often as he can, which is usually at least once a day. As Walther Kiaulehn says, "Anyone who lives in Berlin and doesn't go to a *Kneipe* regularly is either sick or he's no Berliner."

Every Berliner seems to have "his own" *Kneipe*; he tells you it's either right around the corner (*gleich um die Ecke*) or diagonally across the street (*schräjrüber*). Like the English "local," it is as much a place to meet and talk as to drink. *Kneipen* became especially popular in the days after 1871, when thousands lived three, four, five to a room, in wretched *Mietskasernen.* The *Kneipe* afforded them a measure of privacy; it was the only place they could be away from relatives, except on a park bench. Yet that doesn't explain it all, for even Berliners with all the room in the world go to a *Kneipe.*

"Even aesthetes whose apartments are true works of art," writes Kiaulehn, "lock up their cultural possessions at times and go to a *Kneipe*. It doesn't bother them at all that their favorite *Kneipe* happens to have an old bicycle leaning against the piano. It can even be said that the Berliner strongly mistrusts any *Kneipe* which has been made artificially *gemütlich.* He'll accept palatial and pompous decorations only in restaurants. What he demands of any real *Kneipe,* however, is that it be unpretentious to an extent bordering on being uncomfortable, that it be neither too brightly lit nor too dark—and that the owner doesn't lay his comb down in the butter dish. But that ends his list of requirements."

If the people in the *Kneipen* are real Berlinese types, that holds true even more for the owners behind the *Theke,* as the Berliner calls the bar. One can't be certain whether the customers' Berlinese tongues educate the owners, or vice versa, but if anyone has developed a sharp and impudent Berlinese wit, it's usually the man behind the bar. Niquet, a famous 19th-century publican at 24 Jägerstrasse, is still legendary in the city for his Berlinese wit.

When a customer one day wanted to borrow money, Niquet replied, "Too bad, but you came a day too late! Just yesterday, I signed a contract with the Prussian State Bank. From now on, they're not going to sell any more sausages and I promised them I wouldn't loan out any more money."

Our own favorite *Kneipe* owner, Hermann Thibaut, like Niquet, is a descendant of the Huguenots; his family has been in the *Kneipen* business for generations. When Hermann returned to Berlin in 1945 after service as a soldier he became a truck-driver. He was soon singled out by a trade association as Germany's "Politest Long-Distance Driver." He promptly quit driving and opened a *Kneipe,* which he named after the title he'd been given, Zum höflichsten Fernfahrer. His is a working-class clientele. The place is rarely jammed, but is always crowded enough so one can say there's something *"los."* It has two pinball machines, made in Chicago, and a German juke-box, plus two German-built slot-machines, but none of them create much noise. Hermann and his tiny pouter-pigeon wife see to it that no one's bothered.

One sits and talks over the Bärenpils he serves, over a *Molle und Klaren*; regulars are honored by being seated next to Frau Thibaut at the big round *Stammtisch* in the corner, where one plays Skat, the traditional card game. When we left Berlin, Thibaut was horrified. "How can you live in a place where there are no *Kneipen* at all?" he asked.

There is today no *Kneipe* particularly patronized by artists and writers as in the old days, though the café Franz Diener, a former German heavyweight boxing champion, runs on the Grolmann-strasse comes close to it. Still, it's nothing compared to the Roma-nisches Café of the pre-Nazi era, and the new Romanisches that was recently set up in the Europa Center bears no similarity whatever to its predecessor, except in name. It's just a place where elderly widows eat pastries, and actually, a well-known Berlin author was recently denied admission for not wearing a tie.

In modern Berlin, the talent now gathers in various scattered spots throughout the city. The Kreuzberger *Künstlerkneipen* (art-ists' taverns) are among the most interesting and least known to tourists. Shortly after I arrived in West Berlin to research this book, I headed out there with my wife and an American friend, a girl from California then studying in Berlin. With us was a Technical University student named Rolf, who brought along his date, Karin. Rolf, like so many others in West Berlin, is a refugee from the G.D.R.; Karin, again like many others in West Berlin, is a refugee from West Germany.

The section of Berlin in which these *Künstlerkneipen* lie couldn't be drearier—blocks of huge old apartment houses, dark, wet and gloomy streets, occasional moonlit factory sites or railway yards, pavements deserted. Rooms here are cheap, running ten dollars a month or less, and a good many struggling poets, novelists, sculptors, painters, photographers, musicians, and budding philosophers live in them. Many of these come to the Leierkasten (the "Hurdy-Gurdy") in the evening. It's a corner *Kneipe* that in years gone by attracted writers like Günter Grass. Its walls are covered with paintings, some in frames, some murals on the walls, most of them cubist, many of them obscene, with impudent slogans scrawled on them in paint. We sat down with Rosie, the fat, disheveled woman who managed the place, a former artist's model whose full-length portrait, showing her wearing black hose and nothing else, hung framed on the wall. Others joined us: Wolfgang M., a young music student from South Germany now studying in Berlin, and finally, a tall, thin, gentle fellow in his thirties who had chucked a job and family in Frankfurt am Main to write poetry and drift about Berlin. For six years, he'd spent a few weeks on one couch, a few more on another, a constant guest. He's Karl-Heinz Herwig, known throughout Berlin as "Caesar," perhaps because of the Roman row of bangs that cover his forehead above his steel-rimmed spectacles.

A little later in the evening we all went to Die kleine Weltlaterne ("The World's Small Lantern"), a *Kneipe* established by *"Künstlermutter"* ("artists' mother") Hertha Fiedler in 1961. Her crowded *Kneipe* serves as both a gallery for unknown painters and as a salon for poets, several of whom Hertha herself brought to public attention over the years. When she staged her first exhibition shortly after she opened, she mailed out only twenty invitations; today, she sends out seven hundred and the crush is so great that apparently everyone comes, including critics from the papers. From the Weltlaterne, our pub crawl, or *Bummel,* landed us at the Alt-Berliner Wirtshaus ("Old Berlin Inn") near the Oranienplatz.

This is owned by the son of the founder, an old Prussian type, rather strict about the appearance and decorum of his clientele, as well as about the premises. Farmers bringing produce into Berlin used to anchor their barges on the canal next to this inn before going farther into the city. Today, the canal here has been blocked, for the Berlin Wall runs so close to the tavern that those people living alongside the inn must use the rear entrances of their apartment houses, as the front entrances abut onto the wall itself. Still, despite this gloomy sight, there was in the place the kind of *Stimmung* Berliners like. Guests played guitars and accordions, sang old Berlin songs, talked, played cards, and smoked.

We had gone from artists' bars into a working-class district; now we moved on to a *Kneipe* that had a milieu right out of Brecht and Heinrich Zille. This was the former Bei Tante Else, or "Aunt Elsie's," on Oranienstrasse near the Adalbertstrasse, in Kreuzberg. It was a small place, long and narrow, a bar up front, tables in the back. We wormed our way past a score of workers and women. Most of the latter were local prostitutes, all looking forty to fifty years of age, though we were assured they were half that old. Drunks in ragged suits slept with their heads resting on tables, a grotesquely fat prostitute reeled about the floor, dancing with a young worker whom she held up. When they fell against a table, it started a fight with those sitting there. Rolf, a connoisseur of Berlinese milieu, called the proprietress and pointed to the wallpaper with distaste.

"You've redecorated," he complained. "You've ruined the place!"

"Muss ja sein!" she answered. "Has to be! Place was beginning to stink."

When she referred to us as *die Herrschaften,* or "ladies and gentlemen," it was clear she thought we didn't fit in, so we left for Ellie's Bierbar on Skalitzerstrasse near the Görlitzer station where you have to ring a bell and ask to be allowed to enter. Ellie's is one of the oldest *Kneipen* in Kreuzberg, a Berlin tradition, and the people working there boasted that Marlene Dietrich drops in when in Berlin and that Hildegard Knef, Berlin's newer Dietrich-style singer, also pays an occasional call. We didn't see them there that night.

Ellie's happens to be what Berliners call a *Schwuhl-Lokal* or "queers' hangout"; by some unspoken territorial imperative, the front room at Ellie's had been staked out by male homosexuals and the center room, where the dance floor was, by lesbians. Our group was segregated in the back, among the squares, slummers, and doubtfuls. An enormously fat woman of about fifty, who must have weighed at least three hundred pounds, came over after awhile, leaning against our table like some hippopotamus wrapped in a loose black dress. She had a crew cut, looked like Grosz might have designed her, and had a big smile for our Californian girl.

"Na, Puppe?" she asked. "How about a dance?"

When our friend refused (in German, which she'd learned in Berlin), the gargantuan lesbian heaved what may have been her bosoms beneath that enormous black dress, and after trying to cajole our friend for a time, seemed to explode.

"I've been coming here for thirty-five years," she yelled, "and nothing like this has ever happened to me before! I warn you, if I see you dancing with anyone else, I'll tear your throat out! If you're not willing to dance, what the hell are you doing in a *Schwuhl-Lokal?*"

We saw her point and prepared to leave, pushing past several male homosexuals dancing cheek to cheek beside lesbians dancing even closer. Finally we got to the front door, opening it just in time to let three new visitors come in. An elderly man and two elderly ladies, the very picture of respectable German grand-parents out with a friend, stepped past us. It being three in the morning and they being Berliners, they were looking for *Stimmung*. The fact that the *Stimmung* was *Schwuhl* doesn't bother Berliners in the least.

The same cannot be said of tourists, who end up in the commercialized downtown strip joints or transvestite clubs if they want a titillating peek at Berlin's erotic life. The most famous of the latter is the Eldorado on the Lutherstrasse, which features transvestite singers, dancers, and barmaids. It even has a "TV" strip-tease dancer who at the last moment whips off the fur boa clutched about his chest and the wig on his head. The audience, oddly enough, usually includes a number of stolid German families, some even bringing teen-age children. All of them howl with laughter at the *double-entendres* dropped by the square-chinned baritone in the blonde wig and low-cut evening dress standing beside the piano. Usually one also sees a few visiting businessmen, from the United States, West Germany, and elsewhere, sitting about open-mouthed, some of them frozen in horror. Clearly, they'd expected girlie shows; now they weren't sure just what they were seeing.

Shows like these don't bother anyone in Berlin. Neither does the presence of places like L'Inconnue, the lesbian club, or similar male homosexual and transvestite hangouts. No public outcry is raised, no women's organizations flutter about in anger, no preachers demand reform. The Berliners believe there ought to be—within limits—something for everyone; these places, as far as they're concerned, are all good fun, even if the fun isn't for them. The idea that they ought to meddle or restrict anyone horri-fies them, for the simple reason that they don't want anyone to interfere with what they themselves might do. Inevitably, it means that if you know the places, much of West Berlin is "wide open." Certainly the downtown area is as studded with "non-stop striptease" clubs as is London; these, however, are for tourists. Berliners don't go to the Erotik, the Kakadu, the Rififi, or the like; if they want to dance, they go to places like the Neue Welt on the Hasenheide. At night, downtown Berlin is taken over by tour-ists.

What amazed me, however, was how little those Americans stationed in Berlin knew the city. I'd come to know a good many members of the State Department at the United States Mission in Berlin, the very ones who report back to Washington the mood of the cities to which they're sent. When I first spoke to a few of these officials about the *Künstlerkneipen* in the Kreuzberg Dis-trict, they sounded intrigued. They'd been in Berlin for years; they'd heard of them, of course, but hadn't ever seen one. Suddenly it seemed a good idea to meet some of these young intellectuals who might loom big some day. They agreed to come with us the next evening. "Just try not to come on strong, like officials," I said. "If possible, wear casual clothes, so you don't stand out."

The whole affair was a disaster. Communication never broke down; it never even began. No one relaxed and most of the talk was polite and guarded. The three young diplomats, all of attaché or section-chief rank, came directly from a cocktail party, one of those countless "command performance" affairs in the American "ghetto." All social life there is an incestuous round of repaying parties with parties, always talking to the same Americans from the same offices, with a few "Columbus Society" Germans added for flavor. The three officials showed up in dark suits, their elegant, carefully coiffed young wives in tow. Heads snapped and eyebrows flew up wherever we went. Soon they became edgy, defensive and uncomfortable, their wives most of all. The *Künstlerkneipen,* which had at first seemed colorfully arty, soon seemed only drab and wretched. I'd long stopped worrying about the communication, but was sorry they couldn't have a good time here in Berlin, in typical Berlin surroundings.

Finally, they excused themselves. They said the evening had been interesting. We sensed they wanted to go back to be with their own kind, perhaps to their Harnack House Club, where they could have cocktails among Army officers.

Rolf and I saw them into their cars and watched them drive off down the dark Kreuzberg streets.

"Let's find a bar," Rolf said after they'd gone. "I need a drink."

"Let's go to La Perla," I said. "It's no *Kneipe,* but there are compensations."

When we got there, Harry Handwein was just closing up, but he agreed to stay and play for us a while longer. When he started on Cole Porter, I felt better. Nothing would ever fundamentally change about nighttime Berlin. It would survive everyone, even the times and benefactors like us from across the seas.

chapter twenty-one

IT'S A SIGN OF THE TIMES THAT, WHEN A WEST BERLINER TODAY
wants debauchery, he goes to Hamburg. Berlin used to be known
all over the world as "Sin City," but that was long ago, when it led
every other German town in everything, including corruption
and depravity. It's different today. Just as a lot of other big business has moved from West Berlin, so has commercialized sex and
serious crime. You can find crime and vice in Berlin still, but
it's not big business any more. It's a cottage industry.

What the Berliner finds in Hamburg is harlotry and bawdy shows
neatly confined to the St. Pauli District; the Reeperbahn and
Grosse Freiheit ("Great Freedom") streets, touted in official
guides as "amusement centers," are tourist attractions—and traps.
One can shop along the store windows of Herbertstrasse as though
for clothes; the merchandise displayed behind the plate glass,
however, are girls, wearing few of them. The business of sex is
being mass-produced in West Germany today and Berlin is being
left behind.

Of course, the basic commodity remains the same; only the
packaging is new. It may be part of that general shift from prewar
heavy industry to consumer goods and it is greatly influenced by
American mass-production and marketing methods. Being bright
and adaptable, the Germans have fallen in love with United States
merchandising techniques: Entrepeneurs apply them to all areas
of endeavor, including the peddling of flesh. Bordellos are legal
in West Germany, but the old-fashioned bordello, with its red
lamp, piano, plush sofas, and *fin de siecle* air has no place any more.
It is giving way to the high-rise whorehouse, the multi-story apartment house filled with one hundred prostitutes or more, each ob-

taining for a monthly rental approximating $150 to $200 a Danish-modern studio apartment with kitchenette and bath. Each is fitted out like the next, down to the emergency buzzer that summons the bouncer should a customer get violent. The rent is high by German standards and so are the profits to the developers, usually a syndicate of realtors, financiers, and businessmen, but the girls benefit from standardization, security, and services such as linens, meals, medical attention, and emergency aid. Hamburg has an "Eros Center" and "Palais d'Amour"; in Stuttgart, the Dreifarbenhaus, or "Three-Color House," is home to seventy prostitutes, while Wilma Adamitz's four-story Düsseldorf establishment houses 228. There are others elsewhere in Germany, in Frankfurt am Main and in other large cities that similarly offer the latest model in mass-produced sex.

The small businesswoman, working on her own, still does have a place, but in West Germany that place is not usually on street corners. She cruises the hotel, amusement, and business sections in an expensive Mercedes, sometimes not even leaving her car to conduct her business. The police usually harass such private entrepreneurs as public nuisances. City governments throughout the Federal Republic are unofficially pleased to see the emergence of the high-rise whorehouse, for they vastly prefer prostitution neatly confined, registered, restricted to certain districts, and subject to regulation by bureaucrats. Just about everything is orderly in Germany, even disorderly conduct.

Berlin, on the other hand, continues to operate in the old manner. This means that no real-estate developer can erect a really supermodern brothel in that city and that the population must make do with the old-fashioned, illegal bordellos that exist. No one knows for certain how many of these operate in West Berlin, but there seem to be enough. Police officials say there are "dozens"; one responsible press estimate claims there are 380.

Finding them seems to provide half the excitement for a lot of people. Many houses have a special character of their own, allowing one to "discover" them as one might discover a small restaurant as yet unspoilt by success. Berliners appreciate the fact that much of the charm, not to speak of the illusory romance, disappears when one takes the sin and effort out of illicit sex. There certainly seems to be little adventure in checking oneself into an easily accessible "whore's Hilton" on the Reeperbahn. These are not sinks of sin and debauchery but shopping centers. That sort of supermarket lacks something; Berliners know what it is—style.

"Old-fashioned" prostitutes still lazily swing their handbags along the streets of West Berlin, just as they did in the fabled 1920's and for hundreds of years before that. They continue their sauntering down the Kurfürstendamm, and they chatter in small clusters on certain street corners. They still lean against jukeboxes in certain *Nuttenkneipen,* the "whores' bars," or prop themselves against the city's walls or its *Litfass-säulen,* as Berliners call their street-corner advertising pillars.

Some of those who don't walk the streets, sit in the bars, or work in brothels operate as "masseuses." Indeed, West Berlin has a number of massage and sauna establishments that seem more erotic than invigorating. There is a place on the Heerstrasse where men and women can sweat it out together. Swedish-massage fanciers can get rubdowns in West Berlin from topless masseuses, or if they prefer, be visited in the privacy of their own homes.

The existence of 380 bordellos in West Berlin cannot be firmly established, for if the vice squad or *Sittenpolizei* (literally "morals police") knew the accurate count, they could close down each one of them. Such a number would have to include every bordello, from the smallest two-woman partnership to the biggest bagnio, as well as a lot of those small hotels (*Pensionen*) and rooming houses populated with a heavy proportion of professionals. Altogether, the police believe there are about three thousand full-time professional prostitutes working the streets of the Western sectors, but they admit that there are also many housewives earning secret pin money at this trade while their husbands work. The best-looking, best-dressed, and most expensive prostitutes patrol the Kurfürstendamm; lesser lights frequent its shadowy side streets. The best-known of these is the Augsburger Strasse, just a block from the Kudamm. It is studded with bars and cheap strip joints, all of them hangouts for whores; its corner with the Joachimsthaler Strasse, just a block from the decorous Café Kranzler, is decorated with a bevy of bawds every night.

Housewives who "moonlight" at daytime prostitution are not the only annoyance aggravating the professionals. Amateur competition in general has cut into sales and reduced their overall share of the market. This being a permissive, erotically charged postwar society, young students no longer frequent prostitutes; they don't need to. The Pill and other devices have reduced maidenly inhibitions and removed many a ground for morality, while antibiotics eliminate fear of the "poison concealed among the roses of lust," as Goethe once described VD. Just as elsewhere in the Western world, sexual stimulation is everywhere in West Berlin, whipped on by music and films, magazines, books, and advertising. The young West Berliners of today are probably more sexually emancipated than they have ever been and those young men who go to the city's "beat clubs" to pick up girls may be said to stand a better-than-even chance of ending up in bed with them, as the majority of girls seventeen years of age are no longer virgins. If a young student does end up with a girl who is determined to maintain her virginity, then the times have introduced a means of relief said to be new to Germany. "Petting to climax," *Der Spiegel* says, was previously regarded by Germans as a United States phenomenon, an American "way of having your cake and eating it, too."

Petting to climax appears to be an urban and upper-class activity in Germany. Rural youths regard it as unnatural and tend to lead their rustic girls into the hay directly. Berlin psychologists point out that class barriers are retained in bed, despite postwar Germany's supposedly classless society; working-class youths, like their farmland counterparts, are often far more direct than the students. A young Berlin worker points to one of the problems when he says he can't occupy himself in intelligent conversation with the working-class girls he knows; his boredom makes him more mindful of physical desire. Students, on the other hand, have other outlets for their energy: the theater, protesting against Viet Nam, and being outraged by their elders and society. Sexual intercourse, in short, is not the only form of intercourse they have with girls, but the one thing *all* Berlin youngsters seem to have in common today is a relatively easy access to "free" sex, should they seek it. They can afford to abandon the prostitutes to men who need to pay. Some of these are businessmen and tourists, others are workers no longer young enough to attract pretty amateurs, and still others are the foreign workers and soldiers who are often isolated and lonely.

295

Call-girl operations are against the law in West Berlin; prostitutes are not permitted to arrange their affairs over the telephone. There is no telephone company in Germany. The telephone and telegraph system is operated by the postal system, and the use of a Government agency to support organized vice is plainly regarded as intolerable. While prostitution per se is permitted, the girls are hemmed in with restrictions. Berlin prostitutes, like those in London, are not allowed to solicit business by accosting potential customers on the streets; they are compelled to carry a medical-inspection book with them, showing they've submitted to periodic VD checks; they are not allowed to turn over any of their earnings to a procurer, as pimping and any other form of living off the earnings of a prostitute is illegal; they are forbidden to operate houses of ill repute or to work inside them, and they are not allowed to station themselves within a set number of yards of any church or school.

The girls generally operate out of rooms rented in the city's small hotels, those *Pensionen* of which there are scores in the downtown area. The prostitute will usually rent a room other than her business apartment and the ten marks extra that she normally charges for that room pays for the rent of her own room as well. In addition to the fee for the room, she charges anywhere from twenty to two hundred marks for the rent of her body, the average going rate being fifty marks, or $12.50. Few of the prostitutes manage to save money. Most girls spend it as fast as they earn it, usually on drink or on the pimps they are not "permitted" to maintain. One unusually thrifty girl came to the attention of the *Kriminalpolizei,* the criminal-investigation branch of the police, when she charged that her boyfriend had absconded with the savings tucked in her mattress. She claimed he'd filched thirty-five thousand marks, or $8,750, a small fortune by Berlin standards. Such, of course, are the occupational hazards involved in a milieu all too often composed of thieves and confidence men. There are others as well. A prostitute in West Berlin has no recourse to law if a customer refuses to pay after he has enjoyed her favors; on the other hand, the customer can charge her with fraud if she refuses to render services paid for in advance. Needless to say, the girls are smart enough to demand payment first, and generally speaking, they carry out their duties conscientiously.

Traffic in homosexuality has always been a prominent aspect of Berlin vice. For generations boy prostitutes, or *Strichjungen,* have operated at the *Bahnhof Zoo* railway station and elsewhere, and today, one can even order a "boy" over the telephone. These youngsters, in their late teens, are very often not homosexuals themselves, but only lend themselves to homosexuals for money.

Just as common are transvestites. There are a lot of them in West Berlin. *Der Spiegel* goes so far as to call the city "the Mecca of Europe's transvestites" and the police regard them as a growing and aggravating problem. There is no law today (as there was under Hitler) forbidding men to dress up as women, nor is there a law prohibiting them from receiving their weekly injections of Progynon and Proluton, female hormone preparations that raise their voices, add bosoms, and remove body hair at five dollars a shot. The transvestite prostitute, however, often proves to be a thief more adept at rolling drunks than at gratifying them; this often makes him as much a target for the *Kriminalpolizei* as for the *Sittenpolizei* vice squad. "Some of them," a police official told me, "are so adept that they pick up men, get them drunk, and lure them to bed without ever betraying the fact that they are not women. They are so clever in their manipulations that the men remain convinced they are in the company of women while in bed with them. Their aim, of course, is to rob these people of wallets, watches, and other valuables."

That transvestites are not new to Berlin may be seen from the following article which appeared in a Berlin newspaper eighty years ago:

"Almost every social element in Berlin has its social reunions —the fat, the baldheaded, the bachelors, the widowers—and why not the woman-haters? This species of men, so interesting psychologcially and none too edifying, had a great ball a few days ago. 'Grand Vienna Fancy Dress Ball'—ran the notice. The sale of tickets is very rigorous; they wish to be very exclusive. We enter the hall after midnight. The merry dancing is to the strains of a fine orchestra . . .

"But what is that? The lady in rose tarletan, that just now passed us, has a lighted cigar in the corner of her mouth, and puffs like a trooper; and she also wears a small, blond beard, lightly painted out. And yet she is talking with a very *décolleté* 'angel' in *tricots,* who stands there, with bare arms folded behind him, likewise smoking. The two voices are masculine, and the conversation is likewise very masculine; it is about the 'd--- tobacco smoke, that permits no air.' Two men in female attire! A conventional clown stands there, against a pillar, in soft conversation with a ballet-dancer, with his arms around her faultless waist. She has a blonde 'Titus-head' sharp-cut profile, and apparently a voluptuous form. The brilliant ear-rings, the necklace with a medallion, the full, round shoulders and arms, do not permit a doubt of her 'genuineness,' until, with a sudden movement, she disengages herself from the embracing arm, and, yawning, moves away, saying, in a deep bass, 'Emile, you are too tiresome today!' The ballet-dancer is also a male!

"Suspicious now, we look about further. We almost suspect that here the world is topsy-turvy; for there goes, or, rather, trips, a man—no, no man at all, even though he wears a carefully trained moustache . . . How he dances and turns and trips and lisps! And yet kindly Nature made this doll a man. He is a salesman in a large sweet shop, and the ballet-dancer mentioned is his 'colleague' . . .

"On closer examination of the assembly, to my astonishment, I discover acquaintances on all hands: my shoemaker, whom I should have taken for anything but a woman-hater—he is a 'troubadour,' with sword and plume; and his 'Leonora,' in the costume of a bride, is accustomed to place my favorite brand of cigars before me in a certain cigar-store . . . Right! There is my haberdasher, also; he moves about in a questionable costume as Bacchus, and is the swain of a repugnantly bedecked Diana, who works as a waiter in a beer-restaurant . . ."

That article appeared in February, 1884, and caused Dr. Richard von Krafft-Ebing to proclaim that "these facts deserve the careful attention of the police, who should be placed in a position *to cope with male prostitution, as they now do with that of women.*" * He says that a high Berlin police official informed him that the police were conversant with their city's "male *demimonde* . . . and

* Emphasis is Krafft-Ebing's, as provided in his *Psychopathia Sexualis.*

do all they can to suppress blackmail among pederasts—a practice which often does not stop short of murder."

The same might be said of the police today. They seem almost as troubled by transvestite prostitutes as are the female prostitutes who resent their competition. In late spring, 1967, an argument between the whores and the transvestites over a certain strip of territory ended in a street fight.

It began when three miniskirted transvestites called Sabrina, Oora, and Audrey were patrolling the Kurfürstendamm in search of customers and were physically attacked by a battery of bawds armed with umbrellas and high-heeled shoes. When the police arrived (they had been summoned by an outraged female prostitute), they had a hard time sorting the real girls out from the phoney ones and finally had to demand that all those involved produce the identity books German citizens are compelled by law to carry. The "internal passports" of Sabrina, Oora, and Audrey showed that their real names were Karl, Wolf-Rüdiger, and Walter.

The West Berlin police have about one hundred transvestites registered, but no one imagines that this remotely approaches the real total. It's hard to count them for the simple reason that a great many of them don't look like men dressed up as women. They look like women, period, and as a matter of fact, many of them even look like movie starlets.

Miljöh is the Berlinese slang spelling for "milieu"; *Berliner Miljöh* means only one thing: the milieu as portrayed by Heinrich Zille, or perhaps, by Bert Brecht and Kurt Tucholsky. The setting is typically tawdry and the characters are unfortunate, and sometimes, depraved. One finds this Berlinese milieu in many smoky corners of the city but certainly there is no place that provides it better than the city's *Nuttenkneipen,* the whores' bars. These don't just supply prostitutes, beer, and liquor; they dish out authentic Berlinese as well. Here one encounters the special vocabulary, the impertinence, the boastfulness, the famous joviality.

One such *Kneipe,* since threatened by commercial redevelopment, was the White Moor (Der Weisse Moor) on the Joachimsthaler Strasse, on the very same corner with the Augsburger, which is so regularly populated by prostitutes. It was 8:30 on a Saturday morning that a friend of mine and I entered this *Nutten-*

kneipe, seeking coffee of all things, the cafés on the Kurfürsten-damm, a block away, not being open yet.

"Coffee? Did I hear *coffee,* fine gentlemen?" the waiter said with a contemptuous grin. He'd addressed us, with feigned humility, as *meine Herrschaften* and then went back to wiping a glass behind the bar. "Certainly!" he called over. "We're serving it immediately—over there at the Café Kranzler!"

So we ordered brandies instead. His name was 'Achim, short for Joachim; he was in his early twenties, blond, and with a ready smile. "What the hell kind of a place do you think this is?" he asked, handing us our Weinbrand. We walked to one of the two elbow-high wooden tables off the bar. Across from us was an enormous woman who must have weighed two hundred pounds, standing next to a young fellow in his early thirties. She wore a conservative black dress that discreetly concealed the huge breasts that ballooned over the table, had neither lipstick nor a trace of other make-up on. Her face was as round as a big cheese and as free of wrinkles as a blown-up balloon. She introduced herself as Ilse and told us the fellow standing beside her sold hot sausages from the curb-side *Wurstwagen* regularly stationed on the corner. He saw we were interested and realized that we were strangers.

"Sure Ilse's a streetwalker," the sausage peddler said and Ilse nodded solemnly in agreement. "But, listen, I've worked this corner for years and I know every girl in the neighborhood. I've watched them all, the ones on the Augsburger Strasse and the fancy whores on the Kudamm over there."

We asked him if there were any difference and he burst into a short laugh as though we were fools.

"I call them 'Playboys,' those hoity-toity whores on the Kudamm! The ones who go to the Kranzler, they're all trash! They put on airs over there and then they come to me and ask for a curry-wurst—'But with a napkin, *if you please!*' "

He minced about, miming feigned elegance, and Ilse laughed.

"You know the truth about *our* whores here?" he asked. "You can't count how many times I've loaned these girls twenty marks to tide them over! And every time, I get it back, right on the dot. There's not a whore on the Augsburger Strasse who isn't a decent, honest girl!"

There were three other prostitutes in the White Moor along

with Ilse, together with perhaps a dozen men. At 8:30 in the morning, all of them looked the worse for wear. Berlin's *Kneipen* may stay open at the discretion of the owner; the White Moor, open twenty-four hours around the clock, sheltered many a customer throughout the night and picked up more of them in the early hours, as other places closed. Two of the girls in the place were pretty and in their twenties, one must have been fifty, and all except Ilse were very drunk. The oldest one was fat, wrinkled, heavily painted, and had black pouches under bloodshot eyes. She winked at us, then got into a fight, shoving one of the men across the room, cursing. Finally she retreated to the far corner of the bar, where she stood, crying into a handkerchief.

"Sooner or later," said the young Berliner with whom I'd come, "they all break down and blubber. They have the sentiments of bourgeois housewives."

This was confirmed by Ilse, who wanted us to listen to a tale of mother love and self-denial, which we did, in return for the brandies she insisted on buying us.

"I've got a twelve-year-old daughter," she told us. "That's the only reason I'm on the streets! I had that girl with my mother until she was six. What do I find when I go to fetch her? She was absolutely *depraved!* The old lady let her out until ten! I grabbed that kid by the hair and told her, 'No more of that crap! From now on, you stay in the house after six!' So I sent her to a private *Internat* for two years and that cost me a thousand marks a month. But I didn't care, because that kid's going to get the best education there is. And if I ever catch her not studying, I'll break her head!"

"Maybe that's not the best way," my friend suggested quietly. Ilse looked about her in amazement and slammed the palm of her hand on the counter as though it were her daughter's skull.

"You crazy?" she blurted out. "You think I want her to end up like me? You really must be nuts!"

"I didn't mean . . ." my friend tried to interject.

"Listen, little boy! I've been on the streets for years and there's absolutely nothing that I haven't done. Now, why the hell do you think I do it, if not for her? You know what I'll do if I ever see her walking the streets? I'll break both her legs, that's what!"

A moment later, she recovered her good humor and ordered another brandy over our protests.

"No, these are on me," she insisted. "I can see you're from out of town and you're a guest. It's only right!" She addressed the last remark to me and then casually asked if I were in Berlin with my wife. When I nodded, she shrugged her shoulders, abandoned the line of questioning, and told us a little more about herself. She'd been to Italy, Spain, and finally to Australia, where she said she'd worked in a gasoline station and a rifle factory before returning home to begin her career on the streets. We asked her where she'd lived in Australia, but she couldn't remember the names of any towns. She brushed the question aside and announced she was retiring that Christmas.

"I'm going to Switzerland with my little girl," she said with satisfaction. "Start all over. I'll have saved up enough by then. From Christmas on, I'm off the streets!"

The sausage peddler nodded gravely, but when Ilse turned away for a moment, he shot a knowing grin at us. He knew the truth.

Another night, at that *Künstlerkneipe* called the "Leierkasten," Rosie, the manageress, seated me at the regulars' table beside a slovenly harridan who looked sixty years old but who turned out to be only forty-five.

"You know why I look like this?" she asked defensively, though I hadn't said a thing. She stared belligerently until I bought her a beer, then smiled, showing a gap where the two lower front teeth were missing.

"I spent three of the best years of my life, when I ought to have been dating like anybody else, in a concentration camp!"

"Are you a Jew?" I asked.

"Jew?" she laughed. "A stupid big-mouth, that's what I am! In 1942, they hauled someone off from the factory where I worked and I called them filthy swine. Two days later, they came to my door. Inciting to treason, they called it. They said I undermined the morale of the troops at the front. I shouted, if what I said could do that, then they better call it quits; the war's as good as lost! So they sent me to Ravensbrueck. I had fifty Russian and Polish women under me. They made me a *Kapo*."

302

After another beer, she began talking about the recent trials of Auschwitz guards.

"They got all the wrong guys!" she claimed, angrily. "I knew those kind of fellows! Some of them were simply terrific!" She kissed her fingertips.

"Listen!" she continued. "They had guns in their backs! Sure there were some who were swine! I'd kill them myself if I saw them! But all they got were small fry!"

An acquaintance of hers joined us. He shared her view of the Auschwitz trial and assured me she had never known of any mass murders, despite being a trustee at Ravensbrueck.

"Damn right I knew!" she interrupted contemptuously. "What the hell do you think they did when those trains rolled in and the camp was already overcrowded? They just handed them a piece of soap and a towel and marched them off to the showers. Then they turned on the gas."

She started crying and banged her fist against her thigh. I thought some memory from those years might have overwhelmed her, but I was wrong.

"What the hell am I doing, drinking in this joint?" she groaned. "It's just that I go crazy at home and have to get out!" (She used the Berlinese expression, "I have to see some other wallpaper [*andere Tapeten*]!")

"You see what I look like!" she blurted out angrily, exasperated. "I got a great husband at home. He's eight years younger than me and I look ten years older than I am! But when I want to go out, he just says, '*Dicke* ["Fatty"], have yourself an evening!' It isn't that I do anything bad. I don't screw around. If I slept with you, he'd kill you; he's like that, someone I can trust. He'd never leave me! He's a guy to count on! So what the hell am I doing sitting around a place like this?"

Ultimately she left. I asked if she were going home, but that only set her crying again. "Tomorrow!" she moaned. "Oh God, how I'll feel ashamed of myself then!"

After she left, I asked her friend at the table where she would spend the night. "She's got a *Klammottenladen*," he said, meaning a rags-and-junk shop. "It's a block away. She'll sleep it off in the back. She's got a lot gnawing on her mind—and not just her man either."

"We'd be much better off with brothels than having whores all over the streets," said a young Berlin police officer, Fred Brandt, over a half-liter of Bavarian beer at the Kudamm's Munich-style Hofbräuhaus. "We have a good deal of trouble with these prostitutes, but we have even more trouble with the men who hang around them. There's a constant succession of barroom brawls over whores and a lot of petty thievery and crime as well. And not all the crime is petty. Prostitutes get killed, too."

One of these was "Cognac-Edith," a thirty-six-year-old streetwalker whose real name was Edith Ziebeck and who was well-known in the Augsburger Strasse. A twenty-two-year-old bartender had picked her up, taken her to his flat, downed a bottle of cognac with her, and then strangled her during intercourse. Her case recalls two others, also strangled during the sex act: Ilse Frahn, fifty-two, nicknamed "Mohrchen" ("Little Moor"), and Margot Borkowski, forty-six, called "Acker Margot" because she lived on Ackerstrasse, both of them killed within a little more than a year in the same building in District Wedding. Since both of them frequented local *Kneipen,* most of them criminal hangouts, to find their customers, the results were perhaps predictable. None of the three prostitutes seem to have been killed in quarrels, nor apparently subjected to sexual-sadistic mutilation; all were apparently strangled in sexual excitement. Ilse Frahn's killer, a twenty-five-year-old, received but twelve months in prison for the murder he committed, the court calling it "negligent homicide."

When sexual violence takes the form of rape and does not involve prostitutes, justice can be more stern, though much of it still seems remarkably merciful compared to sentences imposed by United States' courts. One young man who was in despair because his girl friend left him decided to assuage his grief by raping a florist's eighteen-year-old assistant. He ordered a dozen roses for a Frau Müller by telephone, and when the salesgirl brought the flowers to the address he'd given, he raped her twice, at knife point, in his mother's apartment. "I defended myself as best I could," the girl told police afterward, "but I finally stopped struggling because of the knife." Afterward, he offered to brew her some coffee, which she refused, and then he begged her to wait twenty-four hours before she reported him to the police, because he didn't want to spoil the day for his mother. He got five years.

304

A much more brutal attack on a girl brought an even lower sentence. A twenty-seven-year-old man from District Moabit, enraged after a quarrel with his pregnant wife, entered the U-Bahn subway after a tour of Kurfürstendamm bars, and spotted a pretty nineteen-year-old girl in an empty carriage. When she left the train at the Britz-Süd Station, he followed, and just before she got home, seized her, choked her into unconsciousness, dragged her limp form across the street, threw her onto a construction site, raped her—and then apologized. He got two years and nine months in prison.

Neither of the two rapists seem "maddened sex fiends," despite the second man's brutality, and this helps account for their light sentences. The first man wanted to "assuage his grief," the second to "assuage his anger."

One of the most bizarre Berlin cases of sexual misconduct did not even end in rape. It began with a young Berliner celebrating his twenty-sixth birthday. The gift he longed for most—a girl in bed—had eluded him throughout the evening; drunk, and still hunting, he strolled through the streets of one of West Berlin's prosperous, residential villa sections. He couldn't find any girls on its quiet streets, so he decided he'd try inside one of the villas. Brashly, he began looking for an open bedroom window. He found one at the home of an attorney whose wife had already gone to sleep in one of the twin beds, while her husband remained in the living room. A baby, sleeping in a corner, shared the bedroom. Quietly, the man crept through the window and sat down on the bed beside the sleeping wife. She half awakened in the dark room and softly murmured her husband's name. The intruder, taking no chances and displaying a degree of Berlinese brashness that can only be called *chutzpah,* remained silent as she raised herself, helped him out of his jacket, and embraced him lovingly. Things were going better than he had dared to expect—that is, until a moment later. The lawyer husband entered the room; some premonition had told him something was wrong. On seeing him, the intruder leaped up, fled through the window, leaving his jacket behind. The attorney telephoned the police, and a nearby patrol car seized the young man a few minutes later. He was sentenced to a year in jail for violating paragraph 179 of the criminal code, which related to obtaining extra-marital relations through subterfuge. "It's a bit much," the judge remarked acidly, "when one can't even leave a window open in a remote villa district without fearing someone might climb in!" As for the mortified wife, Berlin journalists commiserated with her for her "Fatal Error," her inability to differentiate between her husband, the lawyer, and the young intruder whom she had embraced and kissed.

The courts deal much more severely when children are the victims than they do in "ordinary" sexual offenses. A ten-year prison sentence, for example, was meted out to Peter Klein, who stabbed and raped the sixteen-year-old sister of one of his football-club friends, the court taking into consideration the fact that he'd already served time in the past for other sexual offenses. A case that especially horrified the city concerned a baby boy who died at the age of sixteen days after being slowly tortured to death by its twenty-nine-year-old foster father. The baby was illegitimate and its sixteen-year-old mother had come to West Berlin to find its father. Instead, she found and married Ferdinand Robbel while she was still pregnant. Weakened by childbirth and in any case unable to interfere with her husband's actions, the child bride watched as Robbel mistreated the infant so badly that it died of pneumonia and of a cerebral hemorrhage. Robbel was sentenced to life imprisonment, while she, as a juvenile, received four years. The state's attorney, or prosecutor, had asked for a sentence of only twelve years for Ferdinand Robbel, because he was not at all convinced Robbel had actually *intended* to murder the child. (Robbel had even booked tickets for a flight to Hanover for himself, his wife, and the infant, for the very day on which the baby died; the prosecutor was convinced that the sadistic stepfather never meant to commit murder and that the crime was manslaughter.)

"I can understand your anger and outrage at what has happened, and I share these feelings," he told the jury, "but the facts must only be determined by means of cool reason and all emotions must be silenced . . . You must take into account the slightest doubt you have which favors the accused. Put away your anger and outrage and do not be tempted to violate the laws and thereby to commit an injustice yourselves!"

The plea was ignored; the jury concluded the baby had been killed because it was "in the way." Not only did the defense attorney protest against the sentence, but so did the state's attorney. Unlike many another prosecutor elsewhere, he did not seek society's revenge, nor even a maximum punishment. Instead, he sought justice.

As in any other large city, there is a good deal of criminal activity in West Berlin, but the Berliners have been spared any kind of Mafia, Cosa Nostra, or Syndicate. The closest they ever came to organized crime along Sicilian or American lines was between the 1880's and the 1920's, when Berlin criminals established a number of so-called "Savings and Social Clubs" (*Spar- und Geselligskeitsvereine*), with high-sounding names like "Forever Faithful" (*Immertreu*) and "German Strength" (*Deutsche Kraft*). Thus they imitated the example set by law-abiding burghers in their city—and, indeed, in all Germany—who at that time formed social, singing, drinking, hiking, cardplaying, sporting, and dancing clubs in numbers impossible to count, all of which were given similar lofty, patriotic names. If transvestites could stage their own ball and establish their own groups in 1884, why not pimps, safe-crackers, murderers, burglars, and confidence men? Their annual banquets were elaborate affairs, often held in fine public restaurants and beer halls, and were sometimes even graced by the presence of high police officials. When *Deutsche Kraft* celebrated at the Rheingold Restaurant on Potsdamer Platz, the high point of the evening was reached when a police officer stepped to the bandstand, picked up the baton, and led the orchestra.

There were as many as fifty such criminal clubs in Berlin, with an average membership of two hundred each, and the police looked on them with a benign eye, preferring to have the criminals grouped together where they could easily be watched. The clubs were tolerated until the 1920's when they began to get more ambitious and aggressive. They started to adopt American "teamwork" methods, imitate American gangsters, and launched protection rackets against *Kneipe* owners, breaking up the taverns of those who refused to pay. When they started shooting each other up in the streets and began to take revenge against disloyal members, executing them, Mafia-style, Berlin's police lost patience.

One roundup took place at Schmöckwitz, an excursion target for many Berliners, which today lies in East Berlin, in the southeast corner of the city. It occupies a hilly peninsula where River Dahme meets Seddinsee, Langer See, and the Grosse Krampe; all this water makes Schmöckwitz a favorite weekend resort for Berlin boating enthusiasts and it was only logical that a criminal club, seeking a summertime retreat for its members, should come to Schmöckwitz under the guise of a water-sports club. The gangsters in question enjoyed the bourgeois resort pleasures while living in the small boathouses surrounding an inn called the Grosse Zug. Fortunately for them, the inn was inaccessible except by boat and all the motorboats that ferried guests over from the other bank were owned and operated by the criminals themselves. Consequently, they felt certain no one could spoil their holiday and that the police could never stage a raid.

The Berlin police, however, were determined to do just that and began trying to devise a way that would not cause a lot of casualties. If criminals could masquerade as members of a water-sports club, then the police reasoned that they themselves could also masquerade. They knew that there is one kind of club all Germans, criminal or otherwise, particularly welcome and so they called themselves a *Singverein,* or "male choral group." Handsome and impressive *Singverein* stationery was printed and a letter was dispatched to the Grosse Zug, announcing the arrival of the male chorus on a certain day. Then they assembled a group of policemen with passable voices, dressed them in civilian clothes, took over an excursion steamer, and set forth. When the boat anchored at the Grosse Zug, the criminals welcomed them with warmth and enthusiasm. The police responded just as courteously. They formed themselves into a long line facing the assembled gangsters, opened up their song books, and broke out into the traditional, "Who owns you, beautiful woodland?" When they were finished, each officer clapped shut his song book, whipped out a revolver, and pointed it at the flabbergasted hoods. A moment later, the gangsters were all marched onto the excursion steamer and hauled off. The police had rounded them all up without firing a shot.

Hitler put an end to the criminal clubs, clapping their members into concentration camps. After the war, there was a brief attempt at establishing a "Savings and Social Club" in District Neukölln, but it was quickly squelched. Organized crime of that kind no longer exists in Berlin today.

The average West German city registers one crime for every twenty-two inhabitants; West Berlin, which has exactly that rate, is therefore distinctly average. The *Kriminalpolizei* has its hands full, nevertheless.

A good many arrests can be traced to the Berliners' partiality for beer and booze; offenses connected with drunkenness resulted in almost four thousand convictions in one recent year, most of them for drunk driving. The number of Berliners who were convicted of *Volltrunkenheit,* which means "complete inebriation" or being dead drunk, came to eight hundred. In fact, an enormous amount of police time is spent chasing drunks in Berlin—and not just in the "entertainment section," but in residential districts as well. To be sure, the citizens of upper-class villa districts get in trouble less often on such counts than do Berliners in the city's "proletarian" neighborhoods. Wedding is a good example. Every third policeman assigned to Wedding apparently does nothing but deal with drunks and with offenses committed by them, for one-third of the hours worked by the district's 750 police officers are devoted to such matters. About 240 Berliners each month got in trouble due to drink just in this one district alone, which creates the bizarre picture of 250 Wedding policemen working full time trying to handle 240 drunks each month.

The population of West Berlin has over the past years held pretty steady; during this same period, there has been a constant, gradual increase in the crime rate. Its crime rate is lower than that of most large American towns, but higher than any of Britain's "top ten crime cities."* Still, Berlin is not a dangerous city, seen non-politically, and one feels safe in its streets—with one exception. Germans—Berliners included—are not the best of drivers. An official West German source, the Federal Statistical Office, reports that one's chance of being killed due to an automobile accident is about twice as high in Berlin as in New York and even

* The total number of crimes investigated in West Berlin rose from about 91,000 in 1963 to more than 126,000 in 1967. The crime rate is 5,774.9 crimes committed per 100,000 inhabitants. London by contrast has 3,378 and Britain's top crime city, Newcastle, has 5,055.

higher than it is in Paris, where drivers are supposed to be particularly reckless. The number of deaths due to automobile accidents, per 100,000 inhabitants, comes to 14.6 in West Berlin, versus 7.4 in New York and 11.3 in Paris. Your chances of being injured, rather than killed, are just as good, or bad. Non-fatal injuries caused by automobile accidents run to 651.2 per 100,000 in West Berlin versus 500.3 in Paris. Comparisons are admittedly approximate, for systems of measurement vary; in Paris, for example, deaths are only registered as being due to automobile accidents if the victims die within three days of the accident, while in Berlin the police allow a whole month. The figures, however, do tend to confirm most foreign visitors' private impressions that Germans—Berliners included—are dangerous behind the wheel of a car. Three times as many of them get killed as do Americans. It almost seems that what "German aggressiveness" remains, a quarter of a century after World War II, is expended on the roads. Driving on an *Autobahn* is like being caught in a *Blitzkrieg*.

In East Berlin, crime and vice have virtually ceased to exist—if one accepts the word of the G.D.R. "No one needs to be a criminal in the socialist society," claims their chief prosecutor, following the traditional line that capitalism breeds criminality. The G.D.R. claims West Germany has four times as many murders and manslaughters as East Germany, six times as much robbery and blackmail, seven times as much "fraud, treachery, forgery," and ten times as much "abetment and receiving of stolen goods." In fact, East German crime data are extremely hard to verify. The press is regarded as a weapon of the "socialistic" regime; the information it provides in this very sensitive area is also meant to serve political ends.

Yet the G.D.R.'s chief prosecutor is probably telling the truth when he claims there is more crime in the West than in the East, since crime doesn't flourish in a police state. Whether an East Berliner is law-abiding or not, he is subject to a great deal of direct and indirect supervision. He is spied upon at his job by factory or office informers; he is spied upon when he comes home from his job by house trustees. He is drummed into mass organizations and much of his free time is taken up in political, cultural, athletic, paramilitary, or organized social activities. He finds it hard to gather with friends (or accomplices) without attracting attention or being reported. If he is not engaged in productive work, he can be jailed for being unproductive. "Do-nothings" and "good-for-nothings" have little opportunity to loiter, hang about, or get into trouble. Questionable bars, those attracting an even more questionable clientele, are simply *verboten,* as are bordellos and prostitution.

This is just one side of the picture, however, the repressive side. Escapees from the G.D.R. have suggested other reasons why there seems to be less crime in the East. In West Berlin, they say, they see cheap values, a tawdry materialism, the lack of an ennobling purpose. They feel their (admittedly well-paid) jobs in industry "only enrich the owners" and do not serve society. They are left alone after their job is done. Those befriended by West Berlin's students may find intellectual companions, but many escapees become industrial workers and soon learn that their colleagues don't care much for "politics and culture."

"You from 'over there' all talk alike!" a young West Berlin worker said to one escapee. "With you, it's always politics. Why not have fun instead?"

A generation of schooling and adult political education in the G.D.R. has made many—but not all—East German workers differently disposed. Of course, a lot of them are attracted by Western "culture," but a surprising percentage have had their interests broadened and many escapees complain that the "fun" urged upon them by their co-workers amounts to nothing more edifying than getting drunk, playing slot machines, going to a sex or crime movie, or "finding a promiscuous girl."

"Doesn't West Berlin have anything better to offer," one of them asked me, "than just hoping for a faster car, more money, and more sex?" Despite the fact that he had risked his life to find that "chaotically" free society he later criticized, this escapee spoke with a certain nostalgia of the "meaningfulness" with which his earlier life had been imbued. He was not alone, he said; others "over there" were also made to feel that they worked for a goal greater than their own self-interest. East German educators and propagandists, of course, try hard to inculcate this sense of communal

311

effort and the Berlin Wall has helped in that it brutally underlined the fact that everyone in the G.D.R. was now in the same boat and either had to pull oars together or sink.

Despite this, East Berlin undoubtedly has "asocial" elements and outright criminals; it even admits some of their crimes in its press. Car thefts and burglaries are common: one East Berliner, aged twenty-one, was jailed after burglarizing more than ninety automobiles in Districts Pankow, Weissensee, and Mitte, while two others confessed to burglarizing more than eighty apartments, schools, and kindergartens. Embezzlements are also sometimes admitted. Herbert Glumm, owner of a theater-ticket agency on East Berlin's Rathaus Strasse, is one example. He was charged with defrauding theaters out of 22,500 marks, while another example is provided by a thirty-three-year-old woman who served as budget expert for the Cultural Department in East Berlin's Pankow District Council. She was jailed for embezzling 41,109 marks over three years. The urge to enrich oneself has apparently not been eliminated even among Communist functionaries.

One of the biggest bank holdups in West Berlin since the end of the war brought in only 106,000 marks, or $26,250, and the "gangster" who made himself famous with this record loot turned out to be an amateur, apparently motivated less by greed and criminal instinct than by a wish to help his fellow-man. The case of Viktor Recker demonstrates the fact that the day of the professional gangster is waning in West Berlin. A lot of amateurs and part-time hoods are at work. Recker, for example, held up the Volksbank's branch office in Neukölln because a friend of his, who owned a failing business, suggested Recker rob the bank to help him out. Recker obliged and handed the largest portion of the swag over to his bankrupt friend. This character thereupon decided not to bother saving the business, but to save himself instead, and fled to Prague. Recker made it to Switzerland, where he deposited his portion of the take, and then made the mistake of returning home to visit a girl friend. He was arrested and brought to trial; the Swiss seized his bank account. Recker's attorney pleaded insanity, which perhaps shows what society thinks of misguided good Samaritans.

The same kind of amateurism marked two other bank robberies held a week apart, one in Moabit and the other in Tempelhof. In the first, the robber stormed into the ABC Credit Institution, scooped up some money, overlooked a great deal more, ordered the bank manager to open the safe, then lost his nerve and fled before it was unlocked. He escaped with only $325. The Tempelhof operation was a bit more efficient and earned two robbers ten times that amount. They burst into the Kundenkreditbank branch office on Tempelhofer Damm at four o'clock both wearing mirrored sunglasses and one of them an "American-style" straw hat. While one of them held customers and employees at bay, the other leaped the counter and collected the loot. They made certain no one would surprise them, for they had brought along a sign reading "Closed at 4 P.M.," which they hung outside. They reasoned that such a sign would keep the orderly Berliners, even policemen, firmly at bay. It worked, but it appears that their plan was not original. Instead, it was copied, in most essentials, from a television play shown on the previous Sunday. The "criminal masterminds" would seem to have been the scriptwriters.

Robberies such as these are relatively rare. Most crime in West Berlin, as previously noted, is simple thievery. As for crimes of violence, a good many Berliners are beaten up and some are even murdered, but premeditated "cold-blooded" murder is rare. In fact, the murder rate seems low. There were only fifty-six attempted murders in 1967; the number of murders actually committed came to forty-six. (By way of contrast, more than three hundred and five hundred murders are committed annually in Chicago and in New York; Houston, Texas, with only half of West Berlin's population, had 244 murders in 1967.)

Most West Berlin murders seem to be "crimes of passion." Lovers kill each other, rejected suitors do away with the girls who spurn them, husbands murder wives suspected of infidelity, and an argument over a game of cards can erupt into bloody violence. Thus, most Berlin murders seem conducted in white heat. *Raubmord,* as the Germans call murders committed during robberies, is relatively rare. Two recent victims of that kind of murder were taxi drivers; the first, Herbert Köppen, was shot and killed by Roman Köcher, who was later sentenced to life imprisonment. In a third such case, the victim was battered to death with a blunt object. He was fifty-four-year-old Alfons Rosenthal, whose death aroused particular indignation because Rosenthal had brought his family home to Berlin just three years earlier after fleeing the Nazis in Berlin in 1933. Shocked and angry, West Berlin's hackies assembled on the Street of the 17th of June (which commemorates East Berlin's 1953 uprising) and drove to the Rosenthal home in Lichtenrade, a part of District Tempelhof. There were one thousand taxis in the procession. When they reached their destination, they handed over money they had collected (in pails) to the family.

Precisely because premeditation and killings in cold blood are rare, most Berlin murders seem excessively violent, and often sadistic. This is partially due to the fact that few Berliners possess guns (illegal in West Berlin because of the tense political situation) and instead use knives, clubs, or their bare hands.

One murder came to light in East Berlin when a zinc bathtub containing a corpse was washed up on the banks of the Friedens (for "Peace") Canal in the suburb of Schönwalde. The dead man turned out to be Lothar Block, whose continued presence had proved a burden to his wife, Siglinde, and her lover, Gerhard Loose. Lothar Block was axed to death by Loose while he slept in his bed; afterward, Frau Block helped Loose dump the corpse into the tub and drive it out to Schönwalde, in the surrounding G.D.R. countryside. They slid the bathtub into the canal, where it subsequently drifted to shore like Moses in the bulrushes, a circumstance leading to the arrest of the murderers.

It is noteworthy that the East Berlin court could have, but didn't, impose the death sentence. East Germany, unlike West Germany, has retained capital punishment, but all Loose got for his ax murder was fifteen years in prison, while Siglinde Block, charged with being an accomplice, got ten years. Such clemency is not unusual: The killers might be regarded as victims of their passion for each other, and such considerations are taken into account. Another East Berlin court, however, sentenced one young man to life imprisonment even though his victim did not die. This was Horst Hinze, twenty-eight, who climbed through an East Berlin bedroom window and attempted to rape a housewife. When she resisted, he battered her so badly that she was sent to the hospital in critical condition. Clearly, the man was of unsound mind, as East Berlin medical authorities told the court, but pleading insanity didn't help in this instance. A West Berlin court also sentenced

Matthias Baltes, twenty-three, to life imprisonment, the maximum under the law. He was convicted for strangling Marlene Oeser, nineteen, his ex-mistress. He blamed her for the breakup of his marriage, as well as for the burden that 350 marks a month alimony imposed on him. After Baltes had made a last unsuccessful effort at reconciling himself with his ex-wife, he chose to revenge himself on his ex-mistress. A court psychiatrist said Baltes regarded her as "the incarnation of Evil itself." The argument failed to impress the court.

One factor generally assessed in West Berlin courts is the defendant's previous way of life: whether he had a steady job, was regular and punctual at it, and showed a general willingness to work hard. The case of forty-four-year-old Heinz Brandt, who killed the woman with whom he had been living for two years, is an example. The victim was five years older than Brandt, an alcoholic, nagging and argumentative, and slovenly about both her appearance and that of her home. He, on the other hand, incorporated many a Germanic virtue. The court noted that he was sober and hard working, that he arrived punctually at work every morning, and that he had tried to convert her to his own "ordered way of life." "This woman," the prosecutor explained, "was the embodiment of his own weakness, and attempting to break out of the fateful entanglement, he wanted to kill her." The murder took place in a bar in Wedding. Brandt had tried with soothing words to get the woman to stop the torrent of abuse she directed at him, but she had kept it up, and had even struck him in the face. Brandt lost his head and battered her with a barstool—though, as the court took pains to note, he had never before been violent. It decided that the act was "foreign to his personality," and that excessive provocation had combined with drink to make him less than fully responsible. It sentenced him to five years for manslaughter.

If dedication to one's job rates high in the Berliners' code of ethics, the converse applies as well. It sometimes seems as though the accused is judged as much on the merits of his way of life as for his crimes, at least by the press and public, if not always by the courts. If a defendant has held few, if any, jobs, the press plays him up as a "ne'er-do-well and good-for-nothing," a lazy bum who is finally being brought to account.

An example is a thirty-seven-year-old with a record of previous convictions who was tried for cheating a taxi driver. He was certainly a questionable type, if also the victim of an unsettled childhood. Brought up in a welfare home during the Hitler era, he had volunteered for the Storm Troopers at the age of sixteen and joined the S.A. *Standarte "Feldherrnhalle,"* from which he deserted a short while later. "Although strong and healthy to the core," the prosecutor complained in court, "this man has never worked, but has always lived at the cost of other people and mostly let the paternal state take care of him . . ." He said it was high time the accused went to a penitentiary for a few years and the court agreed. "A bungled life," Berlin's *Tagesspiegel* headlined. "This time it's the penitentiary for a lazy good-for-nothing."

Another case showing the same attitude concerned a thirty-one-year-old whose wife had worked at the "Pension Clausewitz" on the Kurfürstendamm, a notorious bordello whose owners also maintained connections with the Ministry for State Security in East Berlin. The prostitute's husband, charged with illegally living off her earnings, was sentenced to a year in jail. The prosecutor told the court that it was perhaps difficult for the accused to give up his former high standard of living, but that he was "obligated to do so and to go to work on his own." In fact, of course there was no such *obligation* at all; the accused was legally obligated only to stop living off a prostitute's earnings. Legal obligation aside, however, this accused *did* have a moral and social obligation "to go to work," for not doing so is apparently intolerable to the citizenry. Other people work to live, but the Germans seem to live to work.

It must be remembered that the children who entered kindergarten as Adolf Hitler was entering the Reich Chancellery in 1933 spent all their formative years under National Socialism. They were in their middle teens when Nazism—and all they had been taught to venerate—went down in ashes. These youngsters had not only been given an outlet for their hates, but for their love as well. Patriotism and heroic self-sacrifice were their ideals. They worshiped the dashing *Luftwaffe* pilots, the bronzed colonels leading *Panzers* in sweeps across the desert, and the young officers in turtleneck sweaters who stalked convoys from beneath the sea.

When the war ended, it was difficult for them to accept that what they had thought was noble was now being called criminal. As the truth about the Nazis gradually became accepted, the youngsters grew angry and cynical. They—and their heroes— had been used "to further the aims of a concentration-camp regime," as one of them said to me.

Then came the misery, despair, and hunger of the immediate postwar years, and all about them, they saw only greed, corruption, and crime. Black marketeering was illegal, but even good, law-abiding Berlin families traded on the black market; some even sent their children out to risk arrest for them. A stolen ration book, coal obtained by burglarizing a warehouse, or food earned by means of teen-age prostitution seemed justified. The times were tragic and moral values meant next to nothing; Berliners chose to survive and ask no questions.

Each month throughout those years, the juvenile crime rate rose. In January, 1946, 567 youngsters were brought to trial; by March, the number had risen to 925. The year-end total of convicted juveniles came to 3,200. A year later, it had reached 4,500 and in 1948, 4,800. The judges understood the motives and were merciful. Fines, short periods of arrest, and probation were the norm; few youngsters were sent to prison. The spirit of revenge which characterized Berlin "justice" during the Nazi era had vanished; the spirit of reform and rehabilitation had returned. What could a judge do with a boy caught black marketeering, a boy who had never learned a trade and who had never held a job since the war ended? More than a third of Berlin youngsters were unemployed and it was not easy to find work which might help the process of rehabilitation. Furthermore, placing a juvenile offender into an open job meant closing that job possibility to an unemployed youngster who had never run afoul of the law. Attempts at reeducation were made, however. In October, 1945, the first Youth and Sport Department was established in a Berlin district government, this being the one founded by Leonore Jacobi in District Reinickendorf. Another Berlin woman prominent in this field was Ella Kay, postwar head of the city's Youth Bureau (*Jugendamt*) and later Senator for Youth in the city government.

It seemed to most people that only prosperity was needed to end juvenile delinquency. As it turned out, they were wrong. The affluent society seems to breed more crime than a hungry one.

The Berliners had a respite from juvenile crime from about 1948 to 1954, but from then on, the rate began to climb. In recent years, it has leveled off, but the *Kriminalpolizei* still had to arrest 8,712 juvenile criminals in 1965. This total is almost three times greater than the number of youngsters brought to trial in 1946.

Such youngsters are registered in the *Kriminalpolizei* Youth File, where their names are kept until they reach the age of twenty-one; it is an attempt by the police to determine how many are multiple offenders and to assess the extent of juvenile delinquency. It is a startling fact that one out of every five young Berliners has run afoul of the law and has his name in that file, a figure that does not even include traffic offenders. Uwe Schlicht of the *Tagesspiegel* says it represents "an unimaginable degree of depravity" and he asserts that only the low postwar birth rate is the main reason why juvenile delinquency in West Berlin appears to be declining. There are fewer juveniles in the city, so there are fewer juvenile crimes.

In fact, more youngsters between the ages of fourteen and eighteen get into trouble in West Berlin than elsewhere in West Germany; the figure for Berlin is also higher than that for large West German cities such as Hamburg and Bremen, although West Berlin has a somewhat lower rate of crime among youths between eighteen and twenty-one than does the Federal Republic. What is happening in West Berlin is similar to what is happening elsewhere in the Western world: A lot of youngsters who seem to have everything want more. Some of them "borrow" other people's cars just for an evening's fast ride along the Berlin *Autobahn,* driving it until it runs out of gas and then abandoning it. Others commit petty thefts. Schlicht points out that the offenders are more prosperous than any Berlin youngsters in the past, but says they feel a disparity between what they have and what advertising and the mass media prompt them to want. They are filled, he says, with envy and greed.

Perhaps there is yet another reason, however, and one which helps, too, to explain why West Berlin's juvenile crime rate is higher than West Germany's. In cities like Munich, Frankfurt, and Hamburg, youngsters can find an outlet for their energies by doing what all German youngsters have always loved to do most: going out into the countryside, hiking, or traveling. West Berlin's youngsters are all locked up. Perhaps its delinquents are just beating their fists against the bars.

chapter twenty-two

ESPIONAGE IS SUCH BIG BUSINESS IN BERLIN THAT FICTION CAN'T
keep up with it. "Books like John le Carré's *The Spy Who Came
in from the Cold* aren't in any way exaggerated," says Dr. Hans-
Joachim Kausch, of Axel Caesar Springer's conservative paper, *Die
Welt.* "They're probably underplayed. Attempts have been and
still are constantly made to recruit spies for the East. Before the
wall went up, a Czechoslovak diplomat, whom I met at a party in
East Berlin, even tried to persuade *me* to supply the Soviet bloc
with information. Of course, I refused to do so."

Had he acceded, he might have found it very hard to disentangle
himself later. Blackmail and threats are used both to recruit agents
and to keep those who later prove recalcitrant. For example, West
Germans visiting East Berlin or other cities in the G.D.R. have
been falsely accused of attempting to help East Germans to escape.
Threatened with long prison terms, they are forced to agree in
writing that they will cooperate with the G.D.R.'s State Security
Service (S.S.D.) after returning to the West. Others who actually
were captured while trying to help would-be escapees are promised
a remission of their sentences if they agree to help. Homosexuals
visiting the G.D.R. are another target; they are threatened with ex-
posure if they fail to cooperate upon their return to West Germany.
Sometimes, innocent people are seized while en route through the
G.D.R. from Berlin to West Germany. One West Berlin customs
official, heading for his honeymoon, was coerced into signing a
similar agreement after he was threatened with arrest and detention. When he later failed to cooperate, he received several threatening telephone calls and letters, and still later, his wife received

a letter accusing him of adultery. The envelope contained a photograph of a nude woman.

Still more elaborate means were used to enlist a secretary to a high West German Government official into the G.D.R.'s service. The girl in question was very fat and so obsessed by this problem that she spoke constantly of her endless and futile efforts at reducing, a fact that had come to the attention of the S.S.D. One day, while at home, she received a visit from a slender, elegant woman who introduced herself as the representative of a "reducing institute" and who spoke glowingly of its successes. When the secretary's interest had been aroused, the visitor said that her "institute" insisted on having in its files a nude photograph of every new client, "for the purpose of evaluating progress." The naïve secretary, desperately anxious to qualify, allowed herself to be photographed in the nude. A few days later, a man contacted her and said that if she did not supply photocopies of information in her employer's files, he would send out hundreds of prints of that photograph, one to every employee in her office building. The girl, who was all the more embarrassed because of her obesity, did summon up the courage to confess everything to her immediate superior, who notified West German counter-intelligence. By this time, the East German contacts had vanished—but at least they never carried out their threat, presumably because it had failed its extortionary purpose. The "catch-all" technique employed by the East Germans doesn't always work, as these cases show, but they work often enough to supply the G.D.R. with a great deal of intelligence information. The method reminds one irresistibly of the seducer who says his technique is simply to proposition every single girl he meets. Asked whether he doesn't get a lot of slaps, he replies, "Yes, I do. But I also get a lot of girls."

The energy and ingenuity of East Berlin's Ministry of State Security can be gauged from its complicity in building up West Berlin's branch of the "neo-Nazi" N.P.D. (National Democratic party). The branch was opened in March, 1966; four months later, it was revealed that the "deputy Führer" of West Berlin's N.P.D., Rolf Richard Voigt, was in fact an agent of the East German S.S.D. A short while later, the N.P.D. chief in District Kreuzberg, Lothar Ernst Rikowski, was unmasked: he had spent sixteen months in jail for espionage on behalf of the S.S.D. There is no doubt that the State Security Service in East Berlin was instrumental in launching the neo-Nazi movement in the Western sectors, and for good reason. The G.D.R. would like to prove that West Berlin was turning into a hotbed of neo-Nazi activity. It has, however, miscalculated badly. The N.P.D. proved a flop in Berlin, so much so that it chose not to enter candidates in any elections there. Of thirty thousand West Berlin university students, many of them conservative politically, only twenty joined the National Democratic University Federation, a group close to the N.P.D. *Der Spiegel* calls West Berlin's N.P.D. "pitifully weak"—and this at a time when the N.P.D. was gaining seats in every other *Land* parliament in West Germany. The N.P.D.'s prospects soon seemed even dimmer in West Berlin, for they declined in West Germany after the humiliating defeat the N.P.D. suffered in late 1968 in the very state which gave the party its birth, Lower Saxony. The fact that the S.S.D.'s activity on behalf of the neo-Nazis became known has, of course, not helped the Right Wingers, but merely confirmed what most Berlin voters suspected all along, that birds of a feather flock together. In winter, 1968, after the mayor of West Berlin asked the Allied commandants to ban the party, the N.P.D. decided to dissolve its West Berlin branch altogether, before the generals could act. By scuttling the branch, the N.P.D. also neatly avoided the humiliation of counting its ballots in the next election.

Intelligence, of course, works both ways and a large number of Western intelligence agencies maintain offices in West Berlin, so as to operate behind the Iron Curtain. Some of their methods may not be much prettier than those employed by the Soviet bloc, but just as the East often uses idealistically motivated Communists in the West as agents, so does the West use idealistic anti-Communists inside East Berlin. I came to know several such men, one of whom I shall call Horst. He was in his late twenties when I first met him in West Berlin, a good-looking, fair-haired young man of slender build.

Horst spent four years spying in East Berlin, photographing Soviet Army installations and supplying the West with other intelligence data of a military and economic nature, before he was arrested and sentenced to nine years in prison. After he served three, the West German Government bought his freedom for ten thousand dollars at a time when a good many other political

322

prisoners in the G.D.R. were being similarly traded for money and Western food products. (Press estimates place the total figure of those involved at twenty-six hundred.)

He didn't work for money and he never received any payment (though he was reimbursed for expenses such as gasoline). He was motivated entirely by his hatred of the S.E.D.'s regime. "If I were still living in East Berlin now," Horst told me, "I'd certainly be more careful—but I'd also do it all over again."

Horst, born in what is now East Berlin, was only seven years old when the war ended; this meant his entire education was in Communist schools. Despite this, he remained unaffected by the propaganda, largely because of the home atmosphere provided by his foster parents, who were German Baptists. "Then came the Berlin Blockade," he says. "I was only ten years old, but it was then that I had my first political thought: that it was wrong to try to starve a people into submission." The years that followed made him increasingly hostile to the regime, and he successfully avoided membership in the Free German Youth, and later, in the F.D.G.B., the Government-run trade union.

The events which led to his spying began during his twentieth year while he worked as a clerk in the Polish Mission in East Berlin. A minor car collision took place outside the building and Horst became acquainted with the man involved: a member of the Bulgarian diplomatic mission whom he calls "Kostov." Horst had by this time married the daughter of a minor People's Police official and Kostov, now a friend, often visited the couple in their new flat, where Horst spoke—at first hesitantly, then passionately—against the regime and its injustices. Kostov listened; when he finally commented on Horst's tirade against the East German Government, it was to ask him if he wouldn't like to do more than just rant and rail.

"How would you like to join me," Kostov asked, "in working for the Americans?"

"I was stunned!" Horst told me after his release from prison. "This was just what I'd been waiting for: a chance to transform my loathing for the regime into action. I accepted immediately."

Horst was captured in 1963, a circumstance he attributes to his own carelessness. While most of his reports were given to Kostov by means of a number of secret drops in East Berlin, some of them were written in invisible ink and mailed to Hamburg, to a man with the cover name of Furtwängler. "Foolishly," Horst says, "I sent one of these letters to Hamburg from the local post office in the Berlin district in which I lived."

He had fallen victim to the extensive surveillance surrounding every single East Berlin inhabitant. All East Berlin apartment houses contain "house trustees" (*Hausvertrauensleute*) subordinate to police headquarters on the precinct level; these men are required to file a monthly report detailing anything they may have observed in their buildings that seems out of the ordinary. Anxious to prove themselves vigilant, they report the most banal activities, often so as to make them seem suspicious: Last month, Herr A. came home late at night on three occasions; B. has visitors each Sunday; C. bought himself a new overcoat. Such reports are routinely put away in the file maintained at district level, and if any inhabitant's file grows suspiciously, that person's local post office begins to intercept all his mail. Horst is convinced that it was in this way that the State Security Service obtained one of his letters to Hamburg and learned of his activities.

He was arrested at the Hotel Sofia in East Berlin, just after arriving there to join his wife and some friends for dinner. Kostov, who was supposed to have joined them, hadn't shown up. "The two men who picked me up didn't even have to show me their identification," Horst says. "I took one look at them and knew they were from the S.S.D."

"Go get your little overcoat (*dein Mäntelchen*)," they said patronizingly, "and come along with us."

Wrap-around sunglasses, their lenses covered with black paint, were placed on Horst's nose once he had seated himself in the S.S.D.'s sedan outside the hotel. "That didn't work, however," Horst says, "because I was born in East Berlin and knew it so well that I could identify every street along which we drove."

They were heading towards the Alexanderplatz and Horst hoped the car would stop at the "Alex" police headquarters, for that would mean he had not been picked up on political charges.

"Then I felt the car swing around the traffic circle," he says. "When it did that, I knew it wasn't any minor matter. When the car later headed up an incline, I knew where we were going. I

324

still didn't know what the charges were, but I said to myself then, 'Now it's all over!' "

The S.S.D. men seated on either side of Horst had remained silent throughout the drive, nor did Horst ask them questions. "It's useless," he says. "No one asks the S.S.D. anything. One finds out soon enough. Furthermore, it's none of your business why you're arrested. Those are things every single East Berliner knows, whether he is in trouble or not. Everybody keeps his mouth shut and avoids contacts with any official. If one does have to deal with an official, one says as little as possible and then only in reply to a question."

The drive ended in the courtyard of the S.S.D.'s interrogation prison. "The first thing I saw when I was allowed to remove my 'blindfold' was Kostov's Mercedes Benz, no doubt parked there for my benefit," Horst says. " 'So they got him, too!' I said to myself, 'but on what charge?' "

It need not have been espionage, for Horst had also helped two persons escape to West Berlin in the trunk of Kostov's automobile, which carried diplomatic license plates and was therefore exempt from inspection at the G.D.R. checkpoint between East and West Berlin.

He was interrogated by five S.S.D. officers for nine hours. "While it was strenuous," he says, "it was never brutal. I was never molested in any way, and aside from an occasional jab in the chest with an index finger, they never touched me physically."

It was obvious they knew that he had been spying—but also that they didn't know too much. "All they had," says Horst, "were two items. The first was a photograph of me near a Soviet air base, which must have been taken with a telephoto lens because I had not been aware of anyone near me. I had been counting the number of gasoline trucks and other vehicles entering and leaving the base, but I told the S.S.D. I'd simply found myself near the base while on excursion in the countryside. The second piece of evidence, however, was more damning: it was one of my letters to 'Furtwängler' in Hamburg."

Horst was charged both with espionage and "trafficking in human beings" and remained in solitary confinement for ten months before his trial began. Because his foster mother had obtained his lawyer, Horst got a spirited defense. By the time he came to trial, his wife had divorced him, for which he does not blame her, as she is the daughter of a People's Police official. ("She's remarried since," Horst says. "I don't mind, but I do miss our daughter.")

He came face-to-face with Kostov in the courtroom, though they were not allowed to exchange more than glances. Kostov, being a diplomatic official, had been under house arrest for the past ten months, and after the trial, was expelled to Bulgaria. "The judge," says Horst, "did a great deal of shouting at me, but he sentenced me only to nine years in prison. Some people who did much more than I did received even lower sentences in other trials and some who did less got longer prison-terms. It's often a matter of luck."

He spent the next three years in an S.S.D.-operated part of the Berlin-Rummelsburg Prison, repairing motor vehicles belonging to the S.S.D. Food was adequate and the treatment was decent. None of the prisoners were molested by the guards. He was housed in a cell inside a long barrack and the doors to the cells were left open for much of the time. Prisoners also had the run of the yard. About sixty percent of the prisoners were there on "political charges," mostly espionage and helping people to escape. "There was no question about their guilt," says Horst. "All of them spoke openly about the fact that they were guilty—and none of them were ashamed of it. Most of them would do the same again if they had the chance."

This may well be one of the reasons Walter Ulbricht was willing to trade political prisoners for cash and food. Once released, such prisoners would be a problem, for they could never be trusted.

"Of course, the S.S.D. told me I was released on the initiative of the G.D.R. and only for humanitarian reasons," Horst says. "I was put on a bus with thirty-two other political prisoners and we drove eight hours to the *Autobahn* crossing point at Wartha, where a West German bus picked us up and took us to Frankfurt. We were too exhausted to have a big celebration, but you can imagine how we felt. Those ten thousand dollars purchased six years of my life!"

The West German authorities offered to relocate the former prisoners anywhere they liked. Horst chose West Berlin, as did several others in his contingent. "After all," he says, "I'm a Berliner and I would never think of living anywhere else."

In West Berlin, Horst was interrogated by American, British, French, and West German intelligence agencies. He was then allowed to rest in a Red Cross home, after which he was given a job as a laboratory technician in a West Berlin company. It was at this point that I met him. He was still very nervous and extremely cautious. His eyes avoided mine throughout our talk, leading me at first to be suspicious, for Berlin is full of people who invent tales for reasons of their own. My confidence in him increased that evening when he casually dropped the name of a secret United States intelligence installation in West Germany of which I had personal knowledge from my earlier service in the United States Army Military Intelligence. Not only did Horst know its location, but some of its functions as well. I afterwards checked him out with the West Berlin "Political Police"; they knew all about him and corroborated his story.

It had not been too difficult for me to arrange the meeting with Horst. That very fact indicates some of the weird atmosphere of West Berlin. A step farther in investigating the investigators becomes even stranger. One finds oneself quickly enveloped in a delicate and annoying cobweb, dealing with faceless individuals who have no names, waiting for telephone calls from offices the existence of which one is not supposed to know, and being involved with people who all seem vaguely disreputable, no matter their origin. There are writers who are fascinated by espionage, but after having served in Intelligence, I am not one of these; I found myself increasingly repelled by the lies, half-truths, and distortions. One of the more innocent examples of this Byzantine atmosphere was provided when I first tried to contact an official of West Berlin's "Political Police," its counter-intelligence force. That would be impossible, I was told; they would contact me, for their address was "secret"—although in fact it is well-known. I finally received a telephone call from a man who refused to give his name; he said I had been checked out and that he would meet me in a booth at Mampe's Gute Stube, an old Berlin restaurant of quality on the Kurfürstendamm. He recognized me there (how?) and proved helpful within limits, but insisted that all future contacts be arranged in the same mysterious manner. A huge, burly official with an enormous square jaw, he could have made a killing in Hollywood playing German villains, though he proved soft-spoken and courteous enough. We chatted for an hour or so, during which time he provided me with a certain amount of information regarding Soviet bloc espionage activities. He proved more secretive, though, about his address, insisting that in the future I was to wait for his telephone call. When I pressed him for some way of contacting him, he finally gave me a number where I could leave a message, asking him to call back. It was all very Kafkaesque and seemed suitably conspiratorial for this city of intrigues.

Similar security precautions prevail among Allied intelligence agencies in West Berlin. For good and valid reasons, those Central Intelligence Agency officials who work at the United States Mission in the city maintain secure cover identities, and no one knows exactly how many C.I.A. people work in offices bearing more innocent titles. The general assumption among Americans in West Berlin is that the mission crawls with "spooks," as Mission employees call C.I.A. and other American intelligence personnel. As one gets to know Americans in Berlin and to attend their social gatherings, one also begins to suspect that the presence of these "spooks" accounts for much of that extreme caution one observes in American conversations in Berlin, even when they are among their own colleagues. Every Mission employee knows that anything he says could be reported; as a result, everyone "plays it very close to the vest." This caution is not prompted by actual *fear,* but the degree of caution observed in conversations seems vaguely demeaning for representatives of a democracy. I later came to the conclusion that this exaggerated conformity was not due only to the presence of unidentifiable "spooks" who might report controversial views, but also to those same social pressures which operate within large American corporations like A.T. & T. Careers are at stake and those involved learn quickly to assume the viewpoints demanded, denying that any pressure brought them to heel. In Berlin, this creates a particularly depressing atmosphere, for C.I.A. officials really *are* listening; those diplomats who do their conscientious best under difficult circumstances have become depressingly inured to it all.

Big Brother, of course, watches much more intensely in East

Berlin than in the West.* The network of spies and informers that comprises the G.D.R.'s Ministry of State Security is organized according to function: Secret Main Informers (G.H.I., *Geheime Hauptinformanten*), Secret Informers (G.I., *Geheime Informanten*), and Secret Collaborators (G.M., *Geheime Mitarbeiter*). Ever since the 1953 uprising in East Berlin, people employed in Government- and state-owned industries have been enrolled into Factory Fighting Groups (*Kampfgruppen*), heavily armed and structured in military fashion from the squad to the regimental level. Twenty-five thousand such troops are stationed in East Berlin. In addition, there are the N.V.A. border guards in or about East Berlin, as well as sundry "auxiliary organizations." The most important of these is the Society for Sport and Technology, in which the very young, aged fourteen upward, are enrolled. Finally, there is the People's Police itself, and its emergency unit, the *Bereitschaftspolizei.* This does *not* take into account the sprawling network of police spies and informers, specialized organizations such as the Transport Police, the Soviet divisions ringing the city, nor the number of House Trustees. As there are more than forty thousand apartment buildings in East Berlin, it is no exaggeration to suggest that there may be a like number of House Trustees.

Erika von Hornstein, who provides the stories of seven East German political prisoners in her book, *The Accused,* charges the S.E.D. regime of operating "according to methods customary in the Middle Ages . . ." Others compare it to the Nazi dictatorship, finding virtually no significant differences between the two. Actually, the comparison with the latter isn't completely valid. East German Government policy does not include genocide, racial and religious hatreds are not fomented, and the fate of political prisoners differs significantly.

Nazi Germany killed tens of thousands of political prisoners in concentration camps or Gestapo prisons, often after subjecting them to torture and mutilation. None of this seems to exist in the

* His name is Erich Mielke, a colonel-general and Minister for State Security ever since 1957. From headquarters at Normannstrasse 22 in District Lichtenberg, Mielke's fourteen thousand S.S.D. men operate a network of agents so elaborate that East Berlin has become the center of agitation, sedition, subversion, and espionage of the Soviet bloc in Central Europe.

G.D.R., though its political prisons are bad enough for them to be called "monstrous" by Amnesty International, a nonpartisan organization that recently undertook a study of political prisoners and their fate in East Germany. Despite that assessment, Amnesty International reports that "actual cases of physical violence used on prisoners are extremely rare" and that each appears "to be the action of individual warders rather than the result of policy." Imprisonment itself was for many prisoners less of an ordeal than the pre-trial examination by the State Security Service, where such intense psychological pressure was applied that the minds of some prisoners snapped under the strain. Yet, even during this part of his experience, says Amnesty International, "no prisoner claimed to have been subjected to any kind of systematic torture or beating." The absence of physical violence is certainly an enormous improvement over Nazism. Whereas an apprehended spy like Horst only had a finger jabbed in his chest by the members of the Communist secret police, the personal aides and secretaries of Germany's vice chancellor, Franz von Papen, were kicked and trampled to death by S.S. men's boots during the 1934 blood purge. Nor is the absence of torture and murder of prisoners the only difference. Sentences for political crimes, which in the Nazi era were all death sentences and which during the worst Stalinist years in East Germany often ranged as high as fifteen and twenty-five years, have dropped sharply. Many political prisoners are sentenced to prison for two to ten years today.

Because not all sentences are published by the East Germans, it is impossible to tell just exactly how many political prisoners are jailed in the G.D.R. in any one year, but it appears that their number has been dropping annually ever since the Berlin Wall "stabilized" the G.D.R.'s political and economic situation. In 1961, the year the escape route to the West was sealed, East German courts sentenced 1,598 people to jail for political crimes; by 1967, this number had dropped to 327. The year the wall went up, three persons were sentenced to death and sixteen to life imprisonment on political grounds; in 1967, four of the 327 were sentenced to fifteen years and the remainder received somewhat lower sentences. One West German accused of espionage in the G.D.R. was recently sentenced to life imprisonment, but the tendency toward imposing lower sentences seems clear. "When I was tried and convicted," says Paul Norden, "sentences of either fifteen or even twenty-five years in prison weren't unusual. Today they are."

Three main prisons are used in East Berlin to house political prisoners, along with others convicted for criminal offenses. East Berlin's Rummelsburg Prison usually contains almost two thousand men, more than half of them political prisoners. The Barnimstrasse Prison houses nearly three hundred female prisoners, sixty percent of whom are political prisoners, while the S.S.D.-run Berlin Hohenschönhausen work camp contains between close to one thousand male prisoners, of whom about half are "politicals." Thus there are about eighteen hundred political prisoners in East Berlin alone and an additional estimated six thousand in the rest of the G.D.R.

"One of the more encouraging features of East German policy over the last few years," says Amnesty International, "has been the large-scale releases of political prisoners that have taken place. It is estimated that over three and a half thousand political prisoners benefited from these releases since 1964. On the other hand, while more than twice the number remain in prison and more are continually being sentenced . . . one cannot unfortunately conclude that political imprisonment in East Germany is, in any way, a feature of the past."

A new criminal code introduced in 1967 sharply decreases punishments for *non*political offenses, while increasing them for political crimes. In fact, a host of new "political offenses" have been written into the law (including "Terror" and "Diversion," two entirely new catch-all categories), and of these, *eleven* threaten life imprisonment or death by firing squad "in extreme cases." On the other hand, punishments for crimes against property have been reduced and the number of punishable sex offenses has been cut in half. East Germans today have twice as much sexual freedom as they had before, as if to compensate them for the loss of their political liberties.

The new criminal code (*Strafgesetzbuch*) is the work of a commission headed by Dr. Hilde Benjamin, who is an interesting example of the Communist functionary in East Berlin. She stems from prosperous bourgeois parents, her father having been a company director in the Berlin district of Steglitz. In 1926, Hilde Lange married Dr. Georg Benjamin, a physician who was a Communist party member and who then operated a clinic for the poor in Wedding. So dedicated was he to social improvement that Hilde Benjamin joined the K.P.D., and being a lawyer, ran a free legal-aid bureau for Communists who required assistance. In 1933, the Nazis forbade her to practice law; in 1936 her husband, a Jew, was arrested by the Gestapo and was murdered in the Maut-hausen concentration camp in 1942. She survived the Nazi era in Berlin, supporting herself and her son by taking odd jobs in shops and as a steno-typist. When the Soviets conquered Berlin, they appointed her chief prosecutor in District Lichterfelde and it was from this position that she rose, step by step, up the East Ger-man judicial ladder, until she became Minister of Justice, a post from which she recently retired. More than anyone else in East Berlin, Hilde Benjamin exemplified the suppression of human rights under Communism. Hated, she was called the "Red Guil-lotine." As one-time vice chairman of the G.D.R. Supreme Court, she meted out sixty-seven political sentences, two of them death sentences. Ironically, she also instituted some legal reforms as Jus-tice Minister that actually reduced the Red terror.

While Hilde Benjamin had always been a dedicated Communist and a victim of Nazi persecution, the same cannot be said of every functionary in the East Berlin regime. Most surprising of all is that former Nazis should have risen to positions of considerable promi-nence under Communism, should even have been allowed to as-sume cabinet-level ministerial posts in the G.D.R., despite the fact that East Berlin belabors Bonn so stridently for the ex-Nazis in the service of West Germany.

West Berlin's "Free Jurists" have published what might be called a "Brown Book," listing former Nazi party members who hold prominent positions in the East German Government, the S.E.D., and other puppet parties making up East Germany's "Na-tional Front." * This documentation charges that five G.D.R. min-

* *Ehemalige Nationalsozialisten in Pankows Diensten,* or "Former National Socialists in the service of Pankow." East Berlin's District Pankow is commonly used (pejoratively) to describe the East German Government, much as "the Zone" is used by West Germans when re-ferring to the G.D.R., belittling it as the Soviet Zone of Occupation. This is because Castle Niederschönhausen, located in Pankow, until

isters, men of "cabinet rank," were former Nazi party members, that twelve former Nazis are members or candidate members of the S.E.D. Central Committee, and that fifty-three are delegates to the East German "parliament," the *Volkskammer*. Siegfried Dallmann, for example, joined the Nazi party in November, 1934, and was Nazi youth leader in Thuringia.* Heinrich Homann, also of the N.D.P.D., is one of six deputy chairmen in the "State Council" headed by Ulbricht; he joined the Nazis in 1933. Professor Dr. Peter-Adolf Thiessen, a member of this same State Council from 1960 to 1963, and later, chairman of the research council of the G.D.R. Ministerial Council, joined the Nazis as early as 1925. Kurt Blecha, head of Ulbricht's personal Press Bureau, is a former Nazi party member; Professor Kurt Schröder, a president of East Berlin's Humboldt University, is also a former Nazi, and a great many Communist journalists (who polemicize against Nazis in West Germany) were also members of the N.S.D.A.P. Some former Nazis were ousted—*after* West Berlin's Free Jurists published details about their past—but most continue in high office.

One who was dismissed after the Free Jurists made known his past was Ernst Grossmann, "Hero of Labor," member of the East German delegation to the nineteenth Congress of the Soviet Communist party, and member of the powerful Central Committee of the S.E.D. When his membership in that august group was revoked, the East Berlin press stated only that he had lied about his past, but did not tell what that past was, nor was Grossmann stripped of his membership in the S.E.D. itself. In fact, this high S.E.D. official had joined the Nazis in 1938, had become an S.S. noncommissioned officer, and had later served in S.S. "death's-

---

recent years served as the official seat of the G.D.R.'s Government. Until the death of President Wilhelm Pieck in 1960 abolished his office, it served as presidential "White House" in East Berlin; from then until 1964, the castle was the official seat of the "State Council," whose chairman is Walter Ulbricht.

* He is now a member of the Council of Elders (*Ältestenrat*) of the *Volkskammer* and head of the forty-five-man-strong N.D.P.D. delegation in parliament, this "National Democratic" party of East Germany having been set up specifically (and cynically) to attract Right-Wingers, nationalists, ex-Nazis, and former *Wehrmacht* officers into the S.E.D.-run National Front coalition.

head" units at two notorious Nazi concentration camps, Oranien-burg and Sachsenhausen.

To mention all this raises the question of whether East Berlin has any moral justification for denouncing Bonn's employment of former Nazis against whom no war-crimes charges have been preferred. Further, this is not just a case of the pot calling the kettle black, for fundamental differences are involved. Former Nazi party members holding prominent positions in West Germany are at least in the service of a democratically elected, constitutional government, while those former Nazis in the service of the S.E.D. dictatorship continue as before to serve a police state.

Their prominence in the G.D.R. also tends to confirm the widely held suspicion that many Nazis—perhaps most of them—never really cared a fig for the Nazis' "ideology," but were mainly attracted by the authoritarian nature of Hitler's regime. What they despised then and what they despise now are free political parties, parliamentary democracy, democratic institutions, and guarantees of personal freedoms; they have now once more fitted themselves into the kind of despotic structure they always preferred. The fact that they mouth the slogans of Communism rather than Nazism means nothing. Britain's A.J.P. Taylor, writing of Germany in the Thirty Years' War, said:

"In every age rulers, fighting for their survival or for the extension of their power, have to talk the claptrap of the time; in the 17th century the claptrap happened to be religious."

So it is with these ex-Nazis in the service of East Berlin. They are, after all, more than just careerists or mere opportunists. They are *professionals*.

The People's Police of East Berlin grew out of the police force that the Soviets put together during May and June of 1945, when they controlled all four sectors of the city. Its future course was set during those two months by Berlin's first postwar police chief, or *Polizeipräsident,* Paul Markgraf. He was a former Wehrmacht colonel whom the Russians had captured at Stalingrad and reeducated at one of their Antifa (for anti-fascist) schools in the U.S.S.R. He arrived in Berlin just as the city surrendered to the Soviet forces. While Ulbricht put together a city administration, Markgraf recruited its policemen. He had only sixty days before the Western

Allies would enter the city in July, 1945, which may account for the fact that most of the uniformed policemen he recruited proved an embarrassment. As the United States Military Government reported later, the uniformed police, which numbered eleven thousand men, had a turnover in the first two years of ten thousand in this group alone.

Markgraf, it appeared, had recruited twenty-five hundred past or present crooks and about five thousand former Nazis. Nor were these his only blunders. The man the Soviets placed in command of the uniformed police (as distinct from mufti-clad detectives and officials) was an old-time police officer, Major Karl Heinrich. Far from being a crook or a Nazi, he was a competent and democratic police official of the Weimar Republic, whom the Nazis forced out of office as soon as they came to power. Markgraf should have suspected that a man who was anti-Nazi might be anti-totalitarian by nature, but apparently he didn't. Heinrich resisted Communist pressure as much as he had resisted the Nazis. Then in the summer of 1945, this high police official vanished. The United States Military Government reported that he "disappeared and has not been heard from since," but a West Berlin agency notes he was arrested on August 2, 1945, and lists him as having died on November 3, 1945, in "Concentration Camp Hohenschönhausen," the S.S.D.-operated East Berlin prison work camp.

He was not the only opponent of the Soviets who vanished in those postwar months. In 1949, the Office of Military Government, United States Sector, reported, ". . . there can be no doubt that the great majority of the thousands who have disappeared did so on Russian Communist orders, or were abducted."

The Western Allies struggled with the Russians, trying to counter the kidnappings and abductions, to regularize police procedures, and to influence police actions. Markgraf, however, was *Polizeipräsident* for all four sectors of the then united city; he had his headquarters in the Soviet sector of the city, took his orders from the Russians, and was contemptuous of Western efforts at influencing the police. The Western Allies were powerless, blocked as they were by the Soviet veto in the four-power city. Still, efforts were made at the appropriate Kommandatura meetings. Early in 1948, for example, the Soviets announced the resignation of a police official for reasons of "ill health," but the Western Allies discovered that the man's criminal record had come to light. It involved four previous convictions and current dealings with a gang of criminals. When they confronted the Soviets with this information at a meeting on May 13, the embarrassed Russians walked out in anger. Shortly thereafter, the Russians had further reason to be irritated, for police works-council elections had resulted in a solid anti-Communist vote. Of 233 works councillors, only ninety were Communists and all but four of these were elected in the Soviet sector of the city, where pressure could be exercised. Yet even in the Soviet sector, the policemen had elected thirty-two non-Communists.

Police problems continued to plague the Western Allies until the city government was split in mid-1948, resulting in two separate police forces. Dr. Johannes Stumm set up West Berlin's force in the United States sector's Friesenstrasse on August 2, 1948. Like the abducted Heinrich, Stumm was a pre-Nazi police official whom the Russians mistrusted. By 1948, however, the Soviets began to mistrust even their own Paul Markgraf, who remained in his post in East Berlin only until 1949. The United States Military Government says that "Markgraf seemed gradually to be realizing that it was the Western representatives [on the Public Safety Committee of the Kommandatura] who wanted a democratic police department and increased pay, pensions, and the necessary equipment and supplies to permit the building of a good police force, and that it was always the Russian representative who vetoed improvements proposed by the other committee members."

In June, 1949, the Western Allies made the West Berlin city authorities fully responsible for the maintenance of their police force. This Allied order also made policemen individually responsible for their actions and subject to the rule of law, made the force responsible for its own administration, and stressed that West Berlin was to allow "no secret police . . . or force of police other than is already in being" to be established.

West Berlin's police have since then developed into a tidy military force. Maybe this was inevitable, considering the threats to which the Western sectors were exposed. The U.S., British, and French armies in West Berlin wanted the city to be able to suppress uprisings and unrest by itself. Only a strong, mobile, heavily armed, and well-disciplined police force could act effectively against Communist-inspired riots and disturbances, and at the same time relieve the Western Allies of any embarrassing need for armed intervention. Thus the Allied armies could restrict themselves to their primary duties: guarding the city and its access routes against any direct military threat, which their very presence was meant to deter.

Today there are more policemen per inhabitants in West Berlin —one for every 197 West Berliners—than anywhere else in West Germany. Hamburg has one policeman for every 308 of its citizens, while the state of Northrhine-Westphalia has one for every 718.

There are almost twenty thousand policemen in the Western sectors, if one counts the Volunteer Police Reserve, as one should, for it is meant to relieve the regular force in times of unrest. The force is divided into three main groups: *Schupos, Bepos,* and *Kripos.* The *Schupos* are members of the ten-thousand-man *Schutzpolizei,* which is the ordinary uniformed force and means "protective police"; the *Bepos* belong to the three-thousand-man *Bereitschaftspolizei,* or to the paramilitary "emergency police," and the *Kripos* are members of the fourteen-hundred-man *Kriminalpolizei,* or criminal investigation branch. The F.P.R. Reserve totals about five thousand men. Maintaining this large force costs about ten percent of the city budget, or twice as much as West Berlin spends on all its streets, highways, and U-Bahn underground railways systems. As one result, police arsenals are so jammed with modern weapons that the fire power the force possesses is said to be greater than that of one of the Wehrmacht infantry divisions that rolled over Europe during the *Blitzkrieg* years of World War II.

The most "military" element in the force are the *Bepos,* the emergency police, trained, housed, and disciplined like soldiers; they are kept in their barracks or on maneuvers until the Allied military commandants in the city give the order to unleash them. They take the place of West German *Bundeswehr* soldiers, none of whom may be stationed in West Berlin, and are so firmly restricted by the Western Allied commandants that they tend to seem even more ominous than they are, like some warhead that cannot be armed or employed without consent from the highest quarters. In fact, during one recent year in West Berlin, I saw the *Bepos* used only once—and this time to shovel snow during a blizzard that had paralyzed the city. Even then, it had taken the Allied generals a couple of days to come to the decision to let these troopers man their shovels.

The F.P.R. reserve is yet another "military" force in West Berlin, a cross between a civilian Home Guard and an American-style National Guard unit. Any eighteen-year-old Berliner can join; after an initial two-week training period, he attends a week of maneuvers twice annually. (Employers provide full wages throughout, being reimbursed out of public funds.) This "reserve army" of policemen is meant to protect and defend about two hundred essential West Berlin installations in the event of serious civic disturbance, relieving the regular police of this duty. It also allows a lot of West Berliners a chance to play soldier without joining the military. F.P.R. fatigue-style combat uniforms certainly look military, as do their weapons and methods of training, the latter conducted on maneuver terrain usually reserved for Western troops. The Springer newspapers are enthusiastic supporters, urging Berliners to join the F.P.R. and to swell its ranks even more.

Seven thousand West Berliners have over the years been trained in the F.P.R. reserve and two-thirds of them are city employees of one kind or another. Those with whom I talked not only like their service, but are thoroughly convinced that there remains a need for this kind of force. The overwhelming majority of ordinary West Berliners firmly reject the idea that the Cold War has ended.

There are some Berliners who believe that it isn't just the police uniforms, weapons, or arsenals that are "military," but that some of the military spirit has been retained as well. An early example of this was provided just two years after West Berlin's separate police force was established, during Christmas of 1950. The director of a troupe of political satirists, invited to perform at a police function, was shocked by what he encountered. The evening's performance, before officers and wives of the force, was a disaster.

"Our show poked fun at army life and sang the praises of being civilians again—but it wasn't going over at all," he says.

"Then came intermission. All those policemen and their wives were sitting in civilian clothes at tables decorated with candles and other Christmas trim. Suddenly, a man who must have been their

338

commanding officer leaped up and stepped out into the center aisle.

" 'All right, men!' he yelled in that special barracks-square voice we all got to know in the war, 'we're all sick and tired of these civilian clothes, so let's remember who we are and what we are! Fall in!'

"And all the policemen leaped out of their seats, fell into ranks, and started parading around the hall, singing marches like *Erika,* while their wives stood up on the benches and clapped time to the beat. Now you tell me: Could something like that, just five years after the end of the war, happen in any other country except Germany?"

In Spandau, there's a West Berlin police school named after Joachim Lipschitz, the late city Interior Senator who had particularly emphasized the civic and civilian character of the city police and who was replaced by Heinrich Albertz (to later serve a brief, inglorious term as mayor, succeeding Willy Brandt). Lipschitz's name on that school seems all that remains of Lipschitz's spirit. Under Albertz, much more of the management of the police was surrendered to police officers. If it is true that war is too important to be left to generals, it may be equally true that police matters in Berlin are too important to be left to policemen and that these "watchdogs of democracy" need to be watched carefully by democratic civilian officials. Lipschitz had been such an official; indeed, he went so far as to put the police into "civilian-type" uniforms. Under Albertz, however, much of this seems to have been scrapped. Military-style uniforms replaced the ones Lipschitz had selected; Albertz is said to have snapped that one ought to be able to tell a policeman from a trolley-car conductor. Today, there's little confusion: policemen are equipped with jackboots, Walther pistols, machine guns, grenade launchers, and armored cars. The Interior administration has received a bombproof underground bunker, as well as a *Hauptführungsstab,* or army-style staff organization. This latter was meant to supervise the senior staff headquarters of Police President Erich Duensing, who in turn supervised separate staff headquarters established in military fashion for the three main divisions of the police.

Duensing has been replaced, but he is a man who put his stamp on the force. Like Paul Markgraf, he was a Wehrmacht officer (a major) who belonged to that elite fraternity of men who wore the Knight's Cross of the Iron Cross. Markgraf became a Communist supporter; Duensing traded his field-gray tunic for a membership in the S.P.D. Neither man was popular. Duensing won the nickname *Knüppel Erich,* or "Truncheon Erich," because of the command barked during student demonstrations: *"Knüppel frei!"* or "Unsheath night-sticks," which told the police to make free use of their truncheons. In 1967, that command sent billies crashing into skulls, policemen kicking and pummeling students who had already fallen to the ground, and resulted in such a bloody fracas that a policeman shot and killed a student, Benno Ohnesorge. Ultimately, this student's death brought so much criticism of the police that "Truncheon Erich" Duensing retired prematurely and the government of Heinrich Albertz was replaced by that of Klaus Schütz. There was then a big debate over who was was to succeed "Knüppel Erich." The man ultimately chosen was Georg Moch, his deputy, who had a reputation as a moderate. Hope of change seemed briefly to fill the air—but it vanished during the riots of 1968, following the attempted assassination of Rudi Dutschke, the Left-Wing student leader in Berlin. Now Moch has been replaced, and a liberal, non-professional heads the force.

Actually the possibility of real change was always slight. The military-style drill and discipline Duensing instituted encouraged militaristic thinking and that *Kadavergehorsam* or corpselike obedience that has been the bane of the uniformed German for a long time. To be sure, the city's police academies urge policemen to think for themselves and tell them that their job is to protect the "constitutional order," presumably including civil liberties, but these lessons often do not seem to have been absorbed. How could they sink in, when military drill and army-style discipline were stricter in West Berlin under Duensing than in any other police force in all West Germany? (As *Der Spiegel* pointed out, West Berlin policemen who passed examinations in civics received praise under Duensing, but those who made up their bunks along tight army lines got extra time off. Such subtle lessons sank in.)

One West Berlin policeman spoke frankly about these matters, on the promise of anonymity. He was a rookie policeman who had just finished his training, was in his late twenties, and liberal in his thinking. He says he was horrified by the attitudes he encountered among the others in his class.

"As part of our training," he told me, "we were shown films of Nazi atrocities, to show us the horrors of the past, so that such terrible deeds could never happen again.

"The films were horrible," he continued. "But what horrified me even more was the reaction of the other young policemen watching the films. 'They are all lies!' they told me afterward. Others protested, 'Why do they show us these things? All that ought to be forgotten!' Still others said the films were 'staged' by the Allies. I protested, pointing out that these films were actually official German films, made by Germans who took part in the atrocities, but not a single one of my comrades wanted to face these facts. 'All lies!' they kept saying. 'All lies!' "

The commandant of the West Berlin *Schutzpolizei,* the ordinary uniformed police force, is Hans-Ulrich Werner, a former S.S. officer. East Germany published denunciations of *Kommandeur* Werner and he, in turn, went to court, where he defended himself successfully against "slander." The charges that he committed crimes while in the S.S. proved to be unfounded. In fact, Werner cannot be condemned merely for having belonged to the S.S., for it was actually a fact that all members of the criminal-investigation branch of the police (*Kriminalpolizei*) were during the war years placed under the command of *S.S. Reichsführer* Heinrich Himmler, a circumstance that even put such active anti-Nazis as Arthur Nebe into the uniforms of S.S. generals.

The West Berlin Senat states that in general it is the practice to enlist the services of police officers with previous police experience, even former Nazis, so long as specific charges of wrongdoing had not been made against them, and that West Berlin checks out its officials more carefully than does any other *Land* in the Federal Republic. Despite this, many liberals in West Berlin are dismayed that this "bastion of democracy" feels it needs to rely on former Nazis to defend the democratic, constitutional order of the city. Their presence, like the leadership of men such as "Truncheon Erich," does not assist the average policeman in developing a passion for defending the civil liberties of the Berliners.

The first article of the policeman's catechism in West Berlin seems to be *Ordnung muss sein!*—"There has to be order!"—and this is not always compatible with guarantees of individual liberty. The second seems to be Count von der Schulenburg's admonition to the Berliners in 1806: *"Ruhe ist die erste Bürgerpflicht!"*—"The citizen's first duty is to keep the peace—and remain silent!"

It was inevitable that policemen inculcated with attitudes like these overreacted in the face of student protest demonstrations. For one thing, policemen are not immune to propaganda. The policeman in West Berlin reads the same newspapers as do civilian West Berliners: in the main, these belong to the mass-oriented Springer-owned press. Reading these newspapers, one gets the impression that West Berlin's dissidents, demonstrators, and protesting students are all radicals, beatniks, anarchists, or pro-Communist agents. The students are defamed as *Radikalinskis,* a favorite epithet meaning radicals and given a Russian suffix to drive the point home. Further, the dirty, hirsute appearance of many demonstrators infuriates the proper German burgher. Show them or their policemen these students, suggest they are in league with Ulbricht, and the rection is predictable. It is clear that the average West Berliner agrees with the Springer press' assessment of the students, and what is more, that the liberal city government agrees with it as well. So do the Western Allies. In 1967, all officials demanded swift, stern action against those "disturbing the peace." Then, when Ohnesorge was killed, it became clear that the police had been incited to violence. Briefly, everyone admitted that charges of police brutality were well-founded.

In September, 1967, an American psychiatrist from California addressed West Berlin police officials and urged them not to take the student protests so very seriously, but to regard them instead as a world-wide phenomenon and to respond to them with tolerance and even some good humor. He urged them to get their priorities straight: It was more important that they protect free speech and dissent in West Berlin than just "maintain order." He also urged them to stop thinking of all dissenters as enemies. The discussion which followed this talk showed that most of those attending dismissed the lecturer as a wooly-minded intellectual who theorized about things of which he had little practical knowledge.

The lecturer's remarks paralleled those of Helmut Kentler, a psychologist whom the police briefly employed as a consultant

342

in the wake of public criticism. Kentler, however, failed to white-wash the police, criticized them instead, and soon became the target himself of furious police criticism.

Kentler had not, however, put all the blame on the police. He had said they'd been left holding the bag for the city fathers, trying to "solve" by means of force what the politicians had failed to solve peaceably. He warned that if the city government continued to offer only force as an answer to its confrontations with dissidents and rebels, then the city's students might make common cause with its industrial workers. If this were to happen, West Berlin might have its own June 17th uprising, as East Berlin did in 1953.

Psychologist Kentler observed special psychological problems among West Berlin policemen. He said the policeman takes out on the dissenting student the impotent rage he feels towards the wall and the "enemies" behind it. This rage, bottled up within him during long service at the frontier, explodes into action and dissenters become whipping boys. Kentler also complains that the West Berlin police still think in terms of "mass or mob psychology," which regards the mob as dumb, dangerous, and easily swayed.

When *Polizeipräsident* Georg Moch assumed office, he promised that a "turning point" had been reached. The command "unsheathe truncheons," Moch told a press conference, would never again be given to a unit of the West Berlin police. He would order the police to use restraint, to protect the dissident minority from the fury of the outraged majority of West Berliners, and would allow all citizens the full exercise of their freedoms. Even as he said it, there were doubts whether he could eradicate the spirit of Duensing.

Such fears were tragically proven right when the attempted assassination of Rudi Dutschke in April, 1968, prompted massive student demonstrations. Ten thousand policemen were used against twelve thousand demonstrators. The number of persons arrested rose to almost four hundred, the number of injured demonstrators (and innocent passersby) came to two hundred, and fifty-four policemen were hurt. The riots quickly spread throughout most of Germany; everywhere, the pattern was the same. The police used a maximum of violence and savagery. Dozens of people in West Berlin were clubbed, kicked, and beaten by the police; others were hauled out of cars and belabored with night-sticks. According to massive documentation provided by *Der Spiegel,* policemen charged automobiles, smashing their windows and demolishing headlights. Innocent people, pleading for mercy, were beaten to the ground. In Schöneberg, a news photographer was clubbed to his knees and had a handful of hair pulled out of his head by a police officer. Elsewhere, Günther Zint, photographer of *Der Spiegel,* was spotted while photographing police officers who were kicking a young man in the abdomen. "Get that guy!" a police officer yelled and Zint was also beaten to the ground. Then one policeman stamped on the hand in which Zint still held his camera, while another jumped with both feet on the camera itself, demolishing it. When Zint finally tried to complain to the police officer in charge, he was told, "Get going—or haven't you had enough yet?" Another policeman jostled Zint meanwhile, calling out a sarcastic and laughing "Excuse me!" with each shove.

At the Friesenstrasse police precinct in Kreuzberg, a couple of dozen persons were peaceably awaiting the release of some students who had previously been arrested. They had driven up in cars, not to protest or demonstrate, but simply to drive their friends home after their release. This, however, did not suit the policemen. They prefer to take prisoners to the outskirts of the city and set them free, singly and far from each other, in the woods or in remote streets. Faced with the cars outside, the police decided to attack. Two waves of policemen charged them, the first smashing their windows and headlights. Then a second wave of policemen charged, dragged the people seated inside the cars out onto the street and clubbed them down to the ground or sent them fleeing on foot, abandoning their automobiles. Among those beaten were the middle-aged parents of one of the arrested students, who had been waiting in their Mercedes-Benz for their son.

Outside the Kaiser Wilhelm Memorial Church, where not only students but also passersby and Berlin visitors had gathered on the Saturday before Easter Sunday, a police loudspeaker warned that everyone found in the center of the city was "an offender."

"Merely being here is a criminal offense!" the police loudspeaker called out. "You are all offenders! You will all be photographed and afterwards suffer the consequences!" A troop of mounted policemen trotted up the steps of the church, chasing a young student, while another student, running across the street, was struck across the back of the head by a police truncheon, swung by a policeman in a passing police van. Another student was caught seated in his car in Spandau. Three policemen pulled open the car door and beat him up with their night-sticks. When one of his feet projected outside the car door, the police officers repeatedly slammed the door shut on it.

At the Halle Gate, policemen chased a young demonstrator and beat him so savagely that he collapsed on the street, whereupon still more policemen rushed over to beat and kick him, until there were ten belaboring the screaming young man. An outraged electrical engineer, who witnessed this while driving by, jumped out of his car and demanded to know the shield numbers of the policemen, whereupon he was struck full in the face with a truncheon. Then the policemen turned to attack those still seated in the electrical engineer's car, beating them up as well. One of those hit in the face with a truncheon while seated inside was an elderly art historian.

Elsewhere in West Berlin, a British correspondent witnessed how a group of demonstrating students had peaceably gathered together against a wall after police had promised to let them go if they would stop rioting. Once they did so, the police herded them together—and then swarmed over them, beating them with their night-sticks. Other eyewitnesses watched as young girls, suspected of being "demonstrators," were kicked in the abdomen, how others fell down and were trampled in the stomach, and how one policeman actually swung his truncheon up, full force between a girl's legs.

Police brutality, like student provocation, seems to be a worldwide phenomenon today, with only the London police excepted. The police in Paris, Mexico, Japan, New York, and most notably, in Chicago, have handled students just as savagely. And, just as most Americans apparently approve of firm repression of the student demonstrators, so do the West Berliners; only a third of them thought their policemen had been "too rough." These aggressive students, obviously bent on provoking officials and burghers alike, horrify the West Berliners. They are offensive personally and politically. Instead of attending to their studies, they riot in the streets, outraging the Berliners' sense of probity and devotion to industriousness. Further, the demonstrations against the war in

Viet Nam inevitably took on an anti-American character: This also outraged the West Berliners, who are among the most *pro-*American people in the world. The students' chants of "Ho-Ho-Ho Chi Minh" and their placards showing portraits of Che Guevara drove the West Berliners past the limits of their endurance. They were pleased that the police treated the students roughly. The fact that a few innocent spectators got clubbed down in the process is something the Berliners are willing to shrug off. This is a city, after all, that has never really understood how to deal with dissent. It has always understood truncheons better. The old, bitter joke seems to still hold true: Hell is a place where the mechanics are French, the cooks are English—and where the policemen are all Germans.

chapter twenty-three

THE FIRST SIGHT YOU ENCOUNTER AS YOU DRIVE IN FROM HANOVER on the *Autobahn* is Renee Sintinis' statue of the Berlin bear, sculpted as a cub. It is an apt symbol of the Berlin that grew out of the rubble of 1945, but there is one that might have been better. Perhaps there ought to be a statue of Baron Münchhausen, that legendary Germanic Paul Bunyan, executing his most spectacular maneuver: pulling himself out of a swamp by grasping his own hair. That's what the Berliners did with their economy after the war was over.

Air raids knocked out so many Berlin factories that twenty-five percent of the city's industrial capacity was destroyed by bombs and Russian artillery shells, but that was only the beginning. The Soviets had sixty days to themselves in the city, and they picked Berlin clean. This was not dismantling for reparations along the lines of the Yalta agreements, but neither was it indiscriminate looting. The Soviets knew their sphere of influence would soon be restricted to the Soviet sector of Berlin, and they concentrated on stripping the West. Furthermore, they wanted to be able to claim reparations for years to come from East Berlin's factories. When they were through the Soviet sector of Berlin was left with fifty-two percent of its industrial capacity intact, while West Berlin was left with only about twenty percent. The United States Military Government noted with dismay that most of West Berlin's industry "had been destroyed, dispersed, or looted." The effect, of course, was devastating for West Berlin.

In the months immediately after the war, the Berliners were forced to establish a crude kind of barter economy. Everybody after all, had something, even if it was only a blanket, and everyone needed something else, even if only a kitchen pot. They spent their time swapping the few, shabby goods that remained. Smashed shopwindows, boarded up, were covered with slips of paper, each offering something in trade for something else. Newspapers, as soon as they appeared again, were just as crowded with classified advertisements offering items in exchange for needed goods. Businesses pleaded for equipment so that they might start up again. A bottling plant asked for "corks, new or used," a funeral parlor advertised for nails, a clothing firm offered to swap two thousand yards of gray thread for one thousand yards of red or white. A company offering anti-rust paint warned purchasers they'd have to bring along their own containers. A marmalade factory advertised for barrels, buckets, or any other appropriate container for its products, as well as for machinery with which to start up again. Helmets were turned into kitchen pots; demolished tanks lying about the city were broken up for scrap. When Berlin's machine industry held its first postwar "trade show" in autumn, 1945, it had so little to offer that it staged the event in the gymnasium of Spandau's Public School No. 8. Even so, it created a sensation at the time. All sorts of products had been ingeniously fashioned out of Wehrmacht war materials: scythes, saws, hoes, and shovels. One Berlin factory, which had earlier exported engines throughout the world, had only a primitive stove to show; another company, known for its fine machine tools, proudly displayed its latest product, a wheelbarrow. Plows were being fashioned out of swords.

The first Berliners to pull the city out of its 300 million cubic meters of rubble were the city's *Trümmerfrauen,* or "rubble women," who collected bricks, knocked the plaster off them, dusted them off, and piled them up for reconstruction purposes—200 million bricks in all. Streets were cleared and pedi-cabs—assembled by connecting a bicycle to a motorcycle sidecar—began to pull British Tommies and American GI's through the city. Virtually no other transport was available: of 655 city buses, only 87 remained.

Nor were these the only handicaps. All of the city's banks had been closed on Soviet orders. No money was available; Berliners had to work for I.O.U.'s. Political pressure increased, and no sooner had a very modest start been made in cranking the economy up again, than the Russians blockaded the Western sectors. Lack of raw materials again compelled West Berlin factories to shut down or to curtail production. Construction was halted; the only big industrial project completed by the end of 1948 was the rebuilding of Power Plant West, renamed for Ernst Reuter, which made West Berlin independent of East Berlin power sources.

The end of the Berlin Blockade did not, however, signal any automatic boom. In fact, it left the city even more behind West Germany than before. The Federal Republic of Germany had been receiving Marshall Aid since 1948, while West Berlin did not even begin to receive it until late in 1949. West Germany's industrial index, at the time the blockade ended, stood at ninety percent of 1936, while West Berlin's stood at seventeen percent. A year later, West Germany's hit 113 percent, while West Berlin, with only thirty percent, had three hundred thousand unemployed, or one worker out of every three.

Recovery came gradually, after 1952. More than three billion marks worth of Marshall Plan and other American aid was pumped into the city. A "Long-Term Plan" also began to bring in about two billion marks annually of West German aid. The city still receives financial assistance, and indeed, could not prosper without preferential treatment since its isolation from the Western world and from its own natural hinterland continue to pose enormous problems. It has never fully caught up with West Germany, however; by the time it seemed to be well on its way toward that goal, Khrushchev's ultimatum of 1958, and later, the erection of the Berlin Wall provided additional setbacks. Its industries began to establish branch offices in West Germany. Then they began to move part, and finally, all of their managements over to the prosperous and safe West, while West German investment in the city's industry was cut. The central state bank in Berlin (*Landeszentralbank*) says that the wall and Khrushchev's threats against the city cost West Berlin 2.5 billion marks in capital investment. Today, West Berlin is a regional processor for West German corporations, the tail end of an assembly line that begins more than one hundred miles away.

Depending on the way you measure it, West Berlin's industry is either very impressive today, or pretty disappointing. City boosters like the *Tagesspiegel* call it "the biggest industrial city in all Europe" and point to a gross annual product of more than 17.5 billion marks (more than that of all Greece), and to the facts that its production index stands at 186 percent of 1936 and that its industry produces as much as Denmark or Norway. West Berlin's exports today reach 140 countries and are valued at 500 million dollars, or twice the exports of Ireland. Every fifth West German light bulb, every fourth dress, every third cigarette, and every third film are produced in West Berlin.

On the other hand, its production index, compared with 1936, has consistently lagged behind West Germany's. The fact that West Berlin is the nation's largest industrial city is due mostly to its population, the largest of any West German city. It is misleading, says the *Landeszentralbank* in Berlin, only to consider such absolute figures as annual industrial turnover (more than 12 billion marks). If one looks at industrial production relative to population, a different picture emerges. West Berlin, "Germany's biggest industrial city," then comes in not first, *but fifteenth.* Stuttgart, Frankfurt, Hamburg, Düsseldorf, Cologne, and Munich produce goods valued at between 10,200 and 11,700 marks for every one of their inhabitants; West Berlin's figure is 7,250 marks, or one-third less, due largely to its political isolation. Those fourteen West German industrial towns which outrank West Berlin in this listing do so because they draw much of their labor force from the surrounding countryside. Commuters swell the level of production for each one of their citizens. Such workers, however, are completely missing in West Berlin. Sixty thousand of them used to commute into the Western sectors from the surrounding East German countryside, but that all ended in 1961. In addition the city's industry also has no room in which to grow. Unlike West German industrial cities, it cannot expand into the surrounding territory; its boundaries are fixed and it can grow only within itself.

Thanks to massive help, it has done pretty well. It continues to have a trade deficit, caused by prosperity and the increasing demand for consumer goods, as well as by the need to import raw materials and semi-finished products, but it has full employment today and there is always at least the hope that West German industries may increase their capital investments in West Berlin. A Berlin Aid Law, expanded in scope after the wall went up, offers huge inducements to businessmen willing to do so. Not only are income taxes about thirty percent lower in West Berlin than they

350

are in West Germany, but corporate taxes are lower as well. An extremely high rate of depreciation is granted and anyone investing in West Berlin can have the value of his investment increased ten percent from available public funds. Most important, products finished off in West Berlin are exempt from West Germany's four percent "turnover tax" and the ultimate purchaser in West Germany can apply for a further four percent reimbursement allowance. Investors who loan out money for construction projects in West Berlin can deduct up to twenty percent of the amount of the loan from their income or corporate taxes, and finally, ten-year credits at only four percent are granted to those either building or expanding commercial or industrial enterprises in the city.

The exemption from the turnover tax is responsible for the fact that West Berlin is in large part a finisher of West German products. Some Berliners complain bitterly that appliances seem to arrive in West Berlin factories requiring only a handle or a hinge before they are shipped back to West Germany, exempt from this four percent tax. They complain that capital investments, despite the benefits offered, are low. The *Landeszentralbank* says that they should have come to 12.1 billion marks between 1958 and 1965, but came to only 9.6 million, meaning a loss of almost three billion marks during that period. Any such loss threatens stagnation and the city is afraid, as Willy Brandt put it while he was mayor, of being "sidetracked historically"; he warned that West Berlin could not survive if it just held its own and that it had to grow "dynamically."

Considering what it began with at war's end, the growth has, of course, been impressive. West Berlin's biggest single industry, the electrical industry, has grown six hundred percent since that year. Other major companies include food processing, mechanical engineering and machine tools, clothing, cigarettes, chemistry, printing paper, and steel. But the fact remains that they still cannot keep up with general West German prosperity.

Frankfurt is again the financial capital of West Germany (as it was before 1866), and it is there that most financial institutions maintain their headquarters. Frankfurt also contains the most important German stock exchange. West Berlin, by contrast, has what one of its city senators calls a "rather pitiful little stock exchange" and only branches of major West German banks. Not a *single one* of West Germany's postwar corporations maintains headquarters in West Berlin. A laudable exception is the Springer newspaper chain. Axel Springer, a passionate supporter of West Berlin, built a huge headquarters and printing complex in West Berlin, abutting onto the Berlin Wall, transferring his main office from Hamburg. This has helped with jobs, but also provides a political irritant, for tens of thousands in West Berlin would prefer to see Springer return to Hamburg—or better yet, close up shop altogether.

Four out of every ten West Berlin workers are employed in industry and another two are on the city payroll in one capacity or another; the rest work either in commerce, services, or the building trades. The electrical industry, with 112,000 workers, employs the bulk of West Berlin's 300,000 industrial workers; construction, with 65,000, is second largest in terms of payroll, and the clothing and textile industries are third with 47,000. The number of city employees, 110,000, in West Berlin is, of course, enormous, as is the city's payroll, which comes to more than two billion marks a year. West Berlin outranks all other West German cities in the size of its bureaucracy, with 51 government employees for every 1,000 of its inhabitants, while Hamburg has 42, Bremen only 36, and the other German *Länder* only 25.

The need for industrial workers is constant and an annual inflow of at least eighteen thousand is required if the city's population structure is to remain secure until 1980. New workers are needed to replace those who reach retirement age, as well as those who annually leave Berlin after working there for a year or so. Many workers seem reluctant to move to West Berlin factories because these, in many instances, do not have the modern equipment to which they have become accustomed in West Germany, again the result of a lack of capital investment in the city. At the present time, the influx of workers from West Germany averages about fifteen hundred a month and, while a large percentage of these actually settle down in West Berlin to stay, an enormous effort has to be mounted constantly to bring in more and to keep them there. Inducements include not only exemption from West German military service, but financial aid. Any worker who accepts employment in West Berlin is paid all his travel costs to the city;

he receives his return fare to West Germany as well if he stays a year. The city pays for his visits home to West Germany every six months if he is unmarried, every three months if he left a wife behind; wives, in turn, can come to West Berlin free of charge to visit their husbands. Moving costs are reimbursed, as are incidental expenses. A marriage loan of three thousand marks is offered; this is repayable over eleven years at one percent interest, is reduced with the birth of each child, and is considered paid in full when a third child is born. This cash payment is largely responsible for the fact that the annual excess of deaths over births in West Berlin has been reduced.

Lower taxes in West Berlin can increase a worker's net pay up to 107 marks a month but many of them note that this only serves to make up for the fact that industry often pays less in West Berlin than it does in West Germany. Nor is this the only revelation troubling newly immigrated workers. The city recruiting agents paint too glorious a picture. Many a West German worker arrives in West Berlin convinced that he will be greeted as though he were liberating the city from economic disaster. In fact he finds not only a housing shortage that makes it difficult for him to find proper accommodations, but finds also that he is often blamed for it. "When we show up at our jobs," says one such worker, "the Berliners tell us they need us like a hole in the head and accuse us of stealing apartments from them." Another complains that West German workers are treated "like Negroes in the U.S.A."

Many young, unmarried workers are quartered in special settlements that the West Berlin city government tries to make as attractive as possible, often closing an eye when furniture in them sometimes gets smashed and obscenities are scrawled on the walls, and to the endless succession of brawls. Officials are well aware that these workers are lonely and feel themselves strangers in the city and efforts are constantly made, if often unsuccessfully, to keep these young men busy. Social workers and civic officials offer reduced theater and concert tickets, only to find few workers are interested; they bring lecturers to youth clubs, only to find that the attendance is pitiful. An English-language course that began with an enrollment of 350 dwindled rapidly to eighteen, and finally, to five. If the authorities invite the workers to voice their complaints, they often find that only one man bothers to show up. Yet the complaints remain. Because the officials know this, they conscientiously redouble their efforts. They spend, for example, five hundred marks every two weeks to arrange for amateur and professional entertainers to serenade the workers at Kreuzberg's *Dachluke* youth club under the motto, *"In Berlin lässt sich's leben"* —"In Berlin, one can really *live!"* The workers watch and perhaps have a good time, but whether they believe this slogan is another question.

Not that their working conditions leave much to be desired. Trade unions like IG Metall have enormously improved the lot of German workers. A metalworker in 1891, when the union was first founded, earned eighty marks a month gross for sixty-three hours work a week; he received three months sick leave but had neither a paid vacation nor, of course, any vacation bonus. Today, such a metalworker earns 895 marks a month, works 41¼ hours a week, gets twenty-two days paid vacation, a holiday bonus of about three hundred marks, six weeks wages if he falls ill, and eighteen months sick leave—all this at a time when his money purchases more than three-and-a-half times what it did in 1891.

One might imagine that the constant labor shortage would prompt West Berlin businessmen to automate not only assembly lines but office procedures as well, cutting all nonessential time-consuming work, but such is not the case. A great deal of machinery in factories is necessarily modern, being of postwar manufacture, but the work methods one sees being employed in almost all offices strike American observers as incredibly antiquated. Not only do bureaucrats move ponderously; so do businessmen. Because the Germans are inordinately fond of forms and of all paper work, an extraordinary and unnecessary amount of it is carried on in Berlin offices, everything being laboriously quadruplicated, generally without the help of modern duplicating machinery. Filing systems and office procedures in general do not seem to have been modernized since Bismarck's day and the supplies and equipment used, while often brand-new, is of the same type used decades ago. Bank procedures are laborious and seem right out of the roll-top desk era: often they require filling out one form after another while the clerk behind the counter does much the same. Even the slightest transaction takes undue time—even more so if one arrives at an office or a bank in mid-morning or mid-afternoon, while everyone takes an elaborate break, not just over coffee, but also over layer cakes with whipped cream.

Some of these inefficiencies are the result of overstaffed bureaucratic structures (incredible considering the chronic labor shortage), but others seem due to an unusual amount of stubbornness and inertia. The building in which I maintained an office provides one example, though it is perhaps untypical in that it may be a bit *better* than most, being located just a few yards from the fashionable Europa Center office building and in the very heart of the city. Actually, no one kept the lobby, hallways, offices, or lavatories clean except the tenants, when they found the time. Wastepaper and other garbage was never picked up; it had to be carried downstairs by the office staff, usually by secretaries, to be thrown into the overflowing garbage cans in the building's backyard. The washrooms and toilets on each floor were modern enough, but as no one cared for them, they always were littered with newspapers and other debris, and usually stank. Each suite of offices on each floor had its own commode assigned to it with its own key; it was the responsibility of the office staff to see that this commode was kept clean and supplied with tissue. As no one was responsible for the wash basins, these were never cleaned at all. No towels or soap were provided, which made going out to wash one's hands seem somewhat like an excursion since one marched off, carrying one's own towel and soap dish back and forth. All this was perhaps due to West Berlin's labor shortage; in any event the landlord assumed no obligations of any kind, so far as I could determine; he existed merely to collect the rent. These were high enough by German standards and he was reputed to be rich.

The fact that realtors can write off seventy-five percent of their investments in their first year resulted in a lot of highly speculative —some disastrous—building schemes in West Berlin. Ludwig Erhard, watching the process, is said to have groaned, *"Die Leute verdienen sich an Berlin kaputt!"*—meaning, in effect, "People are cleaning up like crazy on Berlin!"

The inducements that lure speculators to West Berlin are in large part responsible for some of its more spectacular building schemes, such as the Europa Center and those other complexes which sprang up afterward in emulation. A radio wholesaler named Karl Heinz Pepper, today "Mr. Big" in West Berlin, slapped the center together partly with money provided by investors and partly with public funds. Its twenty-two-story Tower Building not only dominates the Breitscheidplatz and the Kaiser Wilhelm Memorial Church, but all of West Berlin and has even become symbolic of the city, much as the Brandenburg Gate and the *Funkturm* formerly were. Tourists gawk at the city from the building's rooftop observation platform and visit the I-Punkt cocktail lounge and restaurant on its top floor, in which they can sit luxuriously over sizzling steaks and chilled American cocktails, watching the distant vista of the wall and East Berlin without needing to feel involved or disturbed. At ground level, the Europa Center contains two courtyards, one with a skating rink, as well as a lot of expensive and fashionable stores, located in three-story shopping arcades. In addition there are a modern hotel, a twelve-story apartment house, a cabaret, two cinemas, as well as a four-story Haus der Nationen, which contains *ten* separate restaurants, decorated in the various styles of German provinces and the café that was for sentimental reasons given the name of the old Romanisches Café.

When the Europa Center's office building remained largely vacant of tenants for some time because of its prohibitive rents, few people were bothered, perhaps not even Herr Pepper. This complex of buildings, after all, is as much a monument as a commercial enterprise. It is regarded as proof of that Berlin "vitality" and is viewed as a wonderful amalgam of what Berliners love: work, beer, entertainment, cakes, chic, sausages, modernity, and strong coffee.

No one can fault the urban planners for any lack of imagination. The sheer extent and scope of construction in West Berlin is amazing. Even more so is the idea that it is almost all the result of a scheme put together more than twenty years ago, when the possibility of reconstruction seemed hopeless. Perhaps it was because no one had the energy, materials, money, or faith to build anything right after the war that the city planners managed to find time to produce an intelligent, coherent, and even a bold plan for the city. That this plan has been adhered to ever since 1946 certainly seems the result of West Berlin's consistent Social Democratic voting record, for "socialist planners" have kept entrepreneurs carefully in check and curbed exploitation of the city. They encouraged building, but only if the plans and proposals were in accordance with specifications set down by the city planners themselves.

Few architects ever faced the unlimited opportunities provided by the nearly destroyed Berlin. Recognizing this circumstance, in 1946, Professor Hans Scharoun, one of the city's leading architects and then building commissioner, assembled a team to devise a completely new city, one which would serve generations to come. The plan encompassed all Berlin, West and East, for the city was not officially split until 1948 and what is perhaps most amazing about this early plan is that it is still followed today, despite the division of the city.

The center of old Berlin, which had always been the financial, business, and government heart of the capital as well as its fashionable entertainment center, was called the "City," in the same way as London refers to its financial quarter; this section fell to the Soviets after the war, which meant that West Berlin needed to establish its own commercial and cultural district. It has been careful, however, to avoid creating a rival "City" to the one East Berlin is now busy building, for West Berlin planners are happy to note that the East Berlin authorities appear also to be faithful to much of Scharoun's original plan. This means that, as far as the city planners are concerned, there is no wall, no artificial barriers of any kind. Indeed, many of the maps they use do not show the division of the city. The financial institutions that are today established on the Hardenbergstrasse, near the Kurfürstendamm, are expected some day merely to augment the ones which are again to be reestablished in the Eastern "City."

Part of Professor Scharoun's plan consisted of two separate "belts," one cultural and the other commercial, so situated that their buildings march inexorably *toward,* rather than away from, the old "City" in East Berlin. These belts may be followed today, beginning at the banks, wholesale houses, and office buildings of the Kaiserdamm. They proceed to the Bismarckstrasse with its new cultural buildings, such as the German Opera and the Schiller Theater, then join the multi-story office buildings, such as the IBM headquarters on Ernst Reuter Platz, going on to embrace the new Technical University buildings, the Academy of Fine Arts, and the Academy of Music. On the far side of the Zoo Station, they take in the headquarters of West Berlin's big clothing industry and run on to the Europa Center and the Kurfürstendamm, with its shops, theaters, and restaurants. In the nearby Lützow Quarter, these belts take in a number of new hotels as well as office and residential buildings, and farther on toward East Berlin, they include the Philharmonic Hall, the Congress Hall, the American Memorial Library, and a new National Gallery, designed by Mies van der Rohe, and completed in 1968. Eventually restaurants, shops, and recreation facilities are to be added. Future city plans include a transformation of the Friedrichstrasse from Mehring Platz to Bahnhof Friedrichstrasse in East Berlin into a beautiful pedestrian mall, closed to all motor vehicles. Once Berlin is reunited, it is to become a shopping and entertainment boulevard.

This seems hard to imagine. Much of the Friedrichstrasse, in both West and East Berlin, looks as it did at the end of the war, though the ruins have been cleared away. Yet the very fact that this area continues in many places to be empty of buildings or still filled with damaged, decaying structures is proof that the plans are taken seriously, for the West Berlin authorities are saving this section for the future. Those new buildings permitted into this central part of Berlin, like the headquarters of the Springer newspaper chain, the Excelsior project at the ruins of the former Anhalter railway station, and the new business center at the corner of Friedrichstrasse and Lindenstrasse, are admitted because they conform to the architectural plan of the future. The Excelsior project, for example, consists of an eighteen-story "skyscraper" apartment house offering 550 luxury flats at five marks a square meter (about $1.25 a square yard) and containing a restaurant on its seventeenth and eighteenth floors, a bowling alley, a movie theater, a rooftop heliport, a swimming pool, and a sauna bath.

Though many such private projects have been started partially with public funds, most housing put up in West Berlin after the war is public housing or what the Germans call *sozialer Wohnungsbau*, "social apartment construction." This was necessary not only because of the extent of the damage done to the city by wartime air raids and Soviet shelling, but also because West German financial institutions were investing in West Germany and leaving West Berlin housing to the city. The extent of bomb damage to Berlin residential districts has already been noted; what is remarkable is the fact that missing apartments have virtually all been replaced.

That part of old Berlin which now makes up West Berlin used to contain 979,000 apartments; today, the number of apartments is almost equal that figure. Yet the demand for new flats, especially from young West German workers entering the city, continues to exceed the supply.

Of the present apartments in West Berlin, about one hundred thousand are more than eighty years old. Rents in the antiquated flats are about a third as high as are the rents in low-cost housing developments put up by the city (about thirty-five cents versus one dollar per square yard of living space). Because tenants of condemned buildings receive priority in new housing developments, a lot of the one hundred thousand West Berliners who are looking for new flats condemn the city for tearing down old buildings too hastily. It is true, they say, that a great number of apartments still have no toilets and that almost twice as many have neither a bathtub nor a shower, but the latter group, it is pointed out, comprise only a third of all apartments, while in Paris and Vienna eighty and eighty-six per cent of apartments are reported to be without such facilities. The old buildings, however, understandably continue to affront the city planners and architects, whose own vision of Berlin is more ambitious. They prefer huge public developments like Gropius Stadt, described in an earlier chapter, or its northern counterpart, the Märkisches Viertel. While more than fifteen percent of apartments in public housing developments have no warm water and only 62.4 percent have central heating, such buildings are more in line with West Berlin's modernistic conception of itself. It should be noted again, however, that both the Gropius Stadt and Märkisches Viertel sections are more popular among the planners than among the people inhabiting them. They are barren and, says *Der Spiegel* of the latter development, turning into "slums." Berliners find them examples of "brutal architecture," the "rental barracks" of the 20th century.

There are so many new buildings everywhere in West Berlin today that you have to look awfully hard to find any war damage, just as you once had to look hard to find a structure that was not at least partially ruined. There are estimated to be about six hundred ruined buildings left in West Berlin even today, almost eighty of them in District Tiergarten, much of which is being reserved for future development as Berlin's "diplomatic quarter," once the embassies move from Bonn to a reunited Berlin. This district also contains Mies' Gallery and Scharoun's Philharmonic Hall, which the Berliners call "Circus Karajani" after the conductor of the Berlin symphony orchestra, Herbert von Karajan, and because of the tentlike roof covering the dramatically unsymmetrical structure. These two buildings are not the only strikingly modern public structures in West Berlin. Still another is the largest apartment house in the city, the Corbusierhaus, which the architect called *"Unité d'habitation, type Berlin."* The building houses 1,400 tenants in 527 apartments close by the Stadium Hitler built for the 1936 Olympic Games. Corbusier originally planned his apartment building to be part of the Interbau Competition of 1955-1957, but as it measured 184 feet in height and 148 yards in length, it was considered too large for the Hansa Quarter then being constructed. This Interbau (or International Building Exhibition) was a stroke of genius on the part of the city and sparked a great deal of the modern architecture of later years. Architects from all over the world were invited to enter and forty-eight of them, from thirteen countries, joined in. The result of this, the Hansa Quarter off the Tiergarten, is a complex of all sorts of buildings consisting in places of one-family detached houses with gardens, in others of sixteen- to seventeen-story apartment houses and smaller blocks of flats. Two churches, a public library, schools, shops, a cinema, and a restaurant are included in what came to be a completely self-contained neighborhood. Walter Gropius of the United States and Alvar Aalto of Finland are only two of the famous architects involved. The United States was not officially represented, a troublesome omission to a lot of people in Washington at the time. The one who was most concerned was Eleanor Lansing Dulles, sister of John Foster Dulles, then Secretary of State; on her initiative, the Benjamin Franklin Foundation in the U.S.A. built West Berlin's Congress Hall, designed by Hugh A. Stubbins in the form of a great shell, supported by two lower stories and buttress pillars and resting on one thousand concrete supports. The acoustics in its auditorium are so good that a speaker can be heard in every one of the 1,264 seats without using a microphone. The Berliners speak of it as "the pregnant oyster," a reference to its shape.

Religious architecture also received an impetus in West Berlin after stagnating during the Nazi era; fifty-seven new churches have

360

been built since 1950 and many others restored. The Jewish Community Center, which serves both as a cultural center and a synagogue, was built in 1958 to replace the Central Synagogue the Nazis had burned down during the *Kristallnacht* twenty years earlier. The old synagogue's doorway was incorporated into the main entrance, along with a column containing fragments, as a reminder of the past. Another house of worship with such reminders in it is the Kaiser Wilhelm Memorial Church, originally built in 1895 and never very attractive. The only part of it that survived after the war was the old tower, gutted by fire, and reduced to about half its old height. A debate raged after the war whether the old ruin should not be completely torn down and demolished, especially as it did not seem a symbol of democratic Berlin, having been built during the reign of Kaiser Wilhelm II, but it was finally decided that the tower (which Berliners call "the hollow tooth") ought to be kept as "an eternal reminder" of the destruction caused by war. A new octagonal church now stands to one side of it and a new tower on the other side. The double walls of the new church are of a honeycomb concrete, its recesses filled with colored glass, mainly blue, designed by Gabriel Loire of Chartres; the walls insulate the interior against the noise of the traffic roaring about Breitscheidplatz and also allow for a built-in lighting system that gives both the new church and the new tower a mysterious ice-blue radiance after dark. The carillon that was installed in the old ruined tower, as a gesture to the House of Hohenzollern, which the church, after all, celebrates along with Christ, tolls a composition composed by Prince Louis Ferdinand of Prussia.

One of the happiest decisions the West Berlin city planners made after the war was to extend what they call their *Grünanlagen* or "green spaces." These do not only include parks and woods, but also trees along the avenues, grassy strips in the center lanes of the city's boulevards, flower beds everywhere, and lawns in front of most new apartment houses.

"We'd rather put up landscaped areas than hospitals," a city construction official told me. "The city needs to be aired out. So we plan wide, tree-lined streets divided with landscaped strips, allowing the wind to blow through them and chase away the exhaust fumes from the very cars the streets attract."

As the houses are built farther back, to make room for widened traffic arteries, they also provide space for grassy and flower-planted "front lawns," even in the middle of the city. Almost a quarter of a million trees have been planted along West Berlin's streets and about 120 million marks has been spent in landscaping the city.

It was not until after the blockade ended that work began restoring the city's trees and parks. An emergency program was launched in 1949 by Mayor Ernst Reuter. Seven years later, almost all wartime losses had been replaced, though one-third of the trees lining Berlin's avenues, which have always added so much to the charm of the city, are still missing. Yet today, *two-thirds* of West Berlin consist of woods, farmland, water, lawns, gardens, recreation and sports fields, and of landscaped "belts" alongside downtown avenues and canals. In West Germany, where space might be said to be ample, urban and industrial developers chew up sixty-five thousand acres of "green space" every year; West Berlin, despite its desperate need for space, resists this ferociously. In fact, the city constantly hunts for new places in which to plant grass, trees, or flowers. The Spree River, which used to run through stone embankments, presents a completely different vista today as a result of this policy. More than forty miles of landscaped walks have been planted along it and along the banks of canals, a good many of them in the very center of the city. In Gesundbrunnen, part of District Wedding, the hunt for natural beauty caused the city planners to dig up a small and legendary underground river called the Panke, which is now pleasantly landscaped along its banks.

The Lietzenburgerstrasse, in the center of West Berlin, provides a good example of what conscientious planning can do for an otherwise uninteresting major traffic thoroughfare. The center strip of the avenue is not only lined with grass, but also with trees; these originally stood directly in front of the buildings on one side of the Lietzenburger Strasse, when it was half its width. The bombs cleared the front houses away, the city cleared the rubble away, the planners added another lane to the street, but they chose to leave the old trees standing in what came to be the dividing strip, rather than to uproot them.

Planting trees is one thing; working around them to save them in new construction projects is more difficult, yet this is also the practice in West Berlin. It's seen most dramatically on a visit to the Freie Volksbühne Theater, built in 1963. The architect was charged with not disturbing the grove of trees on the building site and construction was carried out, in effect, under and among the branches. "Of course, it's easier to build the way you do in the States," an official admitted, "by first bulldozing down all the trees and leveling the ground, but we prefer it our way."

As a result of this policy, Berlin becomes quite lovely every spring and summer, even though it has never been considered to be beautiful architecturally. The new modernistic buildings are, of course, a pleasing and dramatic improvement over the old, late 19th-century structures, but even the latter look attractive behind the trees lining the city's avenues and boulevards. On those narrower residential streets with new buildings, the trees sometimes tend to be smaller but the houses are deliberately set back far enough from the sidewalks so that landscaped strips may be planted in front of each. There are a lot of these narrow streets around, despite the fact that Berlin has always been known principally for its extremely wide boulevards and avenues. "We keep them narrow," I was told, "because we have no wish to turn every street in Berlin into an automobile race track." There is good reason for this: West Berlin has more than a quarter of a million passenger cars today and expects to have almost four hundred thousand by 1970, not counting buses or commercial vehicles.

Berlin's landscaping, its green aspect, strikes visitors immediately; after awhile, one realizes this is not the only way in which an attempt is made to beautify the city. Decorative elements are incorporated in many building façades, often on those sides of office buildings that, elsewhere, might carry advertising. Mosaic murals cover some of them; others are just decorated with multi-colored intersecting lines or some other simple device. This is also the result of city policies. Any builder using public funds receives an extra allocation of one- to one-and-a-half percent of the building costs for such purposes.

One of the major problems in modern West Berlin is that not only does the city have to import supplies for all reconstruction and expansion, but it also has to haul almost all its food supplies in as well. Every egg, liter of milk, or bockwurst that arrives overland in West Berlin from West Germany needs to be accompanied by a bill of lading and be registered with the East Germans. The sheer extent of this is staggering. Every day, thirty-seven shipments of milk, each consisting of twenty thousand liters, arrive in the city through the G.D.R. Sometimes, West Berlin even has to air lift its meat in from West Germany, because the G.D.R. imposes restrictions to prevent hoof-and-mouth disease, or just to harass the city. The higher living standards rise in West Berlin, the greater is the volume of food and drink consumed, which only aggravates the problem, even if it does make life in the city more palatable.

Although West Berlin contains 835 farms, cultivating more than 10,000 acres, these can only supply a fraction of the demand. More than 200,000 metric tons of potatoes and a like amount of fruit, as well as more than 150,000 tons of meat and meat products have to be shipped in each year. Locally produced milk accounts for 25,000 liters daily, but that satisfies only eight percent of the demand, even though it is the most popular type of milk sold in the city. Milk from West Germany may be more than twenty hours old, and in some cases, requires special preservatives; local milk, called *Vorzugsmilch,* "preferred milk," is more fresh, but the city's cows produce only one glass of such milk a year for every West Berliner. (These cows, incidentally, are brought in as calves, are milked for eight months, and then slaughtered.)

Berlin's downtown dairies and urban pigsties date back to developments almost one hundred years ago, during the *Gründerjahre* of the 1870's, when farmers became millionaires by selling their land to slum landlords. What they kept in many cases were their barns. Cows and pigs required little space and their products were both in great demand and profitable. Thus, even today, West Berlin maintains a pig population of almost nine thousand, feeding them the refuse of restaurants, homes, and police barracks. Plans have recently been announced for a 12-story "farm" that could house thousands of chickens, vertically. Unlike the cow and pig farms, Berlin's poultry industry did not have its roots among the farmers of the "founding years"; chicken farming started as a hobby in Berlin many years ago, the amusement of factory and white-collar workers, and developed into an industry only because prices suddenly rose and modern feeding methods made profits possible. This is even more the case today, for the city's chickens

364

now live in climate-conditioned "comfort" and do nothing but produce—on the average about 200 to 250 eggs per year each.

The amount of food West Berlin stores to guard itself against another blockade is another of those "closely guarded secrets." Actually, the East Germans (and therefore the Soviets) are able to keep an exact count of the food traveling through the G.D.R. but are uncertain exactly what quantity is preserved and stored. "We want to keep them guessing a little bit," says a West Berlin official, "though we also want them to have a pretty good idea about how much we've got. It will make them think twice about imposing another blockade. They know that we can last about a year on what we've put away and also that any lift will be more effective now that planes are bigger and faster, airfields have been expanded, and everyone has experience in supplying the city by air."

The costs of storing such food runs to about 90 million marks a year. Most of it is sold periodically at low prices, as it is replaced; some stored food lasts twelve months, while meat and butter are sold after six or seven months.

Transport of live animals to West Berlin occasionally causes a scandal. Forty pigs were once found to have suffocated to death because they had been too closely crowded into an airplane. The Berliners raised such an uproar that the city parliament investigated the matter, ultimately finding the shipper, not the airline, guilty. A similar case concerned a quantity of carp which a West Berlin retailer had bought at a wholesale market. The man in question was not a fishmonger, but a butcher, who had picked up the carp because customers had asked him to supply them for a holiday. Perhaps because he didn't know better, he dumped three hundred pounds of the fish into a herring barrel, so tightly that a number of them suffocated. He brought this barrel to one of the city's outdoor markets, where the condition of the fish was noticed by knowledgeable customers. They immediately telephoned a veterinary doctor, who rushed over to examine the carp and who afterward called the police.

Outdoor markets, such as the one in which this carp butcher was discovered, exist all over West Berlin. These are weekly markets (*Wochenmärkte*), held in open squares on a specific day each week. There is even one in front of the Rathaus Schöneberg, the seat of West Berlin's Government; once every week, stalls selling both foodstuffs and dry goods cover the John F. Kennedy Platz, the same square on which tens of thousands of Berliners massed to hear the President during his 1963 visit. They sell fresh fruits and vegetables, fish, eggs and other dairy products, kitchen gadgets, clothing—indeed almost anything in the low-price range. We shopped at such a market regularly in our own section of Berlin, Marienfelde; there it was held every Thursday morning and was situated right next to the established local shops, which included a large supermarket as well. Berliners like to buy in weekly markets, not only because doing so is an old Berlinese custom they would never wish to abandon, but also because the dairy products, vegetables, and fish are all fresher. Despite their infatuation with modernity, Berliners find it more pleasing to buy a pound of cottage cheese when it is spooned from a large vat and a pound of butter when it is cut from a large block, rather than buy the same products prepackaged in the supermarket down the street. While such supermarkets have in recent years become very popular, most food purchases are still made at the small, neighborhood shops whose number and variety have always been impressive and regarded by the Berliners as a typical feature of this city's scene. Not very much has changed in these shops over the years; they all still look the same, smell the same, and have the same atmosphere as they did when I was a child in Berlin—and very likely, years before that. *Drogerieen* still smell of pine-scented soaps; *Feinbäckereien* still give off the heady odor of those hundreds of freshly baked, crisp rolls that lie in large bins behind the counters; *Metzgereien* still have the same robust white-gowned, pink-cheeked, butcher women swinging strings of sausages or slicing at whole sides of beef; shops selling *Tabakwaren* still reek of those fat, dark cigars Germans like to smoke and are still crowded with old men and young boys buying *Lotto* lottery tickets and the weekly tickets for the bus company; shops still pump milk into the bottles or milk pails customers bring with them, and one can still buy that *Bauernbrot,* farmers' bread, each slice as big as a plate, and order it cut down to manageable size. There was a shop in Marienfelde that sold nothing but potatoes. Inside there were just a scale and three small mountains of differently priced potatoes the proprietress would attack as you would a hill of coal—with a shovel, tossing the ones you bought onto the scale and then into the nylon net bag one brought along.

The supermarkets, of course, tend to sell mass-produced food and food products; cold cuts in these stores are as antiseptically sealed in plastic as they are in the United States. They also, of course, sell a great many more products than do the small corner store, even including wines, spirits, and beer.

The maddening thing about West Berlin food shops, and about the city's retail industry in general, is that, to everyone's discomfort, antiquated laws regulate their hours of business. All food stores close at six every evening, which makes it almost impossible for office and factory workers to shop after they come home and the shops overcrowd toward the end of the working day with a flood of latecomers. One would imagine that, under the circumstances, the Berliners would be allowed to shop all of Saturday, but that is true only on the first Saturday of every month, when stores are allowed to stay open until 6 P.M. On every other Saturday, the stores must close at 1 P.M., which makes Saturday shopping frantic and overcrowded, too. Even the exceptions to these rules are maddening and confusing to Berliners, not to speak of visitors. Florists, for example, are allowed to stay open until 5 P.M. on Saturdays, but only if they are located within three hundred yards of a cemetery. Barbers can stay open until 6 P.M. on Saturdays, but are then required to stay shut until 1 P.M. on the following Monday. Newsstands have to close on Sundays at 1 P.M. Chain stores selling food must close at 1 P.M. on Saturdays but independent food shops can stay open an extra hour, until 2 P.M. Of course, the ordinary Berliner is disgusted with these laws but all attempts at reforming them have so far failed. The unions are dead set against any changes. Retail clerks work 42¼ hours a week and apparently do not want to work overtime. The result of this, however, is not merely to inconvenience the Berliner. The reason why many city officials are disturbed by these laws (Brandt, while mayor, said, "They make us look very provincial.") is that they annoy tourists, since most visitors arrive on the weekends, when the shops are closed. The city's newspapers are constantly crusading against the "shopping-hour laws," but it all has little effect. A kind of hypnotic inertia seems to grip the Senat, the retail associations, and the trade unions whenever the subject even comes up for discussion. These laws, says one Berlin newspaper, will continue forever—until the shoppers stop acting like frightened sheep. No one knows when that day will arrive. If reform ever comes it will probably again be due to foreign intervention, in this case by means of the tourists from abroad, all of them ready to spend in the chic Kurfürstendamm shops on Saturdays, only to find they cannot do so. The only place they can buy anything in the city after closing time on Saturday is at Tempelhof Airport, where they can buy a souvenir or a bunch of flowers.

The sight of these tourists strolling about West Berlin on weekends, each of them unable to spend the hundreds, perhaps thousands, of marks, francs, lire, kroner, or even dollars in their pockets, is enough to make West Berlin's merchants and city fathers weep. These tourists represent very big business indeed in West Berlin: More than two million arrive each year, six hundred thousand of them foreigners and the rest West Germans. The number of foreign visitors coming to the city has gone up five hundred percent in the past decade, the largest single contingent being American—followed by Swedes, Frenchmen, Britons; and then by Asians, Swiss, South and Central Americans, Danes, Dutch, Italians, and Austrians. West Germans particularly like to come during holiday weekends and incredibly vast numbers have arrived in the city for Easter holidays, creating unbelievable traffic jams at the G.D.R. checkpoints on the *Autobahn*. No matter how fast the East German customs officials work (and sometimes they drag their heels deliberately), visitors driving in by car on such weekends have to bank on a four-hour wait at the checkpoints; the line of cars queueing up for processing at the Marienborn checkpoint sometimes stretches six miles, bumper to bumper.

Every tenth West German has visited West Berlin at least once during the past ten years and thirty-six percent of all West Germans at least claim that they would pick Berlin if they were given a choice between a holiday there or in Hamburg, Bonn, or Munich. Yet West Berlin is not the most popular German tourist spot it was before the war. It is now in fourth place, but even that is an improvement over a few years ago, when it was in seventh.

The city works very hard to stimulate tourism, not just for economic reasons, but also because it is so desperately concerned with keeping the idea of Berlin alive. Cultural festival weeks and about six hundred conventions and trade shows a year bring in large numbers of visitors. Tourist brochures flood the world and are now even being printed in the Russian, Romanian, Polish, Czechoslovakian, Yugoslavian, and Bulgarian languages. Special fares and package tours are offered to any interested group. West Germans under twenty-five, for example, are invited to spend six-day holidays in West Berlin for a total cost of only sixty-five marks ($16.25)—and that includes the bus fare to and from Berlin, full room and board at a youth home, as well as visits to theaters, concerts, and cabarets. In urging West German educators to bring student groups to the old *Reichshauptstadt,* the Senat offers aid in staging special tours and lectures, emphasizing any number of political themes: the division of Germany, the status of Berlin, the development of East Germany, and also the nature of National Socialism. It urges that these youngsters be taken, not only to the Berlin Wall, but also to places evocative of Nazi terrorism: to Berlin's Plötzensee Prison and to the memorial on the Stauffenbergstrasse (the former Bendlerstrasse), where Count von Stauffenberg and his co-conspirators were executed after the failure of the July 20, 1944, plot against Hitler.

The very first civilian passenger plane to bring tourists to West Berlin from the United States after the war landed at Tempelhof on May 20, 1946. It had begun the journey with twenty-five passengers, most of them newsmen who chose to debark at Amsterdam. Only four traveled on, thinking "Berlin was worth a trip"— in the words of the city's official tourist-promotion slogan, *"Berlin ist eine Reise wert."* In those early days, only passengers paying dollars could fly in or out of the city and it was not until 1948 that any Germans holding marks were allowed aboard the planes; even then, only ten seats per flight were allocated to so-called "DM passengers." Finally, in 1950, a real passenger service was instituted, one which accepted any person who had the fare. Today, Boeing 727 trijets link Berlin with West Germany, carrying 128 passengers on each flight. It now takes less than three hours to get from London to Berlin, only eleven hours and twenty-five minutes to get there from New York, and about an hour from most of West Germany. The passengers come—by the tens of thousands. "I see these people all the time," says Pan American Flight Captain Bill Fish. "They come in for a couple of days from Frankfurt or Munich or Hanover and then hurry back. I often ask them what they saw in Berlin. 'The wall,' they say, 'and then we went over to East Berlin for the afternoon, and at night we went to drink at the Resi.' Others just stay at the Hilton. What can they learn of Berlin in that time and doing those things?"

Actually, it is surprising how quickly tourists form vivid impressions of Berlin. It leaves few people indifferent. Michael Ratcliffe of *The Sunday Times* of London, who called Berlin "the fantastic metropolis," came back from a visit to report:

"The whole city is one great image, or rather a collection of contradictory images, a place whose ceaseless exhilaration is impossible to envisage until one has actually been there. For all manner of reasons, it is a terrific place to spend at least a week at almost any time of the year—for it revitalizes, as all good holidays should. Experience suggests it is most enjoyed by those under thirty-five. The mind requires a kind of double vision, assimilating both the ambiguous present and the gaunt, nudging past. Surely no city in the world—not Rome, not Pompeii—suffuses such an appalling sense of history. Quite apart from its wealth of music and theater, the point about a trip to Berlin is this: Nothing bores. The questions never stop . . .

"One never ceases to marvel, of course, that the city 'lives' at all, that one does not, in fact, feel as if one were on Alcatraz. Much of the rebuilding is shoddy, but nowhere would this seem to matter less. For West Berlin really does *work*—an effectiveness one attributes less to the magnificent transport system than to the native Brandenburger resilience; the exhilaration of the Mark. There is a tremendous sense of *dash* to the place; it is a tonic simply to walk about . . ."

While everyone seems to have a personal reaction to the city, some visitors feel compelled to mouth set pieces or give vent to preconceptions. BBC, for example, sent a London journalist to Berlin to offer his views of the place; the television documentary took a position 180 degrees removed from Ratcliffe's, and was studded with factual errors and oversimplifications. It showed Berlin only as a gloomy, leaden city populated entirely by the ghosts of Nazism; when the journalist in question visited the memorial at Plötzensee Prison, he made no mention at all of the anti-Nazi Germans murdered there but only wondered what sinister motive could have led the West Berliners to make "a shrine" out of a Nazi jail. Berlin in fact seems one of those cities which reflects any bias one brings along, and it therefore seems little wonder that most Americans see it in terms of Cold War clichés.

Every foreign official who goes to Berlin knows in advance that he will be photographed peering over the wall and that he is expected to offer a comment for publication. Most of these appear to have been composed and memorized before the trip. Former United States Secretary of the Interior Stewart Udall, for example, arriving to study the way Berlin deals with air and water pollution, gazed over the wall and remarked, "Berlin has a special kind of pollution problem; the wall pollutes both the landscape and the spirit of the city." Queen Elizabeth, Prince Philip, and the Crown Prince of Japan, on the other hand, merely stared icily across the wall and maintained regal and enigmatic silences. Others find their tongues strangely loosened. One of the most flamboyant descriptions provided by a tourist was offered by one Panagiotis Papados, who translated Berlin into the idiom of Greece: "The political horizon beyond the wall is determined by chthonic gods," he said, "gods of the chaotic depths. The gods and people of West Berlin are different. Gods like Pallas Athene, with her clear, ethical commands, govern here . . ."

Papados' remarks, along with those made by almost anyone else who has a nice thing to say about West Berlin, are reprinted by the city and circulated around, for they all add to the chorus of outrage and draw attention to the city's biggest tourist attraction, the wall. City officials like Dr. Ilse Wolff, who is in charge of tourist promotions, have traveled as far as South America in hunt of visitors to Berlin and hotelier Klaus Winkler has toured the world to drum up business—if not for Berlin, then at least for the Berlin Hilton, of which he is the manager.

The Hilton, like the Europa Center, was put up with a lot of public funds and its construction caused a storm of protest from other Berlin hoteliers, all of whom felt left out in the cold. Dr. Paul Hertz, who was Economics Senator in the city government when Conrad Hilton opened his fourteen-story, 604-bed tower in 1958, defended it passionately, arguing that it would bring in tourists and was therefore well worth the 27 million marks it cost. It seems he was right, for the Hilton, despite its prices, always seems to be crowded, mostly with the kind of American tourists who travel the globe but only move from one Hilton or Intercontinental hotel to another, without ever encountering any "native atmosphere." There is no doubt, however, that something like the Hilton was needed; before it went up, there were only two other major hotels, the Hotel Berlin, which also opened in 1958, and the "Bristol Hotel Kempinski," the first important hotel to open after the war, in 1952. Most of the old hotels of prewar Berlin had vanished in the air raids—the Eden, Excelsior, Fürstenhof, and Kaiserhof among them. The city was left with only a small fraction of the number of hotels, hotel beds, and guesthouses it had in 1937 and it has not yet caught up with the prewar standard.

Economic considerations aside, there are other reasons why West Berlin needs tourists. When they stop pouring into the city, it will mean that the Berliners have been forgotten by the world outside. West Berlin needs to be reassured, especially since the G.D.R. in 1968 made the transit of goods and visitors to and from West Berlin more difficult and much more expensive. The presence of tourists is taken as proof that the world outside remembers West Berlin exists. "Courage is fine," as an old Berlinese saying puts it, "but endurance is better."

Competition is the keynote in Berlin. If West Berlin competes with West German cities, East Berlin today competes with West Berlin. Nothing irks the S.E.D. leadership in East Germany more than the fact that no Western nation regards the G.D.R. as a legitimate state; it works furiously at making East Berlin into a showcase for Communism, trusting that buildings will lend prestige to the government and give East Berlin the appearance of a major capital. Political power, national prestige, and international status all are given more consideration than people.

Nowhere is this more apparent than in the field of construction. Political considerations alone even govern housing. As a result, construction of new apartments in East Berlin rose only seven percent during a period in which construction in industry rose three hundred percent. Streets everywhere but downtown are full of potholes; because consumer goods are neglected in favor of heavy industry, there is little automobile production in the G.D.R. and, therefore, no urgent need for improved streets except where tourists might see them. Again, because industry takes priority over everything except the quest for national status, new housing is usually concentrated around or near factories, while much of the rest of East Berlin is neglected. In 1955, a decision was apparently taken to reduce the amount of floor space per apartment, because ever since then, East Berlin flats have become smaller and smaller. At the Schillingstrasse, for example, there's a handsome modern seventeen-story apartment house with 240 apartments; it turns out that these are all one-room flats. A lot of old apartments have been repaired—but then split into smaller units. Almost two-thirds of East Berlin's 460,000 housing units consist of one- or two-room apartments (not counting kitchens or toilets), and of this total, about 120,000 are either new or renovated. Two-thirds of post-war housing consists of new flats, usually in developments adjacent to factory sites. In recent years, East Berlin has been building or renovating 7,000 apartments a year, but because it combines the figures for both categories, it is impossible to tell how many of these are new. In any case, the construction rate lags far behind West Berlin, even taking into account the population difference. West Berlin has been building 18,000 to 20,000 new apartments annually and this does not count old ones which have been repaired or modernized.

In the East very little construction went on until 1950, when the G.D.R. decided to build its Stalin Allee, renamed the Karl-Marx-Allee after "de-Stalinization." It was not until 1964 that all its sections were completed, but, despite the enormous effort and propaganda invested into this one-and-a-half-mile-long avenue, it never attained any popularity. The Communist leadership hoped that it, rather than the "imperial" Unter den Linden, might become the center of East Berlin, and it was for this reason that Unter den Linden was so long nelgected.

While the East Berlin authorities concentrated on Stalin Allee, the Russians were busy building their embassy on Unter den Linden, choosing a site previously occupied by the old Czarist Embassy, the Hotel Bristol, and the Archbishop's Palace. This four-hundred-foot-wide structure, containing some 320 sumptuously decorated rooms, set the tone; the East German authorities began to follow suit. A number of new office buildings and ministries were planted on the avenue, along with some new trees, and by 1952, it was decided also to restore the historic buildings on Unter den Linden. It was not until well after the Berlin Wall went up and the G.D.R.'s economy was forcibly stabilized that this reconstruction activity went into full swing. Today, Unter den Linden has been almost completely restored or rebuilt and the East Berlin authorities have conscientiously maintained the architectural integrity of the avenue by keeping all its new buildings to a maximum height of about seventy-two feet.

Some of the restoration activity is very ambitious indeed, most notably that of the Crown Prince's Palace. This had been bombed down to its second story. In 1961 its ruined shell was completely demolished, nothing being worth salvaging except a few cornices showing the heads of bearded men. It is now being completely reconstructed and the palace, which served as a museum after 1918, is to become the official "Cultural Center of the Capital's Magistrat."

The Berlin Palace of the Hohenzollerns was less fortunate in that it was razed to the ground in late 1950 before Ulbricht decided to restore the glory of old Prussia. The only part of it that was saved, for reasons rooted in the Communist catechism, was Andreas Schlüter's decorative portal, which contained that balcony from which Liebknecht proclaimed a "soviet republic" in Germany in 1918. This is today incorporated into the front of the State Council Building, which stands where the palace once stood on Marx-Engels-Square, next to the new Foreign Ministry Building. Both structures support Ulbricht's contention that the one-party state run by his S.E.D. is here to stay.

If anyone entertains any doubt about the fact that East Germany is today the richest country in the Soviet bloc (excepting the U.S.S.R.), then the new Alexanderplatz complex is meant to dispel it. An enormous television tower almost 1,200 feet high (362 meters), containing a restaurant 680 feet (207 meters) off the ground, dwarfs everything around it. It is almost 200 feet taller than the Eiffel Tower in Paris. Only Moscow has a higher TV tower. It would, after all, have been an impertinence for the East Germans to try to exceed that. The tower, incidentally, was built over the protests of the Western Allies, who pointed out that it interfered with air safety and who had repeatedly turned down

374

requests from West Berlin's Radio Free Berlin (S.F.B. for *Sender Freies Berlin*) that it be allowed to build a similar tower.

Spinning around this enormous shaft will be the completely reconstructed Alexanderplatz. A new shopping center, S-Bahn station, new office buildings, and restaurants are being added to the House of Teachers and *Volkskammer* Congress Hall already standing there for some time, but the most spectacular building on the square, aside from the TV tower, will be a new two thousand-bed hotel, the second largest in all of Europe and certainly the largest by far in all of Berlin.

Even churches have been and are being restored, including the Berlin Cathedral, or *Dom,* at the Lustgarten, whose cross today looms high over Marx-Engels-Platz, as though delivering a blessing or perhaps absolution to the marchers passing beneath it on the high holy days of Communism. Historic churches like the Nikolaikirche, the Parochialkirche, and the Marienkirche are all being restored. It is clear that East Berlin's authorities have in recent years decided not to leave any of their historic downtown buildings in ruins, for the gutted shells of these buildings had too long been a reproach and an affront to East Germany's prestige.

On the other hand, there remain twenty-eight thousand gas-burning street lamps in East Berlin, and the streets they illuminate, being outside the downtown area, are in pitiful condition. There's no crash-building program under way to restore these, it being observed that the absence of automobiles in East Berlin today makes such an effort a waste of time and money.

The desire to make downtown East Berlin into the showcase of East Germany may, however, actually bring the East Berliners some new flats. There's already one new apartment house on Unter den Linden, near the corner of the Friedrichstrasse, and plans are afoot to encircle all of downtown East Berlin in a ring of twenty-one-story apartment houses, but like many other G.D.R. projects these may never get off the drawing board. In one section of East Berlin, for example, where plans called for twenty-four apartment houses containing a total of ten thousand apartments by 1970, the actual number of flats completed annually keeps sinking in relation to the plan and at times the goal was fulfilled by only twenty-two percent. Construction of housing units is impeded not only by the low priority assigned to it but also by a shortage of materials, by poor planning and management, and by the use of antiquated construction machinery. East Berlin has almost forty-nine thousand construction workers; in relation to its population, it has about twice as many as West Berlin and, therefore, might be expected to build at twice the rate, but actual construction per worker runs about seventy percent of what it does in the West.

That new thirty-nine-story hotel on the Alexanderplatz, the tallest in all of Europe, points to one of the central reasons why East Berlin is so concerned with its downtown image. The G.D.R. reports that more than 640,000 tourists a year come to East Berlin and that almost half of these come from so-called "capitalist countries." It hopes that the number of Western visitors coming to the G.D.R. by 1970 will increase, and as most of these will come to East Berlin for at least part of their stay, accommodations are desperately needed. Nothing was done about hotel construction until about 1962, when it was suddenly realized that East Berlin needed hotels if the G.D.R. were ever to secure a first-rank position in the Soviet bloc in terms of prestige. Until the thirteen-story Hotel Berolina off the Karl-Marx-Allee was built, about the only place one could stay in East Berlin was in the old Adlon Hotel—or rather, in the ruins of it, for this former elegant Berlin establishment had been reduced by the war to one small wing containing 129 beds. There was also a scattering of small inns and *Pensionen,* enough of them so that East Berlin could claim to have one hundred places offering three thousand tourist accommodations, but none of them ensured a memorable visit. A new magazine about Berlin, launched by the G.D.R. in December, 1968, makes the preposterous assertion that East Berlin has sixty hotels (and twenty department stores); tourists hunting for these will discover that terms like these mean different things on either side of the wall—like the term "democratic" in "G.D.R."

The East Berlin propagandists can give you any number of good reasons why you should visit East Germany, but the East Berliners' own feelings about tourists is somewhat different. According to a popular joke, Walter Ulbricht once staged an international competition in which the first prize consisted of one week's free vacation in East Germany; the second prize, of two weeks, and the third prize, three weeks' free holiday in the G.D.R., and so on down the line. The legendary loser, one can imagine, was invited to stay permanently.

The regime does not like to go into details about the kind of Western visitors it gets to come, for the fact is that many aren't typical tourists. A great many are West Germans who aren't "touring" East Germany at all but are over there to visit relatives; a great many others, from France and Italy, are Communist party members who take advantage of cheap package tours through "Socialist" Germany. East Berlin often refers to the many visitors it gets from Scandinavia but it forgets to mention that most of these are in transit to Austria and Switzerland. They used to stop in West Berlin before the liquor taxes were raised; many of them now go to East Berlin for cheap booze and cheaper beds, but they don't come to tour or to admire.

Promoting tourism into East Berlin is the job of an agency entitled the "Department of Foreign Traffic, Tourism, and Berlin Promotion," which is the counterpart of Dr. Ilse Wolff's West Berlin tourist office. Oddly enough, the official who heads East Berlin's agency is also a Dr. Wolff, though no relation. Both have something in common other than their names, however, for both wish to promote tourism in East Berlin. When Heinrich Albertz was mayor of West Berlin, he told an interviewer that he intended to buttonhole every West German and every foreigner whom he met and tell him, "Go to East Berlin! Because that's the way in which Berlin can continue to play its role as a bridge," meaning a bridge between the Soviet bloc and the West. Brochures West Berlin hands out to visitors stress the same thing.

"You really should—you really *must* go over there!" one brochure tells West German tourists. "You are in the fortunate position of being able to prove to the people in the Soviet sector that they have not been forgotten, that one is willing to come to them and to be with them quite naturally, simply as one German among other Germans in a section of the German capital. That's important, *very* important—of that you may be certain!"

East Berlin welcomes them all, if only for the money they bring. The visitors' reactions are usually less welcome and the only ones reprinted in such East German foreign-language magazines as *G.D.R. Review* are made by the kind of tourist who yearns to see

"Socialism in action" and who even approves of the wall. Most tourists are not favorably impressed. Amos Elon of Israel wrote that East Berlin, twenty years after 1945, still looked as though the war had ended the day before yesterday. *Giornale d'Italia* recently published the comments of some young Italian students that are typical of many Western reactions. It quoted Simonetta Curcio as saying "East Berlin feels like a concentration camp," and mentions that the photographs she had taken of the wall had been confiscated by Peoples' Policemen and destroyed—"as though one could destroy a reality by tearing up pictures," she concluded. Annamarie Di Serio commented on the "tragic" look of the city's exterior. "But what is even stronger," she said, "is the feeling one gets everywhere of oppression." Renata Serbioli was most impressed with "the general poverty and the complete absence of cheerful spirits or happiness" on the other side of the wall. Primo Selani felt that "everyone looks old, poorly dressed, in a hurry, lackluster and depressed." Finally, Mario Tabanelli suggested that it might be a good thing if every politician and statesman in the non-Communist world went to see East Berlin "to learn the value of freedom."

That comment concerning the confiscated photographs is reminiscent of pictures one sees of the Brandenburg Gate both in the *G.D.R. Review* and on postcards sold in the Soviet sector. The Berlin Wall, which stands west of the gate, is clearly visible in any photograph taken from Unter den Linden, but not in these printed pictures. The image gets hazy and it is clear that the wall has been erased by Communist retouchers—as though, to paraphrase Miss Curcio, one could destroy reality with a retoucher's brush.

In fact, the reality is known to every East Berliner, for the wall is its primary evidence, though corroborative evidence exists as well. While tourism, for example, is encouraged even for the East Berliners, the tours offered only head East. Every third East Berliner has taken advantage of government-sponsored tourist trips, mostly to inexpensive state-owned resorts within East Germany itself. The Baltic seacoast and the Thuringian forest are popular and there are any number of scenic holiday centers in the G.D.R. that are among the loveliest in Germany. The all-inclusive cost of a two-week holiday is very low: between thirty and one hundred marks, or up to twenty-five dollars at the official

G.D.R. rate of exchange. In the summer, East Berlin's *Ostbahnhof* is crowded with vacationing Berliners, some of whom take the Moscow Express or the Baltic-Orient Express, which start here. This railway station, the fourth to be established in Berlin, was opened in 1841, and in later years came to be known as the Silesian Station, being renamed "East Station" only in 1950. Trains leave or arrive there every two minutes; those Berliners who do not use them make use of the hundreds of buses that also take group and package tours throughout the G.D.R.'s vacationlands. As for foreign travel, sixteen days on the Soviet Black Sea coast can be bought for 930 marks ($232.50), a fee which includes the cost of air travel via Moscow or Kiev; a two-week camping trip in Bulgaria can be bought for 760 marks ($190); and an East Berliner can even visit Cuba for 5,800 marks ($1,450). Most East Berliners who go abroad for a holiday choose Romania, Bulgaria, or Hungary, but they could even take a trip to Mongolia or North Korea, if they wanted to.

The West, of course, is prohibited to them, and ever since the Dubcek-era began in January, 1968, so is Czechoslovakia. The prohibition against Yugoslavia has been in force for some time, though small numbers of East Germans were, until the Czech crisis, annually allowed to visit that country. They did so in strictly-supervised groups, whose leader was in all cases an S.E.D. functionary and usually a *Vertrauensmann,* a trustee or agent, of the S.S.D. Strict limitations were imposed because too many East Germans made it to the West via Yugoslavia or found political refuge there. One reporter who asked a young girl in an East Berlin tourist office why trips to "Socialist" Yugoslavia weren't possible any more received a mumbled reply about "lack of security arrangements" and was then assured "Bulgaria is just as pretty."

All travel is well supervised. Group tours are one way of controlling individual defections and they are about the only means an East Berliner has of traveling abroad, even to the approved Bulgarian and Hungarian resorts. Pocket money is strictly limited so as to restrict freedom of movement and none of the tourists are allowed to carry passports, all of them being registered in a "group passport" carried by the tour leader.

Such precautions are necessary even on trips to distant Bulgaria, because its Black Sea coast and frontier with Turkey provide a way of escape to the West. The owner of a West Berlin *Kneipe* whom I came to know quite well was instrumental in arranging several such escapes for friends in East Berlin. The East Berliners would join a group tour to Bulgaria and he would meet them there, having brought along an extra airline ticket as well as a forged passport for their use. Armed with these, the East Berliners climbed aboard a commercial Western airliner in Bulgaria and flew off to West Berlin. The escapees in question lived only a few blocks from the Western sectors but getting to them safely called for a round-trip via the Black Sea.

One East Berlin girl, the manager of a hairdressing salon, tried to escape to Turkey, together with her West Berlin fiancé, while she was on holiday in Bulgaria. Both of them were apprehended, however, and detained by the Bulgarians for some time. The young man was then expelled from Bulgaria to West Berlin, while she was returned to East Berlin. The S.S.D. interrogated her for hours but did not arrest or punish her. She was even allowed to go back to work, but the trade union on whose behalf she managed the salon announced she was unwelcome—whereupon, to the girl's amazement, the East Berlin authorities told her to leave for West Berlin to join her fiancé.

Such cases, in which an East Berliner is allowed to "travel West," do occasionally occur and seem to reflect the fact that East Berlin is happy to get rid of troublesome people, though they may be motivated in part by compassion.

The biggest group of East Berlin "tourists" visiting the West are, of course, the pensioners. Ever since November 2, 1964, when the G.D.R. first gave people over sixty-five permission to leave the country, they have been coming by the hundreds of thousands. During the first two months, a quarter of a million of them visited West Berlin and more than a million took advantage of the travel permit during 1966. They may spend up to four weeks in West Berlin or West Germany, and if they choose, they may remain there. Most of them return, however; only 2,078 chose to stay in West Germany during 1966.

"My first thought, as I stepped on West Berlin ground," says one of them, "was this: here I am a man, here I'm allowed to be a human being!" Pensioners such as this old Berliner are among the most moving people one can meet in West Berlin. Their gratitude at being outside the G.D.R. even for a brief time is genuine and always pitifully touching. They visit all the shops, tour the housing developments, tramp along scores of streets, gawk at all the displays, read all the newspapers and magazines, watch even the worst films and plays with childlike delight, and stand about in a kind of wide-eyed trance along the Kurfürstendamm, staring at the traffic, the well-dressed people and the animated faces of West Berlin. A great many have been so moved by their experiences that they have written the city government of West Berlin to thank them for the courtesies it extended and also to unburden themselves, in unsigned letters, of some of their feelings concerning life "over there."

They sometimes call it "the shady side" of the wall, even though it's been getting a bit brighter for a while. In mid-1967, East Berlin workers were granted pay increases and extended holidays; most important, they were granted a five-day week. Paid holidays were extended from twelve to fifteen workdays annually. Yet morale remains low, and although the Western press describes East German workers as imbued with a sense of national pride, purpose, and accomplishment, it is hard to find an East Berlin worker who will agree privately. They are proud, as Willy Brandt pointed out, but of what they themselves have achieved in spite of the difficulties imposed on them, proud of how they have endured.

Difficulties continue to be massive, but East Germany has developed the biggest industrial capacity of any country in the Soviet bloc, except the Soviet Union, despite enormous Soviet reparations claims, which Western experts estimate at 100 billion marks (25 billion dollars) but which Ulbricht says were close to 120 billion, and without any foreign aid at all such as West Germany received in the European Recovery Program.

Today, almost every East Berlin industry and business enterprise is either completely nationalized or partly owned by the state. East Berlin's 750 industries are run by twenty industrial trusts whose managers today enjoy a greater degree of freedom in decision-making than they ever had before. The bulk of East Berlin's industry is in electronics, mechanical engineering, chemicals, clothing, and food—the same pattern as in West Berlin. The big electronics enterprises were expropriated from their owners after the war, East Berlin in several cases choosing to keep the old capitalist names because of their high prestige. Berlin-Wilhelms-ruh, for example, contains the Bergmann-Borsig plant; the name Bergmann comes from Bergmann Electrical Works, while the Borsig name was simply usurped without permission. Several plants which had belonged to the A.E.G. (a German 'General Electric') were seized and are, like the others, V.E.B. factories, "People's-Owned Enterprises" (*Volkseigene Betriebe*).

The number of workers in almost every single East Berlin industry has dropped since 1952, because of defections to the West. Of 591,000 employed East Berliners, the only contingent whose numbers have risen steadily since 1952 are the bureaucrats. More than 170,000 East Berliners are Government employees, a figure that reflects how East Berlin fulfills the function of capital for East Germany. Of the remainder, in industry, trade, or commerce, a small number work for private employers, there still being 337 private enterprises in East Berlin. These, however, are insignificant: Only five of these have more than one hundred workers.

The gross national product of East Germany has tripled since 1950 and keeps rising. East Berlin's factories export industrial electronics control equipment and entire factories to the Soviet bloc. Still, factories often produce only about seventy percent of their quota and there remain startling shortages. A textile-research institute, for example, advertised, "Who is in a position to deliver two hundred sheets of sandpaper?" A local school administration advertised for fifty double-bunk beds; a local district council asked for the loan of a steam roller; a People's-Owned Enterprise asked for tires that would fit its vehicles; another enterprise pleaded for three thousand rivets; and a factory canteen asked private hutch owners for rabbits.

Shortages, therefore, don't just plague housewives; they plague industrial managers as well. The causes are many but the situation may be attributed, most of all, to the demands of the Soviet Union itself, which rang from immoderate to rapacious.

Political jokes reflect a good deal of the economic reality propagandists try to hide. One of these tells of a young inventor who has just designed a device for cleaning teeth: a toothbrush. Jubilant, he rushes it to a V.E.B. factory to be mass-produced—but, by the time the first toothbrush comes off the bristle belt, the young inventor's teeth have all fallen out. Another joke in which much truth is hidden tells of an East Berliner who is asked to define the "critical periods" in G.D.R. industry. His reply: "Spring, summer, autumn, winter." A Communist theoretician is asked whether people will still need money after "pure" Communism has been achieved. "No," he replies. "By that time we also won't have any money." As for when the "final stage" of Communism will be reached, the East Berliners' answer is, "When people have had enough of it." Asked what is the difference between capitalism and Communism, an S.E.D. functionary replies, "In capitalism, man exploits man. In Communism, it's exactly the opposite." Finally, a regime functionary is asked whether the nation's milk production could be raised by ten percent. "Of course, it could," he replies. He is thereupon asked if it could be raised twenty percent, to which he also responds in the affirmative. Finally, he is asked if it could be raised thirty percent. "Yes, we could even do that," he answers. "But, of course, the milk would be pretty thin by that time."

Despite the G.D.R.'s constant industrial growth, the milk may be getting a bit thinner for its citizens, due to a five-year trade agreement signed with the U.S.S.R. currently in force. This pact had its roots in the constant and almost paranoid fear of the S.E.D. leadership that the Soviet Union might conceivably make a deal with the West that would abandon them to their own devices, which means to their own people. In late 1965, Ulbricht felt compelled to make some dramatic gesture which would make East Germany absolutely indispensable to the U.S.S.R. for some years to come. He chose a trade pact which would give the Soviet Union more than fifty percent of all East German exports, in exchange for Soviet raw materials. The East Germans would deliver machinery, complete chemical and electronic installations, and other capital goods, including three hundred merchant ships, all at prices below what these would fetch if sold in the West and in many cases even below production costs. In return, the G.D.R. would buy oil, iron ore, and other raw materials from the U.S.S.R. at prices well above the world market.

The job of negotiating this incredible trade pact fell to forty-eight-year-old Erich Apel, East Berlin's State Planning Commissioner, but it appears that the final terms were not his, but reflected Soviet demands entirely. Apel and the younger "technocrats" in East Berlin wanted to increase trade with the West, in exchange for equipment with which to modernize the G.D.R.'s industries; Apel knew that, if this pact were signed, it would mean that virtually all trade between the G.D.R. and the West would have to stop to enable East German factories to fulfill its terms. His protests, however, were in vain; the Soviets refused to negotiate and simply handed Apel the trade agreement along with an ultimatum that it be signed by 11 A.M. on December 3. Apel huddled with Walter Ulbricht and other East German leaders. The S.E.D. leadership knew it was useless to argue with the Soviets, who had twenty divisions stationed in East Germany; for another, their own attitude is that of Erich Honecker, the "Crown Prince" in East Germany, who said "The party has never made a mistake," and also, "The only book worth reading is the history of the Communist party of the Soviet Union." Men like Honecker believed Soviet Russian support needed to be purchased, whether the price was exorbitant or not. Apel, however, was of a different mind. He resisted until an hour before the end of the Soviet ultimatum. Then, still without agreeing to sign, he left his meeting with the other S.E.D. leaders, went into his office, and put a bullet through his head.

His suicide was not a sudden, desperate move; he had earlier told friends he intended to stage a protest against the trade pact in such a way as to attract international attention. He succeeded, even though he did not stop the pact from being signed that very same day, literally over his dead body.

chapter twenty-four

BERLIN HAS IN ONE SENSE ALWAYS BEEN A DIVIDED CITY. THERE have always been those who strove to widen the frontiers of the spirit and others who only wished to expand frontiers. The city's rulers seldom cared about nurturing the arts, and *Kultur* has at times been a dirty word. Hermann Göring is reputed to have said, "When I hear the word 'culture,' I reach for my revolver!" Years before Göring arrived in Berlin, Kaiser Wilhelm II snorted, "Art that goes beyond the limits and bounds set by me is no longer art!" Berliners have always had to put up with this kind of attitude; only a few of their rulers ever were interested in fostering the arts, most of them trying to shape and to use culture for their own ends. An example is provided by an anecdote concerning Hitler's first days in Berlin as chancellor. He and Goebbels had gone to see a popular film glorifying Frederick the Great. Goebbels, whose *Filmkammer* was soon to censor all German motion pictures, returned first, bursting to tell his Nazi cronies about the movie.

"A magnificent film, a remarkable film," he said. "That's the kind of thing we shall need!"

A few minutes later, Hitler came up in the elevator and entered the room. Hermann Rauschnig, an eyewitness, says *Gauleiter* Forster asked Hitler what he thought of the picture.

"A horror!" Hitler replied. "Absolute rubbish! The police will have to stop it. We've had enough of this patriotic balderdash!"

"Yes, my Führer!" Goebbels blurted out, pressing forward to Hitler's side. "It was feeble, very feeble. We have a great educational task ahead of us!"

Change the names to update the characters, move the action forward more than a generation, and the same scene could still be played in Berlin, at least in its Eastern sector. The film in question had the improbable title, *I Am the Bunny* (*Das Kaninchen bin Ich*), and criticized injustices that took place shortly after the war. Kurt Maetzig, who produced it for the East German film monopoly, DEFA, thought the target was safe, for the abuses were a generation old and had occurred during the Stalinist era, but he was wrong. One of Ulbricht's deputies, Alexander Abusch, said *Bunny* really criticized "certain fundamentals of socialism," as though abuses of legality were indeed basic to the system. In the wake of *Bunny,* careers and reputations, if not actually heads, began to roll all over East Berlin.

For a time, the S.E.D. leadership had hesitantly gone along with the wave of cultural liberalization sweeping through many East European "people's democracies," had even found a few kind words to say about the Beatles, but by autumn, 1965, officials became apprehensive. Popular discontent and the disturbing "revisionist" tendencies in the Soviet bloc had prompted second thoughts about relaxing cultural controls. Alfred Kurella, cultural overlord, had already spoken out, damning liberalizing tendencies in the Soviet bloc. By the time the December, 1965, plenary meeting of the S.E.D. Central Committee was convened, the party had decided to crack down hard. Erich Honecker, heir apparent to S.E.D. leadership, expressed some of the factors underlying the regime's decision to resume strict controls. Recent elections had shown that the party had failed to win over "many" voters. Large numbers had voted only "hesitantly," others stayed home altogether, and some even voted *against* the official candidates. Such disaffection needed to be blamed on something other than the regime itself. The communications media and the intellectuals became the scapegoats.

Even rock-'n'-roll music came under attack during the seven-hour speech Ulbricht delivered before the Central Committee. "The eternal monotony of 'Yeah, yeah, yeah,' " he told the functionaries, "is deadly and ridiculous." He set up an advisory body to regulate culture, slashed funds to the arts, and attacked the intellectuals. *"Ja, ja, ja!"* said the functionaries, rushing to proclaim the new hard line throughout the country. In the wake of it, Maetzig's *Bunny* was skinned and roasted.

Another victim was Professor Robert Havemann, who had for

some time been urging the regime to liberalize. His S.E.D. membership had been withdrawn and he had been fired from his post at Humboldt University. Still not silenced, Havemann had allowed West Germany's *Der Spiegel* to print an article in which he called for a parliamentary opposition in the G.D.R., saying, "Any form of socialism that offers fewer democratic rights and freedoms than does the bourgeois state is a distortion." As a result of this, he was fired from the job he held at East Berlin's Academy of Sciences and all his fellow academicians were ordered to avoid his company. By March, 1966, the academy president, Werner Hartke, decided to call for his expulsion from that body. This was accomplished illegally by Hartke, acting on his own in April, after a majority of the Academy members had voted against expelling Havemann. It was noted that Havemann, a loyal Communist since 1932 and one who had narrowly escaped a Nazi death sentence, was ironically being persecuted by an ex-Nazi in the S.E.D.'s employ. Hartke had joined the N.S.D.A.P. in 1937 and had risen under it to *Blockleiter,* and some have alleged, even to *Führungsoffizier.*

The whole East Berlin cultural community came under attack. Writers were acused of "skepticism," "revisionism," "violations of Communist morality," "intellectual arrogance," and of "hypocritical" demands for freedom. They were overly influenced by the West, it was said, and they worked against the interests of the "working classes." Film-makers were charged with "boundless petty bourgeois skepticism" and their productions with promoting "rowdyism, immorality, and anarchist tendencies among the young." Producer Maetzig promptly humbled himself, admitted his errors, and expressed his "great shame." He promised to revise *I Am the Bunny.* Soon the cutting rooms of DEFA were knee-deep in scissored segments. Four other DEFA films were banned, in addition to *Bunny.* Six foreign imports, including *Marriage, Italian Style,* were also withdrawn.

Two writers who came under savage attack were Stefan Heym and Wolf Biermann, both of whom had ironically opted in favor of life in the G.D.R., leaving the West in the early 1950's. Heym was a refugee from Nazism who had won the Bronze Star as a United States Army officer during World War II and who had worked on the American-sponsored *Neue Zeitung* after 1945. His novel, *Day X,* which deals with the June 17, 1953, revolt, still sits unpublished in an East Berlin publishing house. When he was asked about it at Siegmunds Hof, a West Berlin student home, where he appeared for an evening about a month before the hard line was announced, Heym insisted, "I never have any problem about writing the truth." In saying it, however, he emphasized *writing*.

Now, the very fact that he ever wrote *Day X* got him into trouble, as did a satire of S.E.D. literary criticism he had published. The *Kulturbund* denounced him (as well as Havemann and Biermann) for aiding "the worst enemies of the German nation" and the Author's Association called Heym "a particular example of the visible influence of the enemy's ideology."

Wolf Biermann was the G.D.R.'s Bob Dylan, a talented and satirical writer of poetry and songs that he recited to his own guitar accompaniment. The son of an old-time Communist, Biermann left Hamburg in 1953, when he was eighteen, and moved to East Berlin. He assembled a small troupe of actors and singers, and with them, built up a theater of his own, actually laying his own bricks. After the wall went up, Biermann's verse became increasingly critical of G.D.R. policies. The regime broke up his theater by transferring each member of his troupe to another city. Undaunted, Biermann appeared before small groups and at private gatherings, even singing songs criticizing the border guards. When the new harsh course was announced, *Neues Deutschland* singled him out for special attention. "Biermann," it said, "doesn't know how to say 'Yes!' to Germany's socialist state!" Alexander Abusch joined in, calling Biermann's poems "primitive sexual obscenities" used to "besmirch" the working classes; the F.D.J.'s publication, *Junge Welt* (for *Young World*), announced, "Wolf Biermann has written dirty songs, some of them so dirty that common decency forbids us to listen to them. This filth is as politically indecent as it is pornographic!"

Lashing out in all directions, *Neues Deutschland's* editor-in-chief, Hermann Axen, accused writers in general for "their strange idea that in order to tell the truth about socialism one must first of all criticize it," and Kurt Hager demanded they realize that art must primarily be "a weapon in the class struggle." Walter Ulbricht, acknowledging Producer Maetzig's humble apology with a friendly letter, accused East Berlin's artists of indulging themselves in "doubts" about the G.D.R. "Our writers and artists must close their ranks more firmly about the party," Ulbricht said, adding that they "have the greatest amount of freedom to produce anything that serves our state and our society."

When playwright Peter Weiss and novelist Heinrich Böll came to the defense of Wolf Biermann, Hager denounced their suggestion that freedom of opinion ought to exist under socialism as "counter-revolutionary," saying that such freedom is often used "to bury socialism." The S.E.D., Hager also said, was willing to work with all writers "who honestly cooperate in strengthening the G.D.R."

"Louis Fürnberg," said Hager, "wrote that lovely song, 'The Party is right, it is always in the right!' That holds true for the past, it holds true for the present, and it will also hold true for the future!"

"Dear Comrade Ulbricht," said Authors' Association Chairman Anna Seghers in a telegram advising him that the writers now recognized their errors, "We thank the Central Committee and you, Comrade Ulbricht, for your help in this matter." Minister of Culture Hans Bentzien was sacked; Klaus Gysi was put in his place. But this was just a ritual reshuffle, for Gysi is no hard-line Stalinist and both men are loyal party functionaries. Author Werner Bräunig promised to rewrite his novel, *Der Rummelplatz* (*The Amusement Park*) and octogenarian Stefan Zweig, the grand old man of East German letters, proclaimed, "I've said for years there's just no place in which I feel as homey as the G.D.R."

Despite the fact that Ulbricht's December, 1965, speech launched the new line, there were reports that it may have actually been adopted against his wishes and that he attacked the intellectuals only after being faced with a virtual rebellion in the S.E.D. Central Committee, from members who were even more "Stalinist" than he. True or not, books in East Berlin are made to specifications set by cultural commissars. Authors who meet these are coddled, while the others are simply not patronized, which means not published. The situation of some of them is desperate.

An example is Peter Huchel, now past sixty-five years of age, the former editor of *Sinn und Form* (*Meaning and Form*), the only East German magazine that achieved any reputation outside the borders of the G.D.R. Under Huchel, it became a leading Left-oriented literary journal, as highly reputed in the West as in East European countries, but by 1962 it was decided that *Sinn und Form* was "too pro-Western." Huchel, a poet in his own right, was not only fired from his job, but denied all right to publish in East Germany. Today he lives in complete disgrace in Potsdam, a lonely old man whom the G.D.R. at least does not allow to starve to death, for he is still a member of the Academy of Arts and draws his pay from that. Recently he entertained hopes of being able to emigrate to South America, where friends had guaranteed him a livelihood, but the regime refused to grant him an exit visa. The last book of his poems to be published was issued by West Germany's S. Fischer Verlag, a Frankfurt publishing house, in 1963, under the title *Chauseen Chauseen* (*Avenues Avenues*). "Deep down the bones rot," he says in one of his poems, "but the breath flies upward . . ."

Huchel had been a prisoner of war in the U.S.S.R. until 1945. Another East Berlin writer who was a P.O.W. in Russia was Johannes Bobrowski, released only in 1949. Novelist, short-story writer, and poet (*Shadow Land: Selected Poems* is available in English translation) Bobrowski is considered one of the major German writers to have emerged after the war. In 1965, at the age of forty-eight, he became critically ill. When he failed to respond to antibiotics given him in the Soviet sector, Klaus Wagenbach, the West Berlin publisher, tried to rush over additional medication. The G.D.R. refused to allow him to enter East Berlin. When Bobrowski died, a storm of protest arose. Many people claimed the G.D.R. had let him die, though in fact it is doubtful Wagenbach's medication could still have saved him. In any event, the incident proved again the ham-handed disregard for public opinion the East Berlin regime so often displays.

The last East Berlin writers permitted to visit the West were novelist Manfred Bieler and poet Günter Kunert, who attended the Cheltenham Festival in London. Bieler afterward took permanent refuge in Prague, but Kunert still lives in East Berlin. Almost no authors may any longer be published in the West. One exception is Hermann Kant, whose *Die Aula* (*The Auditorium*) was reviewed favorably in West Germany by critics who called it entertaining and readable, which is something for literature emanating from East Berlin. It sticks to the party line, pokes mild fun at G.D.R. accomplishments, shrugs off shortcomings as mere childhood diseases of "Socialism," but has the virtues of being dramatic, ironic, and humorous. The book was first issued by East Berlin's Rütten and Loening publishing house, and later sold to a West German publisher in Munich also called Rütten & Loening, a situation that could only come about in divided Germany, where the property (including the names) of old established publishers were often seized by the Communists. Kunert also is still published in West Germany and some East Berlin writers were for a time given permission to submit manuscripts to *Kürbiskern* (literally, *Pumpkinseed*), a Munich magazine which takes an extreme Left-Wing stance. Recent restrictions, however, have made the East German state solely competent to negotiate foreign contracts for authors, which puts writers in the position of having the regime both as their publishers and as their literary agents.

East Berlin is the center of the G.D.R.'s publishing industry, which claims to issue more books than any other country in the world in relation to the number of citizens, or more than six a year for every East German. Every third day, a new book is published just for the "young adults" (*Heranwachsende*) in East Germany. Volk and Wissen Verlag, responsible for all schoolbooks, has produced about 400 million of them since 1945, along with more than 200 million periodicals. Though by no means all are political, each is subject to political direction. (When Bruno Henschel, whose Henschel Verlag publishes theatrical books, was asked at Siegmunds Hof why he had never published playwrights of the Theater of the Absurd, the old man mumbled, "There is no demand for those.")

In 1959 established authors were ordered to go out to the factories, both to discuss their books with the workers and to find new writers among them. A slogan was publicized in the hope of digging out hidden talent: "Coal miners, grab your pens!" It was not enough to write *for* the workers; one had to write *with* them, according to the "Circle of Writing Workers." The attempt, however, turned out to be a disaster and the entire effort was allowed to peter out quietly, though the regime press still continues to urge all those with the right attitudes to try their hands at producing literature.

Those who interfere with free interpretation in the arts have never been popular in Berlin, as is made plain by a small anecdote about Richard Wagner. The composer was strolling through Berlin one day when he heard the wedding march from his *Lohengrin* issue forth from a barrel organ in a tenement rear courtyard. It was played too fast and without any feeling, so Wagner took a moment to accost the old *Leierkastenmann* who cranked it out. The elderly Berliner laughed and asked Wagner what made him such an expert, whereupon Wagner identified himself as the composer. "So, so, that's who you are!" murmured the old man. "How about showing me how it's done properly?" Wagner grasped the handle and turned it for awhile, afterward handing the man a coin. "I've been cranking this out for a long time," the old man grumbled, "and now you have to come here and hand me those rules and regulations about how I should play it! But, seeing as you're the composer, I'll do it your way." Wagner again passed by that courtyard two days later and once more heard his music being played. Happy to note that his instructions had been followed, Wagner hurried inside to give the man another coin. When he reached the *Leierkasten-mann,* he turned pale. A hand-lettered sign hung from the barrel organ: "Personal student of Richard Wagner."

Even today, Berliners seem able to maintain their independent stance, and in East Berlin, too. Despite all the "reeducation," the refractoriness of the population continues to plague the regime. In March, 1967, the State Council received a report on "Youth and Socialism" from a commission set up to assess public attitudes. Only its favorable comments were published, but the full text reached West Berlin six months later and revealed that "the great educational task" still lay ahead. Western books, called "filthy and trashy literature," remained popular among the young, promoting "objectivism," "questioning," "moral unsteadiness," and "civic decadence." Further, the commission bitterly attacked parents for "tolerating or even supporting" the fact that their youngsters watch Western television and listen to West Berlin radio programs, "imbibing and transmitting the poison of imperialist ideology" and it admitted the regime had failed to inculcate "socialist thinking" among its young people.

The popularity of Western books can be seen from East Berlin's best-seller lists, which, of course, make mention only of books by "approved" Western authors. One such list included a collection of Swedish short stories, a book of Walt Whitman's works, *Modern American Prose,* as well as a Soviet novel, poems by Maya-kovsky and a twelve-volume set of Goethe. Books in general are cheap and plentiful in East Berlin and many a Western tourist buys his Heine and Goethe over there, ignoring the fact that even such classics often contain a party-line preface. Browsing in East Ber-lin's bookshops, one, of course, finds a great deal of Marxist and S.E.D. literature, but there is one kind of propaganda that hap-pily is missing. Memoirs of *Waffen-S.S.* "heroes" and apologias by ex-Nazis, which do appear in West Berlin, are strikingly absent. What is written about the war in East Berlin may serve the S.E.D. dictatorship, but it at least demonstrates a sympathy for peoples overrun by the Nazi armies, never glosses over Nazi barbarities, and is unflinchingly anti-fascist throughout.

The violent condemnation of Western radio and television, contained in the report to the G.D.R. State Council, is occasioned by the fact that East Berlin's more than two hundred thousand tele-vision sets are often tuned to the West. The regime's attitude to-ward this practice was expressed by a member of the S.E.D. Cen-tral Committee who uttered the Orwellian cry, "We want the truth as it is expressed in the G.D.R.!"

This version emanates from a great many East Berlin broadcast-ing stations, several of them aimed at West Berlin and West Ger-many, as well as the neutral and West European world. The G.D.R. even operates two "black transmitters" beaming programs at the West German Armed Forces, whose morale and discipline they seek to undermine. Their conspiratorial tone suggests their scripts are written by West German revolutionaries hiding in some candle-lit Ruhr cellar and that they broadcast from inside the Federal Re-public, in constant danger of being discovered, but this is not the case. "Radio 935" staffers actually operate out of the House of the National People's Army at Regattastrasse 267, in East Ber-lin's Grünau section, while "Radio 904" workers are just up the block, at number 277. Their programs are taped at Nalepstrasse 18-50 in East Berlin's suburb of Oberschönweide and transmitted from Burg, near Magdeburg, in the G.D.R. Both just happen to use frequencies assigned to the Soviet Union.

Headquarters for the East German *Deutschlandsender* station was for many years in West Berlin, having been established there in May, 1945, by the Russians. The building on the Masurenallee was such a hotbed of intrigue that a man who fled East Germany in 1950 and who inadvertently stumbled into it, thinking it was the home of the American-owned R.I.A.S. station, was dragged off and hauled back into East Berlin. After that, the British nailed signs around the building, reading, "*Achtung!* This is not a West Berlin station!" and in 1952 they briefly sealed the building off with military police, barbed wire and anti-tank barricades. It was not until 1956 that the Soviets cleared it completely, eleven years after they first came there, providing an object lesson in how difficult it often is to get the Russians out of territory they occupy.

Television was introduced to the East Germans in 1950 but regular programming was launched only in 1952, in celebration of Stalin's birthday. The Alexanderplatz Post Office was equipped with a set for public viewing. Soon, main post offices in each East Berlin district had viewing rooms. The first sets offered for sale (called "Leningrad") cost 1,450 marks, more than two months' pay for an industrial worker, but they have become cheaper in recent years and the ratio of sets per inhabitant is almost as great as in West Berlin, where there are five hundred thousand sets for about twice East Berlin's population.

Television in both West and East Berlin is an odd mixture of culture and what the Germans call *Kitsch,* "tasteless junk." The latter also seems to be a specialty of East Berlin's motion-picture industry. The DEFA studios in Berlin-Babelsberg have cranked out more than three hundred films since the end of the war, but critics don't think that more than a dozen, to be very generous, were of any cinematic value whatever. One recent film that was popular in the G.D.R. and even shown in West Germany and Britain was *The Adventures of Werner Holt,* a realistic, anti-Nazi war film. DEFA's biggest box-office success, however, seems to have been *The Sons of the Great She-Bear* (*Die Söhne der grossen Bärin*), a cowboy-and-Indian Western directed by a Czech, Josef Mach. Its popularity underscored the real hunger that exists in East Berlin for light, nonpolitical entertainment. *A Wedding Night in the Rain,* DEFA's first wide-screen musical filmed in color, is typical of the *schmaltzy* comedies East Berlin audiences favor. Indeed, Babelsberg seems to have become the "Dream Factory," for almost all DEFA films are opiates and very few touch upon

394

realities of life under Communism. A recent attempt at tackling real issues in a way meant to please the state was DEFA's *Stories of That Night,* the night in question being the one of August 12-13, 1961, when the frontier to the West was sealed. It told the stories of four men involved in closing the frontier and managed to do so in a way that enabled viewers to identify themselves with the characters portrayed, at least for a good part of the film, until each man ritualistically expressed his approval of the wall. "That August night," says one of them, a bricklayer, "a back door was slammed shut, fast as lightning and at just the right moment, but with great calm and forethought, so that war couldn't enter in, so that what we'd built up over all these years wouldn't be stolen." The film even told of a couple who fled to West Berlin: a hysterical wife and her husband, a successful but fuzzy-minded East Berlin professor. Their daughter stays behind to help "build Socialism." When she asks her father why on earth he'd want to go West, he mumbles, "So that we can really live!" That line, however, is played for laughs, being spoken after the audience had plenty of proof that this couple lived very well indeed in the G.D.R., amid all the comforts anyone might want.

Somewhat the same theme was the subject of *Achterbahn (Roller Coaster),* a play performed at East Berlin's Maxim Gorki Theater for about two years. It's about a foundling brought up in the G.D.R., who briefly visits West Germany, only to return again. It is the work of Claus Hammel, whom G.D.R. critics call their most successful playwright. A former writer for *Neues Deutschland* and critic for *Sonntag,* Hammel, now in his late thirties, presents arguments that sound almost convincing, if the audience didn't know better from personal experience. The Maxim Gorki Theater, with about three-fourths of its seats filled for most performances, is not in any case the most popular in East Berlin. Thanks in part to Western visitors, that honor belongs to the Berliner Ensemble, which specializes in Bertolt Brecht plays and which is run by his talented widow, Helene Weigel. It is almost always sold out and the quality of the productions offered here and in the Deutsches Theater have helped give East Berlin a reputation for offering first-rate theater. Plays performed in East Berlin run the gamut from Greek classics to *My Fair Lady,* which enjoyed a huge success at the Metropol Theater. Modern dramas by Peter Weiss

(*Marat/Sade* and *The Investigation*) are also popular and any Western performer, such as Ella Fitzgerald, who appeared at the Friedrichstadt Palast, is assured of a wild reception in the Soviet sector.

East Berlin also has two first-rate opera companies, lavishly supported by the state: Professor Walter Felsenstein's *Komische Oper* (Comic Opera) and Professor Hans Pischner's *Staatsoper* (State Opera), the latter housed in that Unter den Linden Opera built by Knobelsdorff for Friedrich II. These rank among the Continent's finest and if they are not as well-known as they might be outside the G.D.R., this is a result of their restricted foreign-travel schedule —due in turn to that defection rate, the bane of every East German impresario. During two recent engagements in Lausanne, Switzerland, eight members of the State Opera defected. When the Brechtian Berliner Ensemble staged its triumphal visit to London in 1965, it lost Christian Weisbrod, twenty-six, one of its youngest members. Weisbrod, however, proved a tragic figure, both in exile and back home. He returned to East Berlin shortly after having moved to West Germany, unhappy at leaving the ensemble, if not the G.D.R.; a short while later, Weisbrod was found dead in East Berlin's historic Marienkirche, having swallowed pesticide. More recently, East Berlin succeeded in gaining an actor by means of defection, this being Wolfgang Kieling, forty-four, a Berliner who said he was disgusted with West German "complicity with the crimes of the American government towards the American Negroes and the Vietnamese people." He said he was going to the G.D.R. because "it is the only German-speaking country of which I can say with certainty that it does not participate in [these] crimes . . ." Greeted with gusto and fat contracts, Kieling was even promised he could visit the West any time he liked, this being a fringe benefit that sets him apart from his new colleagues in East Berlin. The regime overlooked Kieling's last major Western film, Hitchcock's *The Torn Curtain,* in which Kieling played a sinister East German agent.

Because of the roles they are assigned, it's not always easy for an East Berlin actor to attain the popularity of an actor in the West. In fact, because the East Berlin TV-viewer is for so much of the time glued to West Berlin's *SFB* transmissions, the East Berliners are almost more familiar with Western actors than they are with their own. This usually surprises Western actors who visit East Berlin. One who did a few years back was Rolf Ulrich. His West Berlin company of cabarettists, *Die Stachelschweine,* received an official invitation to attend a performance of East Berlin's own (and only) cabaret, *Die Distel* (*The Thistle*), before the hard line was inaugurated.

"We had just recently appeared on West Berlin television," said Ulrich, "together with cabarettists from Munich, rather savagely caricaturizing everyone from Willy Brandt to Walter Ulbricht. When we arrived at the S-Bahn station in East Berlin, we were amazed to find a crowd of about two hundred Berliners cheering us. They didn't know our real names—they just recognized us as Ulbricht, Khrushchev, and so on. They even followed us across the street to the *Distel* theater and there we also received a huge welcome. It was my first visit to East Berlin in five years and it somehow seemed like taking a trip to Japan, it was that momentous and complicated."

After the show, Ulrich's troupe was invited to a buffet dinner in a room above the theater, where they met the *Distel* actors, other East Berlin culturati, and a number of regime functionaries.

"Wolf Biermann was there," says Ulrich "and he sang a song denouncing the wall. The functionaries were furious, blaming it on us. 'We invite you here and you start provocations!' they said. I chatted with Biermann afterward. He was such a thorn in their side that the functionaries would have been happy if he left for the West, but he wasn't going to do them that favor. Anyway, what would he do in the West? He's still a Communist. It's just that he considers the men running the regime over there to be a bunch of bastards."

Any personal encounter with East Berlin's cultural functionaries seems Kafkaesque to Westerners accustomed to the free exchange of ideas. Like Ulrich, I also met some of them in the building which houses *Die Distel,* for it is also the home of the East Berlin "Press Club." My visit there was occasioned by a meeting in West Berlin, with a Herr X., a minor Press official in East Berlin. X. had come to Siegmunds Hof on an evening when a number of writers, myself included, were being questioned by the students. We spoke later in rather guarded fashion, for he was clearly unwilling to be drawn into a conversation about conditions in the East, though it was apparent how he felt about the wall; when I asked him to join the students and me for a chat, the poor man begged to be excused, confessing with embarrassment that he had to return to East Berlin before midnight struck, as though his S-Bahn train might turn into a pumpkin. He gave me his telephone number, but it was impossible (or impossibly tiresome) to call him from West Berlin. Although we were only a few blocks apart, there are no longer any telephone connections between East and West Berlin* and any calls to the Soviet sector are shunted via long distance through Frankfurt, West Germany, and Leipzig in the G.D.R. before reaching their destination. I therefore waited a week, until I was next in East Berlin, and called him from a public phone booth near the Friedrichstrasse Station. I was connected with a young lady who asked me politely but insistently to identify myself in considerable detail and who then told me to call back in forty-five minutes. When I did, X. himself answered and I repeated my request that we get together for lunch.

"I still haven't had a chance to talk with Professor Eisler about that," X. explained, this being before his boss' death. "Can you tell me if he knows anything about you that might make it easier for me to meet you?"

I thought Eisler probably had never heard of my name and told X. as much.

"Well, does he know anything that's *un*favorable about you?"

Again, I assured X. my name probably meant nothing to Eisler.

"In that case," X. said, "and since Professor Eisler is in the hospital today, I could meet you at 4:30 in the Press Club at the Friedrichstrasse."

The club consists of a large, well-lit room, rather sparsely furnished, located on the second floor of a building housing both the G.D.R.'s journalists' union and the *Distel* theater. Although I arrived there punctually X. had preceded me and was already seated, talking with a woman in her fifties. She was plump, round-faced, and wore a maroon flannel shirt, buttoned at the collar, and a man's necktie. Her hair was also done in a mannish style and she seemed rather masculine herself in general deportment, either proletarian, lesbian, or both. She was introduced to me as a Frau

* Except between Soviet and Western Allied headquarters.

V., an editor at a book-publishing house who lived in West Berlin, who was a member of West Berlin's small S.E.D., but worked in East Berlin. She had been working for the same East Berlin publisher ever since 1945 and soon planned to move over permanently to East Berlin. It was simply a matter of her getting assigned an apartment big enough for her and her books. She was an enthusiastic supporter of the G.D.R. and an eloquent apologist for the wall, so I asked her about all the books she must have collected in West Berlin over twenty years. The G.D.R. would never allow her to move these Western books to East Berlin, I said, but she just smiled and assured me she was bringing them across one by one and would have most of them in East Berlin before she herself made the move.

The *Distel* producer sat across the room with his wife and children. X. offered to talk to him so that I might be permitted to buy some house seats at the box office, since each *Distel* performance is sold out weeks in advance. When that was arranged, I was introduced to one of the *Distel's* leading actors, who had moved to East Berlin from Vienna in the mid-1950's. The fact that one of the *Distel's* leading actresses had just defected to the West during a tour of Yugoslavia came up.

"She behaved herself quite well after defecting," X. said. "She refused to make any statements attacking the G.D.R."

Frau V. agreed, adding that the girl had been motivated entirely by personal reasons. I asked about a star athlete who had also recently left the G.D.R. for West Germany.

"There's no doubt about *him*," Frau V. replied. "He behaved very badly once he got to the West."

"He said everyone would leave the G.D.R. if they had the chance," X. explained.

"Absolute nonsense!" Frau V. said, clucking disapprovingly. I looked at X., who sat shaking his head mournfully, but who had nothing to add.

The Viennese actor, who had been sent over to the table by the *Distel* producer and who seemed to know neither of my companions, began to tell us something about his life. He had lost all his family in Nazi extermination camps during the war and had suffered greatly himself, being a Jew; after the war he joined the Communists. He said he had left Vienna to accept G.D.R. citizenship because he considered the Viennese too anti-Semitic and he spoke also of the "impossibility" of life in West Germany.

"So many," he said, "still harbor nationalist and adventurist resentments. Average people, still thinking in the old Nazi ways! One hears them and wonders how it is possible for people still to think that way."

Frau V. apparently had not been listening too carefully or had misunderstood, because she suddenly blurted out angrily, "But there are a lot of those types also living in the West!"

"I was speaking about the West!" the Viennese replied anxiously. Frau V. seemed relieved.

I had not expected her to stay with us so long, for when I first appeared at the club, she said something about having to leave right away. Yet it was soon an hour and a half later and becoming apparent she was there to stay, perhaps to keep an eye on X., who seemed to say less and less with each passing minute and who looked mournful and abstracted. At one point, when Frau V. excused herself, apparently to visit the ladies' room, X. cast a glance at me that I thought I understood at the time; I felt more sorry than ever for this well-meaning but muzzled official. When Frau V. returned, the Viennese, without any apparent reason whatever, launched into a well-argued, passionate condemnation of West German rearmament, the war in Viet Nam, and NATO, while X. sat silent, nodding his head, and Frau V. sat back in her chair, looking well-satisfied. It seemed to me the Viennese was speaking "for the record," to get his position understood, particularly as we were all strangers. His voice struck me as bored throughout.

He was much more animated when I saw him later on that evening, on stage at *Die Distel,* where he and his company performed several sketches in front of a very enthusiastic audience. The jokes which went over the best were all aimed at minor material shortcomings in the G.D.R. and at bureaucratic petty-mindedness; sketches lampooning the West were less well-received, because they were a bit more heavy-handed and seemed familiar. The essence of the Berlin cabarettist's art lies in the savagery of his satirical attacks against local sacred cows, all of whom the audience must be able easily to identify; these particular cabarettists, despite all their efforts and talents, were allowed to do very little of this. But even their mildest jokes about the regime's shortcomings, extremely tame by West Berlin standards, brought the house down. As I left, I thought of the mournful Herr X. and the generally subdued atmosphere in the Soviet sector. It seemed to me that what the East Berliners want, as much as anything else, is a good laugh.

The last word about that was provided a decade ago by Bert Brecht himself; it was published two years after his death: "To live in a country without a sense of humour is unbearable; but it is even more unbearable in a country where you need a sense of humour."

While East Berlin remains the final goal to be attained by any East German actor or artist, being the capital of the G.D.R., the same cannot be said of West Berlin. Other cities, like Munich, due to their ease of access and lack of built-in tensions, now compete heavily in the arts. The very rich, who are still patrons of culture, especially of painting and sculpture, are not in Berlin; they're in the Ruhr, or in Frankfurt, Hamburg, and Munich. West Berlin's cultural and artistic life would atrophy, were it not for the massive aid it receives, as well as for the fact that the city continues magically to magnetize men and women of talent and intellect. It's also become a mecca for the hustlers, impresarios, fund raisers, and managers of the arts, all of them administering artificial respiration by means of energy and funds expended. They give it the kiss of life, but whether it is usually also the kiss of love is not so certain. Some of the emphasis tends to be quantitative rather than qualitative, a good deal of it centers around promotions rather than productions, and most of it is associated with tourism and with the city's cultural-*political* role.

West Berlin has no cultural commissars but it does have some very influential leaders. One of these is Professor Walter Höllerer of the Technical University; another is the autocratic father figure of the literary Group 47, Hans-Werner Richter. "Group 47," says author Hans Habe, who dislikes it, "is a business enterprise, a public-relations organization, a literature factory, compared with which IBM looks like a sublime academy of poetry." It certainly has for a long time been the most prestigious "in group" in West German literary circles, though those outside its ninety-odd membership generally discount its importance. Richter chooses those to be invited to the group's annual three-day conventions and some who were invited in the past find themselves dropped without so much as a fare-thee-well, while others invited for the first time, learn by means of this that they have been tapped for membership. All new candidates must have had at least something published and all are expected to read from an unpublished manuscript. Prominent publishers also attend, for reasons as commercial as they are cultural; it was thanks to the fact that my own Munich publisher attended that I was able to obtain an invitation to observe—*"ganz anonym"* (completely anonymously), as I was warned by my publisher, Klaus Piper. Happy to agree, I drove out to the Lake Wannsee villa where the group met. This is a large, handsome mansion which belongs to the city, with terraces and lawns overlooking the lake at the rear and a handsome courtyard out front. "Only for invited guests," a hand-lettered sign on the front door warned in mock officialese. "Automatic gunfire and savage dogs for intruders!"

After we went in, Piper assured me that just about all the important writers, critics, and publishers were standing within a radius of a few yards. Most of these seemed in their thirties or forties, as though older writers were passé. In any event, those assembled formed a kind of Upper Bohemian avant-garde, the extreme avant-garde assembling in Kreuzberg's *Kneipen,* not in posh Wannsee villas. I chatted briefly with Peter Härtling, author and co-publisher of *Der Monat,* a magazine Melvin J. Lasky used to run before moving to Britain's *Encounter.* Härtling is a relaxed young fellow with an easy smile who reminded me of an American graduate student, earnest yet boyishly friendly; then I briefly met a lean, slightly stooped, very intense man in his forties, whose eyes darted about constantly as though in search of persons with whom it was important that he speak. This, I learned, was Höllerer, Professor Höllerer, *the* Höllerer. He was interested, charming, friendly; he was also restless, an intellectual table-hopper. A few minutes later, a portly man in his late fifties moved smilingly through the crowd, tinkling a little bell that dangled between the thumb and index finger of his right hand. This was Father, by which is meant Richter, telling us all to hurry along to the next room. We shuffled in, took seats in armchairs facing a table behind which were French doors overlooking the snow-covered lawn and the lake. After everyone had been seated, Richter took his place at the table, beside a cadaverous young man with a thin black beard and moustache, dressed in a dark suit and wearing a white shirt, buttoned at the neck, but no necktie. "Five poems!" he announced and began reading them off without further ado. He was Friedemann Berger, an East Berlin writer. It was then just a month before the hard line of G.D.R. culture was announced, and a few writers were still being allowed to visit Group 47 for the day, as long as they returned each evening on the S-Bahn, before midnight. Berger's poems were highly stylized and had a staccato, abbreviated quality about them, conveying an air of disappointment and frustration. When he was through reading aloud, the criticism started. Berger, seated on what has come to be known as the group's "electric chair," was about to be fried or reprieved, no one knew what in advance. The group exists to discover and supposedly to encourage new writers like Berger, to assess and comment upon their unpublished work; every young German writer seems to slaver after an invitation from Richter; those of them who loathe the group often seem either to be writers who were not invited or those who were torn to shreds in front of it. The group's rules are strict and somewhat sadistic, for the writers are not allowed to defend themselves; they are compelled to listen in heart-thumping silence. Berger was neither condemned nor praised; his poems were casually dismissed as "conventional" and then as "understandable," which ended the discussion. Berger rose, protectively clutching his verse to his bosom, and prepared for the trip home.

The door had opened during the discussion to let someone come in, fashionably late. It was Günter Grass, very quietly making a dramatic entrance. Only a few turned their heads to watch him take a seat near the front of the room, on a bench against the wall; they either knew him too well to bother looking or wouldn't be caught dead gawking at a celebrity. Grass lit a cigarette, then chain-smoked. Not having heard Berger's poems, he offered no comment.

Peter Bichsel, a thirty-year-old Swiss, was called up next. He looked like an undissipated Dylan Thomas: roly-poly with touseled hair, a cherubic face above an open-necked white shirt, his belly protruding over his unbelted trousers. He read two sketches from a forthcoming novel. Bichsel's script dealt with the frustrations involved in restoring a decaying house; it was filled with sketches of the bourgeois world, described in terms of the minutiae cluttering a small room. The plans of a house painter hoping to decorate the hallways attractively brought chuckles and even outright laughter; Bichsel had captured the affection, not only the interest, of the group. I found out later that he was a favorite, a product of the group's workshop, and considered by them a major talent, though his first book had been poorly received by critics. His reading sparked a spirited discussion, lasting twenty minutes. Joachim Kaiser of the *Süddeutsche Zeitung,* an important critic, led off by saying he hoped criticism would be especially severe, because of Bichsel's potential. It was right, he said, to demand the very best of him. Günter Grass said he thought Bichsel's prose was "too perfect," that he "took no risks," and that he was so careful in his writing that Grass missed "a certain daring." Others replied that the care with which Bichsel wrote—"Bichsel," said one, "will probably be careful till the day he dies!"—was precisely the factor that honed his prose to such a witty, satirical edge. Bichsel listened, head down, chin on hand, eyebrows raised puckishly, seeming to wonder what might come next. As it turned out, he won the group's first prize that year, worth five thousand marks ($1,250).

After the room was aired during a ten-minute break, a young, blonde girl in a black turtleneck sweater and tan slacks was led to the electric chair. She was Ingrid Bacher, married, living in Rome, author of two published books. She read from two chapters of an unpublished novel: In the first, the hero buries his father, a former Nazi; and in the second, he rides in a taxi and hears an East German radio broadcast mentioning his father's Nazi past and home address. "Graveyards," said one critic afterward, "are tough material with which to deal." Another said taxicabs, ships, hotels, and other confined quarters in which intimate worlds can be constructed were too conventional to be handled other than brilliantly. Her observations were all obvious, it was said, and her situations were stereotyped. She sat through the ordeal of listening, smoking one cigarette after another, her rather pinched face watching the audience tensely, while Richter sat beside her smiling, perhaps to give her encouragement, perhaps to encourage the critics.

Friedrich Wilhelm Delius was the last author to read that morning. By then it was close to lunch, the critics were edgy, their faculties had been sharpened, and having heard Bichsel, they were not receptive to writing that they considered of lower quality than his. Delius chose the first chapter of a novel about a small German town, some of his details seemed irrelevant, and there were self-conscious references to the role of the author. When he was finished reading, Joachim Kaiser led the attack, swooping down like one of Frederick the Great's hussars. Günter Grass followed, firing volley after volley like a Prussian grenadier. These men were two of the biggest guns in the room, and by the time they and a few others were through, Richter mercifully called a halt, adjourning the session for lunch. One newspaper critic, seated nearby, prepared to attack the turkey leg in front of him and I asked him once more about Delius, who had evoked my sympathy. "It isn't that Delius lacks writing ability," the critic remarked while slicing the meat. "What he lacks completely is talent."

Friedemann Berger wasn't the only East Berlin writer who that year attended the Group 47 meetings. A few others were also present, though the G.D.R. had refused to allow Wolf Biermann, Manfred Bieler, and Peter Huchel to attend. Nor were any East Berlin writers at all allowed to attend the group's meeting at Princeton University in 1966, for the hard line had by that time been set.

This visit to the United States was made on the initiative of the director of New York's Goethe House, and later, on the invitation of Professor Victor Lange, head of Princeton's German Department. The Ford Foundation financed a large part of the eighty thousand dollars it cost to bring over ninety-five authors by ship and plane. Most of these were unknown to Americans, and inevitably, the students flocked around Grass and Peter Weiss, whose *Marat/ Sade* was by then already a great success, while the faculty lionized Professor Höllerer, who won their praise by offering some of his own works for criticism.

Some Americans thought the group was a sort of "Town Meeting, German style," while others disparaged it as cliquish. Back in Berlin, however, it is not the "membership" that comes under attack, but rather its structure and alleged political orientation. One scholar, who gave a balanced account of the group in a talk at West Berlin's Jewish Community Hall, said that while the group has no formal structure, it certainly appeared to have a hierarchy almost clerical in composition. He described Richter as the "Pope," for he apparently means to serve as pontiff for the rest of his life. The college of cardinals surrounding Richter consists of powerful literary and dramatic critics like Kaiser, while the bishops, who, according to him, have less to say each year, are successful authors like Grass. Beneath these are the priests, the large mass of young, relatively unknown authors, who are annually invited to participate in the rites and ceremonies. Though he did not mention it, there are also important "lay observers," these being the publishers and editors who attend regularly, like Klaus Piper of R. Piper & Co. Verlag and Fritz Raddatz of Hamburg's Rowohlt Verlag. These and many others seem to circle the unpublished manuscripts as though they were bonfires, sniffing out the critical reactions and presumably making note of those young writers who are both well-regarded and still unattached.

Group 47 celebrated its twentieth birthday in 1967 and passed its first distinctly "political" resolution on this occasion: Inevitably, perhaps, it condemned press magnate Axel Caesar Springer. Eighty members agreed never again to write for a Springer publication; publishers were asked not to send review copies or advertisements for their books to any periodicals owned by the conservative newspaper czar. Thus the membership had joined the students' barricades, but ironically, it appeared that the students had not joined them. Outside the Landgasthof Pulvermühle, a Franconian inn where the group had assembled that year, there stood a phalanx of picketing students, waving placards demanding the dissolution of the group. *"Lieber tot als Höllerer!"* read one: "Rather Dead Than Höllerer!"

The years, it was noted, had changed Group 47, so often criticized as anti-social, too avant-garde, too "leftist." It seemed to have become fat, old, and prosperous enough to be picketed by the young, almost as though it were part of that very bourgeois world its members deplore. No one seemed to know what to do about the demonstrators. Should one call the police, ignore them, or invite them in for coffee and cake? All these suggestions were voiced, while one or two members ventured outside to "discuss issues" with the pickets. The others remained behind closed doors,

406

looking for all the world like proper burghers eager to avoid the disorder in the streets.

The group continues pulsing largely because its critics keep it in the limelight, for a lot of conservatives in Bonn still seem to see it as some kind of vague threat to public decency. Its power over German literature at one time was very great, but according to Professor Höllerer, is now vastly exaggerated. As for the uniformity of its leftist orientation, Höllerer regards that as a myth as well, pointing out correctly that the group is attacked both by West German conservatives and by the East German Communists. "Its members," he says, "are basically united in their rejection of radical extremism, whether from the right or the left."

There are those who think the group has done some writers a disservice. One prominent Berlin writer feels it has overprotected its authors and in some cases has promoted its favorites too fast. To prove his point, he brings up Uwe Johnson, the thirty-four-year-old writer who left East Germany in 1959, who later lived in West Berlin and then went to work for a New York publisher.

"He is doubtless a talented writer," he said, "but the Group 47 made such a fuss about him after his first book and gave him so much publicity that he now finds it very hard to live up to his reputation. The poor man is so scared he can't find any peace for his work and it's now apparent that his talent never was all that great."

The man who dominates West Berlin's literary life is author Günter Grass, now in his early forties. He does so not only by his prominence, but force of personality. Inevitably, there are those who dislike him. "He dictates who gets published by the Luchterhand Verlag," says one prominent Berlin writer. Another one claims Grass feared for his position when Uwe Johnson turned up and "tried to undermine" him. Grass' friends admit his influence is great, but deny he ever acts from petty motives. They point out he helped Klaus Wagenbach establish his publishing firm in West Berlin; that he convinced Luchterhand, his Rhineland publisher, to establish a branch in District Spandau, and that he has recommended authors to both publishers. Backstabbing, they say, is simply out of character for Grass. "He's much more interested in playing *pater familias* at home than being a celebrity," says a poet and critic who is a long-time friend. "He's got a house now rather than an apartment, but it is furnished as simply as his flat was, before

The Tin Drum made him wealthy. Grass has never let success go to his head."

His politics are unimpeachably liberal and democratic, so much so that he became the first German writer officially invited to tour Israel. Outspokenly opposed to the Right-Wing N.P.D. party ("Vote in a way that you'll be able to approve of when you're seventy!" he urged young voters during a recent N.P.D. campaign), he is also a strong opponent of the S.E.D. dictatorship and has condemned playwright Peter Weiss for his support of Ulbricht's regime. Grass campaigned actively for Willy Brandt before the S.P.D. standard-bearer joined the C.D.U. in Bonn's Grand Coalition; he recently expressed his disappointment with the S.P.D. and has spoken with admiration of Fritz Borm, the elderly, intellectual leader of the Free Democrats in West Berlin. Ever since he came to Berlin in the early 1960's, Grass has involved himself very much with the city's life, both personally and in his writings. *"Gleisdreieck,"* a book of poems, deals with Berlin, as does the play in which he condemns Bert Brecht for his failure in 1953 to support the rebellious East Berlin workers, *The Plebeians Rehearse an Uprising.*

"Authors are never models to imitate," Grass told West Berlin youngsters on one occasion. "They live quite ordinary lives, make mistakes, and have their doubts." Despite the advice, it remains a fact that writers are more highly regarded in Germany than elsewhere. They are considered public figures, representatives of their nation as well as of their generation, even as a sort of public conscience.

"In America and Britain," says one critic, "a writer is just a man who writes, as another might teach or drive a bus, but in Germany their books are reviewed as much for their political orientation as for their literary merits. This leads writers to retaliate if their books are attacked on political grounds; soon their friends and enemies join in, and then there is a battle royal because of a book review. German authors are forever being asked to sign manifestos and petitions, appear on public platforms, voice their opinions on radio and television, and to strike partisan political attitudes. Grass manages to separate the artist in him from the political activists, but others like Enzensberger have got the two muddled."

Hans Mangus Enzensberger is a scholarly poet whose intense interest in public affairs has led him increasingly into journalism. As a result, say his critics, his poetry suffers. Like Uwe Johnson, Enzensberger left Berlin for New York, if only temporarily. Grass recently spoke of spending a year in Britain. "The tense atmosphere in Berlin is at fault," one writer explains. "The city is wearing on the nerves, especially for authors who are at the center of its stage."

If Grass joins the exodus, West Berlin will be left with only a few writers of importance and even fewer who have achieved international recognition. Peter Chotjewitz, born in Berlin in 1934, author of a recent book about the city (*Die Insel,* or *The Island*), is highly regarded, but even he is often away and wrote his latest book in Rome. There are others: Peter Härtling of *Der Monat;* Ingeborg Bachmann, an Austrian; and Robert Wolfgang Schnell and Günter Bruno Fuchs, both identified with the "Bohemian" Kreuzberg scene. Wolfdietrich Schnurre, a co-founder of Group 47, is a widely translated poet who is one of the few writers in Berlin who actually writes *about* the city. Cut off by the Berlin Wall from his father, he feels its presence bitterly and has even produced a book of photojournalism documenting its construction. Hans Scholz, who won the prestigious Fontane Prize for his Berlin book, *Am grünen Strand der Spree (On the Green Banks of the Spree*), subtitled *Almost a Novel,* is considered a major Berlinese writer rather than a "literary" figure in the city. Another Berlinese writer, but one who resided in Munich, is the late Walther Kiaulehn. Günther Birkenfeld, whose *Horizont* brought many young postwar writers to prominence, became a major figure during the first postwar decade after having been part of Berlin's literary scene during the 1920's. Martin Kessel, a novelist now much neglected, is another of that handful who can claim to be real "Berlin writers," having spent his life there. Wagenbach, the publisher, is a prominent writer as well, and *the* German authority on Franz Kafka today.

"Writers are like birds," it has been said. "They travel light and they go to places where they can find food."

Berlin is one such place, thanks in part to that magpie of the arts, the inexhaustible Professor Höllerer. Höllerer helped open the purse strings of the Ford Foundation on behalf of Berlin's literary life; later the Berlin Senat and private German organizations took over his projects, once that source had dried up.

He came to Berlin in 1959 at the age of thirty-seven, accepting the chair of literature at the Technical University. Five years earlier, he had founded *Akzente,* a literary magazine devoted to fostering the work of young writers; he had published a book of his own poems, called *The Other Guest,* and had already enough of an international reputation to be invited to lecture at Harvard, Princeton, and other American universities. Two more books of Höllerer verse have appeared since his arrival in Berlin and his novel, *Die Elephantenuhr* or *The Elephantine Clock,* is awaited with interest for it has been in the works forever, it seems, though actually "only" for ten or twelve years.

Der Spiegel calls him a perpetual-motion machine; in Berlin, he's called a *Kultur-Motor,* which means a spark plug and a dynamo enlivening the world of culture. You name it: Höllerer seems to be everything, in everything, and everything seems to swirl around him. He still operates from his base at the Technical University (professorships being lifetime appointments); he's also director of the university's Institute for Language in the Technical Age. He's been the director of the Literary Colloquium, the co-producer of the intellectual Third Program on both *Sender Freies Berlin* and North German *Rundfunk,* a member of the Academy of Arts and deputy director of its literature department (Peter Härtling is director now and Franz Tumler is his deputy), a member of the German Academy for Language and Poetry, the publisher of *Akzente,* an anthologizer of German writings, the author of many articles, and the organizer of a bewildering array of cultural events.

"The problem with Höllerer," says one critic, "is that no one can identify what he stands for. He jumps from one interest to another." He is accused of using his professorship to involve himself in areas that have nothing to do with literature, an accusation which merely points out that, like most prominent figures in Berlin's "incestuous" cultural world, Höllerer attracts ill-wishers and a lot of nasty and even silly talk. It is whispered that he is dying of cancer (not true); he is charged with nepotism (again not true, being based only on the fact that his wife, a photographer, has taken some pictures for the Literary Colloquium—in which ca-

410

pacity Höllerer met her); he is accused of being "afraid" ever to publish that novel of his; he is charged with making "too much" money from too many interests and of promoting the arts to promote himself.

"Those people who are so much against Höllerer ought to start something themselves!" says a scholar prominent in the Academy of Arts. "There is only Höllerer in Berlin! Who else is there? Why don't others begin something? German inactivity! They only do something when they are told to do it. But on their own accord? Never!"

In fact, others were also active. The city's imaginative and energetic senator for Arts and Sciences, Professor Dr. Werner Stein, is one of them; together with several others, such as Director Barsig of *S.F.B.* and critic Friedrich Luft, Stein is a member of the board of trustees (*Kuratorium*) of the Literary Colloquium. Dr. Walter Hasenclever, an American born in Berlin and today resident there, is the man who conceived the idea of winning Ford Foundation money for the city's cultural life; he won the support of Shepard Stone of the Foundation and of Willy Brandt, then mayor. Höllerer was asked to come up with program ideas in the field of literature. This developed into the Literary Colloquium, which Höllerer says was the smallest of the three projects receiving Ford Foundation aid; an Artists in Residence program and an International Music Institute were larger.

Höllerer over the years attracted the headlines, however. Several of his cultural promotions, each a series of events under one thematic title, attracted many prominent people to West Berlin. One of these was "Literature in the Technical Age," this being the name of the university institute he heads; another was "Modern Theater on Small Stages." The first was under the aegis of the university; the latter produced funds for the Literary Colloquium. For a time, Höllerer free-lanced for *Sender Freies Berlin,* which helped make him even more famous in West Berlin and which led to the (false) report that he was under a "fat contract" with *S.F.B.* In fact, Höllerer's TV fees usually went to the Literary Colloquium, rather than to himself, to help support its efforts on behalf of young, unknown authors. A year ago, he stopped free-lancing altogether. "I'm in favor of change," Höllerer says, "as soon as an activity has been allowed to run for a while. Young people

411

are needed for Berlin. Wolfgang Maier and Wolfgang Ramsbott today head the publications and films operations of the Literary Colloquium and I've helped bring three young scholars to the fore at the Technical University, each of whom today conducts lectures and seminars: Volker Klotz, Gerhard Schmidt-Henkel, and Klaus Baumgärtner. Many of these came to West Berlin from elsewhere: Baumgärtner from Leipzig and East Berlin, Ramsbott from Cologne, and Klotz from Darmstadt. It's absolutely essential for Berlin that young people be offered responsible work in this city: the immigration to West Berlin of young scholars and writers is especially vital."

One prominent West Berlin author, half in admiration and half in envy, calls Höllerer a big *Windmacher,* literally a "maker of winds," a man who creates a lot of activity. An editor of *S.F.B.,* who agrees, says that's just what West Berlin requires. "Höllerer became an institution," he adds, "even though his influence is beginning to be on the wane, due to the radicalization of the university students. They're less interested in literature today than they were a few years ago. They're more political."

The "Artists in Residence" program mentioned earlier allows writers, painters, sculptors, composers, and conductors to spend a year in West Berlin. The city gives them free housing and studios, while the Ford Foundation provided a monthly tax-free stipend. This was supposed to be 1,250 marks but, according to a story which has become something of a legend in Berlin, a typist inadvertently put a dollar sign in front of the figure and the Ford Foundation paid out 1,250 *dollars* a month to each artist, without a murmur. Since the foundation's support was withdrawn, the typographical error has been corrected; the program is now supported by the city and by a German organization, and the artists involved have had their fleshpots drastically trimmed. The city obtained the funds needed to keep these programs running after the Ford money stopped.

When Höllerer won the ten thousand-mark ($2,500) Fontane Prize for Literature, a great many people were absolutely outraged. Noting that it was given to him for his promotions rather than for what writing he had done, the *Tagesspiegel* said the prize had lost all meaning and value and might as well have been given to a publisher. One previous recipient of this most prestigious of

Berlin awards says, "Höllerer simply didn't *earn* the prize for literature. But two out of three people on the jury belonged to the Group 47. So there you are! What can you do?"

"All those people who connive against Höllerer," says one of the Professor's admirers, "could not even succeed if they all ganged up together. There's simply no one in the world of culture who could have achieved all that Höllerer has achieved, even if they had all the money Höllerer managed to find."

"He's not the first *Kultur-Motor* in West Berlin," says *Senatsdirektor,* Harald Ingensand of Senator Stein's office. "Erwin Redslob was another successful one after the war." Redslob, the first *Rektor* of the Free University, was responsible for financing a new museum of Berlin history, the one which is now housed in the old Kammergericht courthouse. Because the old Märkisches Museum lay in East Berlin and was inaccessible to West Berlin youngsters, Redslob founded one on his own initiative so they might know what their city looked like before it was divided.

"Berlin always needs this kind of individual action," one official says. "The city has to have constant cultural promotions simply because West Berlin today lacks a cultured upper class (*geistische Oberschicht*) now that it isn't the center of the nation's wealth."

Lack of substantial money still plagues the city, however, and Berliners are quick to identify Bonn as the pinch-penny villain.

"A few million marks more a year would provide the whipped cream," says a city official. "If Berlin can't be political center, it ought at least to be made into cultural center for West Germany. But Munich is more accessible, so it gets more and more of the funds, at Berlin's expense."

Physical isolation and the political tensions caused by the wall's very presence inhibit the inflow of artistic and cultural influences as much as does any shortage of public funds. "Everything is more difficult and tedious in Berlin," says an official, meaning that everything and everybody has to be hauled through East Germany, often at considerable expense. When a major art exhibit is planned in West Berlin, the city often has to pay the air freight for the paintings and even then has a hard time convincing owners to send them through the "Iron Curtain" into remote Berlin.

"We live on the edge of Germany, on the brink, rather than in the center," says a scholar. "Too many of the people who come

413

here are either 'political tourists' or businessmen in a hurry. They don't have time to appreciate the city's cultural life. Still, despite everything, all of us who *do* live here in Berlin know very well why we stay here rather than live in Munich or Hanover!"

The reason lies, as might be expected, in the nature of the Berliners themselves. No matter what layer of society they come from, Berliners seem to be more interested in culture than many other Germans.

The statistics seem to bear this out. Forty percent of all Berliners go to the theater; only twenty percent go in other West German cities. There are more libraries in West Berlin, in relation to the number of inhabitants, than in any other West German city, and more books are checked out of them in Berlin than anywhere else. Only Düsseldorf, industrial center of West Germany, has fewer inhabitants per bookshop than West Berlin, which has 450 bookstores. Its seventeen theaters caused Switzerland's authoritative *Neue Züricher Zeitung* to claim West Berlin had recaptured its "world-wide reputation as a cultural center," an evaluation the Senat tries hard to justify, spreading a great many marks around everywhere.

One recipient is the Academy of Arts, whose purpose is to promote and present the arts to the public, as well as to advise the city government in matters concerning them. Even here, however, private initiative saved the day, providing the academy with a new home in the Tiergarten's Hansa Quarter. The prewar academy building on Pariser Platz was destroyed, and in any case, the site lay in the Soviet sector; when the East Berlin authorities established an academy in 1950, West Berlin followed in 1954, housing its own Academy of Arts in a villa in Dahlem. There it would have remained, had it not been for a chance encounter a few years later over a cup of coffee at Hamburg Airport. A young architect and urban planner, Werner Düttmann, fresh from studies in Britain, was seated in the lounge, waiting for a plane for Berlin, when he met Henry R. Reichhold of New York. Reichhold had left his native Berlin in the 1920's after failing to interest its industrialists in artificial fibres; he went on to found Reichhold Chemicals in Michigan and to make a fortune. Chatting with the young architect, whom he found agreeable, Reichhold said he had always wanted to give his hometown a gift, preferably a building, where-

414

upon Düttmann immediately proposed a new Academy of Arts, doing a rough sketch then and there in the airport lounge. Reichhold agreed to finance it and Düttmann returned to West Berlin, where he had a very hard time convincing anyone that he had run into a couple of million dollars. Eventually, however, the academy's new home did open and made Düttmann famous in 1960 at the age of thirty-eight. He won the Critic's Prize the same year Günter Grass did, became *Senatsbaudirektor,* or city construction overlord, and is now an honorary professor at the Technical University. His modern academy home on the Hanseaten Weg is today a very busy center of all kinds of activities, from exhibitions of paintings to occasional Friday night rock-'n'-roll dances.

There's also a local *Kunstamt* (municipal arts bureau) for each of West Berlin's twelve districts, it being argued that each of these is in fact a city containing more than one hundred thousand inhabitants. They promote local artists. Some bureaus simply hang a few pictures in the corridors of their district town halls, while others are more imaginative. Once annually, every single artist in West Berlin is allowed to hang a few of his paintings, whatever their merit, in a gargantuan mass art exhibit at the *Funkturm* halls, the show symbolizing the city's hunger for sheer volume in cultural activity of all kinds.

This drive is one of the factors underlying Berlin's heavily promoted Festival Weeks, launched in 1951 by Mayor Ernst Reuter to reinforce the city's disputed claim to German cultural supremacy. The festivals were at first supported by the Western Allies and then mainly featured foreign contributions. Judith Anderson from America, The Old Vic Company from London, and the Comédie Française from Paris came to the first Festival Weeks. Since West Berlin began to pay the expenses, more home-grown talent has been used. The Berlin Philharmonic under Herbert von Karajan; the German Opera under director Gustav Rudolf Sellner; the city's three municipal theaters (Schiller, Schlosspark, and Schiller Workshop), all under producer Boleslaw Barlog, present a large, varied, and often brilliant series of productions during these weeks, as do the thirteen privately owned theaters in West Berlin, among which the Freie Volksbühne, the Renaissance-Theater, the Komödie, the Tribüne, the Hebbel-Theater, and the Theater des Westens are prominent. Artists from abroad still come

415

to each festival, year after year: Nureyev and Fonteyn have danced in Berlin; Olivier and his National Theater performed *Love for Love;* Yehudi Menuhin regularly plays with the Philharmonic; Japan's Kabuki Theater and India's Kathakali dancers have also appeared. (East Berlin countered by launching Festival Weeks of its own.)

The theaters are always crowded, not only during the Festival Weeks, thanks in part to the unusual role which "audience associations" play in Berlin. The oldest of these belongs to the Freie Volksbühne Theater. Members buy cheap season tickets (subsidized by the city); on the evenings they attend, a lottery in the lobby assigns them their seats. Lucky members end up in the front row, while others who paid as much sit in the rear. The existence of these associations is responsible for the crowds of proper burghers who go to even the most radical and avant-garde plays staged at the Volksbühne. Never in their lives would they go out of their way to hear hair-curling obscenities shouted from the stage, but as they bought season tickets, they sit demurely through Pinter's angriest dramas, filling the seats as though their favorite, Marika Rökk, were performing in some *schmaltzy* operetta. These associations guarantee a full house, but not an understanding or enthusiastic audience. Erwin Piscator, who died in 1966, viewed these burghers with misgivings.

"The theatergoing public," he said, "is faithful and well-educated. People go to Shakespeare and Schiller and the newest incomprehensible Playwright of the Absurd. They sit straight in their seats, their hands held properly along the seams of their trousers, and never make a rude noise. What is my complaint? My complaint is that today's theater does not move these people. They come because it is the proper bourgeois thing to do. They do not come to be instructed or disturbed or engaged. They are indifferent. We live in an age of indifference."

Piscator always tried to disturb Berlin audiences, ever since he founded the Proletarian Theater in the 1920's. When the Nazis came to power, he traveled first to Moscow, then to Paris, and finally to New York, where he directed the Dramatic Workshop of the New School for twelve years. He returned to West Berlin in 1951, first to the Schiller Theater and then to the Freie Volksbühne, where one of his protégés was Rolf Hochhuth and where he also staged Peter Weiss' political dramas. Since his death, West Berlin has no comparable *Theatersoldat* (soldier of the theater), but his tradition continues to be carried on at the Volksbühne and elsewhere. If West Berlin's artistic life isn't what it once was in terms of the number of productions or big stars, this is because the icing on the cake is too expensive for a city of few millionaires, a city cut off from the mainland. What West Berlin has instead is something else that it always has had, even in its fat-cat years: daring, experimentation, and above all, enormous *vitality*. Just twenty-six days after the fall of Berlin, thirty-three athletes, weakened by hunger, clambered onto their bicycles, many of these without tires, and staged Berlin's first postwar bicycle race. Bizarre as it was, in amongst the wreckage of the war, twenty thousand Berliners came out to watch Willi Vegelahn, today a prosperous West Berlin newspaper distributor, win that event. The race was symbolic: Despite everything, Berlin was determined "to remain Berlin." A month after the surrender, five plays were running in the ruins; Friedrich Luft, one of Berlin's most important theatrical critics today, reviewed the first postwar production in West Berlin, Curt Götz's comedy, *Ingeborg,* at the Tribüne Theater that July. A year later, six theaters offered daily productions. The Philharmonic started up again, in the Titania Palast, a cinema with wretched acoustics; no matter, Yehudi Menuhin came there to play alongside conductor Wilhelm Furtwängler on an evening in 1947 that moved the Berliners to tears, for Menuhin's arrival seemed to signify their reacceptance into the family of man. Karl Hofer, one of the greatest Berlin painters, came back to his city and his studio in 1945, took note of the fact that some of his most precious works had been destroyed in air raids, and quietly began to paint them all over again, refusing to be ruffled. The cinema started again, showing Hans Albers in *Grosse Freiheit Nr. 7,* made under the Nazis but banned by them; Hildegard Knef, who came to be Berlin's greatest modern chanteuse, a Dietrich for this day, began filming, first for DEFA, in Wolfgang Staudte's *The Murderers Are Among Us.* Tatjana Gsovsky, the grande dame of Berlin ballet and chief choreographer of the German Opera until her retirement in 1966, began resurrecting the dance after twelve years of disrepute during which ballet was despised as "too soft," the Nazi age being that of the boot, not the slipper. Everything be-

417

gan to move immediately after the war, animated not with money but with sheer *Berliner Tempo* and even today there is more excitement and activity in the world of art and culture in West Berlin than anywhere else in Germany. No one knows how many artists live in West Berlin, perhaps five thousand; Kreuzberg alone is home for at least eight hundred. Hellmut Kotschenreuther, the journalist who "discovered" Kreuzberg, calls it "a state of mind, a place where five occasionally is an even number"—a place, in short, where anything can happen. Not only does Kreuzberg have its artists, or *Künstler;* it has its *Lebenskünstler* as well, those who do not so much produce art as try to live it. I am reminded of the incomparable *Märchen,* whose nickname means "Fairy Tale": a young Berlin Bohemian rather than beatnik, who lives in a litter of old, campy Germanic recordings, together with his pretty, blond wife, a stolid peasant girl; he repairs *Leierkasten* as an occasionally profitable hobby, but mainly out of his love for the hurdy-gurdy atmosphere of *fin de siècle* Berlin. Others, like Kurt Muhlenhaupt, are Kreuzberg's successful painters; most of them can be encountered in the *Kleine Weltlaterne,* that *Kneipe* serving as their saloon and their salon. Not even Schwabing, the Greenwich Village of Munich, has a watering hole as crowded with conscientious culturati as the *Weltlaterne;* no other German city, in fact, has as many young people flexing new creative muscle as has Berlin. A list of Berliners influential in the city's cultural world would necessarily contain hundreds of names, few known outside Germany and some not well-known outside Berlin itself; Germany's cultural life has been fragmented ever since Berlin lost its centrical importance, and artistic careers can now be made locally throughout Germany as never before. Höllerer is an example: His has been primarily a Berlin career, though his influence does reach outside the city; Richter is regarded as more "national" in that his Group 47, despite its creaky middle age, continues to be seen as a major force in German literature throughout the Federal Republic.

When Ulrich Schamoni, not yet thirty, produced his first film in Berlin, trying to rescue Germany's film industry from its mediocre postwar traditions, he says he was overwhelmed with help from many quarters, from Senat officials to veteran actresses like Tilla Durieux. "Only in Berlin," he insists, "could such a thing happen"—meaning the welcome given to young talent by a city eager to embrace the future. Critic Friedrich Luft adds, "There's a new generation arising, more demanding and more enthusiastic. Everything's in flux today. Something's cooking everywhere in Berlin."

One senses this immediately—and emotionally—on even a brief visit. One feels the "tremendous sense of *dash*" about its streets, as London reporter Ratcliffe described it; experiences that "it is a tonic simply to walk about." Yet the hard facts and statistics all point in the other direction. In West Germany, one hears only that "Berlin is dying" and the tone in which this is said is often one of *Schadenfreude,* of malicious pleasure. Yet one almost never hears this statement from those who live in the city, who visit it, or who understand the Berliners. They all know—or feel—the inherent, enduring vitality of the city's spirit. It seems almost perverse, but despite all Berlin's problems and pensioners, the city insists on remaining young.

"when the wall comes down"

The obvious division of Berlin is one thing; it takes a while to rec-
ognize that there is even today a united *Berlin of sorts—the Berlin*
of its youth. "We are in the Diaspora here," one West Berlin
student said to me, referring to the alienation between university
youths and the citizens at large, and the remark might just as well
have been made in East Berlin, where the regime has surprisingly
failed to win the allegiance of its young, despite more than twenty
years of indoctrination.

Kurt———, a medical student at Humboldt University in East
Berlin, is one example. He was a reservist in the East German
Army, and despite the fact that he was not allowed to have any
contact at all with foreigners, either in conversations or in letters,
he spoke with us openly and without fear, contemptuous of those
who might be listening. "I'd scram today if that wall weren't there,"
he said. "So would all the other students."

Like his friends, Kurt is proud of East German accomplish-
ments, but specifically proud of what they, the East Germans, man-
aged to do in spite of Communism, and especially in spite of the
Russians. He is proud also of the fact that working-class youths
like himself are encouraged to enter universities in East Germany,
that people without "social background" seem to have a far better
chance at working their way up into top positions than do similar
youngsters in West Berlin or the Federal Republic. But the wall
reminds them daily of their lack of freedom. Furthermore, East
Berlin is not Warsaw, Bucharest, Budapest, or for that matter,
Kiev: it's just a few blocks away from West Berlin's television and
radio transmitters and receives a constant barrage of Western
programming, not to mention propaganda. "That's why we all

know what's really going on," Kurt says. "Not that we believe everything the West tells us, mind you, but it's closer to the truth than what we get here." Despite the Stalinist repression in East Berlin, several youngsters ventured out into the streets to protest the G.D.R.'s role in the invasion of Czechoslovakia, the son of Professor Havemann among them. These youths are the product of a generation of Communist schooling, but their eyes still see the truth and their hearts still yearn for the freedom and national unity denied them today.

Fred Brandt, an East German who made it to West Berlin, recalls the failure of S.E.D. indoctrination programs. "In school," he says, "we had to study the party doctrines or we'd remain behind, so we learned them by heart, ritualistically, just to pass exams. Afterwards, Feierabend!"*—meaning, "an end to it all."*

Karl Silex, chief editorial writer for West Berlin's prestigious Tagesspiegel, *doubts whether Communist indoctrination will have any lasting effect whatever on Germany's young. "Just look at what happened to Nazism after the regime collapsed in 1945," Silex says. "Overnight, you couldn't find a single person who would stand up for his Nazi convictions. Der ganze Spuk—the whole horrible business—was over in a twinkling. That's what will happen when the wall comes down."*

Others disagree and point to the far-reaching social changes made in East Berlin and the G.D.R. It can be stated flatly that none of the youngsters brought up in East Germany want a return to capitalism, unrestricted private ownership of land, utilities, or major industries, nor do they want a return to the social structure of old, so much of which has been restored in West Germany itself. They utterly reject the one-party S.E.D. dictatorship in the G.D.R., they completely reject the police state, but that doesn't mean they are enchanted with what the West so far has offered them.

It is precisely in these sentiments that one encounters the united Berlin of today, for the youngsters in West Berlin feel exactly the same. Both sets of young people, East and West, have the same heroes. These do not include John Foster Dulles, who promised to roll back the Iron Curtain but didn't, nor do they any longer include Willy Brandt, locked in a Grand Coalition embrace with C.D.U. Chancellor Kiesinger, a former Nazi. The heroes are Che Guevara, the revolutionary "saint" for all those who today place

421

more of their trust in bandoliers of bullets than in ballots; in Germany specifically, the heroes include Karl Liebknecht and Rosa Luxemburg, who were assassinated by the Right Wing in 1919.

These student demonstrators in West Berlin (and their silenced brothers across the wall) feel disenfranchised, unrepresented. Thus they make their voice heard where they can: in the streets.

The sight of them rioting frightens the Berlin burghers, of course; the anarchist and revolutionary slogans they chant frighten even West Berlin liberals. Berlin has for such a long time been a symbol of and shrine to the Cold War that it has always seemed enough to prove oneself an anti-Communist, to prove one's democratic credentials. Students today disagree. "Hitler also was an anti-Communist," Paul Norden says. The generation gap in Berlin involves a conflict of consciences.

These Berlin youngsters are like none Germany has ever encountered before. Born anywhere from 1940 on, they bear no responsibility for the Nazi regime or its horrors, yet they are willing to accept a burden of guilt, as though atoning for their parents, who usually reject it. These youngsters are not even "German" as of old, they are European. They travel far—and constantly—to Scandinavia, California, France, Italy, Spain, and Eastern Europe. They go to Israel to work on kibbutzim and they establish German-Israeli societies (as at the Free University). They do this not to clear their consciences (which are clean), but to show where they stand. It is the stand of young people like this that prompts Paul Norden and others like him to say, "This is a city I can trust."

WALTER HENRY NELSON

422

index

423

427

Knobelsdorff (architect), 52, 58, 396
Koch, Mayor, 50
Koch theatrical company, 59
Köcher, Roman, 313
Kollo, Walter, 33
Komorowski, Major, 128
Konev, Ivan, 130
Konietzny (merchant), 147-148
Königgratz, 81
Königsberg, 38, 43, 67
Köpenick, 88-89, 128
Köppen, Herbert, 313
Kops, Erich, 189
Krafft-Ebing, Richard von, 298-299
Kreuzberg, 26, 27, 28, 107, 121, 123, 207, 286-287, 288, 290, 344
Kristallnacht, 116-117, 361
Kroll, Hans, 172-173
Krupp, Alfried, 96
Kunert, Günter, 390, 391
Kürbiskern, 391
Kurella, Alfred, 386
Kusnitzki, Elisabeth, 124

Lange, Fritz, 203-204
Lange, Hilde (later Benjamin), 331-332
Lange, Victor, 405
Lasalle, Ferdinand, 90
Lasky, Melvin J., 402
Leber, Annedore, 125
Leber, Julius, 125
Le Carré, John, 320
Le Corbusier, 360
Leibnitz, Gottfried Wilhelm, 43
Leipzig, 68, 98
Lenya, Lotte, 106
Leonhard, Wolfgang, 132-133, 156-157
Leopold I, Holy Roman Emperor, 41
Lessing, Gotthold Ephraim, 53-54
Leuschner, Bruno, 162
Levin, Rahel, 63, 66, 73
Liberal Democratic Party (L.D.P.), 148, 152, 153
Lichterfelde, 115, 124, 125, 132, 332
Lieber, Hans Joachim, 15-16, 118, 129-130, 139, 176
Liebig, Pfc., 193
Liebknecht, Karl, 27, 96, 99, 100, 100-103, 374, 422
Lindemann, Fritz, 124

Lindner, Klaus, 232
Lipschitz, Joachim, 171, 221, 339
Literary Colloquium, 411, 412
Literature
  in East Berlin, 388-393
  in West Berlin, 401-413
Lobeck, Hans Werner, 117
Loire, Gabriel, 361
London *Sunday Times,* 370
Loose, Gerhard, 314
Losch, Maria Magdalena, 111
Louis Ferdinand, prince of Prussia, 63-64, 283, 361
Louis Philippe, king of France, 74
Louise, queen of Prussia, 64
Lovett, William, 230
Ludendorff, Erich von, 98, 106
Ludwig, Emil, 17, 91
Luft, Friedrich, 411, 417, 419
Luxemburg, Rosa, 99n, 101-103, 422

Mach, Josef, 394
Maier, Wolfgang, 412
Maetzig, Kurt, 386, 387, 388
Magdeburg, 38
Mann, Heinrich, 109, 111
Mann, Lynne, 227
Marat/Sade, 396, 405
Marienborn, 210, 228
Marienfelde, 8
Markgraf, Paul, 334-335, 336, 339-340
Märkisches Viertel, 357
Marriage, Italian Style, 387
Marshall Plan, 157, 235, 349
Martin, Rudolf, 92
Marx, Karl, 73, 74
Matern, Hermann, 152
Matthews, Frederick, 230-231
May, Jürgen, 264
Mayakovsky, Vladimir, 393
Meaning and Form, 389-390
Mehring, Walter, 109, 113
Meierie, 58-59
Mendelson, Franz, 136
Mendelssohn, Moses, 53, 54, 60
Mendelssohn, Peter de, 112
Menuhin, Yehudi, 416, 417
Merker, Rudolf, 174
Merkur, 152
Metternich, Clemens von, 68
Mielke, Erich, 329n

429

431